Toolkit Mediation

Generating Outcomes as Mediator and Negotiator

Checklist for the mediator and negotiator

I. Planning and arrangements

I-1 The initial contact phase (intake)
I-1.1 The initial contact
I-1.1.1 Pre-mediation sessions: The value of individual meetings before mediation sessions
I-1.1.2 Checklist questions to ask during the intake phase
I-1.2 Factors favoring and disfavoring the use of mediation
I-1.3 Mediation, why should you?
I-1.4 Mediation, why not?
I-2 Pre-mediation planning
I-2.1 Style and strategic approach to the mediation process
I-2.1.1 The task-focused mediator
I-2.1.2 The relationship-focused or communication-focused mediator
I-2.1.3 Other styles and approaches to the mediation process
I-2.2 Expertise on content and specialists versus generalists
I-2.3 The approach to the mediation
I-2.4 Getting in the 'mood for mediation'
I-2.5 Managing and structuring tools
I-2.6 Make sure all relevant parties are present and create balance
I-2.7 Authority, power of attorney and constituency
I-2.7.1 Authority and power of attorney
I-2.7.2 Dealing with the parties' constituencies

II. Procedural aspects

II-1 Psychological contract and building trust
II-2 Maintaining and demonstrating neutrality and impartiality
II-2.1 Maintaining neutrality and impartiality during the mediation
II-2.2 Techniques to demonstrate neutrality and impartiality
II-2.3 Mediator bias
II-3 Balancing power
II-3.1 Balancing power in a structured manner
II-3.2 Balancing power during the process
II-4 Interest-based negotiation
II-4.1 Getting to yes
II-4.2 The rules of thumb from 'Getting to yes'
II-4.3 Getting Past No
II-4.4 Effective behavior for negotiators
II-5 Empathy and perspective taking
II-6 Empowerment of parties
II-7 Interests (subjective criteria)
II-7.1 Common or joint interests
II-7.2 Differing interests
II-7.2.1 Reconcilable differing interests
II-7.2.2 Irreconcilable differing interests
II-7.3 Other classifications of interests
II-8 Blocking issues and causes of conflict
II-8.1 The blocking issue
II-8.2 Conflict causes and interventions
II-8.3 The 10-I model

III. Techniques and interventions

III-1 Overview of the key techniques, interventions, negotiation and mediation tools
III-2 Listening
III-2.1 Importance
III-2.2 Active listening
III-2.3 Techniques
III-3 (Let the parties) Paraphrase
III-4 Summarize
III-5 Reflecting
III-5.1 Magnify/reflect on content
III-5.2 Acknowledge/reflect on feelings
III-5.3 Reflect on the progress
III-6 Reframing or recontextualizing
III-6.1 Neutral or positive reframing
III-6.2 Reframing into an interest, option, feeling or objective criterion
III-7 Neutral language of the mediator
III-7.1 Neutral language general
III-7.2 Techniques to deal with risky questions posed by parties
III-8 Distinguish content from the relationship
III-9 Meta-communication
III-10 Asking questions
III-10.1 Questions on a verbal level
III-10.1.1 Closed questions
III-10.1.2 Straight questions
III-10.1.3 Clarifying questions
III-10.1.4 Open questions
III-10.2 Questions on a relational level, connecting questions
III-10.2.1 Relationship questions
III-10.2.2 Circular questions
III-10.2.3 Reciprocal questions
III-10.2.4 Mirroring/parallel situation

IV. Challenging situations

IV-1 Overcoming deadlocks effectively
IV-1.1 Characteristics of a deadlock
IV-1.2 Causes of deadlock
IV-1.3 Techniques and methods
IV-1.3.1 Interim evaluation of the mediation process
IV-1.3.2 Techniques
IV-1.3.2.1 Deadlocks caused by persons
IV-1.3.2.2 Deadlocks about content
IV-2 Differing perceptions
IV-2.1 Reconciling differing perceptions
IV-2.2 The 'ladder of inference'
IV-2.2.1 The development of differing perceptions
IV-2.2.2 Techniques
IV-2.3 Clarifying differing perceptions is difficult
IV-2.3.1 Cognitive dissonance
IV-2.3.2 Naïve realism
IV-2.4 Dysfunctional behavior
IV-3 Tricky tactics and difficult behavior
IV-3.1 Parties experienced as difficult
IV-3.2 Tricky tactics
IV-3.3 Techniques
IV-3.3.1 Do not react
IV-3.3.2 An appropriate reaction
IV-4 Dealing with emotions
IV-4.1 'Emotional pitfalls' for a mediator
IV-4.1.1 Exploring extensively
IV-4.1.2 Pretending emotions do not play a role
IV-4.1.3 Adopting emotions or going along with them
IV-4.2 Positive emotions
IV-4.3 Negative emotions

I-2.8 Procedural consultations with lawyers or other advisors
I-3 Checklist opening statement and ground rules
I-3.1 Issues a mediator needs to address during his 'opening statement'
I-3.2 Ground rules
I-4 Agreements on reporting
I-5 Co-mediation
I-5.1 Models of co-mediation
I-5.2 When is co-mediation advisable?
I-5.3 When should co-mediation not be considered?
I-5.4 A co-mediator, why should you?
I-5.5 A co-mediator, why not?
I-5.6 Agreements with the co-mediator
I-5.7 Collaborating during the co-mediation
I-5.8 A team is effective but not necessarily more efficient
I-6 Preparing a negotiation agenda
I-7 Experts and mediator's proposal
I-7.1 When to call in an external specialist
I-7.2 The advantages of a mediator proposal
I-7.3 Disadvantages of a mediator proposal
I-7.4 Alternatives to a mediator proposal
I-7.5 How to conduct a mediator's proposal
I-8 Administrative kit
I-8.1 Mediation clauses and other contract clauses
I-8.2 Mediation rules, codes of conduct, disciplinary rules and agreements
I-8.3 CPD, Code of Disclosure and code of professional conduct

II-8.4 The Drama Triangle and Winners Triangle
II-9 The stages of a mediation process
II-10 Advancing from positions and the past to interests and the future
II-11 Result and conclusion of a mediation
II-11.1 No (partial) solutions
II-11.2 Interim settlement and partial solutions
II-11.3 Full settlement
II-12 Package deals
II-13 Balanced and SMART agreements
II-14 (Using) Time
II-14.1 Deadlines and the 80/20 rule
II-14.2 Introducing adjournments
II-14.3 The time required for mediation
II-15 Structuring
II-15.1 Managing the process
II-15.2 Structuring thinking
II-15.3 Facilitating communication
II-15.4 Fractionalizing matters in dispute
II-15.5 Distinguishing
II-16 Caucus
II-16.1 The caucus in general
II-16.2 Utilizing a caucus, why should you?
II-16.3 Utilizing a caucus, why not?
II-16.4 Approach and technique of a caucus
II-16.5 Applying caucus in co-mediation

III-10.3 'Peel-off' questions
III-10.4 Confronting questions
III-10.4.1 Confrontation questions
III-10.4.2 Argumentative questions
III-10.5 Strategic questions
III-10.5.1 Tactical questions
III-10.5.2 Verification questions
III-10.5.3 Summarizing questions
III-10.5.4 Hypothetical questions
III-10.6 If there is no (informative) answer to a question
III-10.7 Anchoring and formulating neutrally
III-11 Reality testing
III-11.1 Reality testing: hypothetical/future oriented
III-11.2 Reality testing: risk analysis
III-11.3 NAN
III-12 The one text procedure
III-13 Mutualizing (finding common ground)
III-14 BATNA, WATNA, RATNA, leverage and ZOPA
III-14.1 BATNA/WATNA/RATNA
III-14.2 Leverage
III-14.3 ZOPA
III-15 Generate options
III-15.1 Brainstorming
III-15.2 Other methods for generating options
III-16 Reaching agreement
III-16.1 Develop objective criteria and select options
III-16.2 Other methods
III-16.3 Reactive devaluation
III-16.4 Loss minimizing
III-17 Use of voice and silence
III-18 Non-verbal behavior
III-19 Paradoxical interventions

IV-4.3.1 Offensive
IV-4.3.2 Defensive
IV-4.4 Interventions for managing emotions
IV-4.5 Recognizing your own role in the conflict
IV-4.6 Change is difficult
IV-5 Varying cultural backgrounds
IV-6 Multi-party mediations or mediations with many individuals
IV-6.1 Large groups
IV-6.2 More than two parties
IV-7 Escalation phases of a conflict
IV-7.1 Glasl's stairway of conflict escalation
IV-7.2 The phases of conflict escalation
IV-7.3 Interventions per escalation phase of the conflict
IV-8 Online mediation
IV-9 Dealing with brains, tips for mediators from neuroscience
IV-9.1 Our brain in evolution
IV-9.2 Mirror neurons and body language
IV-9.3 'Neuro'-interventions
IV-9.4 The SCARF model and beyond reason
IV-9.4.1 The SCARF model
IV-9.4.2 'Beyond Reason: Using Emotions as you Negotiate' by Fisher and Shapiro
IV-9.5 A neurocompass for mediators
IV-9.5.1 Neuro tips
IV-9.5.2 Neuroscience tips for different phases of the mediation process

Initial Contact Phase Preparation and agreements (I-1, I-2)

Focus: preparation, lay foundation.

- **Intake/preparation consultation** (I-1.1, I-2.1.3).
- **Conflict of interests check** (I-1 + consult code of conduct).
- **Suitability check** (I-2.4).
- **Managing expectations** (I-1.1).
- **Mediation approach/strategy** (I-2.1.3).
- **Legal and administrative issues** (I-8).

Transition to phase 1:

Arrange the first mediation session.

Phase 1 Opening statements (I-3, I-4, I-5)

Focus: set tone, manage expectations, first dispute scan.

- **Opening statement mediator** (I-3).
  - Check parties' **names**, whether to use first names or more formality.
  - **Mediation process, tasks** mediator and parties.
  - **Caucus** (double confidentiality) (II-16).
  - **Logistical arrangements** (I-1.1).
  - **Time scope, deadlines and commitments** (II-14).
  - **Postponement/suspension of judicial or other proceedings**.
  - **Ground rules** (I-3).
- **Do the parties have any questions or need further clarification?**

Transition to opening statement parties:

'What do you expect from this mediation?' or
'Who wants to start?'

- **Opening statements parties:**
  - Who will go first (I-2.1)?
  - First scan: content and blocking issues, interests, causes of the conflict (II-7, II-8).
- **Main techniques:**
  - **Listening** for content, interests and blocking issues (III-2).
  - **Summarize** (III-4).
  - **Check assumptions** (IV-2.2), ask verification questions (III-10.5.2).
  - **Questioning style:** open, closed, straight and clarifying (III-10.1).

Transition to phase 2:
Joint summary and issue agenda:

'We have to discuss ... and ... and also ...
Can we settle this dispute if we find a solution to all of these topics? Or did we overlook important issues?'

Transition for caucus-mediation strategy:

- Get consent on main rules for the caucus (II-16.4).

'I think it is time now to continue in separate meetings ...'

Phase 2 Exchange and exploration (I-6, II-7, II-8, II-15, II-16, III-1, IV-1, IV-2, IV-3, IV-4, IV-7)

Focus: manage/structure. Move focus from positions & past to interests & future.

- **Setting a negotiating agenda** (I-6).
- **Exploration of interests** (II-7).
- **Main techniques and methods:**
  - **Listening** for content, interests, blocking issues & opportunities (II-7, II-8, III-2).
  - **Structure** the process and communication (II-15).
  - (Encourage the parties to) **Paraphrase** (III-3).
  - **Acknowledgement** (III-5.2).
  - **Reframe**, recontextualize (III-6).
  - **Questions** (III-10) and **reality testing** (III-11).
  - **Summarize** (III-4).
  - **Dealing with emotions** (IV-4).
  - **Dealing with tricky tactics and difficult behavior** (IV-3).
  - Check **BATNA/ WATNA/ RATNA** (III-14.1), **leverage** (III-14.2) and **ZOPA** (III-14.3).
  - **Caucus** (II-16).
  - **Ladder of inference** (IV-2.2), clarify **perspectives** (IV-2.1) and **psychological barriers** (IV-2.3.4).
  - **Balance power** (II-3), **empowerment** (II-6) and **empathy** (II-5).
  - Maintain and demonstrate **neutrality** (II-2, III-7).

Transition to phase 3:
Verify that:

- All interests are on the table;
- Blocking issues are identified;
- Emotions have been dealt with to the extent that they will not stand in the way of reaching settlement;
- There is understanding for each other's points of view; and
- The role of each party in the origin and development of the conflict.

Summarize + 'Now that it is clear that ... and ...
We need to find a solution for ... and .....'

Phase 3 Options (III-15, III-16, IV-1)
Phase 4 Negotiation

Focus: generate as many mutual gain options as possible, reach agreement.

- **Breaking deadlocks** (IV-1):
  - Dealing with tricky tactics and difficult behavior (IV-3).
  - Balance power, make sure all parties participate (II-3).
  - Understand each party's own constituency (I-2.7.2). and their individual scope of authority (I-2.7.1).
  - Develop objective criteria (III-16.1).
  - Set priorities (II-15).

- **Stimulate creativity and 'out-of-the-box-thinking' using techniques for generating options** (II-15):
  - Brainstorming (III-15.1).
  - Expand the pie.
  - Prepare lists and discuss them.
  - Develop one mutual vision.
  - Seek advice from experts.
  - Ask the mediator to suggest additional options.
  - Consult external sources.
  - Use different thinking frames.
- **Aim at package deals:** pay special attention to this aspect when interim solutions are involved (II-12).

Transition to phase 5:

- Summarize results, time and energy invested.
- List decisions to be included in the settlement agreement.

'I think we are ready to draft the agreement.'

Phase 5 Finalizing agreement & closure (I-2.7, II-11, II-12, II-13)

Focus: finalizing agreement, reaching a deal that can be implemented and that is durable.

In case of partial agreement (II-11.2.3)
- Prepare **draft agreement** (if applicable combined with a list of remaining difficulties/options):
  - Check balance (all parties need to be addressed and do something) and use of neutral language (II-3, III-7).
  - Make it SMART (II-12).
    Specific: unambiguous what has been agreed.
    Measurable: clear when agreement is fulfilled.
    Achievable: it can be done.
    Realistic: parties will do it.
    Time limit: it has a defined ending.
  - Avoid dependence on contingencies.
  - Avoid legalese (parties must recognize their solution and own language).
- Check communication with constituencies and related face-saving aspects.
- Stress **importance of compliance**.
- **Provision** in case parties encounter problems during implementation (f.e. mediation clause).

In case of no agreement (II-11.1)
- Positive summary of results and commitment (III-4).
- Make a list of what has been accomplished (f.e. understanding, clarification of the disputed topics, agree to disagree).
- Clarify next steps.

Phase 6 Follow-up and implementation, CPD

Focus: make sure the parties can implement what has been agreed, CPD.

- Be available for the parties, if necessary revisit or readjust the terms of agreement or search for additional solutions if parties encounter problems during implementation.
- Use each mediation for your own Continuous Professional Development (CPD) and review your performance and confidentially discuss dilemma's and lessons learned in your mediator intervision group.
- How did parties reach settlement, what went well, what should be done differently next time, other learnings?

A more detailed table can be found in II-9.

Toolkit Mediation

Generating Outcomes as Mediator and Negotiator

Manon Schonewille

Second edition

eleven

Published, sold and distributed by Eleven
P.O. Box 85576
2508 CG The Hague
The Netherlands
Tel.: +31 70 33 070 33
Fax: +31 70 33 070 30
e-mail: sales@elevenpub.nl
www.elevenpub.com

Sold and distributed in USA and Canada
Independent Publishers Group
814 N. Franklin Street
Chicago, IL 60610, USA
Order Placement: +1 800 888 4741
Fax: +1 312 337 5985
orders@ipgbook.com
www.ipgbook.com

Eleven is an imprint of Boom (Den Haag).

ISBN 978-90-4730-202-5

Table of contents

Acknowledgement 17

Introduction 19

I. Planning and arrangements 27

1 The initial contact phase (intake) 29

1.1 The initial contact 29

1.1.1 Pre-mediation sessions: The value of individual meetings before mediation sessions 31

1.1.2 Checklist questions to ask during the intake phase 32

1.2 Factors favoring and disfavoring the use of mediation 34

1.3 Mediation, why should you? 36

1.4 Mediation, why not? 37

2 Pre-mediation planning 38

2.1 Style and strategic approach to the mediation process 38

2.1.1 The task-focused mediator 38

2.1.2 The relationship-focused or communication-focused mediator 42

2.1.3 Other styles and approaches to the mediation process 45

2.2 Expertise on content and specialists versus generalists 46

2.3 The approach to the mediation 48

2.4 Getting in the 'mood for mediation' 49

2.5 Managing and structuring tools 52

2.6 Make sure all relevant parties are present and create balance 54

2.7 Authority, power of attorney and constituency 54

2.7.1 Authority and power of attorney 54

2.7.2 Dealing with the parties' constituencies 55

2.8 Procedural consultations with lawyers or other advisors 56

3 Checklist opening statement and ground rules 58

3.1 Issues a mediator needs to address during his 'opening statement' 58

3.2 Ground rules 61

4 Agreements on reporting 62

5 Co-mediation 63

5.1 Models of co-mediation 63

5.2 When is co-mediation advisable? 64

5.3 When should co-mediation not be considered? 64

5.4 A co-mediator, why should you? 64

5.5 A co-mediator, why not? 65
5.6 Agreements with the co-mediator 66
5.7 Collaborating during the co-mediation 66
5.8 A team is effective but not necessarily more efficient 68
6 Preparing a negotiation agenda 68
7 Experts and mediator's proposal 70
7.1 When to call in an external specialist 70
7.2 The advantages of a mediator proposal 71
7.3 Disadvantages of a mediator proposal 71
7.4 Alternatives to a mediator proposal 72
7.5 How to conduct a mediator's proposal 72
8 Administrative kit 74
8.1 Mediation clauses and other contract clauses 75
8.2 Mediation rules, codes of conduct, disciplinary rules and agreements 79
8.3 CPD, Code of Disclosure and code of professional conduct 81

II. Procedural aspects 85

1 Psychological contract and building trust 87
2 Maintaining and demonstrating neutrality and impartiality 90
2.1 Maintaining neutrality and impartiality during the mediation 90
2.2 Techniques to demonstrate neutrality and impartiality 92
2.3 Mediator bias 92
3 Balancing power 93
3.1 Balancing power in a structured manner 93
3.2 Balancing power during the process 94
4 Interest-based negotiation 95
4.1 Getting to yes 95
4.2 The rules of thumb from 'Getting to yes' 96
4.3 Getting Past No 97
4.4 Effective behavior for negotiators 98
5 Empathy and perspective taking 100
6 Empowerment of parties 101
7 Interests (subjective criteria) 102
7.1 Common or joint interests 103
7.2 Differing interests 103
7.2.1 Reconcilable differing interests 103
7.2.2 Irreconcilable differing interests 103
7.3 Other classifications of interests 105

8 Blocking issues and causes of conflict 106
8.1 The blocking issue 106
8.2 Conflict causes and interventions 107
8.3 The 10-I model 111
8.4 The Drama Triangle and Winners Triangle 113
9 The stages of a mediation process 114
10 Advancing from positions and the past to interests and the future 122
11 Result and conclusion of a mediation 124
11.1 No (partial) solutions 125
11.2 Interim settlement and partial solutions 125
11.3 Full settlement 126
12 Package deals 127
13 Balanced and SMART agreements 127
14 (Using) Time 128
14.1 Deadlines and the 80/20 rule 129
14.2 Introducing adjournments 129
14.3 The time required for mediation 129
15 Structuring 131
15.1 Managing the process 131
15.2 Structuring thinking 131
15.3 Facilitating communication 131
15.4 Fractionalizing matters in dispute 132
15.5 Distinguishing 132
16 Caucus 132
16.1 The caucus in general 133
16.2 Utilizing a caucus, why should you? 134
16.3 Utilizing a caucus, why not? 134
16.4 Approach and technique of a caucus 135
16.5 Applying caucus in co-mediation 137

III. Techniques and interventions 139

1 Overview of the key techniques, interventions, negotiation and mediation tools 141
2 Listening 153
2.1 Importance 153
2.2 Active listening 156
2.3 Techniques 157
3 (Let the parties) Paraphrase 159
4 Summarize 160

5 Reflecting 161
5.1 Magnify/reflect on content 162
5.2 Acknowledge/reflect on feelings 163
5.3 Reflect on the progress 164
6 Reframing or recontextualizing 165
6.1 Neutral or positive reframing 165
6.2 Reframing into an interest, option, feeling or objective criterion 166
7 Neutral language of the mediator 168
7.1 Neutral language general 168
7.2 Techniques to deal with risky questions posed by parties 169
8 Distinguish content from the relationship 170
9 Meta-communication 170
10 Asking questions 173
10.1 Questions on a verbal level 174
10.1.1 Closed questions 174
10.1.2 Straight questions 175
10.1.3 Clarifying questions 175
10.1.4 Open questions 175
10.2 Questions on a relational level, connecting questions 176
10.2.1 Relationship questions 176
10.2.2 Circular questions 177
10.2.3 Reciprocal questions 177
10.2.4 Mirroring/parallel situation 177
10.3 'Peel-off' questions 178
10.4 Confronting questions 179
10.4.1 Confrontation questions 179
10.4.2 Argumentative questions 180
10.5 Strategic questions 181
10.5.1 Tactical questions 182
10.5.2 Verification questions 182
10.5.3 Summarizing questions 182
10.5.4 Hypothetical questions 182
10.6 If there is no (informative) answer to a question 182
10.7 Anchoring and formulating neutrally 183
11 Reality testing 185
11.1 Reality testing: hypothetical/future oriented 186
11.2 Reality testing: risk analysis 186
11.3 NAN 187
12 The one text procedure 187
13 Mutualizing (finding common ground) 189

14 BATNA, WATNA, RATNA, leverage and ZOPA 189
14.1 BATNA/WATNA/RATNA 190
14.2 Leverage 192
14.3 ZOPA 194
15 Generate options 195
15.1 Brainstorming 195
15.2 Other methods for generating options 196
16 Reaching agreement 197
16.1 Develop objective criteria and select options 198
16.2 Other methods 199
16.3 Reactive devaluation 199
16.4 Loss minimizing 200
17 Use of voice and silence 201
18 Non-verbal behavior 202
19 Paradoxical interventions 204

IV. Challenging situations & selected topics 209

1 Overcoming deadlocks effectively 211
1.1 Characteristics of a deadlock 211
1.2 Causes of deadlock 211
1.3 Techniques and methods 213
1.3.1 Interim evaluation of the mediation process 213
1.3.2 Techniques 215
1.3.2.1 Deadlocks caused by persons 215
1.3.2.2 Deadlocks about content 216
2 Differing perceptions 217
2.1 Reconciling differing perceptions 218
2.2 The 'ladder of inference' 218
2.2.1 The development of differing perceptions 218
2.2.2 Techniques 219
2.3 Clarifying differing perceptions is difficult 220
2.3.1 Cognitive dissonance 220
2.3.2 Naïve realism 221
2.4 Dysfunctional behavior 222
3 Tricky tactics and difficult behavior 223
3.1 Parties experienced as difficult 223
3.2 Tricky tactics 224

3.3 Techniques 226
3.3.1 Do not react 226
3.3.2 An appropriate reaction 226
4 Dealing with emotions 228
4.1 'Emotional pitfalls' for a mediator 229
4.1.1 Exploring extensively 229
4.1.2 Pretending emotions do not play a role 229
4.1.3 Adopting emotions or going along with them 229
4.2 Positive emotions 230
4.3 Negative emotions 230
4.3.1 Offensive 231
4.3.2 Defensive 231
4.4 Interventions for managing emotions 232
4.5 Recognizing your own role in the conflict 233
4.6 Change is difficult 234
5 Varying cultural backgrounds 235
6 Multi-party mediations or mediations with many individuals 237
6.1 Large groups 238
6.2 More than two parties 239
7 Escalation phases of a conflict 240
7.1 Glasl's stairway of conflict escalation 240
7.2 The phases of conflict escalation 241
7.3 Interventions per escalation phase of the conflict 249
8 Online mediation 249
9 Dealing with brains, tips for mediators from neuroscience 257
9.1 Our brain in evolution 257
9.2 Mirror neurons and body language 258
9.3 'Neuro'-interventions 259
9.4 The SCARF model and beyond reason 261
9.4.1 The SCARF model 261
9.4.2 'Beyond Reason: Using Emotions as you Negotiate' by Fisher and Shapiro 263
9.5 A neurocompass for mediators 264
9.5.1 Neuro tips 264
9.5.2 Neuroscience tips for different phases of the mediation process 265

Resources **267**

Resource A	Glossary	269
Resource B	Key procedural drivers	277
Resource C	Indicators predicting likelihood of settlement by mediation	279
Resource D	Checklist Cost – Benefit Analysis mediation vs arbitration and litigation	281
Resource E	Sample mediation agreement	284
Resource F	Sample settlement agreement	291
Resource G	5 NEGOTIATION KEYS to claim & create value	294
Resource H	Consulted Literature and other sources	297

About the author **313**

Index **315**

Acknowledgement

A lot of people contributed to 'Toolkit Generating Outcomes' and to its final form. The idea for the book evolved from my search for a practical book that dealt with the technical *how to* aspects of mediation tools, interventions and techniques. I could not find such book so I started to rewrite my existing training material in the form of this handbook. My trainees confirmed the need for this book and were also willing to test the initial ideas for the toolkit as well as the mediation intervention game.
The Dutch edition of the toolkit was published on November 15th 2005 during Mediation Day 2005 on the occasion of the celebration of the tenth anniversary of the Netherlands Mediation Institute, NMI (Now *Mediatorsfederatie Nederland, MfN*).
For the first global edition several international contributors are involved.
Huub Liefhebber did a great job in preparing the principal translation into English from the Dutch version. **Celicia Vassar** and many other colleagues subsequently edited the language. Finally, editors for this international edition added their helpful information.
For the first edition in 2009 **Jacqueline Nolan-Haley** added input mainly for the UK, USA and Canada, Professor **Laurence Boulle** and **Robyn Hooworth** for Australia, New Zealand and Asia.
Special thanks to **Michael Leathes** for being a driving force in the ADR world.
Moreover, I thank all my wonderful colleagues who have given direct or indirect input on the idea for the toolkit and its execution. By their valuable remarks, these communications, mediation and negotiation experts made sure the toolkit is a user-friendly and readable manual which the reader can flip through at will.

Manon Schonewille

November 2023

Introduction

Toolkit Mediation. Generating Outcomes as Mediator and Negotiator is a manual for how mediation can be used by various professionals for their own purposes. Managers, mediators, negotiators, trainers, coaches, consultants, lawyers, judges and other professionals can all benefit from using mediation techniques. This practical handbook contains an overview of the rich amount of tools a mediator has at his/her disposal and is written to offer a clear guide on how to 'technically' apply these tools. In particular, it includes comprehensive and easy-to-use practical checklists and overviews.

Mediation theories and techniques are based on contributions from social sciences, management theories and research on organizational development. In (social) psychology and business studies (f.e. game theories), much research has been done on how conflicts develop and escalate and how to deal with such conflicts. From these insights, new negotiation theories, like problem-solving negotiation, have developed. Meanwhile, mediation has developed into a self-determining interdisciplinary profession with professional requirements of its practioners and with its own techniques and theories. Mediation techniques can also be applied in a variety of circumstances outside a formal mediation process.

They can offer a valuable contribution to improve the result of a negotiation or in effectively dealing with day-to-day issues as a manager.

Mediation is a method consisting of several phases or stages in which the involved parties, under the guidance of an independent third party – the mediator – attempt to resolve or prevent a conflict, or dispute that has arisen between them in a structured process of balancing interests. The mediator diagnoses the conflict together with the parties and guides the negotiations between them with the aim of reaching jointly supported sustainable solutions based on their real interests, which, when relevant, are recorded in a list of agreements or settlement agreement.

Legal Mediation or Proactive Mediation

As we teach it in The Academy of Legal Mediation, in the Legal Mediation or Proactive Mediation approach, the autonomy, personal, business, and commercial interests of the parties take centre stage. The mediator not only facilitates but is also actively, solution-oriented, and evaluative (light). A legal or proactive mediator, like a facilitating mediator (see I-2.1. on approaches and mediation style), first establishes a relational foundation between the parties and ensures that the interests surface. Subsequently, a legal/proactive mediator actively explores a relational as well as a substantive solution, ideally resulting in a business deal.

A proactive mediator checks with the parties and/or their (legal) advisor whether the arrangement is legally, practically, and commercially feasible, meets the actual interests

of all involved, and aligns with the corporate culture or situation. As a result, the business and legal agreements made by the parties are sustainable. A legal/proactive mediator is specialized and knowledgeable in the field of mediation where they operate, working at the same level as the parties' lawyers and other advisors.
Legal or Proactive Mediation can be seen as 360° mediation, a total solution in the shadow of the law on both a relational, business, and legal level, where the proactive mediator is the organizational pivot.

See the P's of Proactive Mediation (I-3).

A legal or proactive mediator

☐ A legal or proactive mediator actively supports the parties in 360 degrees:

- People, Problem & Process are explored, Perspectives, Planet, (wider scope than just those at the table) & Profit are taken into account. Party Autonomy is the leading principle, leading to a Paradigm shift, resulting in: Potential (potent) outcomes.
- What opportunities are there, and what are the focal points?
- What is the substantive and legal framework, what are the options, and where are the limits?
- In what way can an expert possibly provide a solution?
- Can a mediator's proposal (I-7) break the impasse?
- Does a hybrid process or combining different conflict resolution methods in this case add value?
- Active participation in generating options (III-15)

☐ The added value lies in the (legal) expertise regarding the mediation process itself (knowledge of legal and administrative mediation instruments, the ability to prepare or guide the preparation of a mediation settlement agreement, a professional mediation agreement, knowledge of mediation clauses, (I-8), etc.), as well as specialization in specific areas of mediation with accompanying process, business/subject matter and, where necessary, legal expertise.

Mediation encompasses more than just the application of skills, techniques, and interventions (III). The goal of a formal mediation goes beyond initiating or improving mutual communication and interaction between parties or clarifying perceptions and emotions. Mediation is a phased method (II-9) of conflict or dispute resolution that, like arbitration and conciliation (binding advice), often takes place "in the shadow of the law".[1]

This means that during a mediation process, litigation is a possible alternative that plays a role in the parties' considerations. The law and the legal context form a (reference) framework during mediation, but not a straitjacket.

The way in which the mediation process is carried out in a specific case is flexible and determined by the mediator and the parties. A mediator has their own specialization and mediation style (I-2.1) and their own skills that underlie the specific interventions used and techniques employed. Parties should be able to choose a mediator with a style and approach to the mediation process that they can agree with.

They should even be able to choose a non-independent, partial, or omni-partial mediator, provided it is an informed choice carried and consciously made by both parties (whether it is advisable for a mediator to be partial is a different discussion, see II-2.1). It is known in social psychology that it is not possible to be truly neutral and objective, not even as a mediator (II-2.1).

The responsibility for resolving their conflict or dispute lies with the parties, as well as its substantive aspects. The mediator encourages the self-effort of the parties to get their stalled negotiations back on track and then translates the potential solutions into a business/personal/legal context to reach a settlement agreement or list of agreements.

From my point of view, mediation is simply said adding an impartial or omni-partial third party to a problem-solving negotiation. Through third party intervention, prior negotiation deadlocks between the parties can be dealt with in order to find a solution to the disputed issues. Other mediators regard mediation more as a process to improve the communication and interactions between the parties or to clarify the respective perceptions and emotions. However, mediators with different views regarding the mediation process and differing styles and strategies can use this toolkit. It is up to each mediator to apply the techniques described in this book for his or her own purposes and to the extent they choose.

This publication is a vital guide for anyone involved in a (potential) dispute, or engaged in a negotiation. In fact, a negotiator can use mediation techniques to shape the result of a negotiation favorably. A mediator can learn how to apply other techniques from negotiation theories, f.e. more directive or less neutral interventions. A manager cannot afford to ignore modern conflict management in his/her work. A coach, consultant or (psycho) therapist can apply mediation techniques in interactions with clients. Of course, the objectives for using these techniques differ depending on the profession.

A mediator is a neutral and independent third party who assists others in resolving their disputes, while a negotiator is always involved as a party and, therefore, uses mediation

1 The expression "in the shadow of the law" refers to the article by R.H. Mnookinand and L. Kornhauser (1979), 'Bargaining in the Shadow of the Law: The Case of Divorce', The Yale Law Journal, vol. 88, no. 5, Dispute Resolution (April), p. 950-997.

techniques to improve his/her own outcome. Moreover, negotiation does not necessarily imply conflict. A manager can be involved in a dispute as a party, but can also be consulted to act as an intermediary by others who are in a dispute. A coach, consultant or therapist quite often deals with just one party instead of two.
For mediators, this book can contribute to further improve professionalism. A mediator can utilize many different interventions and techniques to control the mediation process. In practice, however, most mediators mainly apply their own set of preferred tools. During an actual mediation, attention is divided between choosing what interventions should be used (or not to intervene at all) on the one hand and managing the process on the other hand. Also, in most mediation trainings the focus is especially on the process aspect: what should be done in what phase of the mediation? The in-depth technical aspect of the interventions often receives less attention. This book is written to close this gap.
The toolkit has an interdisciplinary approach where mediation is regarded as a self-determining profession. Negotiation theories as well as knowledge from social psychology are addressed. From the teachings of these different disciplines the practical application or consequence of a mediation, negotiation or conflict situation is described.

Cautionary Note

Toolkit Mediation. Generating Outcomes as Mediator and Negotiator gives an overview of the treasure trove of interventions, techniques and methods that can be applied in a mediation or negotiation. The approach of the book is to offer a technical basis, or training on how the technique of an intervention works. This has to be separated from the question of whether and when it is wise to use this particular intervention in a specific context. For many mediators, the feeling that they need to do something all the time is a big pitfall. Ask yourself regularly during a mediation whether it is useful to intervene at that particular point in the mediation, whether you (and not the parties) are the only one who really works during the mediation, or whether the parties are engaged in a productive discussion so that it is wise to just watch and see what happens. Finding the perfect balance in a mediation is the big challenge. It means being directive enough to control the process without letting the communication be inappropriately dominated by the mediator (f.e. constant active listening).

Owners manual of the Toolkit Mediation. Generating Outcomes as Mediator and Negotiator

At the start this book you find a checklist with four rows that provide an overview of the tools mediators or negotiators have at their disposal. This overview is elaborated in the book. The technique, method or situation is described or presented in a checklist or model. The technical application of an intervention is illustrated by an example.

This book is a toolbox: it is not necessary to read it from cover to cover in order to benefit from it. You can browse by using the checklist and the icons. Accordingly, only the tools that are needed at a specific moment can be extracted from the book.
With the help of icons each chapter contains cross-references to other parts of the book where more detailed information can be found on a specific topic or related topics as well as references to other literature or to web addresses. With the help of the 'discussions' icon, contradictory views on a subject are pointed out. Moreover, the toolkit contains many practical hints.

Overview of the icons

'Technical' application and explanation of an intervention, technique or method.

Recommended literature dealing with a theme more in-depth.

Hint.

One-on-one discussion: caucus or negotiation.

This item is elaborated in another part of the toolkit.

This item is elaborated in another part of the toolkit.

Discussions on this issue/ contradictory opinions.

Website for more information.

Definition

Description of the four parts and appendices of the toolkit

Part I (row I of the checklist) **Planning and arrangements**
The first part of the book about planning and making arrangements can be consulted during the preparation for a mediation and while reflecting on how to tackle the proceedings. Here, information can be found about the intake phase, a checklist for the opening statement, ground rules, agreements on reporting and reviewing, about the mediator fee and on collaboration with a co-mediator. Additionally, there are chapters on mediator proposals, seeking expert advice, online mediation and administrative aspects like mediator certification and CPD, where to find mediation clauses, a code of conduct for mediators and mediation organizations.

Part II (row II of the checklist) **Process aspects**
The part on process aspects deals with features of the mediation process and the tools that a mediator needs to encourage the parties to move their conflict toward a solution. This part contains chapters on maintaining and demonstrating neutrality, dealing with biases, maintaining the power balance, empowerment and empathy. Moreover, hints on how to structure the process and staying on track, the one-text-procedure and how to deal with a caucus are described. The Harvard negotiation method (principled negotiation) is briefly explained. Additionally, there are paragraphs on interests and analysis of blocking issues and what interventions or tools can be used depending on the basic cause of the conflict. Last but not least, this part deals with the outcome that a mediation procedure can achieve.

Part III (row III of the checklist) **Techniques and interventions**
The part on techniques and interventions is the core of this practical book. It starts with an overview of the most important tools managers, mediators or negotiators have at their disposal. The overview contains a description or definition of the tool, when and why it is useful and an example of how the intervention is applied. In the following chapters of part III, the interventions and tools are dealt with in more depth. A description is given how to use a tool or technique and examples are provided to demonstrate the application. To illustrate the specifics, similarities and differences between the tools, the same sentences are used for all intervention examples. The tools are also placed side by side to allow easy comparison. Part III also contains handy schemes to support the choice of what tool can be used in a specific situation.

Part IV (row IV of the checklist) **Challenging situations & selected topics**
This fourth part on methods for challenging circumstances or specific topics can be consulted on special occasions. Methods to overcome deadlock are addressed. Answers can be found on how to deal with clients or (legal) advisors that bring tricky

tactics into play. Moreover, much attention is paid to methods on synchronizing different perspectives and psychological processes that can cause differing perceptions. This chapter also contains checklists for mediations with many representatives per party, multiple-party mediations or parties with dissimilar cultural backgrounds. Additionally, there is a chapter with tools for dealing with emotions, insights and tools based on neuro-science and a chapter on the escalation of conflicts and how to deescalate them (conflict escalation phases).

Appendices
As a supplement, a list of mediator jargon with explanations is included (Resource A). There is also a bibliography and a webography (Resource H).
In this book the words *parties, attendants, representatives, negotiators* and *clients* are all used to refer to the parties in the mediation. This is done for language variation purposes only. Moreover, the mediator is usually referred to as 'he' for the sake of readabilty and because the word mediator is masculine in the Dutch language (although there are many female mediators).
'Toolkit' readers who have comments or who would like to share additional hints or models that can possibly be included in a next edition are invited to mail these to: manon@toolkitcompany.com. Up-to-date information can be found on www.manonschonewille.com; www.academylegalmediation.com; www.mundimeditores.com.

I. Planning and arrangements

1	The initial contact phase (intake)	29
2	Pre-mediation planning	38
3	Checklist opening statement and ground rules	58
4	Agreements on reporting	62
5	Co-mediation	63
6	Preparing a negotiation agenda	68
7	Experts and mediator's proposal	70
8	Administrative kit	74

Part I. Planning and arrangements

Row I of the checklist on the inside of the cover contains the outline of part I. The first part of this book, about planning and agreements, can be consulted during the preparation for a mediation. Here, you can find information about the initial contact phase (intake), a checklist for the opening statement, whether to report and if so how, agreements on reporting and mediator fees, and information on working with a co-mediator.
Furthermore, attention is paid to upholding the ground rules, obtaining expert advice, a mediator proposal, and to the administrative context, for example certification as mediator, where to find mediation clauses, a code of conduct for mediators and mediation organizations.

1 The initial contact phase (intake)

1.1 The initial contact

The intake of a mediation is also called the null phase. As soon as the first contact is made by one or more parties, the mediator has to make several decisions, for example on handling ethical issues such as how to react when he is approached by only one party, and on practical aspects such as how to approach the initial contact and managing the mediation.

Topics in the intake phase

- ☐ Are the parties and the dispute suitable for mediation? Is a different method to resolve the dispute more beneficial in this case? (I-1.2 and Rescource C, key procedural drivers)
- ☐ **Should I hold an initial contact consultation and if so what form should it take?**
  - By telephone, online, in writing, or in person?
  - At the beginning of the first mediation session or in an earlier phase (II-9 and I-3)?
  - Separate consultations or a joint intake consultation (II-16)?
  - (Also) a preliminary procedural consultation with the advisors or lawyers concerned (I-2.8)?
  - Does confidentiality apply to the initial consultations? How can confidentiality be assured?
- ☐ **Conflict of interests checks**
  - Am I impartial as a mediator? Facts and circumstances which could raise doubt about the mediator's impartiality include:
    - direct or indirect earlier contacts with one of the parties. For example when the mediator, or his practice or employer, has acted in a professional capacity on behalf of one of the parties, or has personal or business connections;
    - (in)direct interest in the outcome of the mediation;

- possession of confidential information in relation to one of the parties or the subject of the mediation.

(For further guidance you can consult the mediator code of conduct that is applicable in your country, or the country where the mediation will take place.)

- Are there any matters that can influence my neutrality (II-2.1) such as ethical concerns?
- Are there further issues I should inform the parties about?

☐ When I have been contacted by just one party, should I contact the opposing party and invite or try to persuade them to enter into mediation if the party initiating the mediation asks me to do so? Could doing so affect my impartiality as a mediator (II-2.1)? If so, how would I handle the situation (II-2.1)?

☐ Is the dispute suitable for mediation? And are the parties prepared for it (I-1.2)?

☐ **Managing expectations**

What do the parties expect from the mediation? Are their expectations realistic? Can the mediator meet these expectations as to:

- mediation strategies (I-2.1);
- expertise concerning the content of the dispute, specialization and experience (I-2.2);
- approach to the mediation process (I-2.3);
- time scope (do the parties have a deadline (II-14.1)?).

☐ On what particular aspects of the mediation process do I need the parties to consent in advance?

What mediation rules apply?

Co-mediation (I-5)?

Would it be better to refer the case to another mediator (I-2.2)?

☐ **Fees**

- Do parties know what my fees are and what services will be included?
- What is the allowance for traveling expenses and other out-of-pocket costs, traveling time, writing reports (I-4) or preparation and drafting of any settlement or other agreements/ documents?
- Can I give an estimate of the expected time/costs (II-14.3)?
- Would I (at request of the parties) agree in advance to a time-limit for the entire mediation process or a maximum sum in mediator fees?
- How will/should the costs be distributed between the parties?

☐ **Logistical arrangements**

- The time required for the sessions (II-14.3).
- Procedures to decide on:
  - agenda;
  - location;
  - adjournments;
  - actual or potential deadlines (II-14.1).

Consider to follow the Universal Disclosure Protocol Mediation (UDPM) when informing the parties about what they can expect from working with you as a mediator instead of just sending the code of conduct. The UDPM is an important first step in a new generation of ADR standards, whereby each mediation process and the procedural obligations of the ADR-Neutrals can be adjusted to better clarify the needs and interests of the participants in each case. (More on UDPM see I-7 and I-8.3) and universaldisclosureprotocolmediation.com.

Information on mediation rules, mediators' code of conduct and other legal and administrative aspects can be found in I-8.

Ask all parties how you can establish (confidential) contact: can you use their business email address, or is it better to use their personal email? Can you reach someone through their office's switchboard or better on their mobile number, and so on. It is not a luxury to check if others might have access to an email account and whether it is known within an organization that an appointment with a mediator has been scheduled. This holds especially true for employment mediations when the employee is on a long sick-leave.

1.1.1 Pre-mediation sessions: The value of individual meetings before mediation sessions

Business parties and their lawyers often prefer it when mediation begins with an individual intake conversation.[2] Also, from my personal experience as a mediator, I have found that it works well to have separate meetings with each of the parties beforehand:

- You gain information about commitment, alignment with their stakeholders, whether there are other parties involved, and who should (or should not) be at the table.
- You can 'mediate the process' first.
- While the dynamics between the parties are not yet addressed, you already get a good impression of the themes and types of issues in play; this helps in formulating working hypotheses that you will later test.
- If needed, someone can vent their frustrations.
- You can give undivided attention to each party without worrying about the dynamics with the other party at the table. This is an excellent opportunity to build a psychological contract (II-1). People feel heard, and that often adds significant value to a mediation.
- It is also a good tool if parties are not yet sure if they want mediation (with you), allowing them to become acquainted with what mediation practically entails before committing to a complete process.
- From practice (and from research, see below), it is evident that the likelihood of reaching an agreement increases when mediation begins with individual meetings.

2 UU -Montaingecentrum ZAM-ACB onderzoek 2018 and 2024

Of course, you can also choose to conduct an intake conversation with both parties together. An intake can be done in person, but it also works well online, especially if the parties prefer that.

Swaab and Brett conducted research[3] on 1381 Dutch labor and family cases and concluded that individual meetings prior to mediation have a positive effect on achieving agreement between parties at a later stage (resulting in a higher success rate). When a pre-mediation caucus was used, the intensity of the conflict between the parties was found to decrease during the mediation. Importantly, the researchers noted that these positive effects were more pronounced when the mediator's interventions during the pre-mediation caucus were focused on building a relationship with the parties, rather than discussing the conflict or exploring potential solutions. Mediators who do this run the risk of being perceived as less neutral. Recent studies underscore the crucial importance of creating rapport, instilling trust, and building a relationship between the mediator and the parties (II-1). The use of a caucus during the mediation process had less impact in this study compared to its use during the pre-mediation phase, especially in the case of labor mediations.

Swaab and Brett's conclusion and recommendation is that a caucus should not only be seen as an option during the mediation process but as an important tool in the intake phase. According to them, mediators should make a deliberate choice and match between the timing and the objective of a caucus. A mediator should primarily focus on rapport and building a relationship with the parties during a pre-mediation meeting, without delving too much into the conflict and its potential solutions. How can this be achieved? Providing reflecting on feelings (III-5.2), listening (III-2), and being empathic (II-5) are good tools.

In I-1.1.2, there is a checklist with sample questions to ask in the intake.

1.1.2 Checklist questions to ask during the intake phase

Checklist of questions to ask during the Intake phase

Note: An individual intake, with an emphasis on building trust and a good working relationship between you and the parties, has a positive effect on de-escalating the conflict and increases the chances of reaching an agreement (I-1.1.2). Therefore, focus primarily on the People and Process aspects and as little as possible on the Problem.

3 Swaab, R. & and J. Brett (2007), 'Caucus with Care: The Impact of Pre-Mediation Caucuses on Conflict Resolution', IACM 2007 Meetings Paper.

Also business parties and their lawyers often prefer a mediation to start with an individual intake conversation with the mediator.

Sample questions for an individual intake with 1 Party (B is the name of the other party)

People

- ☐ *"Who, in your opinion, is most affected by this issue and who is affected the least?"*
- ☐ *"Does the conflict impact the quality of service/work?"*
- ☐ *"What has been attempted so far to resolve the issue?"*
- ☐ *"Who, in your opinion, has more influence and who has less in resolving the issues?"*
- ☐ *"Why, in your opinion, is the collaboration not working now?"*
- ☐ *"In your view, what's the reason you haven't been able to resolve this together yet? Do you think both of you see it the same way, or could B have a different perspective?"*
- ☐ *"How come you haven't been able to find a solution among yourselves?"*
- ☐ *"What could be a small gesture from B that would make you willing to discuss the issues and commit to trying to resolve them? What would give you hope that it's possible to reach an agreement together?"*
- ☐ *"What would be a small but meaningful gesture from B for you?"*
- ☐ *"Do you think others or B perceive your efforts to resolve the conflict?"*
- ☐ *"What could be a good intention from B, in your opinion?"*
- ☐ *"How do you typically react if B says/does that?"*

Process

- ☐ *"Do you have experience with mediation?"*
- ☐ *"What, in your opinion, would be counterproductive for me as a mediator to do?"*
- ☐ *"What could I, as a mediator, do to best assist both of you?"*
- ☐ *"How do you see my role in the mediation?"*
- ☐ *"Do you have a timeline in mind?"*
- ☐ *"Are there others you believe should participate in the mediation?"*
- ☐ *"Who, in your opinion, from B's side should or should not be at the table to increase the chances of a successful mediation?"*
- ☐ *"How do others (clients, colleagues, other departments, management, employee council, board of directors/supervision, investors, shareholders, etc.) perceive the situation?"*

Problem

- ☐ *"What needs to be discussed during the mediation (or the first meeting) to make it useful for you?"*
- ☐ *"What is the problem or issue that needs to be resolved?"*

- ☐ *"In your view, what is the core of the problem? How do you think B would answer this question?"*
- ☐ *"Where do you agree/disagree with each other?"*

Sample questions for a joint intake

- ☐ *"What is your (joint) objective for the mediation?"*
- ☐ *"Why do you need a mediator?"*
- ☐ *"What do you expect from the mediation?"*
- ☐ *"How would you like me to approach the mediation?"*
- ☐ *"What does it mean if you succeed in resolving the conflict together, or what happens if the conflict is not resolved (in the short term)?"*
- ☐ *"How did you resolve problems in the past?"*
- ☐ *"What are your expectations of each other?"*

The Glasl Escalation stairs (IV-7) can also be used during the intake to assess a party's escalation stage and how they perceive it for the other party.

1.2 Factors favoring and disfavoring the use of mediation

The following list can help to determine whether mediation is suitable for this dispute and these particular parties. The most important factors favoring the use of mediation:

- the parties want to resolve their dispute; and
- they are willing and able to negotiate the conflict, or they at least are prepared to discuss it; and
- the conflict has not escalated too far (IV-7).

REFERRAL TO MEDIATION (Pel, 2007) offers valuable advice for conflict diagnosis and a professional mediation proposal, especially for lawyers, parties and judges involved in court-connected mediation processes. The book also contains countless practical tips based on many years of experience and research.

Other factors favoring mediation

- ☐ The parties want to end their dispute quickly.
- ☐ There is a long-term relationship and the continuation or the thoughtful and considerate termination of the relationship is important.
- ☐ Treatment issue or disrupted communication.
- ☐ The parties have a desire to reach a settlement themselves and on their own terms.
- ☐ A judicial decision does not or would not (totally) resolve the underlying conflict.
- ☐ Confidentiality or privacy is important.
- ☐ There are more than two parties involved in the dispute.
- ☐ The dispute concerns several claims/conflicts.
- ☐ The case is technically and/or substantively complex or requires specialist knowledge.
- ☐ It is an international case (with jurisdictional or enforcement issues).

The main factors disfavoring mediation

- ☐ At least one party benefits from delay and does not want this interest to surface during the mediation (hidden agenda).
- ☐ One of the parties is acting in bad faith. Please note: distrust (of the opponent) does not necessarily imply bad faith. Often it is hard to determine whether a party in a mediation is participating in good faith. This is especially so when parties have come to the mediation table at the request of a third party, such as a judge or the management of a company. When you doubt the motives for participation, you can first explore in a joint session what the parties expect from the mediation. Next you can address the issue in a caucus (II-16) by asking questions (III-10) about the commitment to and the expectations regarding the mediation. If there are strong indications that a party is not participating in good faith, you can ask confronting questions, if necessary (III-10.4).
- ☐ There are no new developments and the same representatives have already tried mediation to solve this conflict at an earlier stage without a positive result.
- ☐ A precedent is needed (for example an explanation of the General Terms) or a principle of law needs to be established.
- ☐ A party is particularly concerned with publicly asserting or proving they are in the right (for example in order to send a wider message).
- ☐ A party is unable or unwilling to take responsibility for decisions or is insufficiently able to represent or protect its own interests.
- ☐ There is an extreme imbalance of power.

1.3 Mediation, why should you?

The main advantages of mediation/arguments of advocates

- ☐ It is fast and efficient.
- ☐ The solution belongs to the parties and is therefore likely to be more sustainable and more readily implemented and observed, than if a third party (for example a judge) had imposed the solution.
- ☐ The settlement does not necessarily have to fit in the (limited) legal spectrum of solutions (right, wrong, compensation or otherwise) and the outcome can be facilitated by drawing on issues far outside the narrow scope of the subject of the dispute.
- ☐ There is flexibility; the parties contribute to the process and can therefore influence that process themselves.
- ☐ A neutral third party is better able to distinguish between emotional and content aspects (III-8) and therefore identify the blocking issues (II-8).
- ☐ The focus is on the parties' interests and on the future instead of (legal) positions and what happened in the past (II-10).
- ☐ A mediator can speak with parties separately (caucus). This allows the real interests to surface, and options for resolving problems can be discussed in confidence (II-16).
- ☐ The parties themselves control the conflict and its resolution. Confidentiality and privacy are guaranteed.
- ☐ A workable relationship can be continued or ended carefully.

Mediation is a powerful management tool. Several books discuss mediation processes and techniques specifically for managers and/or deal with workplace conflict. We recommend:

- *Fowler (2023), RISING ABOVE OFFICE CONFLICT: A LIGHT-HEARTED GUIDE FOR THE HEAVY-HEARTED EMPLOYEE (Volume 4) (The ACR Practitioner's Guide Series.*
- *The Arbinger Institute (2022), THE ANATOMY OF PEACE, RESOLVING THE HEART OF CONFLICT*
- *Grenny, Patterson, McMillan, Switzler, Gregory (2021), 'CRUCIAL CONVERSATIONS: TOOLS FOR TALKING WHEN STAKES ARE HIGH.*
- *Ripley (2021), HIGH CONFLICT: WHY WE GET TRAPPED AND HOW WE GET OUT.*
- *Pollack (2020), CONFLICT RESOLUTION PLAYBOOK: PRACTICAL COMMUNICATION SKILLS FOR PREVENTING, MANAGING, AND RESOLVING CONFLICT.*
- *Falcone (2019), 101 TOUGH CONVERSATIONS TO HAVE WITH EMPLOYEES: A MANAGER'S GUIDE TO ADDRESSING PERFORMANCE, CONDUCT, AND DISCIPLINE CHALLENGES.*
- *Gallo (2017), HBR GUIDE TO DEALING WITH CONFLICT.*

- *Cloke, Goldsmith (2011), RESOLVING CONFLICTS AT WORK: TEN STRATEGIES FOR EVERYONE ON THE JOB.*
- *Crawley and Graham (2005), MEDIATION FOR MANAGERS. RESOLVING CONFLICT AND REBUILDING RELATIONSHIPS AT WORK.*
- *Dana (2001), CONFLICT RESOLUTION.*

1.4 Mediation, why not?

The main disadvantages of mediation/counter-arguments from opponents

- ☐ The only issues that can be resolved in a mediation are those that can be finalized contractually. Some issues require a formal judicial order to be implemented. Agreements on public policy themes like parental control or decreeing a divorce must, by their very nature, be confirmed by a formal judicial order. However, this is by no means an argument against mediation. In most cases it is better to make (prior) agreements oneself than to leave the decisions on such important matters completely to a third party.
- ☐ If the mediation fails, there is no clarity. A follow-up (of a procedure) is needed, with the risk of time loss and having to repeat the process.
- ☐ A mediated outcome, being confidential, does not result in a precedent, and does not advance the development of jurisprudence.
- ☐ A writ of execution or other formal determination, such as a consent judgment is not issued automatically. In most countries converting a mediated outcome into an enforceable title beyond contract law requires an additional step. It is often possible to convert a settlement agreement into a consent judgment by applying to the court. In some countries, especially EU countries, this can also be achieved through an application to a notary. It should be noted, however, that this may become complicated in international cases it must be decided which country's law and procedure will govern.

Books on representing a client in mediation:

- *Jordaan (2022), NEGOTIATION AND DISPUTE RESOLUTION FOR LAWYERS.*
- *Golann and Folberg (2021), MEDIATION: THE ROLES OF ADVOCATE AND NEUTRAL.*
- *Abramson (2013), MEDIATION REPRESENTATION: ADVOCATING IN A PROBLEM-SOLVING PROCESS.*
- *Wade (2013), SYSTEMATIC RISK ANALYSIS FOR NEGOTIATORS AND LITIGATORS: HOW TO HELP CLIENTS MAKE BETTER DECISIONS, Dispute Resolution Centre, Bond University.*
- *Wade (2000), REPRESENTING CLIENTS AT MEDIATION AND NEGOTIATION.*
- *Galton (1994), REPRESENTING CLIENTS IN MEDIATION.*
- *Van Winkle (2001), MEDIATION: A PATH BACK FOR THE LOST LAWYER.*

2 Pre-mediation planning

2.1 Style and strategic approach to the mediation process

Every mediator has his own way of approaching the mediation process. It can either be chosen consciously or used unconsciously. A mediator has his own strategies and tactics, a characteristic way of acting and reacting. Not every good mediator is therefore necessarily suited and qualified for every dispute and all parties.

There are many books and articles on mediator styles. For those who want to dig deeper into the subject we recommend:

- *Schonewille and Lack (2014), 'Mediation in the European Union and abroad: 60 states divided by a common word?', in Schonewille, THE VARIEGATED LANDSCAPE OF MEDIATION: A COMPARATIVE STUDY OF MEDIATION REGULATION AND PRACTICES IN EUROPE AND THE WORLD.*[4]
- *Baruch Bush (2004), THE PROMISE OF MEDIATION, THE TRANSFORMATIVE APPROACH TO MEDIATION.*
- *Cloke (2001), MEDIATING DANGEROUSLY: THE FRONTIERS OF CONFLICT RESOLUTION.*
- *Kolb and Associates (1994), WHEN TALK WORKS – PROFILES OF MEDIATORS.*
- *Kraybill (2005) STYLE MATTERS: THE KRAYBILL CONFLICT STYLE INVENTORY.*

Often a distinction is made between the task-focused style and the relationship-focused approach.[5]

2.1.1 The task-focused mediator

A task-focused mediator generally applies pressure on the parties to resolve their dispute and as a result is inclined to structure the mediation process in such a way that several stages are completed.

- The **solution-focused mediator** from this group is especially focused on reaching an agreement and therefore feels partly responsible for reaching a workable solution. Some of these mediators are even prepared to suggest solutions themselves or to give an opinion, which in some situations can be binding, on how to settle the case (I-7).
- The **problem-focused**, or **facilitative**, **mediator** puts more emphasis on the process, on the underlying interests and on clarifying conflict issues, rather than on finding a specific solution. This type of mediator feels little responsibility for the specific outcome.

4 Chapter 2, p. 19-44: This chapter can be downloaded from the resources section on www.manonschonewille.com.
5 For example Prein (2005).

- A **task-focused** or **evaluative mediator** generally applies pressure on the parties to resolve their dispute and as a result the mediator is inclined to structure the mediation process in such a way that several stages are completed.

Solution focused

A **solution-focused mediator** takes the situation as the clients envision it and what is going well between the parties in spite of the issues that have arisen as a starting point to develop solutions. A concrete goal is formulated to work towards. In the solution-focused approach, attention is focused on the desired state, the future, rather than on what has not worked in the past or an analysis and exploration of the conflict. The focus is on what parties want and what works or has worked (positive exceptions), rather than an analysis of the conflict or exploration of underlying issues. The conflict is a reason to make a change, not the focus of the mediation. The challenge here is asking the right questions (III-10.5.5).

Like solution-focused coaching and other forms of solution-focused work, the basis for solution-focused mediation lies in Solution-Focused Therapy. This is a form of talk therapy developed in the 1970s and 1980s by Steve de Shazer, Insoo Kim Berg, and their colleagues at the Brief Family Therapy Center in Milwaukee (United States). Solution-focused mediation offers several advantages, including its speed and effectiveness in achieving desired outcomes, often resulting in sustainable solutions. It also boasts a high compliance rate, ensuring adherence to agreements, and places a strong emphasis on positive aspects and the future, thus creating room for change. However, it is worth noting some drawbacks, notably the fine art of formulating the right questions, probing deeper, and closely observing (both verbal and non-verbal) responses and effectively building on them. According to Cauffman (2010),[6] solution-focused work encompasses more than simply applying a toolkit of interventions, such as scaling questions, inquiries about positive exceptions to a problem, giving compliments, or presenting the so-called 'miracle question' (see III.-10.5). According to him, the most critical factors for inducing change in clients are as follows: Does the mediator succeed in making clients feel understood? This does not imply that the mediator needs to grasp every perspective of a party but rather that the mediator shows genuine interest in understanding what motivates and matters to individuals. Do clients receive authentic attention? Does the mediator make clients feel genuinely valued (note that authentic attention goes beyond merely providing a reflective response, as per III-5)? Do clients feel respected as individuals? Do they become more hopeful about change and envision alternative interpretations? Finally, the application of specific solution-focused interventions and techniques holds significant importance, including identifying sources of strength and exceptions to the problem. Consequently, solution-focused work

6 Cauffman, L. (2010), Simpel, oplossingsgerichte positieve psychologie in actie. Amsterdam: Boom Lemma. Dutch publication. English version: Solution Focused Coaching, Simple works best, Brave New Books (2020).

encompasses much more than simply asking scaling questions (III-10.5) or applying other solution-focused techniques.
For some matters, people must learn to accept them, or agree to disagree, and it is necessary to examine underlying causes and blocking issues (II-8) or delve into their emotions and feelings. So oftentimes an in-depth exploration is necessary first. As the objective is set at the beginning of a solution-focused mediation without all underlying interests being known, this may limit flexibility. However, it is an efficient way of working.

Evaluative, substantive focused

The **evaluative mediator** is especially focused on reaching an agreement and therefore feels partly responsible for reaching a workable solution. Some of these mediators are even prepared to suggest solutions themselves or to give a mediator proposal (I-7).
In **evaluative mediation**, the focus is on reaching an agreement on substantive issues, often involving separate sessions with the parties (II-16 caucus). An evaluative mediator takes a directive approach to both the process and the substance, feeling partly responsible for the (quality of the) content of the agreements reached by the parties. The result is often assessed by the mediator based on legal or other standards. The underlying assumption (Riskin 1996, 2003) is that parties require support due to a lack of knowledge in the field, unfamiliarity with legal aspects, or industry practices. The mediator feels responsible for alerting parties to these factors and preventing them from shortchanging themselves or making (legal) mistakes.
There is a sliding scale in terms of the degree to which the mediator guides the process and the content, ranging from suggesting options (III-15) → extensive reality testing (III-11.2 risk analysis and III-11.3 NAN) → playing devil's advocate → addressing substantive/legal issues → providing information or making a mediator proposal (I-7) → making a (binding) decision. Therefore, an evaluative mediator must possess a certain level of substantive expertise.
The advantage of an evaluative approach is that there is a high likelihood of reaching a solution, even when the parties cannot agree among themselves. Additionally, the mediator can often provide a reasonably balanced substantive intervention, considering the parties' interests and power dynamics. Many lawyers and companies also find this approach comfortable. However, disadvantages include limited room for addressing emotions and repairing a relationship, the potential for the mediator to exert (unwanted) pressure on the parties to accept a solution or even manipulate them. The mediator may lack sufficient substantive expertise, leading to incorrect advice, and there is a possibility that parties may not share all the necessary information and their true interests with the mediator if they know the mediator is steering the solution based on the substantive aspects. The compliance rate (adherence to agreements) may also be lower when a third party exerts influence.

Facilitative problem and process focused

The **problem-focused, or facilitative, mediator** puts more emphasis on the process, on the underlying interests and on clarifying conflict issues, rather than on finding a specific solution. This type of mediator feels less responsibility for the specific outcome as the parties are responsible for the substantive aspects.

The problem-oriented or facilitating mediator works with improving communication, fostering understanding, the process, uncovering underlying interests, and clarifying conflict issues. More emphasis is placed on these aspects than on finding a specific solution. The conflict is seen as a mixture of communication, psychology and substance. The underlying assumption of a facilitating mediator (Riskin 1996, 2003) is that parties are sufficiently knowledgeable about business practices, legal aspects, and other relevant matters, or they are capable of seeking advice on their own. Facilitative mediators often work in plenary meetings with all parties present (but not exclusively). These mediators can be both strongly directive and facilitating on the process, but they are facilitating on the substance. The division of roles is that the mediator is responsible for the process, and the parties are responsible for the problem and the solution. Parties have a significant influence on the decisions to be made and the assessment of what constitutes a good solution.

Again, there is a sliding scale: from reality testing (future-oriented III.11.1 and risk analysis III-11.2) → presenting different options (III-15) → playing devil's advocate → addressing substantive/legal issues.

Advantages of a facilitating approach include empowering the parties and encouraging them to take responsibility for their own conflict and its resolution. It allows for working on relational aspects, and the compliance rate (adherence to agreements) is generally high. Disadvantages include the possibility of a lengthy process with no guarantee of concluding with an agreement or solution. Questions may arise regarding the protection of a weaker party (II-3) or a party with less leverage (III-14.2) in this mediation style. Additionally, parties may become overly reliant on the mediator if the mediator controls the entire flow of communication through them. There is also a risk that too much emphasis on commonalities (III-13 and III-6.1) may cause some underlying (differing) issues to go unaddressed.

In business-to-business mediations, and especially in Anglo-Saxon countries, most mediators have a task-focused mediation approach. Falling into this category is the (pure) **caucus mediation strategy**, where the mediation takes place almost exclusively by means of individual discussions with one party at a time, unless there are compelling reasons not to do so. Here, the mediation typically starts with a joint meeting to determine the themes and to set an agenda and then proceeds in several caucuses (II-16) between the mediator and the individual parties. In this way, every party can confidentially explain their own point of view and objectives with regard to the mediation.

Only at the end, when a settlement proposal is being negotiated, do the parties meet again in a joint session. A mediation that is based on the principle of confidential listening also falls in this category; here the parties agree to confidentially inform the mediator of their conditions and options to come to an agreement. In this way the mediator can evaluate possible overlap and establish where common solutions can be found. The mediator informs the parties only of a potential ZOPA, Zone of Possible Agreement (III-14), but discloses nothing about the content.

2.1.2 The relationship-focused or communication-focused mediator

A relationship-focused mediator mainly concentrates on the communication between parties and on providing insight into the different perspectives and perceptions and the underlying emotions. The mediation is less focused on the content and the clarification and resolution of the conflict issues. The mediation takes mainly place in joint sessions. The most consistent and distinct form of communication/relationship-focused mediation is **transformative mediation** (Bush and Folger 1994) which strives for total empowerment of (II-6) and recognition by (II-6) the parties involved. Reaching an agreement is not the main goal of this form of mediation. The mediator has a non-directive style and leaves control of the process to the parties involved in order to exclude any influence on the content by the mediator. The mutual interaction and its development (transformation) are central. This changes the parties' perspectives on the conflict and also on their own needs and possibilities. This results in a better understanding of one's own position as well as the other party's position, and parties are therefore better able to resolve the problem themselves.

Advantages of the transformative approach include full empowerment of the parties, with them taking responsibility for their own conflict and its resolution, mutual recognition, and it is a flexible approach in which the parties retain complete control. Communication and interaction are usually improved, and the compliance rate is very high.

The disadvantages are that it may not provide sufficient structure or focus for a certain type of case or parties, such as in business mediations where substance plays a significant role or in mediations involving lawyers. Transformative mediation can be time-consuming, and there is no guarantee of concluding the mediation with an agreement. Additionally, similar to facilitative mediation, questions may arise about whether a weaker party (II-3) or a party with less leverage (III-14.2) is adequately protected in this model.

Narrative mediation (Winslade and Monk 2000) is a relationship-focused mediation style. Narrative mediation develops a new context and description of the conflict in which all parties concerned recognize their own roles in the origin and escalation of a conflict. The dispute becomes a mutual problem, which means all parties involved have

an interest in resolving the conflict. Under the guidance of a mediator, the parties more or less create a (new) narrative by exploring time and place (the setting), the events (the plot) and the parties concerned (the players, roles).
The focus lies on restoring the relationship and reasoning shifts (shifts in logical reasoning). In this approach, the process and substance are not considered separately. The advantage of narrative mediation is that it is suitable for intercultural settings due to its sensitivity and openness to different interpretations and worldviews. The relationship and collaboration between parties are usually improved. Disadvantages are similar to those of transformative mediation, as it may not provide sufficient structure or focus for a certain type of case or parties, such as in business mediations where substantive aspects play a significant role or in mediations involving lawyers. Additionally, the process can be time-consuming, and there is no certainty that the process will conclude with an agreement.

Zumeta (2000)[7] has written a well-readable and clear article that describes and compares the facilitating, evaluative, and transformative styles.

Guidelines for choosing the most suitable mediation approach as a mediator
In our experience for business mediations, the facilitative approach is generally a good starting point. Initially, try to see if it is possible for the parties to resolve their conflict themselves using this approach. However, a certain level of sophistication from the parties is necessary for this, including their willingness to resolve the conflict and their readiness to examine their own contributions to the emergence and escalation of the conflict. If a persistent impasse occurs (see also IV-1) or if forward movement or commitment of the parties is difficult, depending on the cause, you can employ solution-focused or more provocative interventions (III-19), or incorporate evaluative elements such as a mediator's proposal (I-7). Another general rule of thumb is that as the conflict is escalated further, a more directive style is advisable (Glasl escalation stairs IV-7). In addition to identifying commonalities, you can, for example, (in a solution-focused or evaluative manner) help parties identify threats or their mutual worst-case scenario, which they both want to avoid. This often leads parties to see their problems in a different light. When commonalities are also identified, it motivates parties to undergo a mental shift, enabling them to work toward a solution. Subsequently, you can let parties handle more aspects themselves as a mediator.
In summary, as a mediator, consider the various approaches as a menu of choices from which you can select the right interventions for different situations.

Riskin (1994, 1996, 2003) created a matrix of mediation styles known as the 'Riskin Grid'. In this grid, he distinguishes between two dimensions: a narrow or broad problem

7 Zumeta, Z.D. (2000), Styles of Mediation: Facilitative, Evaluative and Transformative Mediation. Availale on IMImediation.org, mediation styles.

definition on one axis and an evaluative/directive or facilitative role on the other. The axes range from non-evaluative to evaluative on content and from facilitative to directive on process. He attempts to indicate in which situation each approach is advisable.
This 'Riskin grid' has been adapted by Manon Schonewille and Jeremy Lack to serve as a foundation for discussions with the parties and their attorneys regarding the process and the preferred style of the mediator, especially in international disputes.

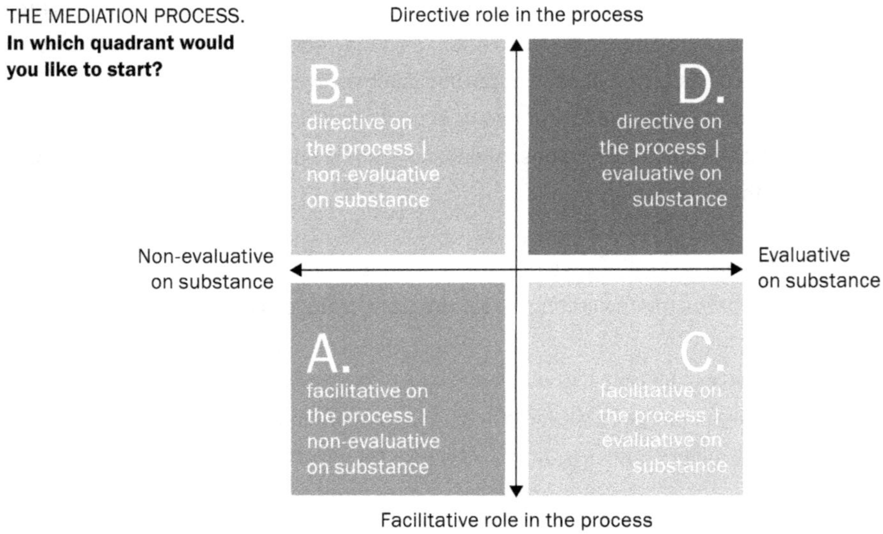

The approach and style of mediation can be defined using two axes:

a) How directive or facilitative is the mediator on **process issues**, such as time management, the use of a caucus or not, exchanging written materials in advance, formal opening statements, etc.; and
b) How evaluative or non-evaluative | facilitative is the mediator on **substantive issues**, such as having no opinion on substantive matters, conducting rigorous reality testing, or being willing to propose a mediator proposal (I-7) if the parties fail to reach an agreement.

This grid leads to a classification into four main types of mediation processes, which can also vary significantly within the same quadrant, depending on the emphasis on process and/or substance. Mediators should ideally be flexible and capable of operating in each of the quadrants, depending on the needs of the situation, the participants, and the stage of the mediation process.
This grid is a useful tool that can serve as a basis for a discussion on the desired type of mediation process among all involved parties. Each type has its advantages and disadvantages.

A comprehensive analysis of the four quadrants is provided in 'Mediation in the European Union and abroad: 60 states divided by a common word?', in: Manon Schonewille and Jeremy Lack (Chapter 2 of The Variegated Landscape of Mediation, (2014)). This chapter can be downloaded from www.manonschonewille.nl under the resources tab and at www.mundimediatores.com.

2.1.3 Other styles and approaches to the mediation process

Kolb (1983) characterizes the fundamental attitude of mediators as 'orchestrators' who support the process, work on the relationship and help empower the parties, or the 'dealmakers' who are directive both in the process and on content. Mediators have their own fundamental attitude regarding the mediation process and they have a specific style.

The professional background of a mediator can play a role in his approach to the mediation process. Every professional group has its own pitfalls as well as positive characteristics that facilitate the performance of mediators. A judge-mediator is often good at listing for interests and issues that are in dispute, but he must focus on not being judgmental about the chosen solution, and be careful not to force his opinion on the parties concerned. A lawyer-mediator is often good at risk analysis and reality testing (III-11) but he must be able to set aside the legal merits of a case. A psychologist-mediator often has very good questioning techniques, but he needs to take care not to spend too much time exploring history and emotions, and also have the parties look at business aspects such as financial consequences.

There is no general recommendation for 'the best mediation strategy'. Much depends, among other things, on the personality of the mediator. The best strategy is the style that most naturally fits the mediator. In addition it depends on the type and the content of the dispute, as well as the parties concerned. Every situation is unique. Accordingly, the process must be adapted to the needs of the parties, not vice-versa. In an ideal case, a mediator can apply different styles and strategies throughout a mediation process. This means facilitating when possible and directing where necessary.

Active self-reflection is very important for a professional mediator. You can use each mediation for your own Continuous Professional Development (CPD) if you review your own performance by taking a few minutes to ask yourself questions like:

- How did parties reach settlement?
- What went well?
- What could be done differently next time?
- Other learnings?

Weblinks about self-reflection can be found in the webography in Resource H.

Schonewille and Lack (2014), Mediation in the European Union and abroad: 60 states divided by a common word? in Schonewille, THE VARIEGATED LANDSCAPE OF MEDIATION: A COMPARATIVE STUDY OF MEDIATION REGULATION AND PRACTICES IN EUROPE AND THE WORLD.[8]
Baruch Bush (2004), THE PROMISE OF MEDIATION, THE TRANSFORMATIVE APPROACH TO MEDIATION.

2.2 Expertise on content and specialists versus generalists

The question whether a mediator needs expertise on content and/or whether he should specialize in certain types of issues, is often debated. Many mediators believe that expertise on content is not necessary for the real 'mediation expert'.[9]
The disadvantage of content expertise is the inclination to aim undue focus on substance. For example, the mediation can focus on whether an angle of x degrees can bring about action y, when it should be about past agreements and expectations between the parties. Or the mediator and parties use jargon amongst themselves but fail to understand that they define the same terms differently, which turns out to be one of the blocking issues (II-8).
An advantage of specialization or content expertise is that the mediator can better understand what the parties are talking about. He will not need to call upon outside expertise (I-7). In complex disputes or a mediation with multifaceted (pre)conditions, the mediator can evaluate possible pitfalls and assess when clients really need the advice or opinion of an expert. For example regarding alimony in a divorce case, a severance package in an employment termination case, or regarding corporate and financial implications in business mediations.
Specialization prevents inappropriate settlements due to ignorance – such as reaching agreements that are unworkable in practice (II-13). This all contributes to the quality and speed of the mediation.
The credibility of the mediator and the confidence the parties have in the mediator and the mediation process are supported by the mediator having a certain background, 'speaking the parties' language', and understanding the issues.
In practice, clients and their lawyers often ask for a mediator who specializes in a certain type of mediation case and has (a degree of) content expertise. A mediator needs to consider what type of mediation cases he is willing and able to take on, how much expertise that requires, and whether he wants to specialize in a certain area or prefers to be a generalist.

8 Chapter 2, p. 19-44: This chapter can be downloaded in the resources section on www.manonschonewille.com.
9 In the Netherlands this is the prevailing line of thought. See also www.mediate.com, e.g. Linden 2004.

In most countries the mediation market shows a tendency towards specialization. There are mediators who are specialized in workplace disputes, divorce and child custody, family mediators, business mediators and mediators who concentrate on (public) administrative matters or neighborhood disputes. Mediators with experience and background in specific areas are more frequently engaged in court-appointed mediations and in mediations set up by mediation providers (organizations offering mediation services).

In preparation for a mediation, the mediator needs to consider what approach and mediation style is best suited for the dispute and the parties concerned (I-2.1). What do clients expect in terms of the degree of expertise and specialization of the mediator (I-2.2)? To what extent is the mediator able and willing to make use of different approaches? And to what extent will he change his mediation style if needed?

If you expect there will be a discrepancy between your offer as a mediator and what the parties expect, it is advisable to manage expectations (I-1.1 and I-2.3) and to clarify or discuss in advance how you will approach the mediation. This requires insight into your personal style as a mediator.

An expert in mediation

As an expert in mediation you need to be able to guarantee professional quality, credibility and speed. Moreover, you must be able to prevent the mediation from getting deadlocked on content or emotional issues. A high-quality mediator has a flexible approach in the mediation process and can adapt his strategy and tactics to changing circumstances. He is also able to employ a range of techniques and interventions during the mediation and, depending on the progress of the mediation and the parties' needs, switch between a style more focused on relationships or communications and a more task-focused style, if necessary. An expert in mediation not only complies with the requirements of (continuing) professional education and has relevant practical experience, he also has the following qualities:

1. Excellent communication skills and a command of mediation interventions and techniques (III-1), is empathic (II-5) and especially a good listener (III-2).
2. Inspires confidence (II-1).
3. Observes (professional) ethical rules and the mediator code of conduct.
4. Creative problem solver who is able to think in terms of 'expanding the pie' (II-7.2.2 and III-15).
5. Ability to communicate with different people in a range of situations and at various levels.
6. Aware of his own prejudices and limitations and learns from his (mediation) experiences (II-2.3).

7. Employs various mediation strategies and approaches (I-2.1).
8. Willing and able to apply hybrid ADR procedures (f.e. Med-Arb or Arb-Med) or to combine several ADR methods when appropriate.

Schön (1983) summarizes it more powerfully: an effective mediator is a 'reflective practitioner', someone who can bring together mediation theory and his own experience with the experiences of others and as a result can select the right approach and interventions for each situation. In commercial business-to-business mediations, a frequently used approach is the rather directive task-focused style combined with, if necessary, evaluative elements. Research[10] shows that companies often prefer a task-focused business mediator and a rather directive style. Mediations that deal with personal relationships or with highly emotional issues in particular often require a more facilitating or relationship-focused style.

2.3 The approach to the mediation

The mediator needs to consider in advance how he is going to approach the mediation and how he will align the expectations of his clients with what he has to offer (I-1.1).

Considerations regarding the approach to the mediation

- ☐ An initial contact consultation (I-1.1)?
- ☐ How to start? Joint session? In a caucus (II-16)?
- ☐ As a solo mediator or with a co-mediator (two equally competent mediators or one professional mediator with one trainee mediator?) (I1-2.5)?
- ☐ Shall I prepare written reports on the mediation sessions (I-4)?
  - What do the parties expect and what has been agreed in this respect?
  - Are there any other parties with whom arrangements have to be made (for example the constituency, the principal who commissioned the mediation)?
  - Do I need an assistant to take minutes or is it better to prepare a (summary) report or action list myself?
  - Or should I decide to dispense with written reports?
- ☐ How much time should be scheduled for the initial mediation session (II-14.3)?
- ☐ Who will attend? What representatives of the parties are required? Are any other parties involved in the dispute (I-2.6)?
- ☐ Do I want information in advance? What information?
  - A (brief) written statement or other documents?
  - Do I read the documents submitted by the parties on their own initiative?

10 For example Schonewille, ACB 2004.

- Or shall I start the mediation without prior information in order to be completely open-minded?
- Did all parties receive all documents?
- Will lawyers or other advisors attend the mediation sessions? And if so are the parties present as well? Should I hold a preliminary procedural consultation with the advisors or lawyers in advance (I-2.8)?
- Shall I send the mediation agreement and make sure it is signed beforehand or would I rather do this at the initial mediation session?

☐ Where will the mediation take place? (Venue, facilities, ambience, accessibility).

☐ What are the seating arrangements (I-2.5.6)? Do I need a table and, if so, what shape should it be and who should sit next to whom? Or will I leave it up to the parties to decide where they want to sit?

☐ Who will make the first opening statement? If lawyers are present, will they (also) make an opening statement?

- Do I leave this up to the parties? (Say nothing and see what happens, or ask: 'Who would like to start?')
- Or do I decide who begins and if so, who will that be, and why?
  The initiator of the mediation or the respondent?
  The lawyers or the representatives of the parties themselves?
  The party who probably:
  - is better at waiting until the other party has finished speaking;
  - is the least emotional so that the opening statement is relative neutral;
  - has the most interest in initiating the mediation so is likely to disclose relevant information and show commitment?
  - The 'weaker party' to give them a psychological advantage and to improve the power balance.
- How long will I request everybody to speak?

2.4 Getting in the 'mood for mediation'

It is advisable to reflect on your mediator role just before the mediation starts and to 'get in the mood' for mediation. To list some basic guidelines: keep in mind that it is important to be perceived as neutral and to be impartial (II-2). Listen carefully (III-2) and try to listen to the parties without preconceived ideas. Search for the interests that lie behind the positions (II-7). And do not move to a solution too fast (f.e. when parties are not ready yet, or when the interests are not fully explored).

Mindfulness can be a good tool to achieve this.

Psychological contract and building trust (II-1).

Valuable background information, opinion articles and a free newsletter can be found at www.mediate.com.

The Center for Mindfulness in Medicine, Health Care, and Society and the Stress Reduction Clinic at the University of Massachusetts School of Medicine are focused on 'mind-body medicine' and are pioneers in integrating mindfulness into mainstream medicine and healthcare. The founder of the institute, Dr. Kabat-Zinn, is considered the one who introduced the practice of mindfulness into various fields, including medicine, education, sports, business, the legal profession, and also mediation.
By practicing mindfulness, it becomes possible to consciously pay attention to oneself and everything around. Living in the moment, the here and now. Attention is a central factor in how people feel, think, and act.

Kabat-Zinn, J. (1990), CATASTROPHE LIVING: USING THE WISDOM OF YOUR BODY AND MIND TO FACE STRESS, PAIN AND ILLNESS (Dell)
Kabat-Zinn, J. (1994), WHEREVER YOU GO, THERE YOU ARE: MINDFULNESS MEDITATION IN EVERYDAY LIFE (HYPERION). More information, including CDs for mindfulness meditation (not to be confused with mediation) practice, can be found on his website www.mindfulnesscds.com.

Riskin is considered the individual who introduced mindfulness to the dispute resolution field. Riskin has been deeply involved in understanding the mindset of lawyers and mediators and was a pioneer in mapping their styles and approaches. An excellent article on mindfulness for conflict resolvers is Riskin (2002), 'The Contemplative Lawyers: On the Potential Relevance of Mindfulness Meditation to Law Students, Lawyers, and Their Clients'.[11]

Mindfulness, as defined by Riskin:[12] paying attention from moment to moment to what is happening in the mind and body without judgment. This means being consciously aware without passing judgment.[13]

11 Riskin, L. (2002), 'The Contemplative Lawyers. On the Potential Relevance of Mindfulness Meditation to Law Students, Lawyers, and Their Clients', Harvard Negotiation Law Review, vol. 7, p. 1-66.

12 Lazarus, L. (2005), 'A Conversation with Professor Leonard Riskin about Mindfulness, Dispute Resolution, and Mind- fulness Resources for Mediators', www.mediate.com.

13 'One way to define mindfulness is that it is a way of paying attention moment to moment without judgment to whatever is going on in the mind and in the body – including thoughts, physical sensations, and emotions. In other words, mindfulness means being aware without judgment. Let me add that one cultivates mindfulness, or the ability to be mindful, in meditation and then brings a mindful perspective or awareness into everyday life.' Riskin, in Lazarus (2005), see footnote above.

According to Riskin, mindfulness can support a mediator on multiple levels. It helps prevent reacting automatically or habitually to events in a mediation. For example, when a client becomes upset and raises their voice, the mediator can intervene by asking them to speak more softly. A mindful mediator observes both the client's increasing stress and their own impulse to correct the client. Riskin suggests that this awareness is often enough to take a step back and prevent impulsive reactions. Because mediation is a dynamic process, and each mediation is unique, Riskin believes that a mediator must be 'present' with their attention from moment to moment. Another challenge where mindfulness can be helpful is preventing the mediator from being distracted by thoughts unrelated to the mediation. Riskin provides an example of a growing aversion to one of the parties: if a mediator notices this within themselves, they can often let it go.

Ury, (2016), GETTING TO YES WITH YOURSELF. HOW TO GET WHAT YOU TRULY WANT.

'Getting to Yes with Yourself' summary

William Ury, the co-author of, among others, 'Getting to Yes' (II.4.1), states that reaching agreement with yourself and self-reflection should be the first step in any negotiation, conflict, or difficult conversation. He believes that the book 'Getting to Yes with Yourself' is a prequel and not a sequel to 'Getting to Yes'.

Have you ever noticed that when we deal with a difficult person, we usually attribute it to the other person or the circumstances and not to ourselves? In a challenging negotiation or mediation, we often focus on how to change the other person. Ury offers a simple yet effective solution: to transform the dynamics of a difficult interaction, it is sufficient – but also necessary – for us to change ourselves. This prevents you from behaving like a difficult person. This is an essential condition for achieving interest-based 'win-win' solutions with others, especially when the situation becomes difficult. In the book, Ury describes a six-step method that allows you to first reach an agreement with yourself, significantly enhancing your ability to negotiate with others. It involves a series of seemingly small changes that combined can 'make the difference'.

Yes to Self

1. **Put Yourself in Your Shoes**
    - Go to 'the balcony' first as Ury calls it (II-4.3): observe yourself, recognize your emotions instead of automatically reacting.
    - Listen attentively and empathetically to your underlying feelings. What are they really telling you?
    - Discover your needs. Determine what you truly need.
    - Seek self-understanding without judgement.

2. **Develop Your Inner BATNA (III.14)**
    - Shift from blaming others when your needs are not met to taking responsibility for your own life, needs, and relationships. According to Ury, your BATNA[14] is the best way to advocate your interests if you cannot come to an agreement with the other party. Attend to your own needs, irrespective of what others do or do not do.

Yes to Life

3. **Reframe (III-6)**
    - Reframing is the skill of giving a different interpretation or meaning to a situation. It helps in accepting things as they are and taking personal responsibility instead of feeling like things are always somehow working against you.
4. **Stay in 'the Zone'**
    - Relax and remain in the present moment. Do not dwell on the past, but accept a situation as it is. Also, do not worry about the future, trust that you will be able to face challenges if they come your way. Any problems can only be resolved in the present.

Yes to Others

5. **Respect Others, Even If They Do not Respect or Reject You**
    - Ensure you do not get dragged into an antagonistic posture by others. Instead of a tit-for-tat approach (IV-3.3.2), surprise others by respecting them and adopting an inclusive approach, even if they are difficult. 'Separate the person from the problem'. The more respect you show, the more you receive.
6. **Give and Receive**
    - When you shift from win (for me) and lose (for you) to 'mutual gain' (win-win), you maximize your benefits. This is the essence of interest-based and integrative negotiation (II.4).

Interest based | integrative negotiation II-4.

2.5 Managing and structuring tools

Below is an overview of regulating and structuring tools available to a mediator to keep the mediation on track and maintaining control over the process.

Important tools to structure and manage the mediation.

14 BATNA: Best Alternative To Negotiated Agreement.

Preventive / Proactive

- ☐ Individual intake session to build trust and get parties in the right mindset at the table (I-1.1, I-2.5, and II-1 psychological contract)
- ☐ Mediate the process first: address issues during pre-mediation (I-1.1)
- ☐ Coordination / procedural meeting with lawyers and preparation of parties (I-2.8)

During the Mediation

- ☐ Opening statement and ground rules (I-3), mediation agreement (I-8)
- ☐ Creating a (negotiation) agenda (I-6)
- ☐ Documentation and written communication (positively influence: notes, interim agreements, top-level agreements) (I-4)
- ☐ Key techniques: LSD with DNA:[15] Listening (III-2), Summarizing (III-4), and Delving into follow-up questioning (III-10) with Do Not Assume (I-2.4 and IV-2)
- ☐ Maintaining power balance (II-3)
- ☐ Effective use of time (II-14)
- ☐ Reframe/recontextualization (III-6), anchoring (III-10.7), and cost-benefit analysis (Resource: D)
- ☐ Reality testing (III-11)
- ☐ The one text procedure (III-12), introducing draft texts
- ☐ Caucus (II-16)
- ☐ Phasing the mediation (II-9)
- ☐ SCARF (I-9 and II-8.5)
- ☐ Breaking impasse (IV-1)
- ☐ Managing perceived difficult behavior and tricky tactics (IV-3)
- ☐ De-escalation (Glasl stairs of escalation IV-7)
- ☐ Interventions based on the cause of the conflict (Moore II-8.2)
- ☐ Involving experts (I-7.1)
- ☐ Mediator's proposal (I-7.2)
- ☐ Process design, mixed modes procedures (I-7), hybrid procedures
- ☐ Sharing unsolicited observations
- ☐ BATNA/WATNA/RATNA analysis (III-14)

After the Mediation

- ☐ Summary of next steps and preparation for the next meeting

15 LSD with DNA is an acronym for Listening, Summarizing, Delve into follow-up-questions, combined with Do Not Assume.

2.6 Make sure all relevant parties are present and create balance

Actively verify whether all parties and people involved in the dispute are present. Sometimes another party plays an invisible role in the background. Try to identify this party and enable them to participate from the beginning, especially if finding or executing a solution is only possible with the commitment of this party. Try to let each party be represented by delegates of relatively 'equal importance', for example with a similar position within an organization or with the same amount of perceived power or decision-making authority. To make sure there is a balance in both the quality and the number of representatives. Also, verify whether the negotiator is accompanied by a (legal) advisor (II-3 and I-2.7.2). For proper balance, it is important that either all parties are supported by their advisors during the mediation sessions or alternatively that none are.

As always there are exceptions to any rules, e.g. if there is a major imbalance between the parties. For example, one party is a repeat player and the other one is a one-shotter; in such situations you may stimulate, suggest or allow in consultation with all parties that the one-shotter is supported in the mediation.

2.7 Authority, power of attorney and constituency

Parties that have to be represented, for example a corporation, require each party to have an authorized and relevant representative. When parties involved in a conflict are private individuals, their actual presence is far preferable to them being represented by someone else, for example a professional advisor.

2.7.1 Authority and power of attorney

Most mediation rules provide that if parties are not personally present at the table and authorized, they must be represented by someone who is authorized to settle an agreement on the spot. For private individuals, this can be achieved with relative ease. In the case of companies or public bodies a complete power of attorney can be more problematic.

Does a power of attorney imply that the representative not only has authority to settle, but also feels endorsed and empowered by his constituency? Is the person who grants the power of attorney also the relevant constituency for the representative? In practice, it is rarely feasible to demand total authority. Subsequent approval of the board of directors is often required in business mediations.

A settlement agreement between parties and a public body is not always the definitive end of the mediation process. Often a formal action by the administration is required to execute the agreement, such as the withdrawal or alteration of an appeal or a resolution, or meeting minutes to endorse the outcome.

In addition to a new resolution, new rules can be necessary. Third parties can complain about a new resolution. Sometimes the consent of another party or another (public) body is necessary for the resolution to be implemented, for example, local government may need to give consent.

Therefore, in a mediation or negotiation with the government, a settlement agreement has the character of a declaration of intent or an obligation for the public body to perform a certain amount of effort (tentative agreement).

2.7.2 Dealing with the parties' constituencies

In almost every mediation you need to take into account the effect of the parties' constituency (the person or group in the background that the parties in a mediation or negotiation represent and/or need to consult with before signing a settlement agreement). The constituency can be obvious or, conversely, hardly detectable.

- It is important to determine which person or group comprises the constituency and how they might influence the process. It can be a formal constituency like shareholders, a board of directors, members of an interest group or a business partner. A constituency can also be informal: family members, colleagues, spouse, neighbors, etc. And it can also be invisible and undetectable – an undeclared boyfriend or girlfriend, a private benefactor, a moneylender. Indeed, anyone whose existence a party does not want to acknowledge, at least in joint session.
- The negotiators need to be given the opportunity to deliberate with and to 'sell' the result of the mediation to their constituency. If necessary you can assist the negotiators and facilitate their deliberations.

It is more important to clarify who is part of the constituency, with whom a consultation is necessary and whose consent is required, than to demand complete authority. When it is clear how far the parties' authorities extend and which steps have to be followed to reach a settlement, you can often settle for less than complete authority, as long as all concerned know the boundaries.

If you fail to clarify this matter, a party could start using the draft settlement agreement as the starting point for further negotiations, because consultation of the constituency results in additional demands (IV-3.2).

Alternatively, a representative could get into trouble with his or her constituency.

It is important to check whether a negotiator needs help to confer with the constituency about a proposal or the (tentatively) agreed upon solution. Check whether there are procedures or opportunities for such a consultation. The less formal or clear the consultation process is, the more difficult it may be to reach an agreement. For more guidance on how to do this you can consult the chapter 'dealing with large group processes' (IV-6.1).

Facilitating consultation with the constituencies

As they consult with their constituency the party representative can be supported as follows.

- Together with the parties, try to find out who is part of the constituency.
- What influence does the constituency have on the course of the conflict, on finding a solution and the sustainability and durability of that solution?
- Discuss whether there is a clear internal decision-making process. When such a process does not exist, let the negotiator develop a proposal for a procedure and discuss this with the constituency.
- Unambiguously agree on how and when the constituency will be involved in the mediation. Make sure the parties regularly involve their constituencies and do not present them with a fait accompli.
- Develop objective criteria for the solution; these are easily explained to the constituency (III-16.1).
- Prepare cost-benefit analyses for alternative solutions and think through case scenarios with the representatives as thoroughly as possible (III-14).
- Clearly state the advantages that a solution can offer to all parties concerned and how it is in their interest (and the interest of the constituents).
- Formulate the settlement agreement in the most balanced and neutral manner possible. All parties need to contribute to the result (II-13).

At the start of the first meeting, make a list with all telephone numbers (including mobile/cell phone and home telephone numbers) and email addresses of the negotiators, the party advisors, lawyers, and their constituencies. In this way everybody can be reached when necessary during the process, even after office hours or during weekends. Try to find out whose consent is required and have these persons be on standby if they cannot participate in the mediation in person.

2.8 Procedural consultations with lawyers or other advisors

When party advisors such as a professional legal firm, accountant, business consultant or an in-house lawyer are involved, you can arrange a preliminary procedural consultation with them before the first mediation session. This introductory discussion can be held by telephone or in person and is especially useful when the advisors have little or no previous experience in representing a client in mediation. But even when advisors are already very experienced in mediation they can play a supportive role for the mediator during the mediation, so setting the stage for this via a pre-mediation consultation could be useful.

Issues to be discussed

- [ ] The **division of tasks** between the advisors, their clients and the mediator.
  The mediator should see to it that the mediation progresses expeditiously.
  - What is the role of the lawyers?
    - An advisor is typically the sparring partner/coach for the principal representatives, who ideally speak on their own behalf. Check whether the parties intend to have their advisors present during the mediation sessions. And if not, how will they be informed about the progress of the mediation and in what circumstances do they need to be involved or consulted? Keep confidentiality in mind, so leave the briefing of the party advisor to the parties (hint I-4) and/or ask the advisor to sign a confidentiality undertaking as well.
    - The advisor is the representative of the party and often takes the initial lead during the mediation session. Check that the parties will be attending the mediation sessions. Double check the authority, mandate or power of attorney of those involved.
  - Who makes the opening statement – the client or the advisor?
- [ ] The mediator **does not impose a decision** and he does not need to be convinced by legal argument.
- [ ] The number of **participants**, who, position, level (I-2.6).
- [ ] **Authority** to settle the dispute of the participants and their advisors (I-2.7.1).
- [ ] Who is the **constituency** and what role do they play (I-2.7.2)?
- [ ] Has a party instituted **legal or other proceedings** in relation to the dispute? If so, how can they be postponed, suspended or otherwise managed during the mediation?
- [ ] The **mediation agreement and the most important ground rules** for mediation (I-5).
  - The mediation effectively begins with the signing of a **mediation agreement**, in the course of which the mediation rules are acknowledged as applicable.
  - Participation is **voluntary**, but once a mediation starts it is **not without commitment**. The mediation agreement normally includes a clause obliging all participants to co-operate actively and in good faith to try to resolve their dispute through the mediation. However, each participant, including the mediator, can discontinue the mediation at any time and without giving a reason. It is advisable to agree in advance that if this happens, there will be an exit discussion to cover issues like next steps, how to inform constituents etc. before the mediation is formally concluded.
  - The mediator may obtain information separately from any party through discussions, correspondence or otherwise, for example in a caucus (II-16).
  - The mediator will treat as confidential any information provided to him by any of the parties, in correspondence, discussions or otherwise, unless otherwise agreed.
  - Parties, their advisors and everyone else involved in the mediation must sign a **confidentiality undertaking** in which they commit to keeping confidential any information supplied and/or recorded in any form during or in connection with the mediation, including

all positions adopted or proposals made by the parties and the progress made in the mediation, unless otherwise agreed.

- Confidentiality should also cover any judges, arbitrators or other adjudicators involved in the dispute.
- The parties are deemed to have waived the right to use as evidence against one another, in subsequent legal proceedings or otherwise, anything that arose during the mediation, including any witness or expert statements.
- Outcomes should be recorded in writing, preferably in a **formal settlement agreement**. On signing this agreement the mediation is concluded.
- Party representatives who participate in the mediation must be **authorized** to sign such an agreement (I-2.7).
- Unless otherwise agreed (in writing), the parties cannot be bound by positions they adopted or proposals they made during the mediation, nor by any statements they have made. In **mediation package deals** (II-12) the parties agree not be bound to anything developed during the mediation until the signing of the settlement agreement (except for explicit interim agreements). Please note that in some jurisdictions (f.e. the Netherlands) package deals must be agreed in writing in order to be enforceable.
- The mediator is bound to a **code of conduct** which covers issues like impartiality, confidentiality and expedition.
- In some jurisdictions, a mediator is also subject to a **formal complaints scheme** and **disciplinary rules**.

3 Checklist opening statement and ground rules

3.1 Issues a mediator needs to address during his 'opening statement'

- [ ] Names of parties involved (check) and of the mediator.
- [ ] Whether to call someone by first name or use last names?
- [ ] What does mediation involve and how are the roles and tasks divided between the mediator and the parties (insofar as this has not already been covered during the start-up phase (I-1.1) and the initial discussions. (I-2.8)). If necessary, this can be explained by going through the terms of the mediation agreement and ground rules (I-2.8):
  - mediation is voluntary and non-binding (until agreements are put on paper and signed);
  - all participants, including the mediator, can discontinue their participation in the mediation at any time (although it is advisable to prearrange an exit discussion to conclude the mediation);
  - commitment of all parties involved;

- no binding decision or ruling is imposed, self-determination of the parties, a resolution of their own;
- confidentiality and privacy.

☐ Neutral attitude and impartiality or omni-partiality of the mediator (II-2.1).

☐ The possibility of holding caucuses (II-16).

☐ If not addressed during the start-up phase, make logistical arrangements, for example the time required for meetings, procedures for scheduling meetings, possible deadlines of parties, etc. (II-14).

☐ Postponement, suspension or other management of any pending legal or other proceedings in relation to the dispute.

☐ Ground rules (I-3.2).

☐ Do the clients have any questions?

The following Acronym can be a useful mnemonic for your opening statement:
1A3C5N[16]

1A Authority to settle
3C • Commitment • Caucus • Confidential
5N • Neutral role • Non-evaluative (unless...) • No Need to answer • Non-compulsory (voluntary) • Non-binding (until agreed and signed)

See definition proactive mediation in Introduction.

You can also mention what mediation entails and use the **9 P's of Proactive mediation** as an mnemonic:

- **P**eople,
- **P**roblem &
- **P**rocess

  are explored,

- **P**erspectives,
- **P**lanet,

  (wider scope than just those at the table)
- **P**rofit

  are taken into account.

16 Inspired by the CAV 4N model of Jeremy Lack: http://lawtech.ch/.

- **P**arty Autonomy
  is the leading principle,

leading to:
- **P**aradigm shift

resulting in:
- **P**otential (potent) outcomes

Proactive mediation process

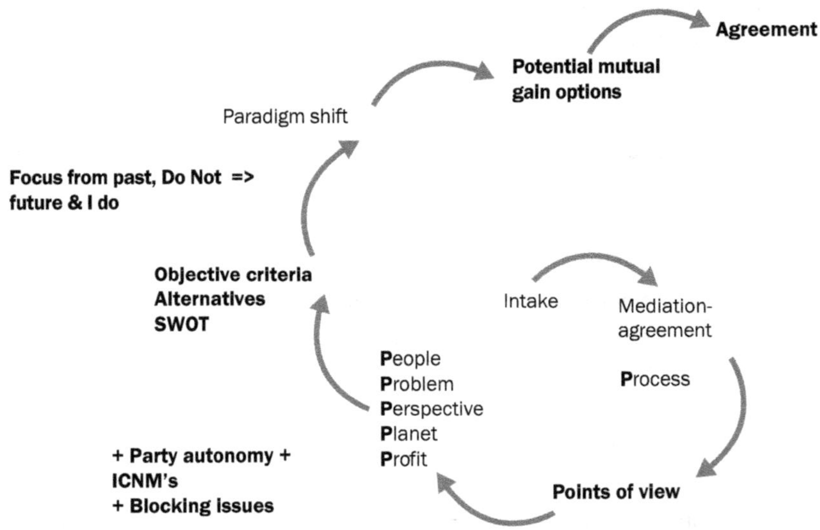

A demonstration of a mediator's openings statement in a cross-border case can be viewed at www.manonschonewille.com under the 'resources' tab.

What is the purpose and goal of an opening statement? And is it always necessary to give an opening statement, or is it only needed when dealing with parties who have little experience with mediation?
The opening statement does not need to be a formal and lengthy monologue by the mediator; you can also ask questions to the parties *("Are you here voluntarily?" "How are you accustomed to addressing each other?")* and address the points to be mentioned by going through the key provisions of the mediation agreement. You can then conclude your opening statement with the signing of the mediation agreement.

It is important to always deliver an opening statement. It is an instrument for the mediator to set the tone, make parties feel comfortable, manage expectations, demonstrate "mastery" as a mediator, and build a psychological contract and trust (II-1).

From a neurobiological perspective, an opening statement also serves a valuable purpose (SCARF and Beyond Reason IV-7). All participants have the opportunity to make an assessment of their relative Status by having an introductory round, and their Status is elevated because the mediator provides positive feedback. For example, by confirming that mediation is a good choice, giving compliments about preparing the pre-mediation briefing, or showing appreciation to the attorneys who have prepared their clients for mediation, and so on. A mediator's opening statement also stimulates Certainty because it is clear what is expected of everyone and what the process involves. The Autonomy of the parties is confirmed: they hold the solution in their own hands and party-autonomy 'is the guiding principle'. By emphasizing that both parties share a similar approach, for example, to resolve the problem through joint discussion, the opening statement initiates a sense of Relatedness between the parties. Last but not least, it confirms that a mediation process means Fairness for all involved, at the very least in terms of transparency, communication, personal involvement, party-autonomy and the ability for both parties to influence the process.
Our brain operates based on deeply ingrained basic principles: minimizing threats (avoiding situations, referred to as "avoid" in SCARF, withdrawing) and maximizing rewards (approaching, called "approach" in SCARF, engaging, being solution-focused). The effect of consciously taking the SCARF principles into account is an increase in the 'approach mechanism' of the parties, a state of mind necessary for a successful mediation, and a decrease in the avoidance mechanism.

More on the SCARF model by Rock and insights from Fisher and Shapiro from 'Beyond Reason' can be found in IV-7. Insights from neuroscientific studies and their implications for various phases of the mediation process are also described from the perspective of the functioning of mirror neurons and facial expressions.

3.2 Ground rules

If a mediator neglects the task of agreeing on the ground rules in advance, he is often faced with negative consequences in later stages. It is therefore wise to agree on the ground rules at the start of the first session and then scrupulously observe them during the mediation process.

Ground rules

- [ ] Mediation is voluntary but is not without commitment. This means that all parties concerned have to make an effort to resolve the dispute. However, everyone - the mediator included - is free to terminate the mediation at any time.
- [ ] The mediator does not impose a binding resolution; the parties are free to choose one themselves. The mediator is the manager of the process and the negotiators are responsible for the problem and its resolution. Mediator and parties together are responsible for the people aspect.
- [ ] The mediator has a neutral attitude and is impartial (II-2).
- [ ] The mediator can meet or communicate with parties and/or their legal representatives separately (for example in a caucus II-16).
- [ ] Depending on their strategy and approach to the mediation process, either the mediator decides if a caucus will take place, or the parties can request one.
- [ ] Confidentiality applies to third parties, but also between the parties (II-16) with regard to what is discussed in private meetings of one party with the mediator, unless other arrangements are expressly made.
- [ ] Communication rules, such as not interrupting and to treating one another with respect.
- [ ] Package deal: the parties can only be bound to a proposal or agreement when all issues are settled and signed (I-2.8, II-12 and II-13) - unless expressly agreed that a partial or interim solution will be binding (II-11.2).

4 Agreements on reporting

Make explicit arrangements on whether there will be any reporting, and if so who will report to whom. Also, agree on the status of the reports to avoid uncertainty and doubt. Clearly stipulate your policy in this respect in advance. This is especially important if only one of the parties has agreed to pay the mediator's fees, or if a third party, for example the employer, is the principal. The codes of conduct for mediators and the rulings of the Dutch Foundation 'Disciplinary Law for Mediators'[17] (I-2.8) are crystal-clear about this. Confidentiality applies not only to what is discussed during the mediation but also to all written documents. This means a mediator can allow inspection of written documents/ reports or report to third parties about the mediation only with express consent of the parties.

17 Stichting Tuchtrechtspraak Mediators, STM , www.mediationtuchtrecht.nl. The Dutch mediators Disciplinary Court rulings are annotated and published on the website of the Mediatorfederation Nederland, MfN: mfn-tuchtrechtupdates.nl.

An exception has been made for the official who deals with mediation parties' complaints as part of the official complaints scheme and for the disciplinary judges. If it is necessary to defend oneself as a mediator in a complaints or disciplinary procedure, documents can be submitted for this purpose only.
In most codes of conduct there is no obligation on a mediator to prepare written reports or notes. However, if it has been agreed that the mediator can or will make a written report, he has to make this available within a reasonable amount of time.
Make sure that the content of every document is fair (all parties and their wishes and interests are addressed), neutral in formulation (III-7), balanced (II-2.2) and where possible emphasizes the progress made and the parties' common interests. It is not prudent, as a rule, to include all points of view and all considerations in a report. It is preferable to just record in writing the outcome of discussions and agreements.

Never give reports or other documents to third parties. No feedback about the course of the mediation (or even that it has taken place) can be given to third parties without the express consent of all parties. However, having approval to release information does not create an obligation for the mediator to do so. A party cannot force the mediator to submit documents to a third party, even if all parties agree to it. A mediator therefore not only has a duty of confidentiality but also the right to remain silent. Make clear agreements with parties in advance on reporting in exceptional cases, for example a mediation initiated after a referral by a judge, when giving feedback is unavoidable, or when a mediation has been terminated (with or without consent). As a mediator, one can ask the parties for express written consent to give feedback information or place a report or other documents at the disposal of third parties. It is even better to agree with the parties that they themselves will report on a joint basis. If so, make sure they agree upon form and content of the report. In a mediation where a settlement agreement has been reached, this can often be included in the settlement agreement.

5 Co-mediation

5.1 Models of co-mediation

Co-mediation – mediation with two mediators – can be performed in several models:

- two equally competent mediators who complement each other. Often a combination of a mediator with content expertise and a facilitative mediator;
- two mediators where one takes charge of the mediation. The co-mediator can play an important role as, for example, an observer, a supporter or as a trainee.

5.2 When is co-mediation advisable?

A team of equally competent mediators can be considered:

- in a very complex dispute, for example many parties (rule of thumb: more than two) or with many participants at the mediation table (rule of thumb: more than four) (IV-6);
- when the case is technically complex, or deals with complicated content issues;
- when the parties are deadlocked (IV-1), for example because the conflict is psychologically or emotionally challenging (IV-2.4 and IV-4), or concerns a protracted or exceptionally escalated conflict (IV-7);
- when different kinds of expertise or skills are required, for example substantive expertise or multilingualism, different mediation experience or mediators with different nationalities to bridge cultural differences in an international setting;
- when parties are in different locations most of the time and it is impractical for them to meet regularly or at all;
- when the parties want more than one mediator;
- when you want to have a sounding board;

A trainee co-mediator can be considered:

- when you need support or a sounding board;
- if you want to offer new mediators the opportunity to gain practical experience.

5.3 When should co-mediation not be considered?

A second mediator is not advisable in the following cases:

- in a (very) simple case with few parties present at the table; two mediators can seem too many, and could result in unnecessarily high costs;
- if the parties object to co-mediators.

5.4 A co-mediator, why should you?

The main advantages of co-mediation

- ☐ The opportunity to complement each other, to give feedback and to deliberate on strategy and tactics.
- ☐ More effective mediation through division of tasks.
- ☐ In a mediation with diverse parties, a mixed team can improve acceptance of the mediator(s) and provide balance (for example male/female, diverse cultural backgrounds, employer/employee).

- ☐ Emotional or difficult themes are easier to deal with.
- ☐ Feelings and non-verbal communication between the parties can be observed better (two mediators see, hear and perceive more than one).
- ☐ To serve as an example of teamwork: seeing others co-operate with each other can encourage collaboration between the parties.
- ☐ Promotes the perception of impartiality and balance.
- ☐ Less pressure on a solo-mediator because tasks can be shared, the mediators can unburden and support each other and distance themselves from incidents.
- ☐ Taking risks is less hazardous.
- ☐ More ideas, options and alternatives are generated, which means a potential for better solutions.
- ☐ Possibility to increase the (time) efficiency of the caucus if both mediators deliberate with a different party at the same time (II-16.5).
- ☐ In case the parties want an evaluation from a mediator at some point, a co-mediator who takes over the lead from that point on can be a real asset.
- ☐ Training prospects and the opportunity to get feedback and learn from each other.

5.5 A co-mediator, why not?

The main disadvantages and pitfalls of co-mediation

- ☐ Extra costs.
- ☐ More time is required to fine-tune strategies and next steps, also during the preparation for the mediation.
- ☐ There is a risk of being more involved with each other than with the parties. For example, the mediators may not be working in harmony because they use conflicting strategies, do not have matching styles, get in each other's way in managing the process, impede progress, or engage in rivalry.
- ☐ Clear-cut deliberation and an evident division of tasks is necessary.
- ☐ Possible coalitions, or parties trying to form coalitions.
- ☐ Inactive, not pro-active, attitude when mediators try too hard to respect each other's style and interventions.
- ☐ Potential for feeling less responsible (bystander effect).
- ☐ The entire process takes more time, scheduling problems.

5.6 Agreements with the co-mediator

To benefit from a team of mediators, it is necessary to agree on clear guidelines beforehand.

- ☐ How are the responsibilities divided? Who is in charge of which task, for example making appointments or preparing a report (I-4) and making the opening statement (I-3)?
- ☐ Should the parties be informed about the specific responsibilities of each mediator? If so, how and when?
- ☐ Can a mediator intervene during a dialogue led by his co-mediator and how will the mediators confer? Can co-mediators consult each other during the mediation session (I-2.5.6)?
- ☐ Are the co-mediators equally competent and both in charge, or is there an experienced mediator with a trainee (I-2.5.1)?
- ☐ What is your fee? Which services will be charged? What is the allowance for traveling expenses, traveling time and preparation?
- ☐ How will the fee be divided among co-mediators?
- ☐ Will the mediators send one joint bill, and if so, who will send it?
- ☐ How will the instructions and set-up be managed (I-1.1)?
- ☐ Who will communicate with the parties first? How and when?
- ☐ With regard to both mediators, what are their approaches to the mediation process and their mediation strategies (I-1.2.1)? How will they collaborate during the mediation (I-2.3)?
- ☐ Will caucus (II-16) be used? If so, how?
- ☐ What are the seating arrangements (I-2.5.6)?

5.7 Collaborating during the co-mediation

Deliberation during the mediation

- How will co-mediators consult each other during the mediation session? In the presence of the negotiators? Or only in private?
- How will one co-mediator indicate to the other he or she wants to confer?
- What subjects can be discussed in the presence of the parties?
- When you confer with your co-mediator without the parties in attendance, do you inform them about this and, if applicable, do you say what you discussed? Do you inform the parties in advance or during the session about the way the mediators will liaise with one another and if and how they will inform the parties about what they have discussed?

Communication topics during a co-mediation session

- How do you intervene in your co-mediators actions during the mediation session?
- Publicly, by asking questions or by sharing an observation?
- Only non-verbally? Discreetly, by means of signs or notes or (text) messages?
- Or only during a break?

What is the seating plan for the co-mediators: opposite each other or next to one another?

- The mediators are seated next to each other.
  - When seated next to your co-mediator, it is more difficult to maintain non-verbal contact (unless you want to communicate by playing footsie under the table! If there is a table!). In this position, depending on the shape of the table, the parties are also sitting closer to each other, so it can be more difficult for them to look at each other and speak directly with one another. As a consequence, there is a risk that all communication goes through the mediators, which inhibits direct communication between the parties.
  - If the mediators are seated next to each other, it is easier for both to observe all the parties. Additionally, both mediators will be perceived to act, and in fact will act, more as a team.
- The mediators are seated opposite one another.
  - In this situation, there is a greater physical distance between the mediators, and as a result it is sometimes more difficult to read each other.
  - However, maintaining eye contact is easier in this seating arrangement.
  - Co-mediators should avoid seating arrangements that can be misinterpreted to imply that each mediator is a 'party-mediator'.

Literature on seating arrangements in mediation

- *Sarah Ater, (June 2019) 'Mediation and Sitting Protocol', www.mediate.com.*
- *Bilikoff (2004), 'Helping Others Resolve Conflicts: Empowering Stakeholders' 19-20. Regents of the University of California.*
- *Starr and Page, (March 2005), 'Dealing with Nonverbal Cues: A Key to Mediator Effectiveness', www.mediate.com.*

There is no 'best seating plan' for a mediation. It depends on the parties and the personal preferences and strategies of the mediators and what they are trying to achieve during the mediation. It is important, however, to make a deliberate choice in advance regarding seating arrangements, the shape of the table or whether a table will be used at all.

However, seating arrangements are not a static feature. Changing places during the mediation can always be considered. This intervention can alter the dynamics of the process and can help break a deadlock (IV-1.3). However, bear in mind that people will subconsciously assume seating arrangements will be the same as on the previous mediation meetings, unless they are told otherwise.

5.8 A team is effective but not necessarily more efficient

The cost-benefit ratio of co-mediation was researched as part of the monitoring of the Dutch Court Connected Mediation Project.[18] Compared to mediation cases with a solo-mediator, co-mediators did not generate any significant difference in the satisfaction rates of parties and their legal advisors regarding the duration and the progress of the mediation. However, the settlement rate was significantly higher in co-mediations (67%) as compared to solo-mediations (59%). Moreover, lawyers were typically more satisfied with the outcome of co-mediation compared to solo-mediation, although the parties did not show a significant difference on that score.
A possible explanation for this contradiction is that co-mediations actually generate better outcomes. Lawyers repeatedly deal with disputes, and they are therefore better able to compare the resolution of one case with outcomes in similar cases. Although it does not require more meetings, on average a co-mediation session (3.42 h) takes longer than a solo-mediation session (2.54 h). Explanations for this could be that two mediators have more (additional) questions and interventions than one. The research also indicated there are more days between the first and the last sessions (62 solo and 87 co). This could be due to the fact that co-mediations are often multi-party mediations or mediations with many representatives around the table, thereby making it more difficult to find dates that are convenient for everybody involved. If so, this can be resolved by planning several dates for possible follow-up sessions during the first meeting.

6 Preparing a negotiation agenda

When it is clear which themes are to be discussed, the negotiators know what to expect and this knowledge empowers them (II-6).
Reaching agreement on the agenda or order of business may help the parties to cooperate again after a difficult moment, and to focus on continuing the mediation. Reaching an agreement about a relatively neutral topic, such as the agenda, can create breathing space and prove that agreement is possible – even on something as prosaic as an agenda. A common approach for setting a negotiating agenda is: categorizing, clustering, fractionalizing and classifying.[19]

18 Nijman (2003).
19 For example Bonenkamp 2003.

Setting up a negotiating agenda

- ☐ **Categorizing:** subdividing topics into logical categories.
- ☐ **Clustering:** placing topics under a common theme or denominator.
- ☐ **Fractionalizing:** dividing complex themes into sub-issues that are easier to review and deal with.
- ☐ **Classifying:** arranging issues, determining an order to discuss themes.

  A rule of thumb for classifying interests and issues to be discussed is:
  - if it is necessary to (re)establish communication between parties, begin with an icebreaker topic. For example, find a topic which is neutral or positive for all the parties (see the hint below);
  - if feasible, start with the blocking issue (II-8), (see below) and then continue with interests. Rule of thumb for the order of raising interests for discussion (II-7):
    1. mutual interests;
    2. differing but reconcilable interests;
    3. differing but apparently irreconcilable interests.
  - within a category, start with uncomplicated issues, then address more difficult topics. However, ensure that you do not save the most difficult topic to deal with for the end.

A blocking issue often boils down to a differing reconcilable interest. For example, it can be about wanting an apology, getting recognition, wanting to be heard, having different perspectives, and distrust. Once the blocking issue is identified, a mediator might consider adopting this as the fist topic to be discussed. This is generally not the most uncomplicated issue, but as soon as the blockage is removed it is easier for the parties to negotiate on the content issues. Verify whether all interests are on the table and the blocking issue is identified. Only then start looking for options (III-15).

When using a flip chart to visualize an agenda, make this a joint effort. Avoid addressing the issues as being a subject brought in by A or B, or, worse, dividing a flip chart page into separate lists for A and for B. Instead, make one common, merged list for all themes to be deliberated, and state them in neutral terms (III-7). See also 'reactive devaluation' (III-16.3).

Moore (2014) describes more methods for setting a negotiating agenda.

- Ad hoc, first in – first discussed basis. Depending on what the parties bring up first, the themes are worked out one at a time before discussing the next issue.
- Taking turns, the negotiators choose which theme will be discussed next.
- Each party chooses its most important theme(s), these are discussed first.

- A common goal or an interest of a higher importance is identified. Address themes in order of importance for reaching this common goal or serving this higher, mutual interest.
- The parties decide which issue(s) should be resolved first, because these lay the foundation for discussion of the other issues.
- Combine a number of themes and discuss them jointly, in order to prevent parties being afraid they will have to give away too much too early without getting something in return.

Another method for setting a negotiating agenda is the *Fruit Tree approach*. This is an extremely effective and visually inspiring process. The mediator draws the outline of a tree on a flip chart. Then the issues are ranked into three categories: High Hanging Fruit, Medium Hanging Fruit and Low Hanging Fruit. The higher the issue is on the fruit tree, the more creative or challenging may be its solution, potentially involving the parties having to build a ladder to get the fruit into a common basket. Very often, the mediator will find that some of the Low Hanging Fruit is actually even easier, and can be classified as Fruit on the Ground – sitting right there to be picked up and placed in the parties' joint resolution basket. This creates quick wins, and builds momentum at the outset, gradually improving the parties' optimism for when they have to go higher up the tree of issues.

A positive or neutral subject

In order to establish communication and let the negotiators focus on matters that unite or on positive experiences from the past, the mediator can introduce a common positive or neutral theme as the first topic of discussion. Make sure that the parties are able to express up front what they expect from the mediation and what the dispute is about. Otherwise, there is a chance they will become (too) impatient.

7 Experts and mediator's proposal

7.1 When to call in an external specialist

A mediator must be able to determine the right time to call in an expert. If this is done too early in the process, the parties can get lazy and rely on the third party to present (parts of) the solution. This may affect their motivation to come up with their own solution. This could also harm the position of the mediator or confirm a party's idea that mediation is a 'soft' process where the mediator just 'cuts the cake somewhere in the middle'. Therefore, it is usually wise not to bring in experts too early in the process. Conversely, waiting too long can lead to a deadlock (IV-1) or wasting time on a solution that will not work or cannot be implemented.

The mediator also has to consider whether and under what circumstances he is prepared and able to advise on content issues or to give an evaluation of how the case could be settled (mediator advice). A number of mediators use the following rule of thumb: mediator advice can only be given when: there has not been a caucus and the mediator did not obtain separate confidential information, the parties expressly request it and the mediator also thinks this is the best way to move the mediation forward.

Others completely disagree with mediators giving advice or an evaluation. Some mediators will frequently give advice or an evaluation if the negotiators ask for it, or if they think they can break a deadlock situation by doing so.

In any case, it is important to discuss the advantages and disadvantages of mediator advice with the parties and clarify the mediator's policy on this issue.

7.2 The advantages of a mediator proposal

Parties can save on time and costs because it is not necessary to find and consult a third party. The mediator already knows what questions have been raised and does not need further information. If all is well, the parties already have confidence in the mediator. It can therefore be used as a pragmatic, fast and economical way forward.

As a last resort, before giving a proposal yourself, a mediator could try another method, such as the one text procedure (I-7.4 and III-12).

7.3 Disadvantages of a mediator proposal

A possible pitfall is that one or even both of the negotiators are disappointed by the mediator's proposal. This could affect the neutrality of the mediator, which in turn could impede the continuation of the mediation. A possible solution is to end the mediation process formally, and then offer the mediator's proposal. In practice, this is not always possible. Sometimes a decision on a certain topic is necessary to enable the mediation to continue. The mediator then has to consider which is more important.

Transparency is the most important aspect. The parties must expressly ask the mediator for his advice. In many rules, a written request is required. Additionally, the mediator clearly has to agree with parties that the 'normal' mediation rules are now suspended, or that the mediation is concluded. The type of the proposal should also be made clear. Is it binding advice or a recommendation? Can a second opinion be requested from another expert?

7.4 Alternatives to a mediator proposal

The mediator can summarize in writing the issues and agreements that have been reached and the issues on which a decision is still pending. This checklist of issues can be presented to a (binding) advisor, an arbiter, the court or the judge. Another tool is the one-text procedure (III-12).

7.5 How to conduct a mediator's proposal

A mediator's proposal, in brief, is a proposal for a possible solution by the mediator when the mediation is at risk of failing. It can be 1) an informal interim oral proposal, 2) only an amount or other limited component (settlement proposal), 3) a settlement range, or 4) a detailed proposal based on the identified interests of the parties and objective criteria and agreements on which all parties agree. With this, the mediator demonstrates that a coherent solution is possible from the puzzle pieces.

Most mediators see the mediator's proposal as a 'take it or leave it' intervention just before formally concluding the mediation (model 2 in the definition above). In this view, a mediator's proposal only pertains to closing a final (financial) gap. The mediator puts forth an amount or limited proposal that can conclude the matter.

If the mediator's proposal is accepted by all parties or if it involves only a range or active collaboration, the mediator can calmly wrap up the mediation along with the parties and document the agreements made (settlement agreement or agreement list).

If the mediator's proposal is not accepted, the mediator must 'by definition' terminate the mediation immediately.

I see the application of a mediator's proposal more broadly than just a take it or leave it regarding an amount (model 4 in the definition above). Besides involving more aspects (interests and other puzzle pieces) in a proposal than just mentioning an amount, I believe that it's entirely possible and sometimes wise for the parties to discuss the proposal with the mediator (if it involves more than just an amount) and make adjustments where they collectively agree. The rule is that this applies to something they mutually agree on.

A mediator's proposal in model 1 can also involve more 'active brainstorming/introducing a solution direction' and serve as inspiration for further discussion and exploring other solution directions.

A mediator's proposal can be made orally or in writing. In model 4, it can also take the form of a procedure of one text (III-12) or creating a draft settlement agreement (I-8.7).

It is crucial to establish clear ground rules beforehand and, as a mediator, to uphold them.

Steps and rules for a mediator's proposal

- ☐ Determine for yourself whether a mediator's proposal has a chance of success: Are the differences small enough to bridge, have you tried all other means such as reality testing (III-11), and have you worked sufficiently on the relationship, communication, and emotions? A mediator's proposal is for the final phase when negotiations are running out of steam, but there's still a sufficient basis to reach a resolution with one last push.
- ☐ Both parties must provide informed consent to the procedure of a mediator's proposal and understand the consequences. Part autonomy is paramount with this instrument. Generally, it's wise to discuss the proposition of a mediator's proposal separately with each party.
- ☐ Clearly define with the parties what the mediator's proposal is about:
  a) an amount,
  b) a specific issue,
  c) a proposal to conclude everything based on the identified interests, objective criteria, and agreements that the parties agree upon,
  d) a range for further negotiations,
  e) ...
- ☐ It might be prudent to first explore each party's reaction to a range in separate discussions before the mediator presents a final mediator's proposal.
- ☐ The mediator presents a proposal (either orally or in writing depending on the situation) that they believe is feasible, meaning it could still be acceptable for all parties involved. Please note that the mediator's proposal should not reflect the position or proposal of any of the parties. A good guideline is to consider what is better for both parties than their alternative (e.g., going to court) and what you think is still feasible for both, considering everything you know about the parties.
- ☐ All participants receive the mediator's proposal simultaneously with a request not to react immediately. They are given time to think about it and may consult with an advisor or their support network.
- ☐ Depending on the agreed-upon rules, it may be a simple yes or no to the proposal (without further negotiation), or the mediator may consult with both parties to see if there are areas they both agree should be adjusted. If it's about a range or more than just an amount, the prevailing opinion is that parties can only say yes or no to the integral proposal. Unlike binding

arbitration, party autonomy remains paramount; parties are never bound to the mediator's proposal.

- [ ] The mediator discusses with each party separately whether they accept the proposal. A good practice is that a party that says 'no' does not get to know the other party's response. Only the party that said 'yes' knows the response of the other.
- [ ] If one or both parties do not accept the mediator's proposal, the mediator ends the mediation.
- [ ] If both parties agree to the mediator's proposal, the mediation continues, and all agreements made can be documented under the mediator's guidance.

For further reading on this topic, see Schutte and Spierdijk in the Tijdschrift conflicthantering: 'The mediator's proposal, a useful last resort?' (in Dutch). Or Hochman's article on mediate.com, 'A Mediator's Proposal – Whether, When and How It Should Be Used.'

An example of how you, as a mediator, can use a range or 'testing the waters' before presenting a final proposal is to ask each party a hypothetical question separately. Pretesting has another desired side effect, anchoring the numbers (III-10.7).

- Check the range: To party A: *'Suppose that B would be willing to settle within a range of €400,000 to €550,000, how would you react?'* To party B: *'Suppose that A would be willing to settle within a range of €550,000 to €700,000, how would you react?'*

- Test: To party A: *'If my mediator's proposal were to fall within a range of €400,000 to €550,000, could you come to an agreement?'* To party B: *'If my mediator's proposal were to fall within a range of €550,000 to €700,000, could you come to an agreement?'* In both cases, in this example, it seems that €550,000 would still be acceptable for both parties if there were a positive response.

8 Administrative kit

The legal aspects of mediation differ per country. Below is an extensive list of literature you can consult on the subject:

- *Calkins and Lane (2022), MEDIATION PRACTICE GUIDE, Ch. 5 'The Attorney and Mediation'.*
- *Menkel Meadow, Love and Schneider (2020), MEDIATION: PRACTICE, POLICY, AND ETHICS (Chapters 7, 8, 9).*
- *Sourdin (2020), ALTERNATIVE DISPUTE RESOLUTION. Sydney: Lawbook Co.*

- *Spencer D. and T. Altobelli (2018), Dispute Resolution in Australia: cases, commentary and materials. Pyrmont: Lawbook Co.*
- *Kovach (2014), MEDIATION (LAW IN A NUTSHEL).*
- *Nolan-Haley (2014), 'Lawyers, Non-Lawyers, and Mediation: Rethinking the Professional Monopoly from a Problem-Solving Perspective,' 7 Harv. Neg. L. Rev. 235.*
- *Golann, and Folberg (2010), MEDIATION: THE ROLES OF ADVOCATE AND NEUTRAL Chapter 13.*
- *Golann (2009), MEDIATING LEGAL DISPUTES.*
- *Nolan-Haley (2008), ALTERNATIVE DISPUTE RESOLUTION, Chapter 3, Nutshell Series.*
- *De Palo and Trevor (2007), ARBITRATION AND MEDIATION IN THE SOUTHERN MEDITERRANEAN COUNTRIES.*
- *Spencer and Brogan (Jan. 2007), MEDIATION LAW AND PRACTICE.*
- *Spiller (2nd edition 2007), DISPUTE RESOLUTION IN NEW ZEALAND.*
- *Alfini, Press, Sternlight and Stulberg (2nd ed. 2006), MEDIATION THEORY AND PRACTICE.*
- *Boulle (2nd edition 2005), MEDIATION-PRINCIPLES, PROCESS, PRACTICE, Chapter 5.*
- *Wissler (2005), 'Barriers to Attorneys' Discussion and Use of ADR,' 19 Ohio St. J. on Disp. Resol. 459.*
- *Goodman (2nd Ed. 2004), BASIC SKILLS FOR THE NEW MEDIATOR (valuable appendix on the rules of evidence).*
- *Kovach (3rd Ed. 2004), MEDIATION PRINCIPLES AND PRACTICE.*
- *Moffitt (2003), 'Ten Ways to Get Sued: A Guide for Mediators,' 8 Harv. Negot. L. Rev. 81.*
- *Deason (2001), 'Enforcing Mediated Settlement Agreements: Contract Law Collides with Confidentiality,' 35 U.C. Davis. L. Rev. 33.*
- *Nolan-Haley (1999), 'Informed Consent in Mediation: A Guiding Principle for Truly Educated Decisionmaking,' 74 Notre Dame L. Rev. 775.*

8.1 Mediation clauses and other contract clauses

Sample Mediation Clauses

A. Mediation

The parties agree that any disputes arising from this agreement or subsequent agreements concluded as a result of this agreement shall be dealt with in accordance with [NAME ADR organization] mediation regulations.

B. Negotiations followed by mediation (with time-limit option)

1. The parties agree that in the first instance they shall endeavor to resolve any disputes arising from this agreement or subsequent agreements concluded as a result of this agreement in mutual consultation.
2. Should it prove impossible to arrive at a settlement during the negotiations (as required: within (***number***) days after the receipt of notification that negotiations are to commence) then the party taking the initiative shall request that this dispute be settled in accordance with the [NAME] mediation regulations.

C. Mediation followed by arbitration

1. The parties agree that any disputes arising from this agreement or subsequent agreements concluded as a result of this agreement shall be settled in accordance with the [NAME] mediation regulations.
2. Should it prove impossible to arrive at a settlement during the negotiations (as required: within (***number***) days after the receipt of notification that negotiations are to commence) then the party taking the initiative shall request that this dispute be settled in accordance with the Arbitration Regulations of the (***select Arbitration Institute***).

D. Mediation followed by legal proceedings

1. The parties agree that any disputes arising from this agreement or subsequent agreements concluded as a result of this agreement shall be settled in accordance with the [NAME] mediation regulations.
2. Should it prove impossible to arrive at a settlement during the negotiations (as required: within (***number***) days after the receipt of notification that negotiations are to commence) then the party taking the initiative shall request that this dispute be settled by the competent court (***or select other city/town***) by the Court of (***city/ town***).

E. Mediation with time limit followed by arbitration for General Terms and Conditions

1. Any disputes that may arise between A (***own organization***) and B (***client/customer, etc.***) pursuant to an agreement concluded between A and B shall be settled in accordance with the [NAME] mediation regulations.
2. Should it prove impossible to arrive at a settlement in the aforementioned manner within (***enter number, for example 30***) days after the other party has given written notification that a dispute has arisen, then either party is entitled to have this dispute settled in accordance with the Arbitration Regulations of the (***select Arbitration Institute***).

Many mediation organizations and their mediation clauses as well as other documents can be consulted through the web. Model mediation and other ADR clauses can, for example, be found at following websites (more and updated links are provided in the resources section of www.manonschonewille.com).

- **Africa:** The Africa Mediation Association (AMA) is a non-profit organization aiming to promote mediation in Africa: https://africamediationassociation.org/.
- **Asia:** Asian Mediation Association (AMA) which includes members from: Hong Kong Mediation Centre, The Indonesian Mediation Center, Malaysian Mediation Centre, Philippine Mediation Center, Singapore Mediation Centre https://asian-mediationassociation.org/.
- **Australia:** www.ag.gov.au/legal-system/alternative-dispute-resolution, www.ama.asn.au.
- **Canada:** www2.gov.bc.ca/gov/content/justice/about-bcs-justice-system/mediation, www.justice.gc.ca/eng/rp-pr/csj-sjc/dprs-sprd/res/drrg-mrrc/04.html, https://adric.ca/rules-codes/national-mediation-rules/.
- **Europe**: https://e-justice.europa.eu/62/EN/mediation.
- **France:** www.cmap.fr.
- **Hong Kong:** www.hkiac.org, www.mediationcentre.com.hk.
- **Italy:** www.adrcenter.it.
- **India:** www.mediationindia.org, www.arbitrationindia.org, www.mediatorscouncil.org, www.icadr.org, www.icadr.org.
- **Kenya:** https://ciarbkenya.org, https://www.nscpeace.go.ke/resources/item/download/6_487289a54d054a46a54ab356b659f3c1, https://www.nscpeace.go.ke/ en https://judiciary.go.ke/?s=mediation.
- **Mediterranean region (southern):** Information on MEDA countries (as well as more information on countries like Barbados, Turkey, Nigeria and Morocco) can be consulted at www.adrcenter.com/international.
- **Netherlands:** https://mfnregister.nl/, https://mfnregister.nl/zoek-mediator/, https://vindeenmediator.nl/.
- **New Zealand:** https://resolution.institute, www.aminz.org.nz.
- **Nigeria:** www.icmcng.org/, www.lca.org.ng/icaa/, www.ciarb.org/our-network/africa/nigeria/ (the Arfrica Mediation Association AMA, https://africamediationassociation.org/)
- **Scotland:** www.core-solutions.com.
- **Singapore:** www.mediation.com.sg, sagemediation.sg, https://simc.com.sg/.
- **South Africa:** www.ccma.org.za, www.conflictdynamics.co.za, www.saam.org.za/.
- **Sweden:** www.sccinstitute.com.
- **UK:** www.civilmediation.org, www.cedr.com, www.lcia.org, www.adrgroup.co.uk.
- **USA:** www.adr.org, www.cidra.org, www.cpradr.org, www.icdr.org, www.inta.org, www.jamsadr.com, www.usam.com.

On the website of the International Chamber of Commerce mediation clauses in several languages can be found: www.Iccwbo.org. The website of the World Intellectual Property Organization also offers mediation, arbitration and expert determination clauses in several languages: www.wipo.int.

Information on Investment Dispute can be found at the ICSIS of the Worldbank group: International Centre for Settlement of Investment Disputes, https://icsid.worldbank.org. The Mundi Mediatores clauses can be found on www.mundimediatores.com.

Newcomers to the ADR field are Mundi Mediatores[20] and InnovADR[21] with new ADR catalyst concepts. Neither of them is an ADR provider and they do not compete with existing service providers. Rather, they are designed to work in a complementary way with ADR services providers, providing new services to lower some of the hurdles that still exist and prevent mediation from growth.
Mundi Mediatores is a catalyst with the mission to address the 'Mediation Paradox': disputants express an overall preference for mediation but in practice mostly resort to litigation or arbitration.
Simply said: Mundi Mediatores is a broker who connects supply and demand in ADR (Appropriate Dispute Resolution) by meeting the users' needs and lowering barriers. The organization builds upon the standards of excellence set by IMI, the International Mediation Institute, and recent contributions to the field like ESG considerations, the Mediators Green Pledge and the Universal Disclosure Protocol for Mediation (UDPM).
InnovADR, based in Switzerland, provides a new model for ADR financing that is very different from litigation funding: paying for the costs of the ADR-Neutrals itself, on a "no-settlement, no-fee" basis, in a way that benefits all of the disputants equally, whether they are defendants or plaintiffs; and not only one party at the expense of another.
Mundi Mediatores (MM) takes a new approach to Dispute Resolution contract clauses by taking in account that that the needs for dispute resolution are often unclear or open to multiple interpretations at the time of inserting a contract clause. The parties do not know what specific dispute will arise, and, therefore, cannot precisely specify the appropriate dispute resolution mechanism in advance.
Parties get flexibility and prevent automatic resort to litigation. MM tackles this issue by enabling parties to engage in process design or request MM to shortlist a suitable mediator.

20 www.mundimediatores.com.
21 www.innovadr.com.

I. Clause to mediate a future dispute

1. The parties agree to first try to resolve any dispute, controversy or claim that may arise between them (the "**Dispute**") through mediation, using the services of Mundi Mediatores ("**MM**") to help them to appoint a mediator by providing a shortlist of one or more mediators (a "**Shortlist**") within thirty (30) days after submitting a case to MM. The mediator(s) that the parties appoint will help them to resolve the dispute, controversy or claim within ninety (90) days from appointment.
2. The seat of the mediation proceedings will be [INSERT CITY AND COUNTRY] although meetings may take place online or in any other physical location mutually agreed to by the parties. The language of the mediation proceedings will be [INSERT LANGUAGE].

II. Clause to solve a future dispute through ADR with process design

1. The parties agree to first try to resolve any dispute, controversy or claim that may arise between them (the "**Dispute**") through an appropriate dispute resolution ("**ADR**") process (e.g., negotiation, mediation, conciliation, litigation or arbitration) or a combination of such processes, using the services of Mundi Mediatores ("**MM**"). MM will help the parties to identify the ADR process or combination of processes that seems most suitable to that Dispute and will also propose one or more neutral, independent and impartial ADR professionals (an "**ADR Neutral**") to handle the Dispute, within thirty (30) days from the date MM was notified of the Dispute.
2. The parties agree to use their reasonable best efforts and to work together in good faith with a MM facilitator to be appointed by MM (the "**Facilitator**"), who will help them to diagnose the Dispute, to design an optimal ADR process and to provide a shortlist of one of more names (a "**Shortlist**") of ADR Neutral(s) who could implement that process and assist them to resolve the Dispute accordingly.
3. The seat of any ADR proceedings will be [INSERT CITY AND COUNTRY] although meetings may take place online or in any other physical location mutually agreed to by the parties. The language of any ADR proceedings will be [INSERT LANGUAGE].

8.2 Mediation rules, codes of conduct, disciplinary rules and agreements

In Resource E you can find a sample model mediation agreement and in F a sample model settlement agreement.
In the Netherlands more and more business mediators in particular use a "notice of conclusion" to provide parties with a confirmation that a mediation has taken place between them. This notice of conclusion is the only document that is excluded from the non-disclosure and confidentiality to which everyone is bound based on the mediation agreement.

The reason for this is that parties often need to prove for, e.g., a judge or as part of a personnel file that they tried mediation. If they do not have an official neutrally formulated form, they may use email exchanges or other documents that can prove that they mediated, which can breach the confidentiality. To accommodate this and ensure confidentiality, a notice of conclusion can be submitted by the mediator.

A mediation agreement template is provided as resource E, you can see this included in article 4.4.

In my opinion the best is to draft the notice of conclusion in an ultra-brief and neutral manner. As a mediator, it is essential to understand the purpose of this message: it is mainly for potential use in future legal proceedings or when revisiting an employee's record. The notice of conclusion aims to show that mediation was attempted, and at what date it ended (and with that the confidentiality obligations for information exchanged after that date) nothing more or less. Therefore, I do not describe the mediation's outcome or specify whose initiative ended the mediation (also not if I as a mediator ended it), how many sessions were held, or the total hours mediated. Some mediators prefer to include this information.

An example of a notice of conclusion:

[Date]

With this message, I confirm the conclusion as of today, [date], in accordance with Article [number] of the mediation agreement signed on [date], between:
[name] with advisor [name] & [name] with advisor [name].
This message, as per Article [number], is the only document outside the non-diclosure and confidentiality stipulated in the mediation agreement, covering all information, proposals, and documents exchanged during the mediation.

Best regards, [name], Mediator

An extensive, annotated list of web sources can be found in: Folberg, Golann, Kloppenberg and Stipanowich, (2005), RESOLVING DISPUTES: THEORY, PRACTICE AND LAW and Goldberg, Sander, Rogers and Cole (6th ed. 2012), DISPUTE RESOLUTION: NEGOTIATION, MEDIATION AND OTHER PROCESSES (appendix I).
Alexander (2006) 'Global Trends in Mediation' offers a rich analysis of mediation models, standards, laws and practices on four continents from a comparative perspective. It covers both common law and civil law jurisdictions with attention to the diversity of legal cultures and systems mediation laws and approaches.

8.3 CPD, Code of Disclosure and code of professional conduct

On the website of IMI an extensive overview of Mediation Rules and Clauses can be consulted: https://imimediation.org/resources/rules-and-clauses/

IMI qualified or certified mediators and CPD

Because IMI was established by and for business users to represent their interests, and it is also an international certification, there is no prescribed single type of mediator/ mediation approach, but various mediation styles are recognized. An important part of the practical exam is for the mediator to demonstrate an understanding of their own style/approach, strengths, and weaknesses and, based on that insight, provide a clear description to potential clients so that they know what to expect when they engage this mediator.

To become an IMI Certified Mediator, an experienced mediator (at least 20 cases or 200 hours in the previous 3 years) must undergo an assessment at one of the IMI-recognized Qualified Assessment Programs (QAPs). In the Netherlands, this includes The Academy of Legal Mediation (part of Toolkit Company). www.academylegalmediation.nl under the tab IMI Certified Mediator.[22] More information and an overview of all QAPs can be found at: imimediation.org tab practitioners.

Code of professional conduct

You can find IMI's code of conduct here: https://imimediation.org/practitioners/code-professional-conduct/

Mediator associations around the world have established codes of conduct for mediators. These codes establish standards that may be appropriate in one country but not in others as they are usually based on a particular way of mediating. With an awareness of the cultural diversity and different mediation models in various countries, IMI has chosen to allow various approaches to mediation (facilitative, evaluative, or directive, on both content and process, transformative, solution focused, caucus-only, etc.). Each country has its own approach and paradigm for what is 'the best practice for a mediator'. So mediators from different countries often employ different approaches to mediation, just like parties from different countries often have different expectations. Some prioritize achieving settlements and concrete outcomes, while others emphasize fostering high-quality dialogues and relationships. Other mediators focus primarily on the procedural aspects and have a strictly facilitative approach towards the substantive aspects.

22 https://www.academylegalmediation.nl/imi-qualifiedor-certified-mediator.

In cases involving parties from multiple countries, it may therefore be challenging to select a mediator or a team of co-mediators, especially when they are subject to widely varying codes of conduct. Some professional codes of conduct offer flexibility, or even a requirement, to adopt an evaluative approach with proposal-making, while others explicitly prohibit from doing so.

To address this challenge, the Universal Disclosure Protocol for Mediation (UDPM) offers a solution. This recent initiative enables to adapt the mediation approach to the cultural preferences and expectations of the involved parties. It ensures that all disputants and the mediator(s) share a common understanding of the specific mediation style and process(es) to be employed in each case.

Gonçalves, Bogacz and Rainey, Create a Universal Code of Disclosure, article 4.4, 4th Key Professionalism in: Michael Leathes (ed.), SEVEN KEYS TO UNLOCK MEDIATION'S GOLDEN AGE, mediate.com 2020.

In a dispute involving parties from different countries or cultures, a disclosure protocol can ensure that all parties and the mediator(s) have a common understanding of the specific mediation process that will be used in that case. This ensures that the parties can fully exercise self-determination and party autonomy by choosing a specific mediator with the corresponding approach. This is the idea behind the Universal Disclosure Protocol for Mediation (UDPM), a recent initiative launched by various international mediation organizations.

The shift from narrowly defined standards in national codes of conduct to disclosure protocols is an important first step in a new generation of ADR processes, where the process, offer, and obligations of the mediator can be better tailored to the needs of all parties involved in a case.

Universal Disclosure Protocol Mediation. For more information about the UDPM and its supporters: https://universaldisclosureprotocolmediation.com/.

II. Procedural aspects

1	Psychological contract and building trust	87
2	Maintaining and demonstrating neutrality and impartiality	90
3	Balancing power	93
4	Interest-based negotiation	95
5	Empathy and perspective taking	100
6	Empowerment of parties	101
7	Interests (subjective criteria)	102
8	Blocking issues and causes of conflict	106
9	The stages of a mediation process	114
10	Advancing from positions and the past to interests and the future	122
11	Result and conclusion of a mediation	124
12	Package deals	127
13	Balanced and SMART agreements	127
14	(Using) Time	128
15	Structuring	131
16	Caucus	132

Part II. Procedural aspects

The structure of part II can be found in row II of the checklist. This part deals with procedural matters and the instruments a mediator has at his disposal to support the parties in order to proceed from conflict to resolution.
Here issues like maintaining and demonstrating neutrality, dealing with bias, balancing power, empowerment and empathy are addressed. Also the structuring of the process and the caucus are described, and principled negotiation (the Harvard method) is explained. Additionally there is an analysis of blocking issues and recommended interventions and instruments (depending on the cause of the conflict). Finally we focus on the outcomes of a mediation.

1 Psychological contract and building trust

At the start of a mediation two kinds of contracts play a role: the formal mediation agreement (I-2.8 and I-5) and the informal psychological contract. The latter is equally important, even though it is not recorded in writing. The psychological contract consists of mutual expectations and responsibilities. These may be expressed implicitly as well as explicitly between the mediator and the parties.
A clear psychological contract:

- stimulates confidence in the process;
- motivates the parties;
- generates mediator credibility.

The psychological contract consists of a combination of factors. The main factors are:

- **The mediator's approach to the process**
  Impartial, as neutral an attitude as possible, show that you are listening, quick grasp of the essence of the problems, and communicate confidence in the process. Also, the mediator's personality, the way he acts and his appearance, must be in line with the parties and their expectations.
  Credibility and confidence in the process can also be generated during the intake phase (I-1.1) by relating comparable mediation cases which were resolved satisfactorily. To the parties, the substance of their conflict is very important and they regard their dispute as unique. You should therefore take care not to give the impression that theirs is a 'standard' dispute which you have seen many times before.
- **Information from the mediator to the parties**
  It is very important for the mediator to be clear, so parties know what to look forward to. For example, how this mediation will be handled and what parties can expect from the mediator and the mediation process; and, equally important, what they should not expect (I-2.3).

- **The expectations of the parties and the image they have of a mediation**
  Discuss with the parties what to expect from the mediator and the mediation (expectation management I-2.3).

Building Trust as a Mediator

The personality of the mediator is a more critical factor for the success of mediation than the ability to apply intervention techniques or having specific legal knowledge at hand. In three studies, Goldberg and Shaw (2007, 2008)[23] demonstrated that successful mediators primarily manage to gain trust and only secondarily possess good process skills. Knowledge and evaluative attributes came in third place. The research was conducted in the United States, where mediators more often tend to use an evaluative style than in Europe.

Earning trust is related to certain character traits, such as kindness, integrity, empathetic listening, and other qualities like being well-prepared. Patience and perseverance were also frequently mentioned. Other characteristics mentioned by parties and their legal advisors but with less significance included diplomacy and tact, offering solutions, creative thinking, and knowledge of the law. It was mainly the combination of qualities that appeared to be crucial for a mediator's success, although it was not necessary for a mediator to possess all of these qualities. No differences were found between male and female mediators.

Characteristics of poor mediators included a lack of integrity (such as sharing confidential information with the opposing party and partiality) and a lack of qualities that could inspire trust (such as egocentrism or a lack of empathy). Inadequate legal knowledge, poor preparation, and ineffective process facilitation were negatively assessed in these studies as well.

Marcil and Thornton (2008)[24] examined the most common reasons for the failure of mediations. They described fifteen factors[25] that, in addition to certain context-related reasons, such as mediation at too early a stage, mediation with too many or too few parties, primarily revolve around the commitment of the parties to the mediation and the skills of the mediator and the parties to effectively communicate about the dispute.

23 Goldberg, S.B. & M.L. Shaw (2007), 'The Secrets of Successful (and Unsuccessful) Mediators Continued: Studies Two and Three', Negotiation Journal, no. 4, p. 393-418. Ook te vinden in Dispute Resolution Alert, Winter 2008, p. 1-12.

24 Marcil, J.G. & N.D. Thornton (2008), 'Avoiding Pitfalls: Common Reasons for Mediation Failure and Solutions for Success', North Dakota Law Review, vol. 84, p. 861-875.

25 (a) Appropriateness of mediator, (b) parties' commitment to resolve the dispute, (c) failure to properly prepare for mediation, (d) incomplete mediation statements, (e) anticipation and discussion of impasse, (f) subsequently scheduled settlement conferences, (g) premature mediation, (h) previous offer exceeds representative's authority, (i) claimant increases demand at mediation, (j) contribution among (multiple) defendants, (k) subrogation interests, (l) insufficient settlement authority, (m) persons with authority to settle do not attend mediation, (n) failure to properly document the mediation settlement, (o) court-ordered mediations.

Poitras (2009)[26] specifically researched how parties come to trust a mediator and concluded that there are five decisive factors:

1. The extent to which the mediator masters the mediation process (not intended as exerting control but rather as a sense of mastery).
2. Explanation of the process.
3. Warmth and consideration (care or attention).
4. A good rapport with the parties.
5. No (perceived) bias towards one of the parties.

Personal qualities, such as warmth and being likeable, play a pivotal role. Conversely, the perception that the mediator favors the opposing party can be detrimental to a party's willingness to trust a mediator.

Guidelines for increasing the chance of a successful mediation outcome:

- ☐ Prepare thoroughly. Support the parties and their legal advisors in their own preparation.
- ☐ Pay attention to your opening statement and make commitment an essential part of the mediation and your opening statement (I-3).
- ☐ Try to build trust by:
  - Being friendly.
  - Providing a clear structure during the mediation and offering a good explanation of it in the opening statement.
  - Acting with integrity: do not disclose information, and give the parties confidence that you handle their information carefully, maintain a neutral and impartial stance (II-2).
  - Showing sincere interest in the parties, being empathetic (II-5), and (actively) listening (III-2).
  - Developing good process skills (II) and effectively facilitating communication between the parties (III).
  - Having patience and perseverance.

An additional benefit of trust is that parties are more likely to share information with the mediator when they trust them. Information is crucial to achieving a sound solution in mediation.

Jennifer Shack, Ava Abramowitz, and Ken Webb are conducting further research into the effective behavior of negotiators based on Rackham and Carlisle's research. In 2023, they began a study to identify specific mediator behaviors that enhance the parties' trust in the mediator. The research involves observing mediators and tracking their behavior

26 Poitras, J. (2009), 'What Makes Parties Trust Mediators?', Negotiation Journal, vol. 25, no. 3, p. 307-325.

on a scorecard. This research will provide more concrete guidance on how to earn the trust of parties as a mediator.

Several initial working hypotheses[27] based on prior research are already interesting to note:

- The success rate decreases as parties have less trust in the mediation and the mediator.
- The success rate increases in mediations where parties talk more than the mediator and attorneys.
- When the mediator frequently makes proposals about the process or regularly outlines possibilities, it has no negative effect. However, if the mediator frequently makes (unsolicited) proposals regarding the substance, trust decreases.
- Mediators who respond sparingly (for example, being very neutral or distant or only working at the content level) can amplify disagreement or the behavior of attacking and defending in parties. Trust, on the other hand, increases with mediators who actively seek information about feelings and understanding, test assumptions, and provide emotional reflections.
- Labeling behavior (announcing what you are going to do) also has a positive effect on trust in a mediator.

These guidelines and research findings align with several key points from the SCARF model: IV-7.

2 Maintaining and demonstrating neutrality and impartiality

2.1 Maintaining neutrality and impartiality during the mediation

Neutrality has its roots in the personal attitudes and qualities of the mediator. Being curious to know what motivates others is an example of having the right attitude. Follow the motto: 'don't get annoyed, just be surprised.' It implies a neutral basic attitude: no prejudice or bias, do not let your own opinions play a part, do not convey more appreciation for one party than for the other, do not show you think that one party is more sensible or rational than the other; try not to judge and especially do not show preferences or disapproval. Impartiality is mainly about having no (business) interest or other stake in the parties or the outcome of the mediation. These are the issues a mediator should investigate before the start of the mediation. (I-1.1)

Impartiality implies a mediator has no business or financial interest in one of the parties, has not acted as an advisor to either of the parties, but also has no other connections,

27 https://static1.squarespace.com/static/583241f7893fc0b69ddde11b/t/65222d4a6621845a6ac14ebe/1696738635425/Abramowitz+%26+Shack.outline.What+Do+Mediators+Do+That+Creates+Trust.pdf 1.

for example as a friend or relative of one party's constituency. For the sake of impartiality, a mediator may not show a preference for one party and also must not have any personal interest in the outcome.

Being (perceived as) neutral and impartial

- ☐ Do not judge the parties involved or the solution chosen by them.
- ☐ Observe your own feelings, but leave your emotions outside the process (IV-4). Pay attention: emotions like anxiety or anger interfere with the human ability to listen carefully.
- ☐ Exclude personal beliefs, values and prejudices from the mediation unless ethical concerns arise. In that event, it is best to terminate the negotiations or the mediation.
- ☐ Focus on separating the content issues from the people issues. An annoying person may still have a good idea or express a valid point of view.
- ☐ Try to formulate questions neutrally, unless you consciously choose to be directive or confrontational (III-10.7).
- ☐ Concentrate on what is being said and on how it is being said (III-9) and not on what you, the mediator, are going to say and how you will intervene (III-2).
- ☐ Check your personal assumptions and those of the parties.

To what extent is it possible to be truly neutral, impartial and objective (IV-2.3)? De Dreu (2005) describes that it is impossible, but does not see this as a problem provided the mediator is open and transparent about a possible conflict of interests or a lack of neutrality. Complete transparency about a conflict of interests that could influence the mediator's neutrality is always required. But transparency does not excuse misconduct. Because of his professionalism, but also because he is bound by the code of conduct (and in some countries, such as the Netherlands, he is subject to a formal complaints scheme and to disciplinary rules), it is not sensible to enter into a mediation with a biased or subjective attitude.

There is always a risk, irrespective of the degree of transparency and openness, that the mediation is eventually subjected to a complaints procedure when one party is dissatisfied with the outcome or the failure of the mediation. A mediator must therefore be impartial at all times. Although demanding complete neutrality from a mediator is not realistic (every mediator brings his own personality to a mediation), every mediator should try his best to achieve a neutral attitude. Moreover, he should constantly demonstrate his neutrality and impartiality during the mediation. A possible lack of neutrality should play no role at all during the course of the mediation. Conversely, an excessive demonstration of neutrality should not be allowed to slow down the mediation.

2.2 Techniques to demonstrate neutrality and impartiality

Explaining your neutrality and even being completely impartial, is not sufficient. You also have to demonstrate it. An important condition to demonstrate neutrality and impartiality is being crystal clear about the purpose and the limits of mediation, and the assignments of the parties concerned as well as the mediator (I-1.1). You also have to be totally open about any circumstances that could compromise your impartiality. If these circumstances could apply, you should not take on this mediation assignment yourself (II-2.1).

Demonstrating neutrality and impartiality

- ☐ Non-verbal behavior (III-18 and III-2.3).
- ☐ Use of language: use neutral language and formulate neutrally (III-7), reframe remarks neutrally (III-6.1) and avoid bias (II-2.3).
- ☐ Balance power (II-3): this can be achieved by the way you: approach and treat the parties, regulate their behavior and the communication between them (III-1) and introduce and uphold the ground rules (I-3).
- ☐ Do not (try to) impose a solution on the parties and also avoid putting too much pressure on the parties to find a solution at any price.

Mayer (2004), BEYOND NEUTRALITY: CONFRONTING THE CRISIS IN CONFLICT RESOLUTION.
Astor on neutrality and impartiality:

- *Astor (2007) MEDIATOR NEUTRALITY: MAKING SENSE OF THEORY AND PRACTICE.*
- *Astor (2000) RETHINKING NEUTRALITY: A THEORY TO INFORM PRACTICE.*

2.3 Mediator bias

You need to be alert to any personal bias and sensitivities you may have. For example with regard to:

- content of the dispute;
- subject matters that can arise;
- communication style of (one of) the parties;
- particular behaviors;
- a specific position;
- a particular solution.

3 Balancing power

Inequality of power plays a role in every relationship and in all conflicts. It is unavoidable and cannot be neutralized completely. Bear in mind that power imbalance is a fact of life, and that it may have played a part in the origin and subsequent continuation of the conflict. Imbalance of power does not just influence the mediation, but could also be an important factor in any other method of resolving the dispute. For example, a wealthy party can engage a number of reputable lawyers or they can easily appeal to a higher court. A more knowledgeable party can negotiate better on a strategic and tactical level. A party with the law or public opinion on its side can exert pressure and refuse to give up a position. Someone with the right to a public defender can 'smoke out the other party' and slow down or prolong the process. A party who feels guilty will be more inclined to make concessions to the opposing party.

Inequality of power plays a part in every conflict. Of course you can try to balance the process, but it is virtually impossible to completely neutralize the differences. Besides, the question is whether this is desirable (II-3.2).

Examples of power:

- expertise;
- pressure or duress;
- constituency or public opinion;
- recommendation by a third party;
- status;
- information;
- the possibility to reward, eliminate or recover;
- economical, financial, property or assets;
- legal;
- emotional.

See also the concept of leverage III-14.2.

3.1 Balancing power in a structured manner

- ☐ Ensure an equal number of representatives and advisors are present for all parties, so that there will be approximately the same number of persons on all sides of the table (I-2.6).
- ☐ Make sure that in principle all parties are supported by (legal) advisors or that none are (I-2.6).
- ☐ In business-to-business mediations or during a negotiation it is important to ensure that the representatives of all parties are equally competent. For example, both are at the level of (project) supervisor or both are members of the Board. In addition, it is important to

determine that they also have a similar functional background (for example both are staff members or operational managers).

- If there is a considerable structural imbalance of power, for example when one of the parties has more information, money or time (III-14), it might be advisable to give the weaker party some extra support. For example by suggesting the involvement of an (additional) advisor, or by giving this party some 'psychological advantage' by suggesting they make the first opening statement (I-2.3). However, beware of the potential 'power of the underdog' (II-3.2). Never lose sight of the fact that David brought down Goliath.

3.2 Balancing power during the process

- Allow all parties equal speaking time and opportunity to contribute.
- Treat the parties as equal partners and ask them to treat each other the same way.
- Empowerment: stimulate autonomy and opportunities to let parties decide for themselves (II-6 and IV-4).
- Ensure that all parties can influence and contribute to the final result of the mediation or negotiation.
- Inequality of power is often the result of having greater financial strength, a higher position or more prestige, the luxury of time, etc. Conversely, the weaker party also can have power. Sometimes the ostensibly weakest party can dominate the entire process by acting as a victim at the expense of the stronger party. So make sure you also control underdogs and victims in a mediation (IV-3.1).

You can ask yourself how far you can or should go in supporting the weaker party, or in reducing the influence of the stronger party, before you risk losing your neutrality. In weighing the pros and cons, you should factor in the extent to which you, as a mediator, should feel responsible for reaching a solution and whether this solution does justice to all parties (I-2.1). One view is that the mediator is entitled to do everything in his power to bring the parties to agreement and that the end justifies the means. And to achieve this you must empower the weaker party or keep the more powerful party under control. For example by asking the stronger party to appreciate and take into consideration the (power) position of the underdog. As a mediator you can even intervene directly if necessary (for example by reality testing III-11, or asking confronting questions III-10.4). The contrary view is that the mediator should not interfere in the content issues of the mediation and should therefore not influence the outcome at all, which implies that he should refrain from intervening in the balance of power as much as possible.
Most mediators adopt a middle course. If the negotiators are satisfied with the solution, the mediator is satisfied as well, unless:

- the mediator feels that one of the parties is being forced to some extent;
- the solution violates the mediator's personal ethical or other important standards;
- the solution is in violation of the law.

In the last two circumstances, the mediator must end the mediation. If the first situation occurs, the mediator can help the compliant party by, for example, advising (both parties) to consult an expert or another sparring partner prior to accepting an offer or agreeing to a solution. For instance the lawyer/family mediator who in certain jurisdictions has to give information about the right to alimony to a party that decides not to ask for it. If the parties consciously choose an unbalanced solution, most mediators will accept that decision. Parties in a mediation or negotiation can have good reasons to relinquish their rights (check underlying interests II-7).

It is advisable to record in the settlement agreement that a party consciously wishes to relinquish its rights, that parties have been advised regarding their rights (for instance the right to alimony) and/or parties have consulted an expert, or that the issue has at least been discussed (II-13). This is especially recommended in jurisdictions where a judge might review the 'reasonableness and fairness' of a settlement agreement if compliance is required at a later date (I-8.7).

See also III-14.2 leverage.

4 Interest-based negotiation

In recent decades a great deal of research has been carried out into the effects of different negotiating techniques. Negotiations can be subdivided into two broad categories: (1) distributive or positional bargaining (based on positions) and (2) integrative (problem solving) or principled negotiation (on the basis of interests). Distributive negotiating can be efficient in simple situations, for example when bargaining at a market stall. More complex negotiations often require integrative/principled strategies or a mix of styles.

4.1 Getting to yes

A well-known methodology for principled negotiating evolved from the Project On Negotiation (PON) of Harvard University in Cambridge, Mass, USA. The classic book GETTING TO YES by Fisher, Ury & Patton (1981) deals with principled negotiation.

The philosophy behind principled negotiation can be seen as the basis for mediation. Trust, the relational aspect, and the business dimension of a negotiation together form the basis for creatively expanding the pie (III-15). They comprise the first step

to an agreement based on the interests of all parties involved (II-7). Trust means having sufficient mutual confidence in the process and in each other as 'partners in conflict', or negotiators, to reach a satisfactory solution. Dealing with personal aspects or relationship issues implies treating each other with respect. The interests (joint or diverging, but not necessarily irreconcilable) form the business dimension. The content aspects must be separated from the relationship issues (III-8).
Conflicting interests are resolved on the basis of a shared sense of fairness, reciprocity, and objective criteria (III-16). At the same time parties are made aware of the alternatives open to them, and the need to reach a positive outcome with or without the other party (III-14). This is an especially important aspect in long-term relationships. Parties often fail to recognize this themselves. Interventions by the mediator or deal facilitator can help them realize this. If you are a negotiator yourself, it is important to understand this.

4.2 The rules of thumb from 'Getting to yes'

- **'Separate the people from the problem' and 'be hard on the problem, be soft on the people'**
  Building a good working relationship is of great importance to be able to (let others) negotiate (about) the content issues (III-8).
  - Make sure the parties 'play the ball', not the person. This prevents the negotiation turning into an ego and power struggle and it helps focus the discussion on the real issues.
  - Work on empathy: try to make the position or the emotions of one party understandable to the other party. Understanding does not necessarily imply agreement. Faith issues aside, people generally cannot accept what they do not understand.
  - Be firm on the content and in clarifying the parties' interests. Simultaneously prevent unneccesary harm to the relationship.
- **Focus on interests, not on positions**
  The interests of all parties is what matters (II-7).
  - Analyze all parties' interests and avoid getting stuck in entrenched positions which were dug at the start of the negotiation or mediation.
  - Interests can be established by exploring the *why?* and *why not?* of a position. You can do this by asking different questions that together generate an answer to the *why (not)?*. Be careful not to ask *why?* too directly. It can be interpreted as confrontational and put people on the defensive (III-10.1.3 and III-10.4). Another, less provocative way of asking *why?* is *'Can you help me understand the reason for ...?'*.

- The most important interests are basic human needs like safety, (financial) security, a sense of belonging, recognition and being in control. 'Needs' have to be distinguished from 'wants'.
- Focus on the future and don't get stuck in the past. The questions *to what purpose?* and *how?* deal with the future and the question *why?* deals with the past.

- **Look for mutual gain solutions**
  Try to expand the pie. Do not assume a 'fixed pie' and do not look for a single solution (III-15).
  - Make sure the solution meets the interests of all parties.
  - Strive for a negotiating outcome that benefits all parties. Do not assume there must be a winner and a loser.
- **Employ objective criteria to be able to assess a solution**
  - By developing objective criteria you can facilitate the negotiation. You prevent power plays about subjective standards (III-16). Moreover, subsequent negotiations with constituents (I-2.7.2) are facilitated.

4.3 Getting Past No

The sequel to GETTING TO YES is the classic GETTING PAST NO by Ury (1991). It describes methods to bring a reluctant party to integrative negotiating.

According to Ury, five important principles have to be observed.

- **Go to the balcony and think first when a party responds unpleasantly; do not react impulsively, consider how you can react effectively**
  Stay in control. Postpone your reaction and take time to reflect. For example, take a mental break by saying nothing for a moment, repeating step-by-step what has been said so far, or take a time out. If you sense that the other party is trying to play a game, you could mention this (IV-3.3.2, naming the game). In any case do not respond to opposition in the conventional way. Resist the natural impulse to capitulate, walk away or strike back. Be the one in control.
- **Make the parties acknowledge each others' position and dissuade them from attacking each other with counterarguments**
  You can only start negotiations when you have established a workable relationship. This can be done by active listening (III-2.2), paraphrasing (letting a party paraphrase) (III-3), reflections (III-5), apologizing (having parties apologize), admitting to a mistake, and looking for mutual understanding (III-13 and II-7).
- **Reframe a proposal rather than (let a party) reject it outright**
  Stay away from 'yes-no' discussions. Do not be colour blind – life is not black and white. Configure the negotiation as a joint process, in which all parties have an

interest in reaching a solution. If a proposal under discussion is unacceptable for one of the parties, do not let it be rejected right away. Try to reframe it into a proposal that may be negotiable. If a party refuses to engage, then try to change the game that is being played or the rules of the game (IV-3.3.2). Important tools to achieve this are asking questions (III-10), using silences (III-17), and most important of all, reframing (III-6).

- **Build them a golden bridge instead of pushing or pulling parties to one side or the other, and let them get closer to each other by themselves**
  Make it easy for parties to say yes. This can be done by mutualizing (III-13), jointly generating options and ideas (III-15), forward-looking reality testing (III-11.1), exploring a party's ideas in more detail (III-15.1) and agreeing on package deals (I-2.8, I-5 and II-12). Take into account the interests of the respective constituencies and support them in preventing a possible loss of face. A paradoxical intervention is another method to avoid pushing and pulling the parties (III-19).
- **Do not let the negotiation escalate, but do try to clarify**
  Make it difficult for parties to say no. Inform or ask about the consequences or how they will react if they don't work things out, ask reality-testing questions, apply a risk analysis (III-11.2) and demonstrate the BATNA, WATNA and RATNA (Best/Worst/Realistic Alternative To Negotiated Agreement) (III-14). And if all else fails, you as the mediator or negotiator apply your own BATNA and terminate the mediation or negotiation. But at the same time let everyone involved know that 'the golden bridge' is still open.

4.4 Effective behavior for negotiators

Rackham and Carlisle ('The Behavior of Successful Negotiators', 1978 Huthwaite) compared the behavior of 'skilled negotiators' with that of 'average negotiators'.[28]

Behavior of skilled negotiators, do's:

- Asking questions – Seeking information instead of 'transmitting'.
- Labeling behavior – Announcing, such as *'May I ask a question...?' 'I am making a proposal...' 'What I am thinking now is...'*
- Actively listening (especially testing for understanding and summarizing).
- Reflecting on feelings.
- Using (a limited number of) strong arguments, not all arguments.

28 Rackham & Carlisle, 'The Behaviour of Successful Negotiators', 1978 Huthwaite.

Other habits of skilled negotiators:

- Thorough preparation with an emphasis on finding commonalities and where value can be created for both parties.
- Exploring multiple options, open to exploring the other party's options.
- Flexibility in the order in which issues are discussed (recognizing the connections between the topics).

In comparison, the behavior of average negotiators, do not:

- Using 'irritators' such as '*generous offer*', '*this is fair*', '*reasonable*'.
- Labeling behavior - if you disagree with something, such as '*I will now explain why this doesn't work*'.
- Interrupting with a counterproposal.
- Defensive and offensive spirals.
- Dilution of arguments (by attempting to be exhaustive).

Other habits of average negotiators:

- Emphasis on preparation for one's own position and how to assert it.
- A limited number of options and mainly one's own options.
- Sequential view of issues (first theme A, then B, then C).

See the beneficial effects of perspective-taking and the detrimental effects of sympathy for achieving the best negotiation result in II-5.

Techniques and interventions in part III and an overview of the (psychological) processes and approaches that can explain why parties act - in the eyes of others - in irrational or dysfunctional ways during a negotiation or a mediation (IV-2.4).

As a negotiator do not try to improve the relationship by conceding on substance. Conceding on content in general does not improve the relationship, consciously working on improving the relationship does.

5 Empathy and perspective taking

Empathy is not the same as sympathy. Empathy involves perspective taking: being able to put oneself in another's point of view and communicate this without getting involved in the other person's feelings (sympathy) or necessarily agreeing with their feelings or point of view.
Empathy is an essential tool for a mediator, especially for building trust with parties (II-1).

Pre-mediation caucuses were found to be more effective when a mediator engaged in an empathetic conversation with the parties, mainly with the aim of establishing rapport and a relationship without delving too deeply into the content. [29] The mediator came across as neutral and trustworthy in this way. If the mediator delves too quickly into the substance of the dispute, they may appear less neutral or impartial. According to some studies, these are critical success factors for a mediator (II-1). Another explanation for the success of an 'empathetic' pre-mediation conversation is that when parties trust a mediator, they are more willing to share information with the mediator. Having sufficient information is crucial to achieving a good solution in mediation.

Galinsky et al. (2009)[30] found that sympathy[31] and perspective taking have significant effects in negotiations. Negotiators who excelled in perspective taking were better at uncovering the other party's hidden agendas and creating value while claiming it for themselves. Having sympathy for the other party is less advantageous and, in some cases, even led to the involved parties being unable to discover enough options for a deal, and the 'sympathetic negotiators' were less capable of claiming value for themselves.

Transference and Countertransference

As a mediator, it is important to regularly assess whether you have entered an unwanted dynamic of transference or countertransference with one or more of the clients. The phenomenon of transference was described by Freud. It involves the repetition in the present of a pattern from the past, with the intention of correcting something that went wrong earlier. Transference refers to the unconscious transfer of old feelings onto another person, particularly from the client to an authority, therapist, counselor, or mediator. The reverse is also possible. The transfer of a professional, such as a therapist, coach, mediator, lawyer, etc., onto the client is called countertransference.

---

29 Swaab, R. & J. Brett (2007), 'Caucus with Care: The Impact of Pre-Mediation Caucuses on Conflict Resolution', IACM 2007 Meetings Paper.

30 Galinsky, A.D., W.W. Maddux, D. Gilin & J.B. White (2008), 'Why It Pays to Get Inside the Head of Your Opponent. The Differential Effects of Perspective Taking and Empathy in Negotiations', Association for Psychological Science, vol. 19, no. 4, p. 378-384.

31 In the Galinsky (2008) research the effects of empathy and perspective taking were compared (in the Toolkit empathy as described in this research is called sympathy, to enable a distinction between sympathy, empathy and introduce perspective taking).

Transference and countertransference unconsciously create an expectation of how the other views you, which in turn affects how you perceive the other person. This can impact communication and hinder your ability as a mediator to effectively guide the process. Transference and countertransference are common, and it is essential for a mediator to handle them properly.
Signs that there may be transference or countertransference at play include recurring impasses, feeling as a mediator that you have lost control over the process, and feeling you are (overly) exerting yourself. You may experience emotions like anger, sadness, irritation, or others. Taking an independent third-party perspective is also crucial for the communication and interaction between yourself as a mediator and the parties.

Do not react directly to the emotions that arise in you, nor suppress them, but instead, observe what the interaction, communication, or person triggers in you and try to understand why that happens and what action-reaction patterns you notice.

The mediator has to find a good balance. This implies understanding and fathoming another person's feelings without compromising neutrality, being influenced by the parties or agreeing with their (possibly rigid) point of view.

Checklist empathy

- [ ] Understand the parties' feelings and translate them into needs and wishes.
- [ ] Show an active interest in the parties and in what motivates them.
- [ ] Perceive and hypothesize new possibilities and options for the parties.
- [ ] Recognize emotions and the impact of power in a relationship, make them functional and neutralize them. Or if necessary, leverage them to achieve a resolution.

6 Empowerment of parties

People can cause a conflict and ultimately they can also resolve it themselves. Empowerment means stimulating independence, autonomy and the ability to make your own decisions. This can be achieved by observing many of the rules included in codes of conduct for mediators:

- neutrality, impartiality;
- responsibility for the chosen solution lies with the parties;
- the mediator respects the choices made by the parties and does not use his values as a yardstick;
- the mediator does not impose solutions.

Checklist empowerment

- ☐ Were the negotiators encouraged to take an active part in the mediation process?
- ☐ Did they treat each other with respect and did all negotiators have the same opportunities to contribute to the final result?
- ☐ Does every party feel (partly) responsible for the origin and the development of the conflict?
- ☐ Do parties appreciate their own and their counterpart's interests, and to what extent does this awareness originate from themselves (or the mediator...)?
- ☐ Have all relevant topics and interests been discussed?
- ☐ Is the chosen solution sourced from the negotiators themselves and does everybody feel responsible for its success?
- ☐ Has the settlement agreement been written in the parties' 'own language'? Do they recognize their own hand in what has been recorded in writing?
- ☐ As a mediator, were you able to keep your opinions and prejudices to yourself (II-2)?
- ☐ Has the dispute truly been resolved, or just papered over? Is the agreement sustainable and will the parties observe it (II-13)?

7 Interests (subjective criteria)

Definition/description	Application	Example of application
Identifying interests (II-7)		
Wants, needs, the reason why somebody wishes something. An interest is a subjective criterion that is often transformed into a position (demands, rights). A position often is the legal or positional translation of an underlying interest. Searching for the subjective criteria, the interests, is one of the essential elements of a mediation or negotiation.	Interests form the basis for win-win or mutual gain solutions. They can support an understanding of the other party's position. In addition, by focusing on the interests, issues that are not part of the conflict can be included in the solution (expanding the pie). By mutualizing topics (III-13) and emphasizing mutual interests, forward movement is achieved as well as a greater understanding of the other party's needs.	**Example interest** (*'You either participate and perform well or leave the team.'*) A: A wants the team to perform well and therefore thinks it is important that the team members cooperate. A's underlying interest is that she wants to score as the team leader in order to further her career. B: B wants clear arrangements while having the liberty to decide the way in which she handles her work. She is also experiencing an extremely busy period and is concerned that she will not be able to finish her regular tasks in time if she does too much work for the team.

Interests can be seen as the subjective criteria that form the basis of a solution, so they need to be identified and brought to the surface in a mediation. Classifying interests as common/joint or as differing interests is customary in mediation theory.

7.1 Common or joint interests

In a mediation or negotiation it is good practice to identify the common interests and to bring these out into the open. Being aware of the common interests gives parties a sense of progress and shows that in addition to the dispute there is also common ground. Maintaining relationships, staying in control, resolving the disputes oneself and striving for a quick solution are all examples of common interests.

7.2 Differing interests

7.2.1 Reconcilable differing interests

Reconcilable differing interests usually concern matters which are important to one party and which can be satisfied by the other at relatively little cost or effort. Examples are: wanting to be taken seriously, demanding an apology or a clear explanation of the background of a regulation or a decision, achieving sales or profits. Also, restoring confidence is generally a reconcilable interest. It is often even a common interest. Reconcilable differing interests can usually be resolved promptly after the interest is brought to the surface; it 'costs' one party only a little while it moves the process a huge step forward.

7.2.2 Irreconcilable differing interests

The term 'irreconcilable differing interests' speaks for itself. These interests are not easy to harmonize. Here, the needs of one party can often be satisfied only if the other party relinquishes an irreconcilable corresponding need. At least that is what it looks like superficially.
In many cases, creative solutions can be generated that result in everybody (partly) getting what he needs, or sometimes even what he wants, but does not necessarily need. Examples of irreconcilable differing interests can be neighbours not accepting noise or smells from a farm versus the farm needing to go about its business without interference (a). Or wanting to retain the exclusive use of one's own technology and claiming compensation because of the infringement on the intellectual rights of ownership versus using (parts of) a technology or even claiming ownership to it (b). Or wanting to divorce versus staying together (c).
Parties have to negotiate (II-4) a solution for irreconcilable interests. Here an important responsibility of the mediator is to explain divergent perspectives and ways of thinking (IV-2). The negotiators can then assess and understand the intentions and perspectives of the other party. Or at least they can agree to disagree. Unravelling emotions (IV-4) and getting a clear picture of the blocking issues (II-8) also play a part.
See generating options (III-15), reaching an agreement (III-16), and the different ways of concluding a mediation (II-11).

In summary, the most important techniques to stimulate finding a solution for irreconcilable differing interests: 1. enlarge it, 2. make it different, 3. concede or be open to a creative compromise.

1. **Enlarge the pie (III-15.2)**

   By including more ingredients in the solution menu than merely the issues at conflict, you ensure there is more pie to divide. In the previously quoted examples this can be: in exchange for certain inconveniences, neighbors can utilize certain facilities on the farm (a). Delivery contracts can be concluded in a mutual agreement instead of negotiating for compensation (b). You get divorced, but you agree to attend the childrens' school evenings together (c). The pie can be enlarged and improved in other ways by brainstorming (III-15.1) and by stimulating creativity (III-15.2).

2. **Make it different**

   A mediator can demonstrate things to the negotiators from a different perspective. *Cannot* then becomes *I choose to. The other is to blame* becomes *We both contributed to the conflict.* Wanting compensation as a means of penalizing the other party then becomes: finding a solution that benefits both. Thinking 'out-of-the-box' can be encouraged in several ways:

   - testing an assumption and asking parties whether this is the only way;
   - asking confrontating questions or making paradoxical interventions (III-10.4 and III-19);
   - reframing (III-6).

3. A possible solution for irreconcilable differing interests in the previously mentioned examples can be the completion of a licence agreement rather than simply being awarded a compensation. Or starting a joint venture instead of competing (b). Or agreeing to relocate instead of checking how much 'odour nuisance' is allowed (a). You are not husband and wife any longer, but you both remain the parents of your children (c).

4. **Concluding a compromise or giving in**

   A compromise does not necessarily mean 'to cut the fixed pie into two equal pieces'. A mediator can help the negotiators find a creative compromise. This can be done by referring to objective criteria (what would a judge say, what is customary, etc. (III-16.1)), or by using methods like: one party cuts the pie and the other gets to choose the first slice. A mediator can boost the willingness of the negotiators to arrive at a compromise by reality testing (a questioning technique to assess the realism of a position and to stimulate the willingness of the parties to come to a solution themselves (III-11)). Another possibility is working with trade-offs (systematically exchanging wishes that are important for one party but less important for the other) is also possible. Also consider 'giving in', or capitulation (IV-3.3.2).

   In a mediation procedure about the liquidation of a partnership, the party who is bought out wants, for example, a fast settlement and delivery of the cash as soon as

possible. The acquiring party could agree (it makes no difference to him when the buyout is concluded) and in exchange wants to keep the library.
Another example of a compromise is the introverted and the outgoing colleagues who cannot work together. The problems are partly caused by conflicting characters, the way they work and how they respond to each other. A possible compromise could be that the colleague with the quick mind and the silver tongue gives the other time to reflect quietly, and thinks twice before responding impulsively if something works out differently than expected. On the other hand the more deliberate colleague who needs more time to come to a decision, gives a clear time frame and indicates where he is in the (thinking) process. Arranging separate rooms also can be a good compromise.

7.3 Other classifications of interests

Moore (2014) uses another classification of interests: content interests, procedural interests and psychological interests.

- **Substantive (content) interests**
  The need a party has for things like money, possessions or time.
- **Procedural interests**
  Wishes regarding the way in which matters in dispute are discussed and the preferred way of implementing the result. Examples of procedural interests are: adequate time to explain a point of view, using a structured negotiating agenda, and employing respectful language. A differing procedural interest can be one party having the need to work out agreements to the smallest details prior to implementation while the other party aims for an outline agreement so that the details can be addressed during the implementation phase.
- **Psychological interests**
  Examples of the emotional and relational needs of the parties are: considering the continuation of the relationship after the negotiation to be important, wanting to be treated with respect, needing to be taken seriously or avoiding loss of face.

The word interest is a broad term. To explore all layers of interests, it is better to speak of Interests, Concerns, Needs, and Motivations. The acronym ICNM's is often used for this purpose. In the Toolkit, for the sake of readability, I mainly use the word 'interests', which however also encompasses other layers like concerns, needs, and motivations.[32]

32 Source: 6 preparation exercises Jeremy Lack, www.lawtech.com.

8 Blocking issues and causes of conflict

Insight into the causes of a conflict is the vital first step towards a resolution.
The mediator analyzes why the parties were unable to solve the problem themselves. Together with the parties he explores the relationships and communications between them. Differences in perceptions can be determined. For example by examining whether different information or inconsistent facts are the real root of the conflict, or whether the conflict is based on a different interpretation of the facts, or because different conclusions are drawn from the same facts. The interests of the parties are explored.
In addition, the more structural causes of a conflict, such as an imbalance of power and incompatible values and principles of the parties are considered.
According to Moore (2014), the types of interventions that are needed depend on the causes of the conflict. Finding the major causes of the conflict also helps the mediator to decide what issues should be discussed, and in what order (I-6). Moreover, this gives an indication of any hidden, underlying interests (II-7).

8.1 The blocking issue

Frequently one of the causes of conflict is a blocking issue (NCRC 1998).[33] A blocking issue is the reason why parties did not manage to resolve a conflict themselves. This is usually caused by emotional considerations, such as an attempt to save face, a breach of trust, the need for an apology, or a belief that the other parties have acted in bad faith.
Blocking issues are often caused by different perspectives, the ladder of inference (IV-2.2) and mutual distrust. This leads to the parties being less able to apply principled negotiation techniques (II-4), or communicate effectively, and therefore to not resolving the dispute.
Clarifying blocking issues and facilitating the discussion about these issues is a great added value of a mediator. It is important that the parties involved obtain insight into the importance of blocking issues (both for themselves and for the other party). Asking the parties to paraphrase the discussion about the blocking issues is a good technique to achieve this (III-3).
As an impartial party, the mediator can listen more neutrally and is therefore better able to analyze the conflict causes. A mediator can help parties to separate the emotional and relationship issues from the content issues. The parties are then free to explore what the core interests are for them (III-8).

33 Training manual San Diego Mediation Center (now: National Conflict Resolution Center) 1998.

8.2 Conflict causes and interventions

In THE MEDIATION PROCESS (2014)[34] *Moore describes the analysis of the conflict causes as a starting point for the mediation process. Based on his observations the mediator builds a hypothesis about the causes of the conflict. Through interventions, the mediator can test his hypothesis. The types of interventions that are necessary depend, according to Moore, on the cause of the conflict. Another book that deals with these issues is Furlong (2020), CONFLICT RESOLUTION TOOLBOX: MODELS AND MAPS FOR ANALYZING, DIAGNOSING, AND RESOLVING CONFLICT.*

- **If the cause of the conflict is rooted in the relationship or in misperceptions in communication**, then stereotyping, ineffective communication, negative interactions or destructive behavior develop.
  For example, Party A sighs because she feels that she has made an awkward remark or because it is difficult for her to put something into words. Party B, on the other hand, interprets the sigh as: 'You see, she is fed up with me'.
  Conflicts that are based on relationship or communication issues can be handled by dealing with emotions (control or vent), clarifying different perspectives, or illuminating and/or changing communication patterns. The mediator can play an important role in this process.
- **If values and principles are the cause, the conflict is difficult to solve.** If you, almost by definition, see, do or judge things differently, it is very difficult to negotiate. Party A, for example, has the strict principle that 'a deal is a deal and you stick to it, even if the circumstances change'. Whereas party B is of the opinion that everything should be interpreted and adapted in the light of changing circumstances.
  The mediator has a toolkit of instruments to help parties reach a solution for conflicts that have arisen from a difference in values and/or principles. A mediator could, for example, help the negotiators agree to disagree or to find a higher and prevailing mutual goal.
- **Structural causes of conflict are also difficult to solve.** These conflicts are usually about a structural difference in power, authority, repeated destructive behavior, different significance placed on factors like time, geographical (dis)advantage or physical differences. An example of structural causes of a conflict is when a housewife, who wants to get divorced but has no capital or income of her own, has signed a strict and unfavorable pre-nuptial agreement, or an employee and an employer in an exit mediation. The 'power of the underdog' can also be a structural cause of a conflict (i.e. the party with – perceived – less power can dominate and dictate a mediation; for example because the party with power feels guilty or because

34 Moore, C.W. (2014), *The Mediation Process*. 4th edition. San Francisco: Jossey-Bass.

the weaker party gets very emotional, causing the powerful party to capitulate in order to avoid the hassle, or the underdog might have more leverage (II-14)). Other examples are parties with a physical or mental disability or a party who is geographically closest to the place of mediation compared to a party who lives on a different continent. Racial and religious issues can also be important.
A mediator can help parties to solve structural conflicts by trying to restore the balance of power (II.3) and making sure that everyone involved can participate equally in the mediation process and influence the outcome.

- **Information conflicts. Evaluation of the roots of a conflict often leads to yes-no discussions between the parties.** It is caused by too much or too little information or by different or wrong information. It can be caused by different ways of gathering information. For example, one party may be convinced that there is a right to alimony but the other party believes that there is no right to alimony because there is a pre-nuptial agreement. An incongruous risk assessment by the respective legal counselors or different recommendations by advisors can also cause an information conflict.
  The solution for this type of conflicts lies in structuring the process (II-15), clarifying data and agreeing on criteria for what information is needed and how and where it can be found. And using the ladder of inference method (IV-2.2).
- **Many conflicts are interest based.** If interests are not clear or seem to diverge, the result is often an impasse (IV-1). Clarification and matching of the diverse interests is one of the foundations of a mediation procedure. It can either be an actual conflict of interests or perceived differences and/or incompatible interests and desires.
  An example of this kind of conflict: two companies that both want to use the same technology to enhance a product, but only one party holds a patent and seeks damages for infringement of its intellectual property rights.
  Conflicts of interests can be solved by enlarging the pie (III-15), using objective criteria (III-6), searching for a creative compromise (II-7.2), reciprocal (systematic) give and take (II-16.2), clarifying interests (II-7) and matching interests. In the case mentioned above, this could result in a license agreement at an enhanced royalty rate, and/or several delivery contracts, instead of damages for what may have happened in the past.

The stairs of conflict-escalation of Glasl: IV-7.

Conflict cause-analysis and interventions. Based on the circle of conflict of Moore (2014)

Cause	Analysis/indicators	Interventions
	Relationship or communication	

- Strong emotions.
- Misconceptions / stereotyping.
- Miscommunication or poor communication.
- Behavior that causes a negative or downward spiral.
	- Hard-line style / hostile behavior.
	- Differing perspectives or assumptions.
	- Recurring interactions with a negative effect.
	- Extreme expression of emotions or refusal to communicate.
		- **Control emotions**:
		  - Reframing (III-6).
		  - Let other party paraphrase (III-3).
		  - Acknowledgement (III-5.2).
		  - Ground rules (I-5).
		  - Caucus (II-16).
		  - Asking questions (III-10 and IV-4.4).
		- **Vent emotions**:
		  - Reflecting (III-5).
		  - Acknowledgement (III-5.2).
		  - Asking questions (III-10 and IV-4.4).
		- **Clarify perspectives** (IV-2).
		- **Regulate communication** (III-1).
		- **Meta communication** (III-9).
		- **Reality testing** (III-11).
		- **Block negative behavior by**:
		  - Changing communication patterns, f.e. who speaks to whom.
		  - Reflecting (III-5.1).
		  - Confronting (III-10.4).
		  - Reality testing (III-11).
		  - Demonstrating how it can be handled differently.

	Interests	
- Differing content (substantive) interests (reconcilable or irreconcilable). - Differing procedural interests (reconcilable or irreconcilable). - Unmet psychological interests.	- Impasse. - Indistinguishable, unclear interests. - Suspicion of a hidden agenda.	- **Emphasize interests** and the **future** instead of positions and the past (II-10). - Search for **subjective criteria** (interests) (II-7). - Search for **objective criteria** (III-16.1). - Develop **options** that take into account the **interests of all parties involved** (III-15). - **Expand the pie** (enlarge it) or **make it different** (II-7.2 and III-15.2). - Search for additional or **different resources** (III-15). - Search for a creative **compromise** or systematically use trade-offs, f.e. by exchanging more and less important needs (II-7.2). - **Reality testing** and NAN (III-11).

Cause	Analysis/indicators	Interventions
Structural conflict cause		
- Destructive behavior patterns or interactions. - Significant difference in influence, resources, knowledge, etc. - Large differences in power and authority. - Aspects that obstruct cooperation like geography, physical limitations or environmental factors. - Structural differences in the importance of time.	- Power and disempowerment. - Quickly giving in. Quick concessions. - Huge power differences between the parties. - Different interests regarding time aspects: accelerating, delaying tactics or time-consuming behavior. - Negative interactions between parties. - Extreme emotions or (emotional) withdrawal.	- Discuss the structural conflict and try to achieve **role reversal**. - **Replace** negative **behavior** with other behavior. - Restore the **power balance** (II-3). - Develop a balanced and neutral **decision-making process** and make sure all parties involved have the same opportunities to participate in the process and the outcome: objective criteria (III-16.1), empowerment (II-6), ground rules (II-5). - Change the negotiation from **positional** bargaining to **principled** negotiation (II-4). - Help a party to analyze or increase **leverage** (III-14.2). - Modify the **manner in which the power is exercised**: f.e. convince instead of steamroll, or content discussions instead of 'underdog' (victim) behavior. - Alter the **conditions of the setting**: f.e. create distance instead of sitting close, different venue, one-on-one discussions instead of joint sessions and vice versa. - Neutralize any **external pressure** from constituents or other parties outside the mediation (I-2.7.2). - Change the role that **time** plays (II-14).
Principles and values		
- Differing criteria to assess behavior and ideas. - Different way of life, incompatible ideology, principles, race or religion.	- Differences and commonalities in approach and reactions. - Very different background or personality.	- **Avoid** formulating in **terms of value** and evaluating (II-2). - **Define** the problem **differently** (II-7.2.2). - Let parties **agree to disagree** (III-11.3). - Develop higher or more important goals or **joint interests** (II-7.2).
Information		
- Too little, wrong or irrelevant information. - Different method of gathering information. - Contradictory interpretation/conclusions.	- Different assumptions or perceptions. - Persistent disagreement about the facts ('yes-no' discussions).	- Let the parties agree on **what information** is important. - Define **how information** will be gathered. - Develop **joint criteria** on how to assess information (III-16). - **Consult** experts (II-7). - **Ladder of inference** (IV-2.2).

8.3 The 10-I model

Application of a model helps to systematically diagnose a conflict and formulate working hypotheses as a mediator.

The 3-I model

In his book 'Mediation Representation: Advocating in a Problem-Solving Process' Abramson (2010-2013)[35] describes mediation as a problem-solving negotiation in which an attorney must achieve two objectives:

1. Address the client's interests.
2. Break potential barriers to reaching an agreement.

Abramson refers to three I's of mediation representation planning: Interests, Impediments, Information.

The 7-I model

In the 7-I model by Euwema and Giebels[36] two approaches come together:

- **Structural approach**
  The situation is examined based on characteristics of structural causes: the conflict issues, the parties, and the context.
- **Process approach**
  The perspective here is the course of the conflict over time: how has the conflict process evolved, what caused escalation or de-escalation, and when did it occur?

The 7-I model can help conduct a quick scan during the mediation intake and analyze the key aspects (the conflict structure and the conflict process): issues, individuals, interdependence, interactions, implications, institutions, and interventions.

The 10-I model

The 7-I model, supplemented with Abramson's 3-I's, results in a more comprehensive analytical tool.

Issues:

What are the conflict issues and problems involved? Do both parties see the same issues? What is the cause of the conflict (interest, structural, norms and values, communication, information)? Refer to conflict categorization and Moore's circle (II-8.2).

35 Abramson, H. (2013), Mediation Representation: Advocating in a Problem-Solving Process, Boston: Aspen Publishing.
36 Euwema, M. and E. Giebels (2017), Conflictmanagement en Mediation. Groningen/Houten: Noordhoff Uitgevers [Dutch].

Individuals:
Who are involved in the conflict? What are the personality traits and conflict management styles of the parties?

Interdependence:
What is the relationship between the parties? Is there mutual dependence, and do both parties perceive it the same way? Is there (im)balance or power (in)equality (II.3 and III-14.2)?

Interactions:
How do the involved parties behave, communicate, and react to each other: cooperative or competitive, counter-behavior or cooperative behavior, superior behavior or subordinate behavior (8.6.1 and II.8.4)?

Implications:
What is the result of the interaction in terms of escalation and de-escalation (IV-7)? has the conflict been ongoing for a long time, and what concrete solutions (both in content and for the parties involved) are conceivable?

Institutions:
In what context does the conflict take place? Are there organizational causes influencing the emergence or course of the conflict? What roles do the parties play, and what are the role expectations and perceptions of the parties involved?

Interventions:
What formal and informal intervention options are available and have or have not been used yet? What procedures or other individuals can play a role? Under what conditions do the parties want and can try to resolve the conflict?

Interests:
What are the joint and individual interests of the parties (II-7 and II-10)?

Impediments:
What barriers exist? What obstructs finding a solution by themselves? What are the blocking issues? (II-8).

Information:
What information is missing or lacking for one of the parties? What information do they want/need to exchange? What information is (currently) missing?

8.4 The Drama Triangle and Winners Triangle

One of the best-known models in Transactional Analysis (TA) is Stephen Karpman's Drama Triangle (1968), a model that makes (repetitive) inhibiting interaction patterns visible. It is a model of dysfunctional social interactions, illustrating an ineffective response to conflict, a power game involving a victim, rescuer, and persecutor. Individuals involved in conflicts and miscommunication often unconsciously take on one of three basic roles. The Persecutor (who does not take responsibility, vents frustrations, judges or verbally attacks others, and feels superior), a Rescuer (who tries to avoid conflicts, takes responsibility, offers solutions, thereby making others dependent and demonstrating their own competence), and a Victim (who complains, does not need to do anything, avoids thinking, leaves everything to others, and does not feel responsible for their behavior).

Drama triangle
Karpman

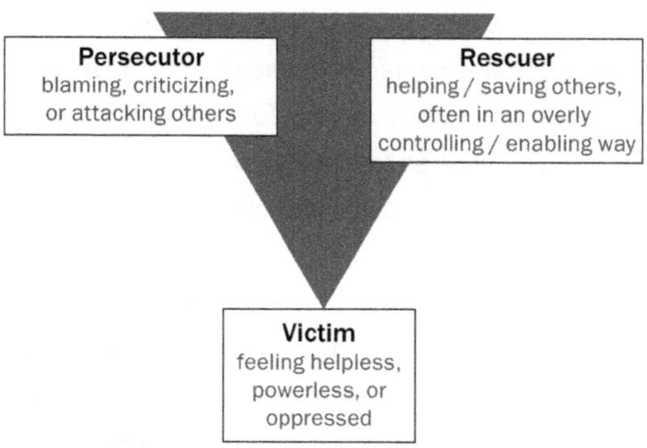

The individuals do not see each other as equals, and none of the actors take responsibility for their own role and behavior; blame is placed on others, diverting attention from themselves. As a result, effective communication or cooperation is impossible. The interaction is not effective but is habitual and can provide short-term satisfaction. It concerns unconscious behavior, which can make this negative interaction pattern persistent.

Roles can also shift: a Rescuer who feels unappreciated can become a Victim ("it's never good enough") or a Persecutor ("I'm just trying to help"). A Persecutor who wants to make amends can shift to the Rescuer role ("let me do it"), or become a Victim ("it's never good enough"). A Victim can become a Persecutor ("I have absolutely nothing to gain from this").

An example of the Drama Triangle: in a mediation, supervisor A believes that employee B needs to perform better and needs to work more effectively with his colleagues on

an important project. A says, "You either participate and perform well, or you leave the team" (Persecutor). B feels unfairly treated: "A just sticks to his point of view. For instance, when I bring up some issues I'm facing, he dismisses them with agreements about targets and responsibilities. Forget it, it's pointless" (Victim). Colleague C responds with: "If you have a good talk together and sort things out, I'll prepare a report with a proposal for a new task distribution next week. I'll take on some of B's tasks" (Rescuer). A reacts indignantly to C: "All this talking and another report won't solve anything" (Persecutor attacks the Rescuer). C: "I'm just trying to help" (Victim).
B tells his wife at home about his work: "A is a blunt person who doesn't listen, he's unfit to be a supervisor, but he'll pay the price soon" (Persecutor). His wife responds with: "Don't think about it anymore. I'll prepare an extra nice dinner and also clean the garage so you can relax" (Rescuer).

The way out of this vicious circle is **the Winner's Triangle,** introduced by Acey Choy in the 1980s, a more constructive and positive approach to addressing conflicts and interpersonal dynamics.
The basis for this is awareness of the interaction and taking responsibility for one's own behavior. The roles then become a Helper (who shows understanding and offers constructive assistance without trying to solve things for others; who takes a caring stance), an Assertive Individual (who addresses issues and sets boundaries), and a Help Seeker (who shares feelings, takes responsibility, and clearly states their needs, not appearing helpless but vulnerable).
An example of the Winner's Triangle: A: "I notice that you're not working well with the team, is that correct? This is an important project, and it's crucial that everyone works together wholeheartedly and performs optimally" (Assertive Individual). B: "I want to perform well and meet my targets. Currently, I'm facing some challenges... I'm quite frustrated myself. What I need is..." (Help Seeker). C: "This project is under significant time pressure, and it's unclear how tasks are divided. Is it worth looking into that?" (Helper).

9 The stages of a mediation process

Almost all mediation literature pays extensive attention to phasing and structuring the mediation process. In this chapter you find a quick 'how-to' reference guide to manage the mediation in every stage of the process.
A mediation procedure goes through several phases, which can change in time and order during the process. Sometimes all phases are passed through within one mediation session, and on other occasions only one or just a few. In addition, during the mediation you often have to return to an earlier phase at a later stage. For example if emotional

issues keep resurfacing during the options phase, or if it becomes clear during the agreement phase that not all interests have been fully explored.

- **Phase 0** **Initial contact phase or intake:**
  Preparation and agreements: (the intake of cases I-1 and pre-mediation planning I-2).
- **Phase 1** **Opening statements**:
  Opening statement by the mediator (I-3) and parties, first inventory of conflict issues, preparing a negotiating agenda (I-6), differing perspectives (IV-2).
- **Phase 2** **Exchange and exploration**:
  Structuring (II-15), analyzing interests (II-7) and dealing with emotions (IV-4). Finding blocking issues and analyzing causes of conflict (II-8), making appropriate use of techniques and interventions (part III), dealing with parties regarded as being tough and tactically difficult (IV-3).
- **Phase 3** **Generating options:**
  Generating options (III-15), developing objective criteria (III-16.1).
- **Phase 4** **Negotiating an outcome:**
  Reaching an agreement (III-16), using objective criteria (III-16.1), using package deals (I-8.3 and II-12). Breaking through deadlocks (IV-1) and negotiating (II-4). See also multi-party mediations (IV-6).
- **Phase 5** **Finalizing agreement & closure**
  Result of a mediation (II-11) and reaching an agreement (III-16), dealing with the constituency (I-2.7), SMART-agreement (II-13).
- **Phase 6** **Follow-up and implementation**:
  Dealing with the constituency (I-2.7), see also multi-party mediations (IV-6).

See also breaking impasse and techniques per stage (IV-1.3), and using time (II-14).

Phase 0 Initial Contact Phase and agreements (I-1, I-2)

Focus: preparation, lay foundation
Approach: directive (or facilitating) on process, initial exploration in relation & ICNM's,[37] limited focus on content, empathetic. Caucus or joint.

Actions and considerations for the mediator, coordination with and information for the involved parties

- **Intake:**
  - How (in person, online, by phone), duration?
  - Separate or joint? (I-1.1).
  - Separate procedural meeting with lawyers? (I-2.8).
  - Confidentiality of intake.
- **Check for independence** (I-1 + consult Code of professional conduct and UDPM):[38]
  - Am I impartial and/or multi-/omni-partial?
  - Are there prior contacts with a party?
  - Do I have an interest in a specific outcome?
  - Do I have confidential information about the parties or the subject, separate from the mediation?
  - What matters might influence my neutral perspective/open mindset?
  - Other matters to inform the parties about?
  - Do I contact the other party if I have been approached by one party?
- **Check suitability for mediation** (I-1.2 + Resource C):
  - Is mediation suitable for these parties with this conflict?
  - Am I suitable as a mediator for these parties with this conflict?
- **Co-mediation** (I-5)?: Collaboration with or referral to another mediator?
- **Managing expectations** (I-1.1):
  - What do the parties expect? Is that realistic: considering my mediation style, mediation approach, procedural and substantive expertise, specialization, and experience as a mediator? (I-2.1 and I-2.3)
  - Do I have enough time, is there a deadline? (II-14)
  - Fee, how are costs divided between parties? Is there a payer/commisioner? How will they be kept informed in conjunction with confidentiality?
  - Do I request an advance?
- **Style, strategy and approach of the mediation** (I-2.1-3 and I-2.3): **preparation:**
  - Who is at the table and who plays a role in the background, are other/additional representatives of the parties desired, or other parties? Advisors? Interpreters?
  - What is my style and approach to the mediation process? Have I communicated that and do parties agree? How do I approach this mediation?
  - How to start, plenary or in caucus?
  - Agreements on reporting? (I-4)
  - Logistics: date, location, time, duration, first meeting. Coordinated with all parties?
  - Do I want (written?) information beforehand? If so, what?
  - Location requirements. Seating arrangement or leave that up tot he parties?
  - Do I ask 'Who wants to start ...' or do I request one of the parties to start?
  - Legal and administrative matters (I-8):
    - Confirmation of engagement / agreement on business terms/fee?
    - Advance payment invoice (paid)?
    - Mediation agreement sent, questions communicated with everyone?
    - Code of professional conduct, mediation rules sent?
    - Any outstanding points from the Universal Disclosure Protocol Mediation (UDPM) to cover?

37 Interests, Concerns, Needs and Motivations, based on: 6 preparation exercises of Jeremy Lack, www.lawtech.ch.

38 https://universaldisclosureprotocolmediation.com/the-protocol/: 6 elements to disclose prior to mediation: Conflict of Interest, Confidentiality, General Process, Role of Mediator/Parties, Technology, Impact of Venue.

Sample questions for the parties in the pre-mediation phase:
"Do you have any experience with mediation?"
"What do you see as the core of the problem? And what do you think the other person would say about it?"
"What are your expectations for the mediation?"
"In your opinion, who is most affected by this situation/issue? Are there others involved?"
"Do you think [name] recognizes your efforts to resolve the situation? Why or why not?"
"Why do you think you haven't been able to resolve this together yet?"

See the checklist for questions to ask during the intake (I-2.5).

Transition to phase 1: Arrange the first mediation session

Phase 1 Opening statements (I-3, I-4)

Focus: set tone, manage expectations, first scan of relationship/communication (substantive aspects) + ICNM's
Approach: directive (or facilitating) on process / content. Joint meeting, unless...)

Opening statement mediator

- **Opening statement mediator** (I-3):
  - Names of parties & advisors, how to address each other?
  - Mediation process, role mediator and parties:

1 A, 3 C, 5N:

- **A**uthority to settle.
- **C**ommitment.
- **C**aucus.
- **C**onfidential.
- **N**eutral role (mediator is omni-partial/impartial).
- **N**on-Evaluative, unless.... but proactive approach.
- **N**o need to answer ...(but everyone can ask anything).
- **N**on-compulsory (voluntary, everyone can conclude the mediation).
- **N**on-binding .... until agreed and signed.
  - Importance of commitment.
  - It's about interests, need, concerns, the future and not about (legal) rights, positions and past.
  - Caucus ('double' confidentiality, now within the mediation process itself) (II-16).
  - Logistics (I-1.1).
  - Timelined, deadlines (II-14).
  - Suspension of any legal or other proceedings / notification.
  - Ground rules (I-3.2):
    - Mediator is a process manager.
    - Parties remain responsible for the conflict and its resolution.
    - Possibly communication rules: no interrupting, treat each other with respect.
    - Package deals (II-12).
    - Mandate, constituency

"Are there any questions or is further explanation needed?"

Transition to opening statement parties and advisors:

Sample questions for the parties to start their opening statement:
"What do you expect from the mediation?"
"Who would like to start first with sharing their perspective?"
"What is the problem that you want to solve in the mediation"

II. Procedural aspects

Initial inventory

- **Opening statements parties:**
  - *"Who would to start with the first opening statement?"* or *"May I ask [name] to start ...?"* (I-2.1).
  - Initial inventory: content, *blocking issues*, interests, conflict causes (II-7, II-8), relationship & communication.
- **Most important techniques and methods:**
  - Psychological contract, building trust (II-1).
  - Listening (III-2) to/ analyze & work with People, Problem & Process, ICNM's (II-7) and *blocking issues* (II-8).
  - Summarizing key words from BOTH parties (III-4).
  - Check assumptions (IV-2.2), *"If I understand correctly you would like to..."* + control questions (III-10.5.2). *"Is that correct..?"*
  - Questions on a verbal level (III.10.1):

    Open ended questions
    - *"What do you expect from the mediation?"*
    - *"What is needed for you to participate and be fully engaged during the mediation?"*

    Closed questions
    - *"Are the ground rules clear?"*
    - *"Are you both still available until 3PM?"*

    Straight questions
    - *"Until what time are you available today?"*

    Clarifying questions
    - *"What do you mean with ...?"*
  - STRUCTURE: pose the same opening question to both parties, ask them not to react to each other, but first present their own perspectives (see structure model of the opening phase below).

Transition to phase 2: summarize issues and statements from both parties (III-4), express joint and individual points and initial inventory of topics to be discussed (I-6)

"We need to talk about... and... and also.... You find... and your view is... You agree that... Are you satisfied when we have found a solution to all these points? Or are there other things that need to be explored?"

+ transition to phase 2 in caucus only mediation:

"I think this is a good moment to continue in separate discussions."

- Ensure both parties can agree tot he basic rules for a caucus (II-16.4).
- Consider to give a task to/homework for the 'waiting' party.

Phase 2 Exchange and exploration (I-6, II-7+8, II-15+16, III-1, IV-1-4, IV-7)

Focus: Structuring the process and communication. Framing topics within a comprehensive framework. Transitioning from positions to interests. Approach: Facilitative and/or solution-oriented on content, directive/guiding and/or facilitative on process. Optionally (more) evaluative (light) towards the end if desired.

- **Preparing a negotiation agenda** (I-6).
- **Explore interests** (II-7):
  - Focus: from past and 'I do not want' to future and 'I do want'.
  - Focus on interest instead of positions.
  - Developing understanding for the other's perspective.
- **Important methods and techniques:**
  - **Listening** for substantive aspects, joint and different interests, *blocking issues* and possibilities communication and relationship issues (II-7, II-8, III-2).
  - **Structure** the proces and the communication (II-15).
  - (Ask the parties to) **paraphrase** (III-3).
  - **Reflect on feelings** (III-5.2).

- **Reframe** (III-6).
- **Questions** (III-10): circular (10.2), mirroring (10.2), confrontational (10.4), 'peel off' questions (10.3), open ended (10.1), relationship (10.5), tactical (10.12), solution focused questions (10.16) and reality testing (III-11)
- **Summarize** (III-4).
- **Dealing with emotions** (IV-4).
- **Dealing with tricky tactics and difficult behavior** (IV-3).
- Check **BATNA, WATNA, RATNA** (III-14.1), **leverage** (III-14.2) and **ZOPA** (III-14.3).
- **Caucus** (II-16).
- **Ladder of inference** (IV-2.2), clarify **perspectives** (IV-2.3) and **psychological barriers** (IV-2.3 and IV-2.4).
- **Power balance** (II-3), **empowerment** (II-6), **empathy** and **perspective taking** (II-5).
- Demonstrate a **neutral mindset** and **omni-/impartiality** (II-2, III-7). Pay extra attention to this at the start of the exploration stage.
- Building trust!! (II-1)

Sample question in the exploration phase

Quick scan and start:
"What do you both agree on?"
"Why do you think you haven't been able to resolve this yourselves?"
"In your opinion, what is the core of the problem?"

Gathering information, linear and open questions:
"What's causing (or preventing) you to...?"
"Is there anything else going on?"
"Could you elaborate on that?"
"When did this issue first arise?"

General open ended questions:
Who? What kind? Where? Where to? Where from? When? How? What time? How long? Why? By what means? To what end? What kind?

'Peeling off' questions and follow-up questions:
"What is your concern?"
"What does that mean to you?"
"What is it really about for you?"

Relational and circular questions:
"What does A need to do for you to...?"
"What can you offer A if...?"
"How do you want the relationship to be in the future?"
"How did you solve problems in the past?"

Reality testing, hypothetical, tactical, and reflective questions:
"Imagine that...; would you...?"
"What if...?"
"What effect would... have?"
"How will XYZ react if this happens?"
"How long did things go well, by the way?"
"What are your alternatives if you can't reach an agreement?"

Solution-focused questions:
"What is going well?"
"What do you want to achieve?"
"How do you want the situation to be?"
"What would it look like at position 10 on a scale of 1-10?"
"Once the problem is resolved, what will you do differently?"

Managing emotions:
"You seem disappointed; is 'disappointed' the right word?"
"I notice that you..., is that correct?"
"What do you need?"

Breaking impasses:
"How would you like to proceed now?"
"Does it still make sense to continue with the mediation?"
"We've made good progress. Points a, b, c are clear. Now we just need to find a solution for x, y, z."
"We're not making any progress. What's causing this?"

Managing the process:
"I suggest providing additions later."
"May I ask you to let each other speak?"
"I'll interrupt for a moment because I'd like to..."
"I'll come back to that later."
"I propose taking a break.

CAUCUS:
Start: confirm confidentiality of the caucus exchange
"Everything discussed during this individual conversation is confidential unless you explicitly permit me to share certain information with the other party."
Questions during a caucus
"Are there any issues that haven't been addressed in the joint meeting but are important to know?"
"What is most important to you?"
"How do you think the other party will react to this proposal?"
"What are the strengths/weaknesses of your case?"
"What else can I do to support you in reaching an agreement?"
"How do you feel the mediation has been progressing so far?"
At the end of a caucus: always check confidentiality
'What can I share with the other party from this conversation?' 'Which information should be kept confidential?'

Transition to phase 3:
turning point – summarize interests and transition to generating options

Check if sufficient progress is made:
✓ Did all interests emerge, are they clear and addressed?
✓ Shifting from accusations and 'you' to wishes and 'I', from the past to the future?
✓ Have the causes of the conflict been identified?
✓ Have emotions been addressed, and are they no longer a hindrance to finding a solution?
✓ Are driving forces and *blocking issues* known?
✓ Has there been mutual understanding of each other's perspectives?
✓ Is the role of each party in the origin and continuation of the conflict clear, including to themselves?
✓ Has the communication between the parties been established?
✓ Control questions you can ask to check if you can move to the next phase:
  - *"If we find solutions for all these interests, will the conflict be resolved?"*
  - *"Imagine that a new discussion about... would emerge in 3 months time... How...?"*
  - *"Are you able to negotiate possible solutions with each other?"*
  - *"Are you willing and able to leave the past and your emotions behind and focus on solutions?"*

Summary of interests and topics: *"Now that it's clear that ... and ..., we need to find a solution for ... and ..."*

Phase 3 Generating options (III-11, III-15, III-16, IV-1)

Focus: Developing several options that meet the parties' interests. Approach: Facilitative and evaluative (light); using solution-focused tools. Joint discussions and caucus as a tool (unless...).

- **Stimulate creativity and 'outside the box' thinking with techniques to generate options (III-15):**
  - Brainstorm (III-15.1).
  - Enlarging the pies.
  - Individually creating lists and discussing them.
  - Developing a joint vision.
  - Seeking advice from experts (II-7).
  - Mediator can propose several options (always more than 1!).
  - Consulting external sources.
  - Using different thinking frameworks or novel frames.

Pay attention to power (im)balance, ensure that all parties can participate (II-3).

Transition to Phase 4: when sufficient options have been generated

Summarize options:
"There are several options for potential solutions, let's investigate..."

Phase 4 Negotiation (II-4, III-14, III-16, III-20)

Focus: Reaching agreement on a specific option. Approach: Facilitative and (mildly) evaluative; solution-focused tools. Joint discussions, and caucus as a tool (unless ...).

- **Facilitate and guide the negotiataions between the parties** (II-4, III-16):
  - Ensure clarity regarding alignment with the constituents (I-2.7.2) and the negotiators personal mandate (I-2.7.1).
  - Develop and use objective criteria (III-16.1).
  - Examine each party's alternatives and check options with the BATNA (III-14).
  - Set and work with priorities (II-15).
  - Consider using the one text procedure (III-12), structured give and take, involving experts, mediator proposal (I-7).
  - Consider tentative or conditional agreements (II-11) or partial agreements.
- **Overcoming deadlocks and impasse** (IV-1):
  - Dealing with challenging tactics and behavior (IV-3).
  - Pay attention to power (im)balance and leverage (III-14.2).
- **Working with package deals** (II-12); pay in particularly attention to this if you work with interim-solutions.

Transition to phase 5: if agreement is reached

✓ Summarize the current status.
✓ Reflect on the effort and commitment of the parties that led to this outcome.
✓ Create a list of agreements that should be included in the settlement agreement.
✓ Stress that the parties themselves are responsible for the agreements made and where applicable suggest they consult their (legal) advisor, allow sufficient time to reflect on the agreements made.

"We can now start to draft the settlement agreement."

Phase 5 Recording Agreement & Closure (I-2.7, II-11, II-12, II-13)

Focus: Recording agreement, ensuring that agreements and deals can and will be implemented. Approach: Evaluative/directive on content and process/Joint discussions, (unless ...)

If closing with agreement (in part) (II-11.2-3):

- Prepare a **draft agreement** (or let the parties or their lawyers do this); summarize any remaining issues or options.
  - Check if the settlement agreement (SA) is sufficiently balanced: all parties must be addressed and do something or refrain from something, use neutral language (II-3, III-7).
  - Make the SA SMART (II-13):

    Specific: clearly state what is agreed upon and by whom, when, and how.
    Measurable: it is clear when the agreements have been fulfilled.
    Achievable: it is feasible and possible.
    Realistic: the parties will adhere to it.
    Timely: clear time limits and specific timing.
  - Avoid dependence on contingencies in the SA.
  - Avoid overlegalization/legalese.
- Verify alignment with the parties' constituencies and note any face-saving aspects.
- Emphasize the importance of everyone adhering to the agreements, **compliance**.
- Include a **provision** in case parties encounter issues during the implementation (e.g., a mediation clause).
- Improve and add/change the draft SA untill all parties fully agree with the text and the content.

If another mediation session is planned (II-11.1):

- Discuss interim tasks and homework for the next session. Confirm this in writing to the parties.
- If it has been agreed that discussing certain points with others who are not involved in the mediation is possible, explicitly address what is confidential and what can be discussed with whom.
- Set a date for the next session.
- Thank the parties for their commitment, (constructive) efforts.

If closing without agreement (II-11.1):

- Provide a positive summary of any results that are achieved (III-3), reflecting on the efforts and commitment of the parties (III-4).
- Create a list of what has been achieved, such as mutual understanding, clarification of conflict points, or agreeing to disagree.
- Reflect on and clarify the next steps. Discuss options like Med-then-Arb procedures conciliation, mediator proposal (I-7).
- Recapitulate the importance of confidentiality of exchanges during and information shared in the mediation.

Phase 6 Follow-up and implementation, CPD

Focus: Ensuring successful implementation, professional aspects for a mediator.

- Be available for any questions or issues that may arise during implementation. Revise agreements with the parties if necessary.
- View each mediation as an opportunity for professional growth. Seek feedback from the parties, for example, for IMI certification. Reflect on your own performance: what went well, what would you do differently next time, how was agreement reached between the parties, lessons learned, and areas for improvement. Share your learnings and experiences (confidentially) in an intervision group and ask for alternative perspectives and insights.
- Consider contacting the parties again after a few months to check on progress and ensure that the implementation is proceeding as desired.

10 Advancing from positions and the past to interests and the future

Focusing on the future offers parties the opportunity to reflect on what is possible and the development of opportunities, and prevents them getting stuck in what went wrong in the past. In this way, the mediator facilitates the parties to take a step towards negotiating a viable outcome. The solution lies in the future, not in the past.

A **position** is a positional or sometimes legal demand, a rigid claim for which, in principle, only one specific solution is possible.

An **interest** is the underlying reason for a position: needs, desires, concerns, ingredients, or conditions that underlie it. To address interests, multiple solutions are possible.
Interests can be categorized as

1) shared/common /joint interests,
2) reconcilable differing interests, or
3) irreconcilable/conflicting differing interests (II-7).

There are different types of interests, such as substantive, procedural, or psychological interests (II-7.3). Additionally, there can be contextual interests related to third parties, the stakeholders, or the context in which the conflict occurs. All of these interests can be shared or different.

See ICNM's in II-7.

At the beginning of the mediation, it is of utmost importance to demonstrate neutrality. Parties are often very sensitive to signals that the mediator may have a preference for one of the parties. As trust in the mediator and the process grows, the mediator gains more leeway (II-2).

Techniques to effectively move parties from positions to interests include:

- ☐ Listening (III-2)
- ☐ If you ask *"What is your interest?"* you often get their position as an answer. Keep digging and asking! Explore further and do not be too quick to accept the first answer.
  The better way is asking multiple indirect questions, 'peel off' questions (III-10.5.3), and hypothetical questions (III-10.5.4) to arrive at the core of the interests by a detour:
  "What makes this important to you?"
  "How do you feel the mediation is going so far?"
  "What are your concerns?"
  "What do you need?"
  "What else.."
  "What does that mean to you?"
  "What could you gain from this?"
  "Suppose that..."
  "If... then...?"
- ☐ 'Maybe...', 'yes, but...', and 'unless...' answers typically mean 'no'. Be sure to follow up with more questions.
- ☐ Structured way for peeling of positions: from reason why, to general interest, to specific personal interest (III-10.5.3):
  "Explain..."
  "What would you like?"
  "What makes that important to you?"
  Summarize (III-4) with a control question (III-10.5.2).
  Substantive reflection (III-5.1).
- ☐ Reframing (III-6).
- ☐ Separate substantive aspects from the relationship and emotions (III-8).
- ☐ Explore the BATNA, WATNA, and RATNA (III-14.1).

- ☐ Silence! (III-17).
- ☐ Paradoxical interventions (III-19).
- ☐ If you use a caucus, you can work with perspective or empathy (II-5):
  "If I were you, I could imagine..." Be cautious with this intervention; it is meant to test where the interests lie, not to provide advice or make partisan comments.
- ☐ In a later stage of a mediation or negotiation, you can use proposals to further search for interests:
  "You don't like that idea; please explain what..."
  "Are there elements in this proposal that you like?"

Especially at the start of the mediation it is very important to demonstrate neutrality. At this stage, parties can be very sensitive to signals from the mediator indicating a possible preference for one of the parties. As the confidence in the mediator and the process grows, the mediator gets more room to maneuver (II-2).

11 Result and conclusion of a mediation

See creating options III-15 and reaching an agreement III-16.

The result of a mediation is often measured only by the agreement being reached or not (by the settlement rate – the proportion of mediations that are concluded successfully). However, monitoring within the scope of several mediation projects repeatedly shows that mediation has positive side effects which are at least as important. The merits of mediation cannot be judged by a high settlement rate alone.
In the Netherlands 94% of the companies that have become acquainted with mediation say they would use it again in a similar dispute. So this must also include parties who participated in a mediation without reaching an agreement, because the settlement rate in business mediation in the Netherlands is around 78%. This means that a mediation that fails to conclude with a settlement can still be regarded as a successful mediation.[39] The reasons for this are, for example, because an agreement may have been reached on certain aspects, or because the mediation has generated a greater understanding for each other's position, or because a business relationship and even the actual negotiation can be continued. Moreover, it could and often does happen that a mediation fails to produce a settlement agreement, but the parties take or waive actions in the periphery of the mediation which effectively resolve the conflict. Also, a party often notices that mediation in general is a valuable method to resolve a dispute, but that no agreement could be reached with this particular party and this particular dispute.

39 These dates are from the quantitative analysis of mediation carried out by foundation ACB Mediation between 1998-2004.

The final result of a mediation can be a (partial) solution, a full agreement or no solution at all. However important the positive side-effects may be, a mediator will generally prefer that the parties reach a full settlement agreement.

11.1 No (partial) solutions

Here it is a matter of:

- deadlock or stalemate;
- no agreement about anything;
- a further escalation of the conflict (fortunately this is quite rare).

11.2 Interim settlement and partial solutions

Possible interim or partial solutions:

- **Interim agreement or partial solution**
  Side agreements can be reached to solve a part of the problem or the whole conflict. For instance because a deadline calls for a partial decision, or work has to continue. This partial or interim solution is already implemented, while other issues, or even the final solution, are being negotiated. The interim solution could also imply that the parties agree to submit a remaining issue to a third party, for example a judge or another expert, or to obtain an expert report if more information is wanted.
- **A trial agreement**
  Parties first want to try out a solution in real terms before committing themselves.
- **A procedural solution**
  Parties agree on the procedure to be followed to solve the dispute. For example, parties agree to disagree and next steps are considered. This could lead to bringing a case, or parts of it, before a binding advisor, a judge or an arbitrator, or to further negotiations with another team, or to initiating hybrid ADR procedures like med-arb (a mediation which results in a binding opinion or an arbitration procedure), etc.
- **Agreement on the way a dispute will be resolved**
  This can be achieved by drawing lots, throwing the dice or by voting. Or parties agree that the mediator's advisory opinion or an expert solution resolve the dispute (I-7).

A mediator or negotiator must be highly aware of the potential intercultural effects during mediation or negotiation. On the other hand, for example in an international setting, they should not attribute all issues to intercultural influences. To recognize when intercultural influences are at play in a conflict, a mediator must possess well-developed intercultural competencies and skills.

An overview of various 'cost calculators' for arbitration and other useful information can be found at http://lawtech.ch/useful-information/. Please note that most calculators only provide an estimate for administrative costs of the arbitration institution. Costs for the arbitrators and your legal representation are in addition to this.

11.3 Full settlement

Potential full solutions:

- **The > 100% solution**
  Mutual gain, win-win, all needs are (more than) fulfilled.
- **The pragmatic solution**
  Although not all interests have been satisfied, the complete package of agreements is good enough to be accepted by all parties.
- **Conceding, giving in or refraining (IV-3.3.2)**
  Parties agree to disagree and leave it at that, or one party yields to the wishes of the opponent. For instance because they recognize their perspective is incorrect, or the other party has a better idea, or maybe their position is not very strong, or the relationship has improved so much that the points at issue no longer appear to be important.
- **Compromise (II-7.1 + II-7.2)**
  A partial solution is found, and a compromise is reached on the remaining issues. This can be achieved by splitting the difference or by allowing one party to make the division and the other party to have first choice.
- **Partial power of decision**
  It is agreed that each party has the power of decision on different aspects of the disputed issues. The other parties must comply with the decision made in that area while they in turn can decide on another selected issue.
- **Deciding on interests or laying down objective criteria (III-16.1)**
  The mediator or the parties make a list of the questions that are to be answered, and a list of common and individual interests. This is handed over to a neutral third party with the request to propose an optimal solution based on these interests. Conversely a third party also can be requested to suggest some objective criteria from which parties can then choose.

12 Package deals

In mediation, parties only commit themselves to a proposal or an agreement when all issues have been recorded and signed in a settlement agreement, or have been specifically agreed upon in a package. Until that moment all consensus is conditional. Apart from legal implications, it can be useful to agree with parties that they will only be bound by commitments or proposals when they have reached agreement on all issues. This makes it easier to secure a partial agreement and at the same time maintain flexibility to change things at a later moment in the process.
This is why it makes sense to include the use of package deals during the negotiation in the ground rules that are established before the negotiation process. One of the recommended ground rules is that package deals are used during the negotiation.

13 Balanced and SMART agreements

Make a SMART agreement:[40]

S pecific:	everybody knows exactly what has been agreed, who will do what, when and how.
M easurable:	it is clear when agreement is reached/implemented, and how the parties will be informed of this fact.
A chievable:	it is feasible and practicable.
R ealistic:	the parties will do it (they will probably adhere to the agreement).
T ime limit:	it has a defined ending which is clear to all parties.

It is furthermore advisable to avoid dependency on contingencies, and take care not to over-legalize (parties must recognize their solution and their language).
An agreement like: *'A transfer of the car's title will be started as soon as possible'*, is not SMART. First, it must be agreed explicitly who will take what action before which date. To party A a transfer of property as quickly as possible could imply party B putting the car at his disposal immediately. When he has possession of the car, he will pay for it. However, party B assumes party A will deal with payment and administrative matters first before he hands over the car.
When an agreement is formulated in this way, it is totally unclear to the parties when the agreement is implemented. How do they interpret transfer of property: is it just a matter of completing legal/administrative matters (changing the names on the registration certificates) or actual physical delivery to the other party? And how do they inform the other party that they have kept their part of the deal? Is such an agreement realistic? Do parties trust each other enough to start paying or delivering the car without providing any

40 SMART is an often used acronym which makes sense in English as well as in Dutch. It is used in many books and web-sources. I haven't been able to locate its original source.

collateral? Would it be sensible to provide collateral or to build in security measures such as a deposit, bank statement, declaration of ownership, etc.?

For a negotiator it is also advisable to record in writing everything that has been agreed upon and to formulate it in SMART terms. Most discussions and disputes arise from the parties having different perceptions and interpretations of settled agreements.

It may involve some effort to be precise, but many conflicts can be prevented by making clear and explicit agreements and by expressing and exchanging expectations at the beginning.

In addition it can be wise to include a mediation clause in a settlement agreement in case a dispute arises in spite of the SMART formulation. As to the use of language, the settlement agreement needs to be formulated in an unambiguous, balanced and neutral way (II-2.2). Describe the precise actions to be taken as a joint or reciprocal effort and ensure that all parties must at some point take action while at other times they leave certain steps to others. This encourages collaboration and partnering. Try to record action items in such a way that they alternate between party A and party B. Take into account that all parties should recognize their own words in the solution as much as possible (II-6), encourage plain language and avoid excessive legalese in the agreement. Moreover, try to be clear and specific, and avoid jargon and vague or woolly language.

In the above case a SMART agreement could be:

'B today (*date*) hands over the registration certificate to A. Within 5 working days A will visit the post office and no later than (*date*) contact B to agree a specific time to collect the car. The transfer of the car will take place no later than (*date*). At the moment of transfer A will pay B the total price of $17.500 in cash. B will then hand over the car with accessories to A'.

If the representatives do not want to sign a settlement agreement, or if there is insufficient time to make a separate written list of what has been agreed, then allow the parties to initial the agreements listed on the flip-chart. Subsequently confirm this in writing, in the shape of a list of agreements. See also the hint at the end of the chapter about maintaining the balance of power (II-3.2).

14 (Using) Time

Take into account:

- deadlines of the negotiators;
- factors which can increase the importance of a prompt settlement or, conversely, could delay or prevent it. The party that expects to gain something from the negotiation or wants something from the other party, is usually the one most pressed for time. (also see Leverage III-14).

14.1 Deadlines and the 80/20 rule

Often the greatest progress is made just before the closing of a deadline or an ultimatum. The 80/20 rule[41] also applies to making concessions in a negotiation.

Apparently most of the concessions in a negotiation are made in the last 20% of the time before the closing of a deadline. A mediator can leverage this reality, for example by introducing an incidental deadline: *'Now we only have 30 minutes left to discuss issues x, y and z.'*
This can also be achieved by introducing a deadline in advance: *'You have indicated that you want a maximum of four mediation sessions.'* A deadline also can be introduced as a last resort when no progress is made at all. *'During the last two meetings we have been going around in circles without making any progress. Do you think continuing this mediation is a good idea? Personally, I am inclined to discontinue the mediation if we haven't made any progress by the end of this session. So we still have one hour. Let's see if we can use this time to break through some barriers.'*

As a negotiator you can also introduce a deadline incidentally in order to achieve faster results and have the negotiations run more smoothly. However, do not use deadlines too often or too rigidly; it can be a difficult or tricky tactic (IV-3.2).

14.2 Introducing adjournments

Introducing an adjournment can be useful in order to:

- sort out a few points yourself;
- consider how to continue the mediation;
- calm down the emotions of the negotiators;
- let off steam yourself;
- consult a co-mediator;
- allow the parties time to consult their advisors or constituencies.

14.3 The time required for mediation

The length of a mediation session can vary from about 1.5 hours to the whole day (and possibly the night). This depends on the strategy of the mediator (I-2.1), the parties'

41 The Pareto principle Around 1900 Vilfredo Pareto established his famous 80/20 rule. Pareto, an Italian economist, observed that 80% of the income in Italy was received by 20% of the Italian population. Since then more and more areas of application have been discovered. The Pareto principle states that only a small part of the causes, effort or input leads to major part of the results or output. Examples of the Pareto principle:80% of the sales are realized by 20% of the products.
20% of the customers determine 80% of the sales.
80% of all complaints are made by 20% of the customers.
20% of the employees cause 80% of the staff problems.
80% of the relevant information in this book can be found in 20% of the pages.
80% of the result of mediation can be reached in 20% of the time.

goals, including their deadlines and whether they can schedule several consecutive mediation sessions. A rule of thumb is that the more emotions are involved, the shorter a session should be. This is why business-to-business mediations often last three to four hours or a whole day while a divorce mediation session takes 1.5 hours at most. Also, one-day mediations or mediations with a time limit (where it is agreed in advance that the mediation will be concluded in a fixed period) are usually applied in a business context. The average duration of the mediation and the time to be planned between two sessions are determined individually and depend in particular on the progress of the mediation and the wishes and agenda of the parties.

There are several articles with quantitative information on mediation performance (f.e. settlement rates, duration, repeat players, satisfaction rates). We recommend:

- *Hanson and Becker (2002), 'Appellate Mediation in New Mexico: An Evaluation'.*
- *Henderson (1996), 'Mediation Success: An Empirical Analysis'.*
- *McEwen and Maiman (1981), 'Small Claims Mediation in Maine: An Empirical Assessment'.*
- *Torregrossa (2002), 'Appellate Mediation in the Third Circuit – Program Operations: Nuts, Bolts and Practice Tips'.*
- *Wissler (2002), 'Court-Connected Mediation in General Civil Cases: What We Know From Empirical Research'.*
- *Wissler and Rack, Jr. (2004) 'Assessing Mediator Performance: The Usefulness of Participant Questionnaires.'*
- *Abramowitz and Webb,*[42] *Bring Objective Science to Mediation, 2nd Key: Data in: Michael Leathes (ed.), SEVEN KEYS TO UNLOCK MEDIATION'S GOLDEN AGE, mediate.com 2020.*
- *Several Model Mediation Surveys to enable courts to obtain high-quality data for evaluating their programs, are developed and made available online by Resolution Systems Institute and the American Bar Association Section of Dispute Resolution. The surveys are meant to be utilized by any court and have an emphasis on civil cases: https://www.aboutrsi.org/model-surveys .*
- *ABA Section of Dispute Resolution Task Force on Research of Mediator Techniques. Jan. 1, 2017, detailed review of 47 empirical studies and four years of investigation.*[43]
- *Wissler and Weiner, 'How Do Mediator Actions Affect Mediation Outcomes? The Report of the Section's Task Force on Research on Mediator Techniques Offers a Few Clues', 24 DISPUTE RESOLUTION MAGAZINE 26 (Fall 2017).*

42 https://mediate.com/2nd-key-data-bring-objective-science-to-mediation/#_ednref3.

43 https://papers.ssrn.com/sol3/papers.cfm?abstract_id=4061216.

On the website IMI, imimediation.org, you can find several resources for statistical data on mediation. On manonschonewille.com there are also surveys and overviews with quantitative data which you can consult.

15 Structuring

Definition/description	Application
Structuring (II-15)	
Empower the parties by introducing structure in the process and thus helping them to clarify the chaos of the conflict.	Structure, conflict analysis, create the conditions under which parties can come to a solution. Set priorities (long term, short term, importance of the issues). Fractionalizing matters of conflict. Prepare an agenda, keep track of timing. Test assumptions.

A dispute means chaos: facts, interpretations, wishes, emotions - present and past - all merged together. By introducing structure, disputes can be resolved more easily and conveniently because structure promotes clarity, vision, restraint, communication and opportunity.

15.1 Managing the process

The mediator can manage the process by establishing ground rules (I-5) and making a distinction between relational and content issues (III-8). Also, dealing with emotions purposefully in the mediation helps to structure the process, for example by letting parties express emotions (only) to the extent necessary or helpful to reach a solution, and identify the blocking issues (II-8).

15.2 Structuring thinking

The facts and points under discussion are listed, interests are analyzed (II-7), different options (roadmaps) to arrive at a solution are considered (III-15), priorities are set and objective criteria to the solution are formulated (III-16.1). Assumptions are tested in the process (IV-2).

15.3 Facilitating communication

Communication between the negotiators needs to be facilitated. This can be achieved in particular by recontextualizing (III-6), reflecting (III-5), paraphrasing (III-3) and summarizing (III-4).

For example, the mediator can make a distinction between communication on the content level (what?) and on the relationship level (how and why?). Intentions and different interpretations, or different perspectives, are explained and clarified (IV-2).

15.4 Fractionalizing matters in dispute

The mediator reduces the issues to clear manageable proportions by breaking up the dispute in several fractions (I-6).

15.5 Distinguishing

1. **Emotions and content**
   Normalizing emotions (acknowledge to the parties that it is 'normal and understandable' to get upset or have strong feelings) without trivializing them (IV-4.4). Distinguish the emotional and relationship aspects from the content issues (III-8).
2. **Main points and side issues**
   Drawing up a negotiation agenda (I-6) and listing the causes of the conflict and the blocking issues (II-8).
3. **Interests and positions**
   Distinguish underlying interests (why does somebody want/need this?) from positions (what does somebody want, what does somebody claim to be entitled to?) (II-7).

A flip-chart or whiteboard can be helpful in structuring. It literally lets the parties look in the same direction. By not being seated opposite, but rather next to each other, they can learn to look at issues under discussion as a mutual problem, a shared experience. Learn to write on a flip-chart without turning your back on the parties (for too long).

16 Caucus

Definition/description	Application
	Caucus (II-16)
Private meeting with one party in the absence of the other party. The mediator will repeat this procedure with the other party in order to maintain balance in the process and to preserve the neutrality of the mediator.	Take the process to the next phase. Explore hidden agendas, allow venting or emotional release, discuss options for a solution in confidence, reality test (III-11), explore BATNA, WATNA, RATNA, leverage and/or ZOPA (III-14), provide an opportunity for parties to confer privately with their own advisors or team.

A mediator has to be able to judge when to hold a caucus or when to conduct the mediation in a plenary session. At the beginning of the mediation or during the intake phase (I-1) you have to examine the best way to start the mediation: in a joint session or in a caucus. In most cases it would be right to start with a plenary meeting. However, if emotions obstruct the course of the mediation or if parties do not want to be in the same room, you could consider starting with a caucus.

The personal style and preference of a mediator on caucus/plenary sessions should be discussed with the parties before the start of the mediation (I-1.1). Caucus is not a euphemism for shuttle diplomacy. With shuttle diplomacy the process takes place almost completely in separate meetings between the negotiator/facilitator (process manager) and each of the parties. There is almost no direct contact between the parties, as a result of which aspects like improving communication are not a (direct) issue. In shuttle diplomacy the facilitator is the key figure in the negotiation which makes him very powerful. Depending on the personality of the shuttle facilitator and his authority, this can play an important role, especially in international settings.

16.1 The caucus in general

In a caucus the mediator consults the party individually and in confidence. The mediator will proceed to a caucus when he sees the discussion is deadlocked, there is no forward movement in the process, or when blocking issues prevent the real interests from being discussed. During a caucus parties can also explore options with the mediator in confidence. When using co-mediation, the mediators should agree in advance how the caucus sessions will be handled (II-16.5).

The benefits of a caucus are valued in different ways. Some mediators feel that caucuses should always be conducted unless there are strong indications not to (the approach in the training sessions by Michael Lewis and Linda Singer, for example). Other mediators are of the opinion that the whole mediation should take place in a plenary session (favored in the training sessions of f.e. Robert Mnookin).

In the Netherlands most mediators occasionally apply a caucus when little progress is being made. In business mediations, caucuses are frequently called. Mediators with a communication or a relationship-driven approach (I-2.1.2) almost never use the caucus (and do so only at the request of the parties).

www.beyondintractability.org has been set up by the University of Colorado and it is designed as an online databank on conflict management. In addition to many articles, the site covers several concepts on negotiating and mediation, which are linked together in background articles.

16.2 Utilizing a caucus, why should you?

The main reasons for using a caucus

- ☐ When the mediation is deadlocked (exploring underlying interests and hidden agendas).
- ☐ When emotions are running so high that adequate communication is no longer possible (vent or control emotions) (IV-4.4).
- ☐ If you want to discuss options in confidence.
- ☐ Providing feedback to a party.
- ☐ If you do not want to apply reality testing in a plenary session (III-11) or ask confronting questions (III-10.4) or if you do not want to explore BATNA/WATNA/RATNA, leverage or ZOPA in a plenary session (III-14).
- ☐ If you want to have a discussion with an (unwilling) advisor or someone who is not experienced in mediation about how things can be better handled.
- ☐ If you always use a caucus.

16.3 Utilizing a caucus, why not?

The main reasons not to use a caucus

- ☐ If parties want a caucus but you feel it is not the right time. Remember, however, that you don't know why a party asks for a caucus. They often have a good reason. It can therefore be useful to hold a caucus if a party asks for one.
- ☐ If you as a mediator typically do not use a caucus, for instance because you do not want to run the risk of hearing secret or disturbing information which puts you in a difficult position. Another reason could be that it is not in line with your approach to the mediation process (I-2.1) or you want to leave open the option to give a mediator's advisory opinion in a later stage of the mediation (I-7.2 and I-7.3).
- ☐ If you consider a caucus useful because you find plenary sessions difficult to handle, seek co-operation with a (more experienced) co-mediator (I-2.5).
- ☐ If you need a break: adjourn the mediation.

If you often conduct a caucus, it can be hard to remember what you have discussed with whom and which information is confidential. It can be of help if you use different colour paper when making notes of each consultation: for example white for joint sessions, yellow for consultations with party A and blue for party B.

16.4 Approach and technique of a caucus

A caucus is a tool for exploring interests, discussing options in confidence and managing emotions. At the beginning of the mediation you should have discussed the possibility that you might have individual consultations, as well as the rules that apply to them.

Approach of a caucus

- ☐ Confirm that everything that is discussed during an individual consultation will be treated **confidentially** (except where expressly agreed otherwise) and will not be disclosed to the other party or third parties.
- ☐ Think about **who** you want to start with.
- ☐ Consider whether the party who has to wait while you are in a caucus with the opposing party should be given an **assignment** to shorten waiting time and to let them be productive, for example:
  - reflect on what they could offer the counter-party;
  - work out a certain issue in detail;
  - consult someone;
  - look for information;
  - take a break.
- ☐ Conclude the caucus by explicitly **verifying the confidentiality of the information**.
  - If you assume that everything that has been discussed is confidential: ask if there is something you are free to convey to the other party.
  - If you feel no or only a limited amount of confidential information has been brought up: ask the party to specify what information is confidential.
- ☐ Maintain **balance** by always meeting with all parties on an individual basis, even if you conduct the caucus merely because you need to consult with only one party. Perception is every bit as important as reality. If you have no specific questions for the other party, you can always ask open questions (III-10), for example how they think the mediation progresses, just to maintain that sense of balance. And who knows what valuable information this might yield.

The structure and steps of a caucus:

I. Introduction to the caucus

1. Hopefully, at the beginning of the mediation, you informed the participants that you can also speak with them individually and explained the rules that apply in such cases. Announce that you will be doing that now. A caucus can also be initiated by one of the parties or their advisors.

2. Decide with whom you want to start (and provide a neutral reason for this), or better yet, let the parties themselves determine who will have the first individual conversation. *"Who would like to go first..."*
3. Provide a time estimate to the party that will be waiting: *"I believe it will take about 30 minutes; if it ends up taking longer, I will let you know."*

II. Caucus 1 with Party 1

4. Confirm the confidentiality once more: *"Everything you discuss with me now is confidential unless you explicitly state that it can be shared with the other party."*
5. Start by asking an open question: *"Is there anything you didn't want to bring up in the presence of the other party, but that is important for the progress of the mediation?"* or *"How do you feel the mediation has been going so far?"*
6. Interact with the party, explore, and ask questions.
7. At the end summarize what has been discussed during the caucus. Be sure to check the confidentiality. *"Is it correct that a...b...c... is confidential information?"* or *"You told me that everything can be shared with the other party? Is there anything...?"*

III. Caucus 1 with Party 2

8. Repeat steps 4 to 6. Provide Party 2 with the same caucus structure and steps as Party 1, as if they were also having a first caucus conversation.
9. After that, you can address issues that were raised in caucus 1 with Party 1 (e.g., a message from the first party). Pay attention to confidentiality and mention that you are allowed to share that information.
10. Summarize what has been discussed during the caucus. Be sure to check the confidentiality as done in step 7.

After one or several individual consultations with both parties, you may wish to return to a plenary session. At the start of the plenary, you might consider giving a summary of the consultations yourself (always respecting confidentiality). In most cases it is best to merely indicate the caucus was useful. Subsequently you can ask the parties if they would like to comment on the separate consultations. After that you can summarize the account given by the negotiators and thereby guide the process and the issues to be discussed. Even if you have not made any progress in the individual consultations, it might nevertheless be advisable to come to the conclusion that they were useful in any event: reframe the fact by noting that progress has been made, thus boosting the parties' confidence that the mediation will lead to a solution (the caucus was not useless, because now you know a caucus does not help this mediation along). On the other hand, you need to take care not to create a false expectation that something happened in another party's caucus which may lead to progress, when this is not the case.

You could also choose to use the technique of asking confrontation questions (III-10) by noting that the individual consultations did not achieve any meaningful progress and then asking the negotiators to analyze why they think that is.

16.5 Applying caucus in co-mediation

When working with a co-mediator (I-2.5), you have to agree in advance whether you wish to use a caucus. And if so, when and how you will handle it. Do the mediators conduct individual consultations jointly or do you want to conduct them separately (as well)? If so, how do you exchange information and who decides when it is time for a caucus?

Each mediator conducts a caucus with one party at the same time

ADVANTAGES:	**DISADVANTAGES**:
- Efficiency. - Needing less time, there is no party waiting and doing nothing.	- You run the risk of being perceived as biased or as one party's mediator. This risk can be neutralized by switching to the other party during the next caucus. - Confusion may arise between the mediators, for example about the confidentiality of information. - Using the mediation process might not fit in your approach (I-2.1).

Both mediators conduct all individual consultations jointly

ADVANTAGES:	**DISADVANTAGES**:
- The mediators see and hear the story at first hand, without the interpretation of another mediator. - Every mediator builds up a (working) relationship based on mutual trust with all parties. - The mediators fulfil the same role to the parties. - Cooperation can improve the quality of the caucus (general advantages of co-mediation (I-2.5.7)).	- It takes more time and one party is (or more are) always doing nothing for a while (except worrying about what is being discussed with the other party). This disadvantage can be reduced by assigning homework, or by making appointments with each party for individual consultations on separate days or at different times.

Do not be tempted to disclose information regarding the caucus or discuss things you learned during the caucus without mentioning that you are allowed to do so. It is no problem to answer to certain questions by stating you cannot comment because of confidentiality: ***'Why don't you ask the other party yourself at the next joint session?'*** This will serve to reinforce confidence in both the mediator and the caucus.

III. Techniques and interventions

1	Overview of the key techniques, interventions, negotiation and mediation tools	141
2	Listening	153
3	(Let the parties) Paraphrase	159
4	Summarize	160
5	Reflecting	161
6	Reframing or recontextualizing	165
7	Neutral language of the mediator	168
8	Distinguish content from the relationship	170
9	Meta-communication	170
10	Asking questions	173
11	Reality testing	185
12	The one text procedure	187
13	Mutualizing (finding common ground)	189
14	BATNA, WATNA, RATNA, leverage and ZOPA	189
15	Generate options	195
16	Reaching agreement	197
17	Use of voice and silence	201
18	Non-verbal behavior	202
19	Paradoxical interventions	204

Part III. Techniques and interventions

Row III of the checklist on the inside of the cover contains the outline of part III. This part, which deals with techniques and interventions, forms the core of this practical book. First, an overview is given of the most important tools that are available to a mediator or negotiator. The rest of part III deals with the interventions and techniques in depth. The techniques and the application of interventions are clearly explained and illustrated. To demonstrate the differences and similarities between interventions, the same example sentences are used for all interventions and arranged in a table. Part III also contains practical schemes to help choose the techniques or interventions which are applicable in a specific situation.

1 Overview of the key techniques, interventions, negotiation and mediation tools

This chapter contains an overview of the most important techniques, interventions and methods as well as examples of how to apply them. Besides discussion/conversation techniques and the interventions from part III, more process-oriented tools from part II, such as the caucus and structuring the process, have been incorporated in this overview. To illustrate, the 'verbal' interventions and communication techniques are applied to the following statement of party A about party B:
'You either participate and perform well or you leave the team.'
Please note: the sentences are not related to a specific case or to the question whether a certain intervention is appropriate in a particular situation. The purpose is to demonstrate the technique in a clear way and make comparison possible.

See also part IV-4.4 Interventions to deal with emotions and II-8.2 Interventions depending on the cause of the conflict.
'You either participate and perform well or you leave the team.'

Definition/description	Application	Example of application
Listening (III-2)		
Listening is a continuing selection process. True listening, and demonstrating that you are doing so, emphasizes your commitment as the mediator, facilitates your ability to hear a message and helps collect information. How to listen effectively and what to listen for depends on what is necessary at this stage of the mediation and what you want to achieve as a mediator. Listening is more than letting someone finish and taking in the words. You also need to demonstrate that you are listening.	Communicating to a party that they have been 'heard' usually ensures that they will stop repeating themselves. It builds rapport and underlines the commitment of the mediator. Moreover, listening is necessary to gather information and to enable proper application of other interventions. Effective listening helps you to manage the process.	**Opening phase mediation**: Handling emotions: let one party listen to the other party, show that the 'emotional party' is listened to and that the message is 'heard'. **Exploration phase**: Gather information to determine which interventions can or should be applied, identify emotions, collect data, and clarify interests. **Option phase**: Factual, data-oriented and solution-oriented listening.
Paraphrasing (III-3) with a verification question (III-10.5.2)		
Repeat in your own words what has been said. Repeat the same statement in other words. The content of the repetition needs to be identical to the original message, with only the choice of words being different. A paraphrase should not include your own conclusions. It is important to check whether the paraphrased account is correct.	**Break through vicious communication circles.** Manage emotions and communications. **Let the parties paraphrase.** Discuss emotional topics or blocking issues (II-8), make the parties listen to each other and convey the message that they have each heard what the other party wanted to say. **Paraphrasing by the mediator.** Clarify issues by using a different vocabulary, let the parties know that you are listening, and thereby build trust.	Paraphrasing by the mediator: *'You would rather have your colleague quit the team if he does not participate properly? Is that what you are saying?'*

III. Techniques and interventions

Definition/description	Application	Example of application
Summarize (III-4)		
Neutral summarizing with a conclusion, followed by a verification question (III-10.5.2)		
Convey the essence of statements of more than one party or of a range of issues. In contrast to paraphrasing, the mediator selects which information is used for a summary and which is not. Additionally, a mediator can incorporate conclusions in a summary. A summary can be combined with other techniques like mutualizing (III-13) or reflecting (III-5). It is an essential tool to structure the mediation process and to guide the communication (II-15). Because the mediator is selective about the information and can also add a conclusion, an evaluative remark can easily slip into the summary. Value-free presentation, while selecting the essential issues, requires practice.	Manage the process, demonstrate progress and structure the dialogue. Connect issues and the contribution of several parties, or enlarge the scope: - Retain or keep track of what is said or clarify topics. - Sum up and (re)structure important issues and themes. - Place issues in a different framework.	*'What I heard is that both of you think it is important that the team functions well. However, you have differing opinions regarding the performance of the individual team members. This means we should address your working styles and the expectations you have of each other, as well as your expectations regarding teamwork. Moreover, we should define the circumstances for potential future teamwork. Have I missed any important issues?'*
Reflecting back general (III-5)		
Magnify positions or topics, point out themes explicitly. This increases the insight of both parties into the other party's position and gives them the opportunity either to further explain their point of view or to revise their opinion.	Reflecting back on the level of: - **Content**: what is being said, magnify key words/parts of a sentence. - **Emotion/intention**: how things are expressed, to clarify the underlying feelings or intentions. - **Process**: emphasize the progress or forward movement.	See below.
Magnify/reflect content (III-5.1)		
Put a point of view or an issue under a magnifying glass in order to make it clear, while offering the parties the opportunity to provide an explanation, or to change their opinion.	Magnify issues, points of view and clarify them. Especially useful for emotional topics and important issues. Repeat key words or (parts of) a statement.	*'She will have to leave the team.'*

Definition/description	Application	Example of application
Acknowledge/reflect feelings (III-5.2)		
With a verification question (III-10.5.2)		
Put an end to recurring (emotional) topics by highlighting the importance of the issue for a party or the feelings associated with it, thereby communicating that the message and the feelings behind a statement are being 'heard'.	Prevent certain topics from becoming recurring themes. Break through resistance.	*'The collaboration with your colleague has been disappointing for you. Is disappointing the right word?'*
Reflect progress (III-5.3)		
Emphasize the progress made so far, in order to manage the process and strengthen the parties' confidence that the dispute can be resolved through mediation.	Stress the fact that the effort of the negotiators is not in vain and that the mediation is moving forward.	*'It is now apparent that you both have different expectations about teamwork and the contribution of each individual team member. Let's elaborate on this issue.'*
Reframing (III-6)		
1. Neutral or positive. 2. Option. 3. Interest. 4. Objective criterion. 5. Emotion.		
Manage emotions and communication by 'translating' statements into a new intellectual framework or placing the issues in another context. Stimulate out-of-the-box thinking and looking at issues from a different or broader perspective. The parties can then let go of their own entrenched perspectives and gradually move away from blame and legal positioning towards taking responsibility and searching for mutual interests.	Make issues subjects for discussion. Develop new intellectual frameworks. Allow the parties space to move from blaming one another to shared interests. Reframing can be viewed as a crowbar to separate the parties from their own perspectives. It goes further than simply reformulating a statement. If you reformulate an issue you are paraphrasing.	1. **Neutral or positive** *'The performance of the team and how the team is structured is one of the issues that we should discuss.'* 2. **Option** *'B can leave the team. Another possibility is that you or C or D leave the team.'* 3. **Interest** *'You want the team to perform well?'* 4. **Objective criterion** *'How is the contribution of an individual team member assessed?'* 5. **Emotion** (with verification question III-10.5.2) *'The performance of the team and B's role in it is such an emotionally-charged issue for you that you would rather have B leave the team than to carry on like this. Is that what you mean?'*

III. Techniques and interventions

Definition/description	Application	Example of application
Distinguish content from the relationship (III-8)		
Clarify what the dispute is really about. Distinguishing between substantive/content aspects and emotional/relationship aspects is a basic requirement of principled negotiation. Also known as: separating the people from the problem (II-4).	Techniques to distinguish between the emotional and the content issues: using neutral language (III-7), reframing (III-6), paying attention to meta-communication (III-9), and structuring the mediation process (II-15). Moreover, a negotiation agenda can be drawn up in which the substantive/content issues and the relationship aspects are separated (I-6). See example.	*'We have to discuss:* - *the cooperation in the team;* - *the performance of the individual team members;* - *the intended results;* - *your expectations.'* (You can also write on a flip-chart or whiteboard to visualize an agenda). *'Can we settle this dispute if we find a solution to all of these topics? Or did we overlook any important issues?'*
Meta-communication (III-9)		
Meta-communication is communication about communicating. The purpose is to point out why certain things are being said and what consequences these (implicit) messages can have. Explaining the intention behind the words can help anticipate and clarify misunderstandings or different interpretations, especially regarding relationship topics.	Communication takes place simultaneously at several levels. To resolve misunderstandings concerning the relationship, the mediator must first move away from the content. Next, he must address what is happening between the parties: describe non-verbal behavior, how do they communicate with each other or with the mediator, what is happening under the surface?	Let us assume that party A strongly emphasizes that the mediator is a team leader in his main occupation, just like he is. Party A finds that favorably, *'because the mediator will understand that, like a chain, a team is only as strong as its weakest member.'* The mediator can bring up the possible impact this might have on party B. For example asking B if in B's opinion the professional background of the mediator can affect the outcome of the mediation. Or, the mediator can enquire whether the remarks of party A adversely affect B's trust in the mediator.

Definition/ description	Application	Example of application
	Asking questions (III-10)	
1. Closed (III-10.1.1). 2. Straight (III-10.1.2). 3. Clarifying (III-10.1.3). 4. Open (III-10.1.4). 5. Relationship (III-10.2.1). 6. Circular (III-10.2.2). 7. Reciprocal (III-10.2.3). 8. Mirroring (III-10.2.4). 9. 'Peel-off' questions (III-10.3). 10. Confrontation (III-10.4.1). 11. Argumentative (III-10.4.2). 12. Tactical (III-10.5.1). 13. Verification (III-10.5.2). 14. Summarizing with a verification question (III-10.5.3). 15. Hypothetical (III-10.5.4).	The mediator asks questions to obtain information and to get important topics out in the open. Moreover, asking questions is a vital tool to manage/ control the mediation and make progress. Not every sentence phrased as a 'question' is an actual question. Often an order or assignment is disguised as a question. A query is a true question if the other party is free to choose the answer they want to give (or to decide not to answer at all). Therefore, a question has to be perceived as such by the receiving party. Whether or not a question is a good one, depends mainly on its impact on the receiving party. Many mediators feel that asking questions is the most important tool for a mediator. However, being able to listen well is actually more important than asking the right questions (so do not forget effective listening!). Some mediators even regard asking questions as the 'only legitimate' intervention. However: please don't forget listening. Being able to listen well is more important than being able to ask the 'right' questions.	1. **Closed**: *'Does the team have an assignment?'* 2. **Straight**: *'How long have you been working together?'* 3. **Clarifying**: *'What do you mean when you say participate and perform well?'* 4. **Open**: *'What aspects regarding your teamwork would you like to discuss?'* 5. **Relationship**: *'When did you start working together? Who initiated it?'* 6. **Circular**: *'What does B have to do to re-establish your trust in good teamwork? What can you offer B in order to make this possible for her to facilitate that?'* and *'What can you offer B to enable her to accomplish this?'* 7. **Reciprocal**: *'If B would change the way in which she works, what could you offer in return?'* 8. **Mirroring**: *'Have you ever experienced that you were dependent on someone else's cooperation and the other person gave you the impression that she did not try hard enough? How did you react in that situation?'* 9. **'Peel-off' questions**: *'Please explain. What do you want? What makes that issue important to you?'* 10. **Confronting questions**: *'Is that really what you want to happen? You say that she will have to leave the team but the way you say it gives me the impression that you doubt this would really solve the problems.'* 11. **Argument**: *'You say that you want B to cooperate well in the team. Could you give an example of a situation where you thought B did not perform as she should? What caused your dissatisfaction? How did this affect the work?'* 12. **Tactical question**: *'How long did you say you have been working together?'* 13. **Verification question**: *'Is disappointed the correct word?'* 14. **Summarizing question with verification question**: *'You have been working together for a number of years. From the beginning, you had different opinions on how the work should be performed, and agreements on deadlines have been a problem. Can I recap by saying that your diverse work styles did not cause difficulties at the start of your working as a team because you felt that the differences in approach also added value to the output of the team? But that now, with the increased pressure of work problems occur more often and you are both affected by this. Is that what it boils down to?'* 15. **Hypothetical question**: *'Suppose we would be able to get everyone to work in the same way, would both of you then be willing to remain on the team?'* (see also reality testing future oriented III-11.1).

Definition/description	Application	Example of application
	Reality testing (III-11)	
To test the realistic nature of a position and to motivate the parties to resolve the dispute themselves. Reality testing empowers parties because it enables them to evaluate their own position as well as alternative solution options more realistically.	Trigger the parties' determination to settle the dispute themselves. Empowerment: by making the parties realize the consequences should they be unable to resolve the dispute themselves.	Test perceptions and expectations. **1. Reality testing hypothetical/ future oriented (III-11.1)** *'What if we could develop a procedure to align all activities, and this enables you to work together in a way you are comfortable with; would you then see a possibility to form a functioning team together?'* or *'What if there was no time pressure at all? How ...?'* **2. Reality testing, risk analysis (III-11.2)** *'How will the output of the team be affected if B leaves the team? And how will the other team members react to that?'* **3. NAN (Negotiated Agreement Now) (III-11.3)** *'What would you be prepared to do to get rid of the whole business today? What are you willing to offer B to make that happen ...?'*
	Mutualizing (find common ground, or joint interests) (III-13)	
Emphasize common facts and mutual interests. Mutualizing offers clients the opportunity to look at themselves, the other party and the problems in a different way, namely not only in terms of your/my point of view, but also from a joint perspective.	Progress can by demonstrated and the understanding of the other party's position increased by highlighting shared interests and common concerns. The negotiators realize that in addition to their differences they also have common ground. Negative stereotyping is avoided, or at least reduced in intensity.	*'You both think it is important that the team performs well?'*

Definition/description	Application	Example of application
BATNA & WATNA & RATNA & Leverage & ZOPA (III-14)		
Benchmark, objective or measure to compare solutions. **BATNA** is the acronym for Best Alternative to Negotiated Agreement. This is the most positive scenario that can be envisaged if the negotiators fail to reach a settlement. **WATNA** is the acronym for Worst Alternative to Negotiated Agreement. This is the most negative scenario if the negotiators are unable to reach an agreement. **RATNA** is the acronym for Realistic Alternative to Negotiated Agreement. This is the most realistic scenario that can be expected if the negotiators do not settle their dispute. **Leverage** is any potential opportunity (power/chances/time/ascendancy, etc.) that a party may exploit to manipulate the outcome of a negotiation in such a way that an agreement is reached on his terms. Whether on a commercial or personal level, the party with the greater need to reach a deal usually has the least leverage. **ZOPA** is the acronym for Zone of Potential Agreement. It is the area within which a settlement can theoretically be reached.	**BATNA** & **WATNA** & **ZOPA** together delineate the potential settlement range. Leverage gives an indication of the power balance that determines where, within the range, the settlement will most likely be reached. Exploration of the **BATNA** ensures that the mediated outcome is better than the available alternatives. The worst alternative, **WATNA**, can provide a basis for reality testing (III-11) and open up an analysis of the **RATNA** (Realistic Alternative to Negotiated Agreement). **Leverage** plays a role in assessing the power balance. It is an analytical tool to assess which party will benefit most from reaching an agreement, which party will be better able to dictate the terms of the agreement, and how one party can potentially gain the upper hand over the other. **ZOPA** indicates the limits to a possible settlement. Remember to expand the pie. Do not limit yourself or the negotiators to ZOPA too quickly. The ZOPA can expand along with the subject matter under discussion.	**BATNA** 1. The company's Board agrees with A, so B is removed from the team. B's replacement quickly adjusts and performs exactly as A wants. 2. The other team members think A is overreacting and do not want to work with A anymore. B forms a new team under her supervision. **WATNA** 1. The project that the team is working on fails and A is blamed. 2. The Board agrees with A, and B is subsequently dismissed. **RATNA** 1. The other team members are affected by the problems and either choose A's or B's side. The team is divided and the output suffers because of the internal problems. This negatively affects the company as well as the image of A and all the other team members. 2. The cooperation between A and B remains difficult and the work suffers. This is consuming a lot of B's energy and enthusiasm, which in turn has negative consequences for the output and B's wellbeing. **Leverage** A knows she will soon be nominated for a position on the Board of Directors. In order to maximize her prospects she wants a perfectly functioning team. She therefore needs to solve the problems with B as soon as possible. However, B does not care how long it takes to solve the problems; after A there will be another project leader who will probably see things differently. Moreover she knows that the company cannot do without her as she is the only employee with specialist knowledge in a particular area. B probably has greater leverage in this scenario. **ZOPA** (a financial example as presented in III-14.3 provides a clearer illustration of the ZOPA concept) At minimum, A wants all tasks that have been agreed to be finished on time and the output to meet minimum quality standards. B wants to determine for herself how she carries out her work and she wants to make sure her other duties and projects do not suffer because of her work for the team. The ZOPA will be somewhere between: (1) the agreement that B determines how and when to carry out the work and (2) the guarantee that the output is delivered on time and in accordance with the specific quality requirements.

Definition/description	Application	Example of application
	Generate options (III-15)	
Develop ideas or ways to arrive at potential solutions and to find outcomes that take into account all identified interests. Stimulate creativity and associative thinking; expand the pie and find optimal solutions.	Enable parties to let go of their initial positions by broadening the horizons. Develop out-of-the-box solutions based on interests. Generating more than one option prevents the parties from hurriedly agreeing to one (potentially sub-optimal) solution. If the parties return to their earlier positions during the options phase, the mediator needs to return to the exploration phase.	**Techniques for generating options** - Brainstorming. - Expand the pie. - Prepare lists and discuss them. - Develop one shared vision. - Seek advice from experts. - Invite the mediator to suggest options. - Consult external sources. - Stimulate creativity and abandon rigid thinking frames.
	Objective criteria (III-16.1)	
An objective standard, principle or benchmark can be used for those components of the dispute that lack sufficient subjective criteria (interests) to enable the parties to reach settlement. The mediator and the parties can look for objective criteria such as market value. The development and application of objective criteria also facilitates reaching agreement with the parties' constituencies.	If the parties fail to generate enough feasible solutions based on subjective criteria (interests), objective criteria can be applied as a second step. These facilitate reaching agreement by comparing a solution with an objective standard.	**Possible objective criteria**: - What output does the Board expect from the team? - How do other teams cooperate? - How were similar difficulties handled within the company or how would another company deal with them? - If the conflict escalated and was brought before a court, how would a judge rule? - What does the human resources department say? - What arrangements were made between the team members at the start?
	Use of voice and silences (III-17)	
Interventions are also possible through use of voice (or, conversely, silence) and the way the voice is used.	Manage communication and control the process by respecting silences and the use of the voice.	**Silences**: - Be comfortable with silences. - Bring prolonged and unhelpful silences to an appropriate end. - Make 'silent parties' participate in the mediation. **Using the voice (technique)**: - Vary with the voice and intonation: volume, pitch, tone, speed. - The way of speaking: hesitant, timid, bold. - In the case of intense emotions or a great deal of noise, speaking slowly and in a clear and quiet tone can be helpful.

Definition/description	Application	Example of application
Non-verbal interventions and non-verbal communication (III-18 and III-17 and III-2)		
Clarify interactions or confront parties, for example, by pointing out any discrepancies between what the parties are saying and how they are behaving. Demonstrate the impartiality and commitment of the mediator. Regulate communication between the parties, and between the parties and the mediator.	By bringing attention to the non-verbal communications of the parties, the mediator is able to clarify or magnify issues or to confront parties (III-10.4). Through body language, the mediator can emphasize his commitment to the mediation and his impartiality. In this way, a mediator can also manage the process.	**Pointing out body language of the parties**: - *'I notice that you are smiling.'* - *'While you are saying this you shrug your shoulders.'* **To show that you are listening (III-2)**: - Facial expression (smiling, looking interested, frowning). - Maintain eye contact without staring. - Gestures (nodding, jotting down key words, hand gestures). - Attitude (relaxed, facing the parties). **Non-verbal communication**: - Give a sign, for example hold the palm of the hand up to indicate 'stop.' (But beware – different gestures may have different meanings in different cultures). - Emphasize verbal communication. - Shrug shoulders. - Express emotions. Reflect feelings in facial expression or body language. - Control the communication. Supporting 'uh-huhs' and 'mmms', nodding, etc. Look somebody in the eye or look away. Stand up or walk around. - Subconscious actions. - Keeping a distance and touching.
Paradoxical intervention (III-19)		
By applying a paradoxical intervention, a mediator can reflect on specific behavior in a contrary way (thus magnifying it in a sense) or break deadlocks. Superficially the goal of a paradoxical intervention appears to be to achieve the exact opposite of what would be expected or appropriate.	A paradoxical intervention is used to break resistance. The parties are given the opportunity to correct inappropriate or unhelpful behavior and at the same time try to get the mediation moving again. A paradoxical intervention causes a shock effect that can break an impasse (IV-1.3.2). Moreover, a paradoxical intervention can make the parties want to prove that things can be done differently.	*'Fine, if she leaves the team the problem is solved. So the dispute is settled now.'* *'Would you like another cup of coffee?'*

Definition/description	Application	Example of application
Identifying interests (II-7)		
Wants, needs, the reason why somebody wishes something. An interest is a subjective criterion that is often transformed into a position (demands, rights). A position often is the legal or positional translation of an underlying interest. Searching for the subjective criteria, the interests, is one of the essential elements of a mediation or negotiation.	Interests form the basis for win-win or mutual gain solutions. They can support an understanding of the other party's position. In addition, by focusing on the interests, issues that are not part of the conflict can be included in the solution (expanding the pie). By mutualizing topics (III-13) and emphasizing mutual interests, forward movement is achieved as well as a greater understanding of the other party's needs.	**Example interest***'You either participate and perform well or leave the team.'* A wants the team to perform well and therefore thinks it is important that the team members cooperate. A's underlying interest is that she wants to score as the team leader in order to further her career. B wants clear arrangements while having the liberty to decide the way in which she handles her work. She is also experiencing an extremely busy period and is concerned that she will not be able to finish her regular tasks in time if she does too much work for the team.
Structuring (II-15)		
Empower the parties by introducing structure in the process and thus helping them to clarify the chaos of the conflict.	Structure, conflict analysis, create the conditions under which parties can come to a solution. Set priorities (long term, short term, importance of the issues). Fractionalizing matters of conflict. Prepare an agenda, keep track of timing. Test assumptions.	-/-
Caucus (II-16)		
Private meeting with one party in the absence of the other party. The mediator will repeat this procedure with the other party in order to maintain balance in the process and to preserve the neutrality of the mediator.	Take the process to the next phase. Explore hidden agendas, allow venting or emotional release, discuss options for a solution in confidence, reality test (III-11), explore BATNA, WATNA, RATNA, leverage and/or ZOPA (III-14), provide an opportunity for parties to confer privately with their own advisors or team.	-/-

Definition/description	Application	Example of application
Clarify assumptions and perspectives (IV-2)		
Clarify differing observations, lines of thought, points of view and perceptions. Clear up and evaluate bias and preconceived ideas.	Through the clarification of misunderstandings and inconsistent perspectives, mutual understanding of the positions of the other party is increased.	**Example of perspective**: A: B is a professional and valuable employee but she fails to stick to agreed actions and thus undermines my authority. B: A is a decisive manager. Unfortunately, her assignments are often unclear to me. Moreover, there are frequent last-minute changes. That is why I usually don't immediately carry out an assignment. These constant changes waste too much time, because I have to do the same work twice.
Play their game (tit-for-tat) or name the game (IV-3.3.2)		
Techniques to manage a complicated conversation or negotiation, to deal with people that act in a way you perceive as difficult, or who use tricky tactics. The objective in using these techniques is to try to change the negotiating style of the (other) party and/or the rules of the negotiation game towards a more effective way of dealing with each other, for example principled negotiation (II-4). Tit-for-tat means doing the same to the other party as they are doing to you. You play the same (negotiation) game they do in order to make them change the way they play it. Another approach to accomplish this is to name the game they are playing.	How to deal with difficult people or tricky tactics: - Analyze what is happening. - Play their game (tit for tat IV-3.3.2). - Give in or walk away. - Change the game and the rules of the game by listening (III-2), reframing (III-6), naming the game or changing the players (IV-3.3.2).	**Play their game (tit-for-tat)** *'Don't project your own frustration on her.'* *'You can't demand that everybody accommodates your style of working.'* **Name the game** *'Do you want to confront her with an accomplished fact?'* *'I'm under the impression that you're trying to power play here. Do you think that will solve the problem? Don't you think it is better to ...?'*
Humor		
Humor is an intervention that is difficult to explain and illustrate. It is, however, of such importance that this critical tool cannot be ignored here. It can be a powerful mechanism for relieving tension or venting emotions. Moreover, laughing together can be a valuable shared experience to help recover common ground. It is a medium through which parties can reconnect.	When in doubt, always test whether the parties are ready for the use of humor and check if the kind of humor you want to use is appropriate. A relatively safe option to test the water is self-mockery by the mediator. This is less threatening in a sensitive situation and it prevents either of the parties feeling they were made to look foolish or not taken seriously, or even feeling under attack.	-/-

Definition/description	Application	Example of application
To give no reaction or to ignore issues		
Many mediators feel that you need to intervene all the time or react to everything. This is an error.	This overview shows all possible interventions and how they are applied. There is no need to intervene in the process constantly. Make an assessment of when it is useful to intervene and when it is better to leave things to the parties and just watch what happens. A mediator should especially not interfere in the flow of productive discussions.	Finding the right balance is a big challenge for any mediator. It entails sufficiently controlling the process and at the same time ensuring that not all communication has to go through the mediator (for example continuous active listening or persistent positive reframing). Parties should be empowered without a 'laissez-faire' approach of the mediator.

On the web a lot of information can be found on mediation techniques and interventions. Examples can be found in the Webography in Resource H.

Make sure that you formulate short, clear and unambiguous sentences. Do not use long monologues, overly informal language or clichés. Avoid posing two or more questions at the same time. For example, not: ***'Why did you choose mediation and what do you hope to achieve?'*** but ***'What do you expect from this mediation?'***.
Do not use too much jargon with the parties. (Resource A at the end of this book includes an explanatory list of mediator jargon.) For example, do not say that you ***'will explore the joint and differing interests ...'***, but rather that you want to ***'look for the topics you agree on and also the issues that are still keeping you apart ...'***
Don't ***'generate options'***, but look for ***'possible solutions'***. In addition, a ***'caucus'*** is better described as ***'an individual meeting between the mediator and one party'*** or simply as ***'a private meeting'***.

2 Listening

2.1 Importance

Listening to the other party is very difficult in any conflict situation. The negotiators are generally inclined to listen selectively. Words are interpreted with a bias and an element of distrust and disbelief. Moreover, parties tend to focus more on finding arguments for not agreeing with the other party than on listening and trying to find what they can agree with. Furthermore, if nobody reacts to what is being said, the speaker will think he is not being listened to and he will merely repeat his own point of view. The discussion then deteriorates into circular argument.

- **Make parties listen to each other**:
  A third party has less stake in the result of mediation and can therefore listen more neutrally to the parties. A mediator can help the negotiators separate the content from the emotional issues (III-8). The parties are then better able to listen to what the other is saying and to analyze the real core of the problem. When a party realizes that the other party really understands what the issue is about for him, he often experiences this as confirmation that his feelings regarding the conflict are acceptable. This phenomenon is known as recognition.
- **Listening as a mediator**:
  Naturally the mediator also has to listen effectively. This is vital in order to decide what interventions should be applied at what time, and to interpret content accurately. The exact nature of effective listening depends on the phase of the mediation; on what is necessary in each specific phase as well as what you want to achieve as a mediator. Listening closely helps build a good working relationship with the parties as well as build trust. Therefore, a mediator should not just listen well but also let the parties know he is listening.

Why is listening well challenging? One reason lies in how our brains function. Below are some numbers and tips for better listening.

Hearing, Seeing, and Processing Information Checklist[44]

☐ **Seeing**:

- Processing visual information: 10,000 kilobits per second
  Researchers at the universities of Pennsylvania and Princeton have measured that the amount of visual information flowing from the human eye through the optic nerve to the brain is 10,000 kilobits per second.[45] This is comparable to the data transmission of an Ethernet connection.
- Sharp vision: a small area is sharp and stroboscopic
  In addition, we can only perceive sharply a very small area with our eyes. Although our eyes are constantly shifting to capture our surroundings as completely as possible, during these shifts, the image briefly goes black, so our brains ultimately receive nothing more than a stroboscopic image.
- If the above is true, how is it still possible for us to perceive our environment so clearly and smoothly? The answer is that our brains create a perfectly running theater performance

44 This checklist is based on the (Dutch) article of Liefhebber, H.J. (2008), 'De vergissing van Descartes en 60 bits per seconde voor ons bewustzijn. Kan modern hersenonderzoek een praktische bijdrage leveren aan de kwaliteit van besluitvorming in conflictsituaties?', Tijdschrift voor Mediation en Conflictmanagement, jrg. 12, nr. 2, p. 44-48. The article can be found on www.manonschonewille.com .

45 Koch, K., J. McLean, R. Segev, M.A. Freed, M.J. Berry III, Balasubramanian and P. Sterling (2006), How Much the Eye Tells the Brain.

from all these fragmentary images. Our brains suggest a complete visual field, but they are actually deceiving us: we see much less than we think, and many things escape our attention. Seeing is, in fact, based on an illusion, but many of our interpretations, actions, and decisions rely on it...

☐ **Information Processing:**

- Conscious: maximum 60 bits per second.
- Unconscious: approximately 11.2 million bits per second.
- Unconsciously, we process nearly 200,000 times more information than consciously in the same time.

Consciousness plays a minimal role in our behavior and essentially witnesses the decisions the unconscious has already made.

☐ **Listening:**[46]

- Speaking at 150 words per minute
- Processing at 1,000 words per minute
- There is, therefore, a kind of surplus capacity. When someone talks, they do so at about 150 words per minute. Since our brains can process more words than the person you are listening to can speak, there is room for our own thoughts, which often tend to wander. For example, because the speaker said something interesting that you continue to think about, or because it is a monotonous story, and you are preoccupied with things like "Is my car parked correctly?" or "Is my mobile phone turned off?" or you are more focused on thinking about your own response or the next question you want to ask.
  Additionally, there is room for absorbing unconscious impressions, sounds from the environment, and movements in the surroundings. All of this comes at the expense of listening quality.
- To function efficiently, our brains work with heuristics (mental shortcuts). Without them, we would need much more brain capacity or many more brains (and a much larger head). Most of the time, these heuristics work well, but they can also lead to errors. Anchoring (II-10-7) or a first impression that exists before we consciously perceive someone are examples of this. It also means that the idea that a mediator can be completely neutral is not accurate (II-2).

- **Tips for effective listening:**
  + Check your assumptions.
  + Listen carefully especially when you think you already know what the other person is going to say or if you are testing/looking for corroboration of your knowledge of the case.
  + Do not jump to conclusions.

46 Thompson, L.L. (2008), The Mind and Heart of the Negotiator (4th edition). Upper Saddle River, NJ: Pearson Prentice Hall.

+ Be aware of your own biases and favorite topics and be extra vigilant when the conversation is heading in that direction.
+ Pay special attention to words said or conclusions that do not align with what you thought, unexpected twists. Do inquire further about those.
+ Talking and listening cannot happen simultaneously. Our brains cannot multitask, even though many people claim otherwise! Someone's brain simply switches more or less quickly from one process to another. So switch your focus to become a listener.

Effective listening is more than just letting somebody finish what he has to say and absorbing what is being said. You also need to communicate that you are listening. See overview 2 in III-2.3.

2.2 Active listening

Active listening by the mediator means ensuring that a speaker feels heard by constantly giving feedback through non-verbal behavior (III-18) and by paraphrasing (III-3), summarizing (III-4), or reflecting back what the speaker says (III-5). Reframing can also be used in active listening (III-6). With the help of verification questions (III-10.5.1) the mediator makes sure the reframe is right and the speaker has been properly understood. Active listening can be used when parties are not yet ready to fully participate in the mediation process or are too consumed by their own thoughts. This can occur, for example, in highly emotional situations.

Take care not to over-use this technique or apply it for prolonged periods. This defeats the purpose and can be annoying. For example, it may be interpreted as patronizing. Additionally, the communication is entirely in the hands of the mediator and this makes the parties dependent on the mediator.

This technique can also be applied in a negotiation or caucus. For example, it can be used when communication is strained, if the conversation keeps going round in circles, and particularly if you have the feeling that the other party is not really listening to you. The technique of active listening:

- forces you to really listen which enables you to analyze why a conversation is lengthy and difficult;
- conveys the message to the other party that you really are paying attention and that you understand what the discussion is about; that you are on the same wavelength;
- can buy you extra time to think through the next step. (This holds true when you apply active listening to an issue that is already clear to you. During the time you have, you can 'play back the tape'.)

For more background information see the websites of the International Listening Association: www.listen.org, www.beyondintractability.org. For exercises to practice listening skills: www.esl-lab.com (intended for English as a Second Language students, but contains useful exercises for native speakers as well).

2.3 Techniques

Definition/description	Application	Example of application
Listening		
Listening is a continuing selection process. True listening, and demonstrating that you are doing so, emphasizes your commitment as the mediator, facilitates your ability to hear a message and helps collect information. How to listen effectively and what to listen for depends on what is necessary at this stage of the mediation and what you want to achieve as a mediator. Listening is more than letting someone finish and taking in the words. You also need to demonstrate that you are listening.	Communicating to a party that they have been 'heard' usually ensures that they will stop repeating themselves. It builds rapport and underlines the commitment of the mediator. Moreover, listening is necessary to gather information and to enable proper application of other interventions. Effective listening helps you to manage the process.	**Opening phase mediation**: Handling emotions: let one party listen to the other party, show that the 'emotional party' is listened to and that the message is 'heard'. **Exploration phase**: Gather information to determine which interventions can or should be applied, identify emotions, collect data, and clarify interests **Option phase**: Factual, data-oriented and solution-oriented listening.

The mediator has to ensure that each party has an equal opportunity to explain their own point without interruption (by the other party or by the mediator). When emotions run high, one tool is to let each party talk for one minute at most (the One-Minute-Rule; Schreuder Tromp, 1997). This is considered to be the maximum time that people involved in a conflict situation can effectively listen to each other. In practice, the One-Minute Rule is very difficult to apply.

Studies in psychology (Roediger, 2003) have shown that the short-term memory can contain about seven pieces of information simultaneously. You retain information by attaching a meaning to it. This illustrates how difficult it is to repeat a conversation accurately. It is an illusion to think that a mediator can reproduce comprehensively and objectively all the information and intentions from what the parties say.

Effective listening as a mediator or negotiator	Active listening by the mediator	Making parties listen to each other	Communicate that you are listening
When			
Always.	Emotional situations, difficult communication, when you are not sure that you understand the parties, when you are going in circles, when you feel the negotiators are not listening.	Important during the entire mediation but especially at the beginning. Can be used for blocking issues (II-8) or in other important or emotional situations.	Vital during the entire mediation but especially at the beginning. Make sure that all parties have the feeling that they are heard. So listen to both parties equally well (and show them that you are listening).
Contra-indications (circumstances where the use of the technique may not be appropriate)			
None.	Using this technique too often (or for a prolonged period) can cause irritation. It furthermore results in the mediator dominating the entire communication.	Using this technique too often (or for a prolonged period) can cause irritations. Additionally, this results in the mediator dominating the entire communication.	None. Pay attention to neutrality. Do not react too often in ways that can be interpreted as approval or disapproval. For example, beware of nodding too much. Emphasize the fact that you are repeating the the statement of one of the parties: *'your point of view is as follows ...; you want to make clear ...; I hear you say that ...'* Another technique to use is mutualizing (III-13).
How			
1. **Attitude**: - Open (not biased), truly interested and curious. - Be honest when you are not able to focus anymore. 2. **Action:** - Ask questions (III-10). - Check your own assumptions and those of others. - Repeat in your own words and verify whether your rephrasing is correct (III-3). This does not mean that you agree with what the other person is saying. - Summarize (III-4). - Give an acknowledgement if appropriate (III-5.2).	- Paraphrase repeatedly (III-3), summarize (III-4), reflect (III-5) or reframe (III-6). - Follow-up with a verification question (III-10.5.2) to make sure the account is correct and to communicate that a party is listened to. - Non-verbal 'attention paying' behavior (III-18).	- Suggest that the parties paraphrase each other (III-3). - Paraphrase as a mediator, make a translation and put things in other words. - Summarize (III-4). - Ask circular or other relational questions, like mirroring (III-10.2). - Check assumptions, if necessary also with the other party (IV-2).	1. **Verbal interventions**: - Helpful 'words' (*'Uh-huh', 'And what else?'*). - Ask questions (III-10). - Paraphrase (III-3). - Summarize (III-4). - Reflect back, magnify/content (III-5.1). - Reframe (III-6). 2. **Non-verbal interventions**: - Expression (smiling, looking interested, frowning). - Maintain eye contact without staring. - Gestures (nodding, jotting down key words). - Attitude (relaxed, turned towards the parties, looking at the parties).

3 (Let the parties) Paraphrase

Definition/description	Application	Example of application
Paraphrasing with a verification question		
Repeat in your own words what has been said. Repeat the same statement in other words. The content of the repetition needs to be identical to the original message, with only the choice of words being different. A paraphrase should not include your own conclusions. It is important to check whether the paraphrased account is correct.	**Break through vicious communication circles.** Manage emotions and communications. **Let the parties paraphrase.** Discuss emotional topics or blocking issues (II-8), make the parties listen to each other and convey the message that they have each heard what the other party wanted to say. **Paraphrasing by the mediator.** Clarify issues by using a different vocabulary, let the parties know that you are listening, and thereby build trust.	Paraphrasing by the mediator: *'You would rather have your colleague quit the team if he does not participate properly? Is that what you are saying?'*

Paraphrasing is to (let the parties) repeat in (their) own words what the opposing party says and verify whether it is done correctly. Invite the speaker to add to or improve the paraphrase. If necessary, repeat the process of paraphrasing in different words.
The mediator can paraphrase or ask the parties to do this. Paraphrasing each other forces the parties to really listen to each other. Moreover, the party who wants to clarify a point gets an unambiguous signal that they are being listened to (II-2.1). In this way, recurring themes can be blocked. This technique is often used for emotional issues (IV-4.4) or blocking issues (II-8).
Asking the parties to repeat what they said and to express the statements using different words can also be applied when you need a mental break in order to think about the next step.
The mediator paraphrases when he wants to make party A's statements clear to party B, for example if it is important that B understands what party A said or meant. Through paraphrasing, you can convey that you are listening as a mediator. This builds a relationship with the parties and generates trust.
Repeating a statement in your own words does not mean that you agree with that statement. You can underline this by following-up with a verification question.

Paraphrase as a mediator:

'As I understand it you say that you want ... is that correct?'

'Do you mean to say that you ...?'

'You feel ... and you think ... Did I miss something?'

Let the parties paraphrase. Do this as a mediator by asking B: *'Could you repeat in your own words how you understood what A just said about ...?'* Next, you should ask A if that is what he meant to say.

4 Summarize

Definition/description	Application	Example of application
Summarize		
Neutral summary with a conclusion, followed by a verification question		
Convey the essence of statements of more than one party or of a range of issues. In contrast to paraphrasing, the mediator selects which information is used for a summary and which is not. Additionally, a mediator can incorporate conclusions in a summary. A summary can be combined with other techniques like mutualizing (III-13) or reflecting (III-5). It is an essential tool to structure the mediation process and to guide the communication (II-15). Because the mediator is selective about the information and can also add a conclusion, an evaluative remark can easily slip into the summary. Value-free presentation, while selecting the essential issues, requires practice.	Manage the process, demonstrate progress and structure the dialogue. Connect issues and the contribution of several parties, or enlarge the scope: - Retain or keep track of what is said or clarify topics. - Sum up and (re)structure important issues and themes. - Place issues in a different framework.	*'What I heard is that both of you think it is important that the team functions well. However, you have differing opinions regarding the performance of the individual team members. This means we should address your working styles and the expectations you have of each other, as well as your expectations regarding teamwork. Moreover, we should define the circumstances for potential future teamwork. Have I missed any important issues?'*

Summarizing is reflecting the essence of the statements of several parties, or of a range of issues of one party. This is done in order to retain what has been said, to clarify topics, to sum up and (re)structure important issues and themes.
Combining a summary with other techniques like mutualizing (III-13) or reflecting (III-5) is also possible. It is an essential tool to structure and control the mediation process (II-15). By giving a summary, the progress in the mediation is illustrated and several themes can be tied together or put in a different, larger frame.
In contrast to paraphrasing, a summary deals with the statements of more than one party, or with several issues discussed over a longer period of time. The mediator selects which information is used for the summary and he can incorporate conclusions in a summary.
Use a verification question to check whether the summary is accurate and complete.
A (partly) incorrect summary is counterproductive and if not corrected, may become increasingly counterproductive in later stages.

Examples of a summary:

'We have discussed a lot of issues. What I heard is that you both think it is important that .... You have different opinions on .... This means that you agree that ... And that we still need a solution for... Is this what it boils down to?'

'You both agree that ... but you both think that ... should be handled differently. Is that a fair summary?'

'You both signed a lease. Until A lost her job the rent was always paid on time. After that, you discussed a payment plan agreeing that A would maintain the garden in exchange for a lower rent. For all kinds of reasons, A did not comply with the agreement. In addition the roof is leaking. This is not being repaired because B wants A should keep to their prior agreement first. Did I sum that up correctly?'

'We talked about ... You think ... I think ... So ... It seems to me that this is what it boils down to. Would you agree with that?'

'We argued about ... and ... and ... We concluded that ... Is our dispute settled if we find a solution to all of these issues? Have I missed something?'

A summary can help to emphasize mutual interests or common themes. Think about making a joint summary after both parties have made their opening statement at the beginning of the mediation instead of separate summaries of each individual party's statement. In this way that the party who was not the first to speak will not feel that the other party's arguments are being 'rubbed in' by the mediator (no matter how carefully or neutrally phrased). Moreover, with a joint summary you can emphasize mutual aspects (III-13) and reframe themes so that both parties are willing to discuss them (III-6).

5 Reflecting

Definition/description	Application	Example of application
	Reflecting back general	
Magnify positions or topics, point out themes explicitly. This increases the insight of both parties into the other party's position and gives them the opportunity either to further explain their point of view or to revise their opinion.	Reflecting back on the level of: - **Content**: what is being said, magnify key words/parts of a sentence. - **Emotion/intention**: how things are expressed, to clarify the underlying feelings or intentions. - **Process**: emphasize the progress or forward movement.	See below.

Reflecting is an intervention that a mediator can use to make things known, for example what a party has said or what intentions or feelings the mediator sees. Or he can comment on the progress of the process. What is said and how it is said is magnified in order to give the speaker and the other party more insight and to offer them the opportunity to think differently. The speaker can clarify, underline or add to the statement, or even take things back. Reflecting plays an important role in effective listening (III-2) and is often used for emotional issues.

Reflecting can be done on the levels of content (magnify key words/part of a sentence), emotion/intention (underlying feelings or the intention) and process (progress).

Because there is a risk of escalating the conflict, some mediators do not like to use this technique; particularly **not the content** magnifying **reflections**. However, the potential gain of using this technique is substantial. Important topics can be brought to the table. A mediator can prevent a certain topic from becoming a recurring theme by explicitly **acknowledging** that the statement is 'heard' and that the importance of an issue for a party is 'understood'. Conversely, an acknowledgement can also cause problems when the feeling is not put into words correctly or when the wrong feeling is labeled, addressed or identified. By **reflecting the forward movement** of the mediation process, the negotiators will get the impression that the mediation is progressing and this can motivate them to work even harder to try to find a solution.

There is a difference between reflecting feelings (acknowledgement) and reframing a feeling (III-6.2).

5.1 Magnify/reflect on content

Definition/description	Application	Example of application
	Magnify/reflect content	
Put a point of view or an issue under a magnifying glass in order to make it clear, while offering the parties the opportunity to provide an explanation, or to change their opinion.	Magnify issues, points of view and clarify them. Especially useful for emotional topics and important issues. Repeat key words or (parts of) a statement.	*'She will have to leave the team.'*

Reflecting the content is referred to as magnifying, parroting or echoing. In this book this intervention is referred to as reflecting or magnifying only. Besides reflecting through repetition of key words or parts of a sentence that one party uses (echoing or parroting), magnifying issues by using different, more accurate words in the reflection can also be very effective in a mediation or negotiation.

It can be seen as the opposite of positive reframing (III-6.1). In reflecting content the mediator does not translate issues into another context or frame, but scrutinizes an issue by placing it under a magnifying glass.

Magnifying is achieved by repeating key words or parts of a sentence that one party uses. In contrast to reframing, it is important to use the exact words and idiom a party uses as frequently as possible. This clarifies a position or theme. In addition, both parties get the opportunity to provide a further explanation or to revise their opinion. Reflecting is often used for emotional themes and key problems.

'It is outrageous ...'

'You find it absolutely incomprehensible ...'

'You want the messing around to come to an end ...'

'You mean take it or leave it?'

5.2 Acknowledge/reflect on feelings

Definition/description	Application	Example of application
Acknowledge/reflect feelings		
With a verification question		
Put an end to recurring (emotional) topics by highlighting the importance of the issue for a party or the feelings associated with it, thereby communicating that the message and the feelings behind a statement are being 'heard'.	Prevent certain topics from becoming recurring themes. Break through resistance.	*'The collaboration with your colleague has been disappointing for you. Is disappointing the right word?'*

By reflecting the underlying feelings that a mediator observes in one or more of the negotiators, the emotion is put firmly on the table. Reflecting that the feeling and the importance of the emotion are 'heard' can prevent the constant repetition of recurring themes. A mediator needs to check whether the reflection of the feelings is correct. Acknowledgement is an interpretation by the mediator of the behavior and other messages of a party. The mediator communicates that the feeling and the importance of the feeling are understood. However, the mediator can make a wrong assumption or interpretation. A wrong or partly wrong reflection of feelings, for example a serious understatement, can be counterproductive. *'This seems to be tough for you'*, when it is only a matter of not agreeing with something. Or even worse: *'I notice that you are not entirely at ease'* when somebody is enraged.

For this reason, it is wise to follow-up an acknowledgement with a verifying question (III-10.5.2). *'..., is that the proper word?'*

Examples of acknowledgements (reflect on feelings) are:

'This is disappointing for you. Is disappointment the right word?'

'I notice that you are not comfortable talking about this topic. Is that right?'

'You have had enough... Does that describe how you feel?'

'May I conclude that this is an important topic for you?'

'You are frustrated by the course of the project so far. Does that express your feeling correctly?'

Be careful with acknowledgements that start with 'I ***understand***...' or 'I **see** that...' This can be interpreted as the mediator thinking it is 'correct' that a party feels a certain topic is important or has strong emotions. Using the words 'I see' or 'I understand', if not conveyed properly, can give the impression that the mediator agrees with the way one party reacts.

5.3 Reflect on the progress

Definition/description	Application	Example of application
Reflect progress		
Emphasize the progress made so far, in order to manage the process and strengthen the parties' confidence that the dispute can be resolved through mediation.	Stress the fact that the effort of the negotiators is not in vain and that the mediation is moving forward.	*'It is now apparent that you both have different expectations about teamwork and the contribution of each individual team member. Let's elaborate on this issue.'*

The mediator can reflect the forward movement when it is necessary to show the negotiators that their hard work is not in vain, by magnifying the progress that is achieved in the mediation process.

'Together you managed to make significant steps forward.'

'We have come a long way during this first hour of the mediation. And we still have 45 minutes before the end of this session.'

In order to illustrate the technique of reflecting, magnifying/reflecting content, acknowledge/reflect feelings and reflect progress respectively are applied to the following sentences.

Reflecting			
	'If they want the license back, they will have to pay through the nose.'	***'You either participate and perform well or leave the team.'***	***'Liar! I don't want to have anything to do with you anymore.'***
1. Magnifying/ content	*'A can have the license back, but then they have to pay through the nose.'*	*'If she does not perform well she will have to leave the team.'*	*'You say she is a liar.' 'You don't want to have anything to do with her anymore?'*
2. Feeling	*'You have had enough of the discussions. Is that right?'*	*'You are disappointed. Is disappointment the correct word?' 'I notice that the collaboration in the team is an important issue for you. Do I see that correctly?'*	*'You are angry about this? Does the word anger express what you feel?' 'I notice that it is not easy for you to talk about this.'*
3. Progress	*'So we can discuss the possibility of selling the license in return for a reasonable compensation?' 'You agree that buying off the license is an option'*	*'It is now apparent that you both have different expectations about team work and the contribution of each individual team member. Let's elaborate on this issue'.*	*'It is a step forward that you have said that you have difficulties with ... it creates clarity ...'*

Please note that the sentences are not related to a specific case or to the question whether a certain intervention is appropriate in a specific situation. The purpose is to demonstrate the technique clearly and make comparison possible.

6 Reframing or recontextualizing

6.1 Neutral or positive reframing

Definition/description	Application	Example of application
Reframing		
1. Neutral or positive. 2. Option. 3. Interest. 4. Objective criterion. 5. Emotion.		
Manage emotions and communication by 'translating' statements into a new intellectual framework or placing the issues in another context. Stimulate out-of-the-box thinking and looking at issues from a different or broader perspective. The parties can then let go of their own entrenched perspectives and gradually move away from blame and legal positioning towards taking responsibility and searching for mutual interests.	Make issues subjects for discussion. Develop new intellectual frameworks. Allow the parties space to move from blaming one another to shared interests. Reframing can be viewed as a crowbar to separate the parties from their own perspectives. It goes further than simply reformulating a statement. If you reformulate an issue you are paraphrasing.	**1. Neutral or positive** *'The performance of the team and how the team is structured is one of the issues that we should discuss.'* **2. Option** *'B can leave the team. Another possibility is that you or C or D leave the team.'* **3. Interest** *'You want the team to perform well?'* **4. Objective criterion** *'How is the contribution of an individual team member assessed?'* **5. Emotion** (with verification question III-10.5.2) *'The performance of the team and B's role in it is such an emotionally-charged issue for you that you would rather have B leave the team than to carry on like this. Is that what you mean?'*

Through reframing the mediator places what a party says in a different perspective or a new context. Neutral or positive reframing makes it easier to transform a difficult issue into a topic that both parties are willing to discuss.

A: *'You really shouldn't complain that I am not listening.'*

B: *'What does that mean? You don't take me seriously and you never listen to anything I say.'*

consequently becomes:

Mediator: *'You both think it is important to pay attention and to treat each other with respect.'*

A positional or oversimplified statement often leads to escalation of the conflict and impedes communication. By recontextualizing what is being said in more neutral terms (neutralizing) or jointly (mutualizing), the edge can be taken off a conflict. Moreover, it helps the parties focus less on the actual conflict and more on resolving it. As a result, a criticism becomes an issue that all involved are willing or motivated to discuss (III-13).

In the example described above, one of the parties - or perhaps both - is not willing to discuss: *'We need to talk about the fact that you should start to listen to each other seriously.'* This sounds more like a confirmation of the accusations. Unless, of course, you want to adopt the confronting question technique (III-10.4.1) or apply a reflection (III-5). *'An interest in what the other person has to say and treating each other with respect is important to both of you. Let's talk about that'* is a topic both parties will probably will even be happy to talk about. Blame can also be reframed in terms of wants or interests. *'You never listen'* becomes *'You want your contribution to be taken seriously?'*

Reframing, especially the neutral or positive variant, is a powerful tool and is therefore often used by mediators. Notwithstanding the fact that this is an important technique, you need to be careful not to use neutral or positive reframing too often, otherwise the real conflict can remain unclear. It can also cause irritation. Sometimes a party wants to formulate things clearly and to the point. And sometimes this is also necessary. If a mediator is constantly smoothing out the issues, the party involved can feel they are not being treated seriously. If the mediator persistently reframes, or does so at the wrong moments, the potential power of this tool declines drastically.

Moreover, the surprise effect of this intervention disappears. In addition, you miss the opportunity to release the parties from their own deadlocked perspectives.
Reframing also has to be technically correct. It goes further than just reformulating a sentence. Reformulating, putting a statement into other words, is paraphrasing (III-3). Some mediators see positive or neutral reframing as an incorrect use of this technique. From this point of view, reframing should only be used to reposition the parties so that they can view their situation differently. Other mediators consider neutral or positive reframing the only proper application of this intervention. They avoid using reframing as described below under III-6.2. In addition, some mediators think reframing is not the correct word to describe this technique and prefer the term recontextualizing.

6.2 Reframing into an interest, option, feeling or objective criterion

When you want to make things clear, you can use reflecting as a technique (III-5) but reframing can also be used for this purpose. Reframing a statement in an objective criterion or in an option can be used to formulate statements in such a way that the parties are turned around, or are able to put 'the shoe on the other (sometimes wrong) foot'. This encourages parties to look differently at issues. These less neutral forms of reframing are also often used in negotiations. They can help to discover new perspectives to counteract tricky tactics or resist negotiators that are perceived as difficult (IV-3).

Reframing is 'translating' and putting a statement into another context for one of the parties. By placing the statement in another context, the effect is: *'Yes, that is another way of looking at it.'* This can be achieved by reframing an interest, an option, a feeling or an objective criterion.

In order to illustrate the technique, different forms of reframing are applied to the following sentences.

Reframing			
	'If they want the license back, they will have to pay through the nose.'	***'You either participate and perform well or leave the team.'***	***'Liar! I don't want to have anything to do with you anymore.'***
1. Neutral or positive	*'You are willing to sell the license if A pays an acceptable sum.'*	*'The performance and composition of the team are issues that we should discuss.'*	*'Your relationship is different from what you would like it to be.'*
2. Option	*'One possible option is to sell the license if a certain amount of money is paid.'* *'A can buy the license in return for financial or some other form of compensation.'*	*'B can leave the team. Another possibility is that you or C or D leaves the team'.* *'The composition of the team could be changed.'*	*'Breaking off all contact is one possible action for dealing with the situation. We could also talk about the way you treat each other. And we can also look at ...'*
3. Interest	*'You would like a clear agreement that you are entitled to the license?'* *'You want a monetary result from the license?'* *'You require a clear understanding of the terms of agreement?'*	*'You would like the team to perform well?'* *'You think it is important that the team cooperates well and you feel that B's input is not sufficient?'*	*'You need clarity?'* *'You say that it is important for you that you treat each other honestly and fairly?'*
4. Objective criterion	*'In your line of business, what is usually paid for a license like that?'* *'In order to arrive at a fair compensation we could, for example, look at how a judge would decide in a case like this.'* *'What does your accountant/lawyer advise you...'*	*'How is the contribution of an individual team member assessed?'* *'We can compare the output of your team with that of department X.'* *'... compare your input with B's input ...'* *'What does the management expect from your team?'*	*'How would other people react in your situation?'* *'What advice would you give your best friend if she were in the same situation?'*
5. Emotion (with verification question III-10.5.2)	*'You have had enough of the ambiguity regarding the license and you want to put an end to the discussions? Is that an accurate description?'*	*'The performance of the team and B's role in it is such an emotionally-charged issue for you that you would rather have B leave the team than to carry on like this. Is that what you mean?'*	*'You are so disappointed about what happened between you that you want to break off all further contact. Is that correct?'*

III. Techniques and interventions

Please note that the sentences are not related to a specific case or the question whether a certain intervention is appropriate in a specific situation. The purpose is to demonstrate the technique clearly and make comparison possible.

The difference between an acknowledgement/feelings reflection and reframing in a feeling

By using an acknowledgement, a mediator pays attention to the feelings or emotions of a party and also communicates that he understands this is an important issue for this party. The feeling is magnified. The party's behavior and what they are communicating is interpreted. The emotion is referred to, as well as the fact that the importance of the feeling for this party is understood. However, no further conclusions are drawn. The aim of an acknowledgement is to put an end to recurring themes (III-5.2).

Reframing in a feeling goes much further than just reflecting a feeling. Reframing means that the mediator interprets the behavior and the communication of a party and this is subsequently traced back to an underlying emotion or need. Finally, the mediator brings this underlying feeling up for discussion. A demonstration of a feeling or a statement is 'translated' or interpreted into the underlying feeling and this places it in a different context. A comment is placed in the context of the emotion that caused the remark. It goes further than observing or confirming that somebody feels strongly about something or thinks a certain topic is of great importance. That is why, when reframing in a feeling, it is even more important to check whether the interpretation is correct. So always follow up a reframe in a feeling with a verification question (III-10.5.2) to check whether you have used the right words and your interpretation is correct.

An example to illustrate the difference between reframing in a feeling and an acknowledgement:

'You either participate and perform well or leave the team.'

Acknowledgement: 'You are disappointed about the teamwork with your colleague. Is disappointed the right word?'

Reframing in a feeling: 'The way that the team and B function is such a big issue for you that you would rather have B leave the team than continue in this way. Is that what you want to say?'

7 Neutral language of the mediator

7.1 Neutral language general

In addition to reframing statements of the parties neutrally and placing them in another context, the mediator can also apply neutral language himself. This promotes balance in the mediation, underlines the neutrality of the mediator and makes it easier to transform a difficult or sensitive issue into a topic both parties are willing to discuss. Therefore, the mediator must ensure he uses neutral language himself (III-6.1).

Part of using neutral language is avoiding giving risky answers. For example to questions that try to extract an opinion from the mediator or otherwise jeopardize the neutrality of the mediator.

Examples of risky questions from parties are:

'Don't you think so?'

'You must agree that this is extreme!'

'You do have children/a beautiful car/animals...yourself, don't you?'

'Don't you think I'm being reasonable?'

'How would you react if you were in my position?'

'You do understand that that is very difficult?'

7.2 Techniques to deal with risky questions posed by parties

- ☐ Ignore this kind of remark or react neutrally: *'The issue is whether you ...' 'My opinion is not relevant.' 'You both look at me expectantly, but I'm not going to answer this question.'*
- ☐ Pass the ball back to the party that is asking the risky question:
  - for example, reframe in an objective criterion (III-6.2): *'What is normal/reasonable/etc. ... for you?'*
  - for example, reframe in an interest (III-6.2): *'Is the opinion of others important to you?'*
- ☐ Pass 'the ball' to the other party:
  - *'What is your opinion about this?'*
  - *'Could you answer that question please?'*
- ☐ Bring up meta-communication (III-9):
  Challenge the party that raises the risky question:
  - *'If I respond to that, don't you think it might compromise my neutrality?'*
  - *'Do you think my opinion is relevant for the further course of this mediation?'*

  Questions for the other party:
  - *'Do the remarks of A affect your trust in me as mediator?'*
- ☐ Confrontation question (III-10.4.1):
  - *'Do you realize that my neutrality is jeopardized if I answer those kinds of questions?'*
  - *'When you ask me a question like that I can't escape the impression that you are trying to pull me over to your side.'*
- ☐ Argumentation question (III-10.4.2):
  - *'What is the reason that you ask me this question?'*
  - *'Could you please explain...'*

8 Distinguish content from the relationship

Definition/description	Application	Example of application
Distinguish content from the relationship		
Clarify what the dispute is really about. Distinguishing between substantive/content aspects and emotional/relationship aspects is a basic requirement of principled negotiation. Also known as: separating the people from the problem (II-4).	Techniques to distinguish between the emotional and the content issues: using neutral language (III-7), reframing (III-6), paying attention to meta-communication (III-9), and structuring the mediation process (II-15). Moreover, a negotiation agenda can be drawn up in which the substantive/content issues and the relationship aspects are separated (I-6). See example.	*'We have to discuss:* - *the cooperation in the team;* - *the performance of the individual team members;* - *the intended results;* - *your expectations.'* (You can also write on a flip-chart or whiteboard to visualize an agenda). *'Can we settle this dispute if we find a solution to all of these topics? Or did we overlook any important issues?'*

A basic rule of principled negotiation is 'separate the people from the problem' (II-4). It is important to distinguish between the content issues and the relationship aspects. This is made easier by: using neutral language (III-7), reframing (III-6) and paying attention to meta-communication (III-9). In addition, the relationship and content issues can be separated by structuring the mediation process (II-15) and by preparing a negotiation agenda in which the content aspects and emotional issues are listed separately (I-6). Consider discussing the relationship or emotional issues and the blocking issues first (II-8). Once these topics are resolved, the negotiators can usually find a solution on the content issues by themselves.

9 Meta-communication

Definition/description	Application	Example of application
Meta-communication		
Meta-communication is communication about communicating. The purpose is to point out why certain things are being said and what consequences these (implicit) messages can have. Explaining the intention behind the words can help anticipate and clarify misunderstandings or different interpretations, especially regarding relationship topics.	Communication takes place simultaneously at several levels. To resolve misunderstandings concerning the relationship, the mediator must first move away from the content. Next, he must address what is happening between the parties: describe non-verbal behavior, how do they communicate with each other or with the mediator, what is happening under the surface?	Let us assume that party A strongly emphasizes that the mediator is a team leader in his main occupation, just like he is. Party A finds that favorably, *'because the mediator will understand that, like a chain, a team is only as strong as its weakest member.'* The mediator can bring up the possible impact this might have on party B. For example asking B if in B's opinion the professional background of the mediator can affect the outcome of the mediation. Or, the mediator can enquire whether the remarks of party A adversely affect B's trust in the mediator.

A verbal message contains more than just the content of the statement. It also says something about how the speaker feels, the state of the relationship between both parties, and possible underlying interests, expectations and wishes. Meta-communication plays a role in the dialogue between the parties and between the parties and the mediator.

For example, if someone dislikes the manner in which something is expressed there are several possible responses. The content of the response is that s/he does not agree with the way s/he is treated but the respective responses give a different impression of the relationship between the parties. And it provides information about feelings as well.

1. *'Don't talk to me like that'* and *'I'm not interested in your opinion.'*
2. *'I do not like it when you address me in this tone'* or *'Why do you speak to me in this way?'*
3. *'You are always condescending'* or *'Another opinionated judgment.'*
4. *'This makes me really sad'* or *'It is not fair.'*
5. *'You must feel terrible.'*

In addition to the content of the message, a remark can also illustrate the relationship between the parties involved in a dialogue, and how they feel about each other. In the examples mentioned above this would be:

1. dominant;
2. formal or polite;
3. irritated or disinterested;
4. 'victim'-behavior (IV-3.1);
5. self-sacrificing.

Communication takes place at several levels simultaneously, especially at the level of content and the relationship between the parties involved.

In DIFFICULT CONVERSATIONS (Stone, Patton & Heen, 2011) three kinds of 'difficult dialogues' are identified that take place at the same time.

1. **The 'what happened' conversation:**
    - *Who is right?*
    - *Whose fault is it?*
    - *Why does the other party do what they are doing?*
2. **The 'feelings' discussion:**
    - *How do I deal with the feelings this stirs up in me?*
3. **The 'identity' dialogue:**
    - *What does this conversation/what do my feelings and these remarks say about me?*

The technique of meta-communication

Misunderstandings about content issues are usually easy to clear up. Misunderstandings about the relationship are usually more difficult to solve. Therefore, resolve content issues first. Next, address the interaction between the parties involved: describe the non-verbal behavior, how do they communicate with each other or with the mediator, what are they doing?

An example: A male and a female colleague are experiencing problems working together. The female co-worker constantly comments that she really appreciates the fact that the mediator is also female *'because this mediator will be more understanding of her point of view'.* The mediator can verbally react to this and explain the concept of mediator neutrality and that gender does not play a role at all. It is far more powerful when the mediator brings up the possible impact of the remarks on the male co-worker. For example, if the mediator, being a woman, asks the male party if he experiences a female bias during the mediation, or if the female co-worker's comments affect how he views the neutral position of the mediator.

See also dealing with risky questions posed by parties (III-7), and the webography in Resource H.

The opposite approach can also be a valuable technique. When confronted with an emotional outburst (relationship level) a mediator can also return to the content level, for example, by asking for information: *'What happened exactly?'*

The mediator can also bring up meta-communication and in this way try to achieve better collaboration between the parties. This is especially important when the communication seriously interferes with the mediation process, or when the performance of the mediator himself is an issue. However, it is not always necessary to bring up meta-communication. The mediator can also use it as a diagnosing tool to gain additional information. See also rationalizations (IV-4.5).

10 Asking questions

Definition/ description	Application	Example of application
	Asking questions	
1. Closed (III-10.1.1). 2. Straight (III-10.1.2). 3. Clarifying (III-10.1.3). 4. Open (III-10.1.4). 5. Relationship (III-10.2.1). 6. Circular (III-10.2.2). 7. Reciprocal (III-10.2.3). 8. Mirroring (III-10.2.4). 9. 'Peel-off' questions (III-10.3). 10. Confrontation (III-10.4.1). 11. Argumentative (III-10.4.2). 12. Tactical (III-10.5.1). 13. Verification (III-10.5.2). 14. Summarizing with a verification question (III-10.5.3). 15. Hypothetical (III-10.5.4).	The mediator asks questions to obtain information and to get important topics out in the open. Moreover, asking questions is a vital tool to manage/control the mediation and make progress. Not every sentence phrased as a 'question' is an actual question. Often an order or assignment is disguised as a question. A query is a true question if the other party is free to choose the answer they want to give (or to decide not to answer at all). Therefore, a question has to be perceived as such by the receiving party. Whether or not a question is a good one, depends mainly on its impact on the receiving party. Many mediators feel that asking questions is the most important tool for a mediator. However, being able to listen well is actually more important than asking the right questions (so do not forget effective listening!). Some mediators even regard asking questions as the 'only legitimate' intervention. However: please don't forget listening. Being able to listen well is more important than being able to ask the 'right' questions.	**1. Closed**: *'Does the team have an assignment?'* **2. Straight**: *'How long have you been working together?'* **3. Clarifying**: *'What do you mean when you say participate and perform well?'* **4. Open**: *'What aspects regarding your teamwork would you like to discuss?'* **5. Relationship**: *'When did you start working together? Who initiated it?'* **6. Circular**: *'What does B have to do to re-establish your trust in good teamwork? What can you offer B in order to make this possible for her to facilitate that?'* *'What can you offer B to enable her to accomplish this?'* **7. Reciprocal**: *'If B would change the way in which she works, what could you offer in return?'* **8. Mirroring**: *'Have you ever experienced that you were dependant on someone else's cooperation and the other person gave you the impression that she did not try hard enough? How did you react in that situation?'* **9. 'Peel-off' questions**: *'Please explain. What do you want? What makes that issue important to you?'* **10. Confronting questions**: *'Is that really what you want to happen? You say that she will have to leave the team but the way you say it gives me the impression that you doubt this would really solve the problems.'* **11. Argument**: *'You say that you want B to cooperate well in the team. Could you give an example of a situation where you thought B did not perform as she should? What caused your dissatisfaction? How did this affect the work?'* **12. Tactical question**: *'How long did you say you have been working together?'* **13. Verification question**: *'Is disappointed the correct word?'* **14. Summarizing question with verification question**: *'You have been working together for a number of years. From the beginning, you had different opinions on how the work should be performed, and agreements on deadlines have been a problem. Can I recap by saying that your diverse work styles did not cause difficulties at the start of your working as a team because you felt that the differences in approach also added value to the output of the team. But that now, with the increased pressure of work problems occur more often and you are both affected by this. Is that what it boils down to?'* **15. Hypothetical question**: *'Suppose we would be able to get everyone to work in the same way, would both of you then be willing to remain on the team?'* (see also reality testing future oriented III-11.1).

The mediator asks questions to obtain information and to get important topics out in the open. Moreover, asking questions is a vital tool to manage or control a mediation and to achieve progress.

Not every sentence that is phrased as a 'question' is an actual question. Orders or assignment are often disguised as questions. A query is a true question if the other party is free to choose the answer they want to give (or not to answer at all). Therefore, a question has to be perceived as a question by the receiving party. Whether or not a question is a good one depends mainly on its impact on the receiving party.

Many mediators feel that asking questions is the most important tool for a mediator (but do not forget effective listening). Some mediators even regard asking questions as the 'only legitimate' intervention.

Listening effectively is more important than asking questions. Listening for answers and information is the objective. Asking questions is merely a means to achieve this core objective.

10.1 Questions on a verbal level

Definition/description	Example of application
	Asking open and closed questions
	1. Closed. 2. Straight. 3. Clarifying. 4. Open.
Gather information, get important topics out in the open, manage/control the mediation and make progress.	**Closed**: *'Does the team have an assignment?'* **Straight**: *'How long have you been working together?'* **Clarifying**: *'What do you mean when you say participate and perform well?'* **Open**: *'What aspects regarding your teamwork would you like to discuss?'*

10.1.1 Closed questions

Closed questions are used to obtain concrete information or when there is a need is for a short answer (for example when the speaker is long-winded). A closed question is one that can only be answered, in principle, with yes/no or comparably limited alternatives. You can use closed questions for the above described purposes as long as you do it consciously. Do not use closed questions as a default setting, or too often, or in quick succession. Otherwise it can turn into a cross-examination. Another (opposite) risk of a closed question is that the expected answer is so short that the person answering the questions seizes the opportunity to start an elaborate speech: *'No, and let me explain to you exactly why'*, getting you the exact opposite of what you intended to get by asking the closed question.

Examples of closed questions:

'Does the team have an assignment?'

'Shall I close the window?'

'Which office is the largest: San Francisco, London or Melbourne?'

'Is the mortgage in both your names?'

10.1.2 Straight questions

A straight question is a request for factual information that is necessary to assess a given situation. It is a direct question, that leaves the respondent little room to dwell on the topic.

'How long have you been working together?'

'What is the team's assignment?'

'What was agreed on this matter during the negotiation?'

'Since when...?'

'What happened when she said that during that meeting?'

'How big is your garden?'

10.1.3 Clarifying questions

A question that is used to shed light on vague or ambiguous comments.

'Could you describe ... in more detail?'

'Where did the car start to break down?'

A more complicated example of a clarifying question:
Party A: *'We don't want a school here. It ruins the peaceful nature of our neighborhood.'*
Mediator (clarifying question): *'What do you mean when you say that the peaceful nature is ruined?'*
Party A: *'There is always a lot of noise, traffic, chaos around a school.'*
Mediator (clarifying question): *'Chaos? Can you give an example?'*

If the answer is vague, the mediator can repeat a question literally.
Mediator: *'How much will it cost you to repair the porch?'*
Party A: *'Well, we are talking about the materials, the wages of the workers, the paint job...'*
Mediator (repeats the question): *'So how much will it cost you to repair the porch?'*

10.1.4 Open questions

An open question is broad and gives the speaker room to elaborate on the answer in his own words. The answer to an open question can therefore offer a lot of information. See also dealing with emotions (IV-4.4).

Examples of open questions:

'What is the most important issue that you want to bring up?'

'What else would you like to add?'

'Can you tell me more about...?'

'What requirements should a solution meet for you to be satisfied with it ?'

'Can you indicate what your main concerns are?'

'How do you feel about the discussions?'

'What is your point of view on that matter?'

Ask questions that can be answered easily and clearly. Resist the temptation to combine too many aspects in one question. If you want information on several aspects, ask them one at the time. For example, if you want to know what B considers the three most bothersome aspects in party A's attitude, it is better to ask: ***'What is the most important problem for you regarding ....' 'Is there another problem?' 'Is there something else?'***

10.2 Questions on a relational level, connecting questions

Definition/description	Example of application
	Asking relationship questions
	1. Relationship 2. Circular. 3. Reciprocal. 4. Mirroring.
Gathering information, getting important topics into the open, manage/control the mediation and achieve progress.	**1. Relationship**: *'When did you start working together? Who initiated the collaboration?'* **2. Circular**: *'What does B have to do to re-establish trust in good teamwork? What can you offer B in order to make this possible for her, to facilitate that?'* **3. Reciprocal**: *'If B would change the way in which she works, what could you offer in return?'* **4. Mirroring**: *'Have you ever had the experience that you depended on someone else's co-operation and the other person gave you the impression that she did not try hard enough? How did you react in that situation?'*

10.2.1 Relationship questions

Relationship questions are designed to find out more about the connection between the parties, how they feel about each other, what they agree on and what is keeping them apart.

Examples of relationship questions:

'When was the partnership established?'

'Who initiated it?'

'What worked/works well in your team work?'

'Can you mention a good quality in A/B?'

'What caused (something in) your partnership to go wrong?'

'What have you done to try to resolve the dispute yourself?'

'How did you resolve your past disputes?'

10.2.2 Circular questions

By passing 'the ball' from one party to the other, the negotiators are actively involved in the search for a solution. Moreover, circular questioning encourages the parties to reflect on their own role in the continuation or solution of the conflict. It illustrates how a chosen behavior can determine the behavior of the other party. There is a recurring pattern of action, reaction and counter-reaction. Circular questions form a special group of relational questions. The mediator puts a question to party A in which a link is made to party B. Next, B is aked a question in which a connection is made to party A. This produces a virtual circle.

Examples of circular questions:
Mediator (question to A): *'What should B do to restore your trust in good teamwork?'*
Subsequently mediator (question to B): *'What can you offer A to...?'*
Mediator (question to A): *'How does your colleague react when you get angry about a comment she makes?'*
Subsequently mediator (question to B): *'And how does she react to that?'*
Mediator (question to A): *'What do you think is the most important reason for B to ...?'*
Next mediator (question to B): *'What can A do to support you on that issue?'*

This kind of questioning can be helpful in multiparty mediations. You can ask party A, for example, what B would need. Subsequently, the mediator can ask C whether C agrees with what A said or whether C can add something or whether he can offer something to support this.

10.2.3 Reciprocal questions

Reciprocal questions are comparable with circular questions (III-10.2.2) but they are put to one party and involve the 'give and take' principle.

'If you want the antique timepiece, then what do you think B should be offered in return?'

10.2.4 Mirroring/parallel situation

Mirroring gets the parties to stand in each others' shoes, like a role reversal. Mirroring a situation or behavior can increase understanding for the other party's point of view and position. It can help break down barriers between the parties, build mutual trust and stimulate the parties' determination to resolve the dispute themselves.

Examples of mirroring:

'Did you ever experience a situation where you... and how did you resolve it?'
'How would you react if it would happen to you that...?'
'What would you do if you were in A's shoes?'
'What if B at the time had done what you propose now? What would the situation be like now?'

Mirroring questions are risky if the presupposed situation did not take place. You then run the risk that the negotiator will give you a 'politically correct' answer. For example that if she were confronted with the same situation it would not be a problem at all, which means a very easy escape. Test the realism and reliability of the answer when using a mirroring question.

This questioning technique can also be used to discover the reverse side of negative aspects ('Every disadvantage has an equal and opposite advantage.')

'Would you miss anything if A no longer...?'

10.3 'Peel-off' questions

Definition/description	Example of application
Asking 'peel-off' questions	
Gathering information, clarifying interests and making progress.	**'Peel-off' questions**: *'Please explain ... '* *'What do you want?'* *'What makes that issue important to you?'*

Peel-off questions get their name from the metaphor: by peeling off the layers of an onion, you arrive at the center. The beauty of the comparison with an onion is that while there may be a center, there is no core, so all the layers are equally important. With the help of peel-off questions, the mediator tries to discover the true interests, deeper down, below the outer layers. The technique involves continuing to ask questions in order to move from positional responses to the actual interests. Good solutions can only be found if the layers of positional posturing can be peeled away to reveal the real interests of the parties.

Barendrecht and Kamminga (2004) distinguish four steps in peel-off questions: start with position(s), move to reasons behind positions, progress towards general interest(s) and finally arrive at personal, specific interest(s).

1. **Position**

   Party A: *'You either participate and perform well or leave the team.'*

2. **The reason**

   Mediator (question about the reason): *'How did you arrive at that opinion?'*

   Party A: *'B does not cooperate and does not stick to agreements we have made. She is costing more in terms of time and energy than she contributes to the result.'*

3. **General interest**

   Mediator (question about general interest): *'What do you want for yourself as well as for the team?'*

   Party A: *'That we all work well together with the same goal so we really get results.'*

4. **Specific personal interest**

   Mediator (question about personal interest): *'Why is that important to you?'*

   Party A: *'It's an important project for our department, and there is a huge time pressure. B has the technical expertise necessary to complete the project correctly and on time.'*

10.4 Confronting questions

Definition/description	Example of application
	Asking confronting questions
	1. Confrontation. 2. Argumentative.
Get important topics into the open, provoke discussion, make the parties look at their situation or behavior differently, make progress and break deadlocks.	1. **Confrontation question**: *'Do you really want that to happen? You say that he will have to leave the team but the way you say it gives me the impression that you have doubts about whether that would really solve the problems.'* 2. **Argumentative**: *'You say that you want B to cooperate well in the team. Can you give an example of a situation where B did not perform as you thought she should? What caused your dissatisfaction? And how did this affect the work?'*

10.4.1 Confrontation questions

The aim of a confronting question is to make parties look at their situation or behavior in a different light. It can be used to achieve forward movement in the mediation or to break an impasse. A question about a discrepancy between non-verbal behavior and what is said is usually also a confrontation question. *'You say the incident is not important but you sigh when you say it. Is it really of no importance to you?'* It is an effective, directive and therefore sometimes risky intervention that has to be applied with care. If a confronting question is incorrectly posed, the neutrality of the mediator and the trust in the mediation process can be impacted. Confronting questions can also be used in reality testing (III-11).

The technique of confronting questions

Be clear, do not use value judgments, keep the tone of your voice neutral. Realize that your own interpretations and opinions also affect how you structure your questions. Go about your questioning in a style that is acceptable to all involved and do not immediately put parties on the defensive.

Examples of confrontation questions:

A party says with an irritated expression on her face: 'Its fine with me, go ahead.'

The mediator: 'You say that you agree but you look angry. Do you really agree?'

Other examples of confrontation questions:

'Are you sure it will work out in practice, the way you imagine?'

'You say that the judge will definitely decide in your favor. I heard the other party say that taking legal action will work out positively for them. How sure are you of your case? Did you discuss it with your attorney?'

'What do you estimate is the likelihood of success? Can you express it as a percentage? 50%, 75%, 90%, 99%?'

'What do you think will happen if you both continue in this way?'

'What will your life be like in five years if ...?'

Confrontation questions and argumentative questions (III-10.4.2) must not be used too early in the mediation process or too often. Moreover, you are well advised to mitigate any harm from an intervention otherwise it may cause a problem later. How to neutralize the negative effects of an intervention and how to prevent escalation is described in the technique 'play along with the game' (IV-3.3.2).

'I'm asking this question because it is important that there is clarity about this matter so that you can look for a solution that meets the interests of both of you ....'

See demonstrating neutrality as well (II-2).

10.4.2 Argumentative questions

A well-known type of confronting questions are the 'why'-questions, known as a type of argumentative questions because of their capacity to provoke defensiveness and strong discussion. These argumentative questions have an important value to clarify the underlying issues of a position. An argumentative question can start with *'why'* or *'what'*. This kind of question can put a party on the defensive so they can only be asked if there is trust and a good working relationship between the mediator and the parties. Even then, it is not advisable to use this kind of questioning too often or for too long. Excessive use may suggest that the mediator doubts what a party is saying or can cause a party to feel they must defend themselves.

'What is the reason for ...?

'Why do you say ...?'

'Why do you want ...?'

A better technique is asking a range of questions that will answer your 'why-or why not' question without using the word 'why'. An example of the use of a range of argumentative questions:

'You are asking for $5 million compensation. How much revenue did you lose because the other party used your technology?'

'Isn't that far less than the $5 million in damages you are claiming?'

'How did you arrive at that figure?'

When you ask confronting questions in a caucus (II-16) there is less risk that a party feels they lose face or that your neutrality is affected. In some cases, however, you cannot avoid using a confronting question in the joint session.

Another technique is to use more open questions (III-10.1.4). For example use *'What happened?'* instead of *'Why are you late?'* or – even worse – *'Why aren't you on time?'* This prevents the addressee being put on the defensive, but still evokes a clear answer to the question

In one-on-one discussions, you can occasionally utilize putting somebody on the defensive with 'why'-questions. It can be deliberately used as a strategy with very difficult parties or parties' attorneys in the technique 'play their game' (IV-3.3.2) or with reality testing (III-11).

10.5 Strategic questions

Definition/ description	**Example of application**
	Asking strategic questions
	1. Tactical. 2. Verification. 3. Summarizing. 4. Hypothetical.
Gathering information, get important topics into the open.	**1. Tactical question**: *'How long have you been working together?'* **2. Verification question**: *'Is disappointed the correct word?'* **3. Summarizing question with verification question**: *'You have been working together for a number of years. From the beginning, you had different opinions on how the work should be performed and agreements on deadlines have been a problem. Can I recap by saying that your diverse work styles did not cause difficulties at the start of your working as a team because you felt that the differences in approach also added value to the output of the team. But now, with the increased pressure of work, problems occur more often and you are both affected by this. Is that what it boils down to?'* **4. Hypothetical question**: *'Suppose we could have everyone work in one way, would you both be willing to remain on the team?'* (see also reality testing future oriented III-11.1).

10.5.1 Tactical questions

If you want to highlight something, you can ask a question you already know the answer to, or just let the parties repeat something in order to emphasize a topic:

'How long did you say you have been working together?'

'Can you tell me once more how often it went well?'

'And you were successful in resolving these problems in the past?'

10.5.2 Verification questions

Verification questions are a kind of strategic questions. They are used in combination with other interventions to check if an interpretation is correct or if something is described and understood properly (III-2.3, III-3, III-4, III-5.2, III-6.2)

'Am I right in saying that you ...?'

'Do I understand you correctly that ...?'

'Angry, is that the right word?'

10.5.3 Summarizing questions

A summarizing question gives a summary or paraphrase of what has been said. The aim of a summarizing question is to determine whether your conclusions regarding the situation and the course of the process are correct, and to control the process (III-4).

'After several rounds of negotiation you have entered into a written agreement on issuing a license. The royalties under the license were lower than expected because of reduced sales. B experienced financial problems and you have discussed an installmentsplan for the license. For several reasons, B did not stick to the agreed installments. Is it fair to summarize that you have made subsequent arrangements regarding the financial aspects of your deal, but you did not stick to the agreement due to changed circumstance?'

10.5.4 Hypothetical questions

The mediator encourages parties to look at different points of views, events or proposals in more detail by asking hypothetical questions. The aim is to gain insight into the possibilities and to stimulate creativity. See also reality testing (III-11).

'Just imagine that financial aspects were not an issue. Would you then be willing to build a new garage together with your neighbors?'

'If the prior owner were still with the company, would you have received the salary increase you are asking for now?'

10.6 If there is no (informative) answer to a question

There are several reasons why somebody does not answer a question clearly. To determine how intervention is possible or if the mediator should intervene at all, the mediator must check why this party does not give an informative answer. The best way to achieve this is to compare this reaction with reactions of this same party to other questions, by assessing non-verbal behavior (III-2.3, III-18) and if necessary by asking a verification question (III-10.5.2).

First, check if the question was clear. For example, did you ask multiple questions in one sentence, was the question too vague or too broad, or was the scope too complex?

A party does not answer a question (properly)

	Reason	Action
☐	The meaning of the question is not understood.	Repeat the question, if necessary in other words.
☐	The question is ambiguous or too complex.	Repeat the question in other words and, if necessary, divide it into subquestions.
☐	A party does not come to the point or is vague.	Repeat the question in the same words (III-10.1.3).
☐	The negotiator does not want to answer because it concerns a sensitive matter or confidential information.	It may be an important subject, possibly even a blocking issue (II-8). Try to discuss the issue through reframing (III-6) or acknowledgement (III-5.2). Consider a caucus (II-16) or consider using confronting questions (III-10.4.1).
☐	The party does not know the answer.	Ask the other party if they know the answer or can give advice. Try acknowledgement (III-5.2). Consider bringing in an expert (I-7).
☐	Insufficient confidence in the mediator or in the mediation process.	Discuss this issue: meta-communication (III-9), change the players (IV-1.3.2) or stop the mediation.
☐	Emotions seriously inhibit communication or are the reason why a party is not able to think clearly.	Alleviate emotions or let parties vent them (relationship or communication is the cause of the conflict) (II-8.2), hold a recess, acknowledge (III-5.2), use effective listening (III-2), use interventions to deal with emotions (IV-4.4).

The way you formulate a question can influence the answer. When you do not want to direct an answer, formulate as neutrally as possible and refrain from using suggestive questioning (III-10.7): *'I assume this really made you mad?'* or *'You must have felt really let down?'*

10.7 Anchoring and formulating neutrally

Experiments prove that it makes a huge difference whether you ask eyewitnesses the question: *'At what speed did the car hit the tree?'* or *'How fast did the car crash into the tree?'* In the latter case, all eyewitnesses indicated that the car went extremely fast. The answer to the first question is usually more moderate. The reason for this is the anchoring effect, as it is known in social psychology. The process of thinking takes a lot of energy, so our brain tries to use shortcuts whenever possible. A familiar quantity is an easy anchor. So the moment a number or proposal is mentioned, it is often used as a reference point.

Turchin & McGuire (2005) described an experiment where the anchoring effect was demonstrated. Two groups were asked the following question: *'How long is the Mississippi River?'* The first group had the words *'longer or shorter than 800 miles?'* added to the question while the second group had *'longer or shorter than 5000 miles?'* added. The average answer in group one was significantly lower than the average answer in group two. So offering an anchor influences the answer even when the researchers clearly stated that the numbers 5000 and 800 were entirely random.[47]

In another experiment (Bodenhausen, 2000) it was even suggested that people who are sad or dejected – a state of mind quite common in a conflict – are even more sensitive to the effect of anchoring even though they took longer to respond.

A proposal or a number influences our ability to judge and can therefore influence the course of a negotiation or mediation. A mediator or negotiator can take advantage of this by deliberately avoiding giving anchors while asking a question. Avoid 'unwanted' anchors from being used as a reference point at an early stage. Be sure to introduce more than one alternative at the same time.

A mediator or negotiator can make use of anchoring by consciously introducing an anchor (for example a number or figure) in a mediation or negotiation where the parties either do not come to the point or are very far apart. Additionally, a mediator can explain the purpose and effect of anchoring to the negotiators to encourage them to put a proposal on the table.

Anchoring can play a role in determining if you should go first in mentioning a sum of money or putting your proposal on the negotiation table. A good rule of thumb is: Be the first to come up with your offer if you can make a realistic assessment of what would be a good deal in this case. You can then use the anchoring effect to make sure your number, proposal or figure will be a reference point in the discussions. In this addition this helps the other party to adjust their expectations to a realistic ZOPA (III-14.2) from the start. However, if you are unable to fully appraise what a good deal is – for example if you are new to the business or the market – it is wise to let the other party put their cards on the table first. It could very well be that their offer is far better or higher than what you wanted to ask for. Be aware of the anchoring effect on yourself in this scenario.

47 In case you are curious: The Mississippi river is 3766 kilometers long.

11 Reality testing

Definition/description	Application	Example of application
		Reality testing
To test the realistic nature of a position and to motivate the parties to resolve the dispute themselves. Reality testing empowers parties because it enables them to evaluate their own position as well as alternative solution options more realistically.	Trigger the parties' determination to settle the dispute themselves. Empowerment: by making the parties realize the consequences should they be unable to resolve the dispute themselves.	Test perceptions and expectations. **1. Reality testing hypothetical/future oriented (III-11.1)** *'What if we could develop a procedure to align all activities, and this enables you to work together in a way you are comfortable with; would you then see a possibility to form a functioning team together?'* or *'What if there was no time pressure at all? How ...?'* **2. Reality testing, risk analysis (III-11.2)** *'How will the output of the team be affected if B leaves the team? And how will the other team members react to that?'* **3. NAN (Negotiated Agreement Now) (III-11.3)** *'What would you be prepared to do to get rid of the whole business today? What are you willing to offer B to make that happen ...?'*

The mediator can test the realism of the parties' points of view, boost the mental process and encourage the parties' willingness to resolve a dispute themselves by asking questions like:

'You are saying this but I am hearing from A that ...'

'How sure are you of your case? 99% sure, 90%, 75%, 50%? Did you discuss this with your lawyer? How does he estimate your chance of success?'

'How much risk are you willing to take?'

'What if you win/lose the lawsuit and you remain neighbors ...'

'What if you are not able to resolve the matter now, what would be the consequences for ...?'

'What will be the effects on your colleagues/children?'

'How would you feel if ...?'

'If you were A and this proposal was presented to you, how would you respond?'

'I have the impression that we are not making any progress. What is the reason that we are not moving forward? I'm wondering if it is useful to continue this mediation?'

With these kinds of questions, the mediator helps the negotiators to think carefully about viewpoints, behaviors or offers. Moreover, he stimulates the parties' willingness to resolve the conflict themselves. In a joint session, a mediator should be careful when using this intervention – especially in the early stages of the mediation. This tool can jeopardize the neutrality of the mediator. See also confronting questions (III-10.4). In a caucus (II-16) or in a later stage of the mediation, (II-16 and II-14.3) it is a powerful intervention.

See also dealing with emotions (IV-4.5) and questioning techniques (III-10).

11.1 Reality testing: hypothetical/future oriented

By using hypothetical questions, the mediator encourages parties to want a settlement as well as thinking out-of-the-box. They are designed to gain insight into possibilities, to stimulate creativity and to make parties think in terms of opportunities rather than problems. *'What if we could develop a procedure you both can agree on, would you then see a possibility to form a functioning team?'*

Hypothetical questions (III-10.5.4):

'What if ...?'

'If this happens ...'

'Imagine ...'

'Suppose that ...'

Future-oriented questions help the parties to take a better look at their own points of view and proposals, as well as those of the other side. They are intended to gain insight in the possibilities and to stimulate creativity.

If you are looking for real answers, do not ask future-oriented reality-testing questions. You cannot test the answer, because in theory everything can become reality in the future. Use these questions to encourage out-of-the-box thinking.

11.2 Reality testing: risk analysis

The mediator can test the degree of realism in the parties' positions by asking risk analysis questions. These questions can also help to explore the realism of perceptions and expectations and probabilities. Moreover, they can support the exploration of WATNA (III-14).

An example of risk analysis:

'You are selling your product worldwide and legal proceedings have been initiated in various countries. What will happen if B wins their case in one of these countries and they are allowed to use your technology? What can you offer them now that would help get this case resolved by yourselves?'

'What do you think the chances are that you will be successful in court and that you can go on using this technology? I just heard you say that the worst-case scenario is that you would have to take the product off the market and pay damages after lengthy court proceedings. How would that affect your business? What can you do to resolve this issue yourself?'

Reality testing can encourage parties to make an effort to resolve the dispute themselves. Therefore, it can empower the parties. It helps them focus on the potential consequences if the dispute is not resolved (by them).

> *'Think about the following scenario ...'*
>
> *'What would happen then?'*

11.3 NAN

Negotiated Agreement NOW (NAN)[48] is a special form of reality testing. The mediator checks with the parties how much it is worth to them in terms of time, money and concessions to get the dispute over and done with (now/today). NAN stimulates the parties to strive for a quick settlement. This creates forward movement in the mediation.

An example of NAN:

> *'How much money would it be worth to you to be done with the whole business today?'*
>
> *'What are you prepared to do to be able to leave all the problems behind?'*
>
> *'What are you willing to do to make sure that this week ...?'*

Articles on reality testing can be found on www.beyondintractability.org and www.crinfo.org.

12 The one text procedure

In a one text procedure, the negotiations do not take place directly between the parties. In successive caucuses (II-16) the mediator explores the underlying interests with the individual parties. Together with each party, the mediator tries to find as many options as possible (III-15) to meet those interests (II-7). The focus is on preparing one joint document. The caucus and detailed exploration of the interests prevent, or at least minimize positional bargaining. Parties are more or less forced to negotiate on principles (II-4). The focus remains on the interests because they are negotiating through an intermediary and they cannot respond to positions and arguments of the other party in a direct interaction. When the previously agreed time expires, or if the joint document is ready, the final version is put before the parties as a 'take it or leave it' choice. They can then either accept or reject the final document. In its purest form, the one text procedure is a very structured mediation variant.

Raiffa (1982) describes the course of a complete formal one text procedure in THE ART AND SCIENCE OF NEGOTIATION.

48 NAN is described in the training manual of NCRC (at the time SDMC) 1998/1999.

The rest of this chapter deals with how to use the 'one text tool' as an element in a regular mediation or negotiation.

The technique of the one text procedure

The one text procedure can be used as a technique within a mediation procedure or negotiation. The formal one text procedure takes place entirely in caucus. As a mediation technique, the one text part also takes place in caucus, but the rest of the mediation can be in joint session as well, depending on the style of the mediator (I-2.1).

The one text procedure can be used as a tool during a mediation if, for example, the interests seem to be clear but the negotiators' conduct remains positional, for example because of unidentified underlying interests. This can first be explored in a caucus (II-16) before the one text procedure is applied. It can also be a useful tool when there is little time to prepare a collective document, for example a statement, formal agreement or proposal.

Prepare a first draft and put this text before the parties. Ask for comments and amendments to the document in successive caucuses. Work out with the negotiators in each round what interests are not yet met in the current text. Parties usually find it difficult to state exactly what they need. Criticizing is far easier. In the one text procedure, the negotiators are asked to comment on a specific proposal and subsequently brainstorm with the mediator and the other party on how to improve it. Prepare a second draft and keep repeating the procedure until all options have been investigated fully. Prepare the final document when you think that no further improvements are possible and put it before the parties as a 'take it or leave it' proposition.

This tool can also be used as a 'last resort' option when every possible alternative approach has been tried but the parties still cannot reach agreement (not even about what other method can be used to resolve the dispute.) In this case, the mediator has a choice between terminating the mediation and proposing that parties ask a third party for advice. Depending on his style, the mediator himself can make some suggestions. This last ditch approach, however, is not without risk (I-7). In addition, a mediator can draw up a list of current options with the negotiators (III-20) or he can apply the one text procedure.

13 Mutualizing (finding common ground)

Definition/description	Application	Example of application
Mutualizing (find common ground, or joint interests)		
Emphasize common facts and mutual interests. Mutualizing offers clients the opportunity to look at themselves, the other party and the problems in a different way, namely not only in terms of your/my point of view, but also from a joint perspective.	Progress can by demonstrated and the understanding of the other party's position increased by highlighting shared interests and common concerns. The negotiators realize that in addition to their differences they also have common ground. Negative stereotyping is avoided, or at least reduced in intensity.	*'You both think it is important that the team performs well?'*

Mutualizing clarifies common facts and interests. This technique advances party A's understanding of party B's point of view. The negotiators realize that besides differences of opinion, there are also common perceptions and interests. Mutualizing helps parties stop blaming the other party entirely for the conflict without taking their own role into account. (IV-4.5).

The technique of mutualizing

Accusations can be characterized as a mutual problem by positive or neutral reframing (III-6).
A says: *'You always criticize everything I say.'*
B says: *'Look who is talking, you never ever listen to a word I say.'*
Mediator: *'You both want the communication between you to be satisfactory.'*

Mutualizing can be done by emphasizing positive aspects or by discovering shared interests and goals. The mediator can ask questions about why the parties started working together, what was good about the teamwork and why, and how conflicts were resolved in the past. The mediator can also ask one party to mention positive qualities or actions of the other party. In addition, the mediator can ask the negotiators what they want and how this can be achieved. For example, let the clients describe the 'ideal' collaboration in a positive future scenario. This often proves to be a difficult assignment. It is far easier to criticize and say what you do not want than to formulate exactly what you do want. In the one text procedure this mechanism is utilized (III-12).

14 BATNA, WATNA, RATNA, leverage and ZOPA

Best/Worst/Realistic Alternative to Negotiated Agreement (BATNA/WATNA/RATNA) and **Zone of Potential Agreement** (ZOPA) indicate the potential settlement range. Exploration of the BATNA assures that the solution reached in the mediation will be

better than the available alternatives. Exploration of the RATNA and the WATNA forms a useful platform to support reality testing (III-11). Leverage means the opportunites (power/ascendancy/circumstances) a party has to reach agreement on their terms. It can be used to analyze which party benefits most from reaching the agreement and which party will be more able to gain ascendancy over the other party. ZOPA indicates the limits for a possible settlement.
The aim is to find a benchmark standard or objective to compare solutions against, and to empower the negotiators.

More about settlement ranges can be found in Moore (2014), who describes the technical procedure. The efficiency of the result of a mediation is dealt with by Raiffa (1996), who uses a quantitative approach.

14.1 BATNA/WATNA/RATNA

BATNA[49] involves determining the best alternative that can be expected if the parties cannot reach agreement, the WATNA is the worst alternative and RATNA is what will probably happen. This technique stimulates the negotiators' determination to resolve the dispute themselves and is also designed to enable the mediated solution to be compared to the alternatives. BATNAs and WATNAs can be regarded as the principled counterpart of the positional bottom line. All negotiators need to focus on the bare minimum they are willing to accept or the maximum they are willing to offer. Some mediators prefer to talk about **Estimated Alternative to a Negotiated Agreement** (EATNA), or **Realistic Alternative to a Negotiated Agreement** (RATNA) because the alternatives as envisaged by the parties are often unrealistically positive (IV-2.3).
For some incompatible differing interests it is not possible to find a joint solution. If the negotiators are also not prepared to compromise on these differences, the mediator can help the parties by discussing their BATNA and then analyze whether another method could be helpful to reach a solution. By reality testing and with the support of the Worst Alternative to Negotiated Agreement (WATNA), the negotiators can check whether it would be advisable to reach a compromise.
The concept of RATNA is based on the concept of MLATNA (Most Likely Alternative to Negotiated Agreement) that was first described in the UK edition of 'MEDIATION: PRINCIPLES, PROCESS, PRACTICE', by Nesic and Boulle (2001), and the second edition (Australia 2005) by Boulle, a reference book that has set a high benchmark for both mediation texts and for mediation practice. Next to giving an overview of the state of the art techniques, mediation methods and choices a mediator faces, the book also deals with the decision-making process in a mediation.

49 The concept is introduced in GETTING TO YES, (Fisher, Ury and Patton 1999).

Definition/description	Application	Example of application
BATNA & WATNA & RATNA & Leverage & ZOPA		
Benchmark, objective or measure to compare solutions. **BATNA** is the acronym for Best Alternative to Negotiated Agreement. This is the most positive scenario that can be envisaged if the negotiators fail to reach a settlement. **WATNA** is the acronym for Worst Alternative to Negotiated Agreement. This is the most negative scenario if the negotiators are unable to reach an agreement. **RATNA** is the acronym for Realistic Alternative to Negotiated Agreement. This is the most realistic scenario that can be expected if the negotiators do not settle their dispute. **Leverage** is any potential opportunity (power/chances/time/ascendancy, etc.) that a party may exploit to manipulate the outcome of a negotiation in such a way that an agreement is reached on his terms. Whether on a commercial or personal level, the party with the greater need to reach a deal usually has the least leverage. **ZOPA** is the acronym for Zone of Potential Agreement. It is the area within which a settlement can theoretically be reached.	**BATNA** & **WATNA** & **ZOPA** together delineate the potential settlement range. **Leverage** gives an indication of the power balance that determines where, within the range, the settlement will most likely be reached. Exploration of the **BATNA** ensures that the mediated outcome is better than the available alternatives. The worst alternative, **WATNA**, can provide a basis for reality testing (III-11) and open up an analysis of the **RATNA** (Realistic Alternative to Negotiated Agreement). **Leverage** plays a role in assessing the power balance. It is an analytical tool to assess which party will benefit most from reaching an agreement, which party will be better able to dictate the terms of the agreement, and how one party can potentially gain the upper hand over the other. **ZOPA** indicates the limits to a possible settlement. Remember to expand the pie. Do not limit yourself or the negotiators to ZOPA too quickly. The ZOPA can expand along with the subject matter under discussion.	**BATNA** 1. The company's Board agrees with A, so B is removed from the team. B's replacement quickly adjusts and performs exactly as A wants. 2. The other team members think A is overreacting and do not want to work with A anymore. B forms a new team under her supervision. **WATNA** 1. The project that the team is working on fails and A is blamed. 2. The Board agrees with A, and B is subsequently dismissed. **RATNA** 1. The other team members are affected by the problems and either choose A's or B's side. The team is divided and the output suffers because of the internal problems. This negatively affects the company as well as the image of A and all the other team members. 2. The cooperation between A and B remains difficult and the work suffers. This is consuming a lot of B's energy and enthusiasm, which in turn has negative consequences for the output and B's wellbeing. **LEVERAGE** 1. A knows she will soon be nominated for a position on the Board of Directors. In order to maximize her prospects she wants a perfectly functioning team. She therefore needs to solve the problems with B as soon as possible. 2. However, B does not care how long it takes to solve the problems; after A there will be another project leader who will probably see things differently. Moreover she knows that the company cannot do without her as she is the only employee with specialist knowledge in a particular area. B probably has greater leverage in this scenario. **ZOPA** (a financial example as presented in III-14.3 provides a clearer illustration of the ZOPA concept) 1. At minimum, A wants all tasks that have been agreed to be finished on time and the output to meet minimum quality standards. 2. B wants to determine for herself how she carries out her work and she wants to make sure her other duties and projects do not suffer because of her work for the team. The ZOPA will be somewhere between: (1) the agreement that B determines how and when to carry out the work and (2) the guarantee that the output is delivered on time and in accordance with the specific quality requirements.

BATNA, WATNA and RATNA also play an important role in caucuses and in one-on-one negotiations (i.e. without a mediator being present). It is always very important to know your alternatives before you enter into any negotiation. This knowledge gives you leverage because you know at which point you can or should walk away from the table and you know exactly what to expect if you do so. Knowing your BATNA is also helpful in assessing the value of a negotiated outcome – is it better than your BATNA? (II-4).

14.2 Leverage

Leverage is the means (power/ascendancy/circumstances) a party in a negotiation has to reach agreement on their terms (i.e. to influence the result). The more leverage you have, the less demand is placed on your negotiation skills. The less leverage you have, the more you need to bring negotiation skills to the table. Shell (2007) describes leverage as: 'The balance of needs and fears' on both sides of the negotiation table.
The party who really needs to achieve a deal within a limited period of time, or who wants to change the status quo, or has the most to lose from not reaching a deal, is the party with the least leverage. The party who has less at stake (if an agreement is not reached), who has acceptable alternatives or who is not pressed for time is the party with the greatest leverage.
For that matter: even if you have a lot of leverage and power in a negotiation, it is rarely advisable to just force your terms on the other party, without taking their interests into account. Apart from the fact that your assessment of the other party's leverage might be wrong, you miss a valuable opportunity to expand the pie together (II-7.2.2 and III-15.2). Moreover, you will probably meet again and you might have less leverage then.

Leverage is also affected by how the other party perceives your leverage, and also your BATNAs and WATNAs. Sometimes, in the real world, negotiators make wildly erroneous assumptions – both positive and negative – about the other party's situation and sentiments. So communicating your BATNAs and WATNAs to the other party can dramatically alter their view of your leverage, and also their assessment of their own leverage. This is why misinformation, bluff, threats, theatrics and even lies are so common in conventional negotiations. All of these effects can be minimized when a neutral third party is involved who helps the parties, in equal measure, switch their focus towards interests and away from tactical positioning.

Leverage can be increased by:

- ☐ Developing **alternatives** and improving your BATNA (III-14.1) to become less dependent on reaching a deal (with this party).
- ☐ Developing alternatives which makes **the other side's WATNA** even worse (III-14.1).
- ☐ Eliminating or reducing **time pressure** on you, and/or increasing that pressure on the other side.
- ☐ Creating a situation in which **the other party has more to lose** if they **do not reach an agreement**. Shell (2007) describes three ways to achieve this:
  - **Positive stimulation**: you are able to offer the other party something they definitely want or need, or you can enable them to obtain or do something they want or need. This does not necessarily have to be in the shape of something tangible or concrete. Immaterial matters such as recognition or appreciation, obtaining a good image or reputation, to be recognized as being 'right', assistance in gaining support from a difficult constituency can all be offered. In order to know what the other party wants, and, more importantly, needs, you need to listen well (III-2) and ask relevant questions (III-10).
  - **Negative stimulation**: the other party wants you to do something or wants to prevent you from doing something. In order to gain negative leverage you can let the other party know that you have the possibility to undertake a certain action or take something away. For example, you could involve the press, change the members of the negotiating team, introduce new terms or start negotiations with a third party. All of these actions make the other party's BATNA less attractive, worsens their WATNA, or improves your own BATNA.

    Don't forget the strong influence of loss-minimizing (III-16.4).

  - **Normative stimulation**: you enable the other party to act consistently with their earlier statements, thereby avoiding loss of face. Examples of consistent conduct are maintaining confidence (i.e. not betraying trust), valuing a fair deal, being perceived as reasonable/right-minded, sticking to objective criteria or principles developed earlier, etc. Reinforce 'irrational escalation of commitment' (IV-2.4) in the other party: so much has already been invested in trying to reach this agreement that we would all lose too much if we withdraw now.

    See IV-2.4 dysfunctional behavior.

    You can also use perspective to increase leverage (IV-2): you only gain leverage if the other party thinks you have leverage, which is more important than actually having it. As a variation on Shakespeare: *leverage can be bought by judgement of the eye.*[50] However, make sure you do not lose credibility as a negotiator. In general, bluffing is not a wise strategy.

50 'Beauty is bought by judgment of the eye', Shakespeare in Love's Labour's Lost. Compare also with the proverb: 'Beauty is in the eye of the beholder'.

The BATNA and leverage evolve during the mediation process or negotiation, for example because new information becomes available, or because circumstances change. Regard the BATNA and leverage as dynamic elements and check regularly if there are changes that require you to readjust your assessment of the position of the negotiators.

Another way to increase the chances of reaching a deal on your terms is to use anchoring (III-10.7): the first figure or value that is put on the negotiation table can form a benchmark throughout the entire negotiation or mediation.

In BARGAINING FOR ADVANTAGE (1999) Shell addresses the concept of leverage in more depth and also provides many examples of gaining leverage.

14.3 ZOPA

The Zone of Possible Agreement (ZOPA) is the bargaining field in which an understanding is possible. The bottom line or minimum conditions to which a negotiator can agree are determined by each party's alternatives and how these are assessed. The zone of possible agreement is between the minimum that will satisfy party A and the maximum that party B is willing to give.

What is ZOPA?
Suppose John wants to sell a second-hand laptop to Mike. If Mike is not willing to spend more than $750 and John wants to receive a minimum of $950, there is no zone in which they can reach an agreement. If, however, Mike is willing to spend up to $1000 and John wants to receive at least $800, the ZOPA is between $800 and $1000.

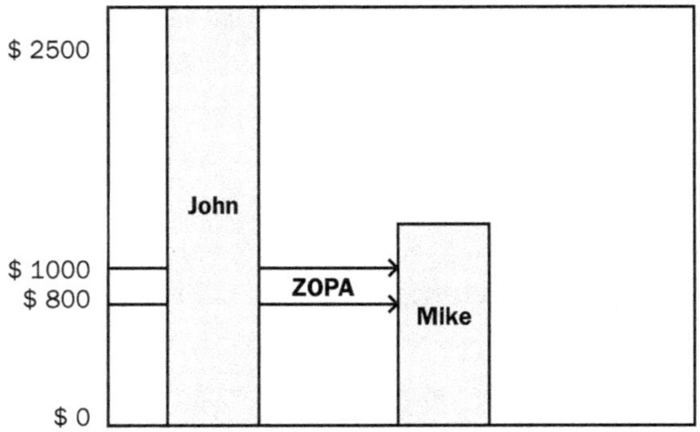

To determine the ZOPA it is necessary to know the parties' respective interests and alternatives. If John received an offer from Pete to buy the laptop for $900, the ZOPA range resets itself to between $900 and $1000. If in addition Mike saw another laptop for $950, then the ZOPA resets itself to between $900 and $950.
Mike can also consider buying a new laptop for $1600 because it is not easy for him to transfer the files of his old PC to the laptop. He hopes that the shop will do this for him if he buys a new laptop. If John offers to sell the laptop for $1000 and promises Mike to transfer his files, the deal can be done because they enlarged the pie.

Do not limit the negotiators or yourself as a mediator to ZOPA too quickly. This can inhibit the opportunities for expanding the pie (III-16) or for completely different, out-of-the-box solutions. Initially, it is better to keep the parties' ZOPA to yourself to use as a broad guideline and not discuss it with the parties too early.

Many weblinks on BATNA/WATNA and ZOPA are included in the webography in Resource H.

15 Generate options

Definition/description	Application	Example of application
Generate options		
Develop ideas or ways to arrive at potential solutions and to find outcomes that take into account all identified interests. Stimulate creativity and associ-ative thinking; expand the pie and find optimal solutions.	Enable parties to let go of their initial positions by broadening the horizons. Develop out-of-the-box solutions based on interests. Generating more than one option prevents the parties from hurriedly agreeing to one (potentially sub-optimal) solution. If the parties return to their earlier positions during the options phase, the mediator needs to return to the exploration phase.	**Techniques for generating options**: - brainstorming; - expand the pie; - prepare lists and discuss them; - develop one shared vision; - seek advice from experts; - invite the mediator to suggest options; - consult external sources; - stimulate creativity and abandon rigid thinking frames

15.1 Brainstorming

After the exploration phase, the mediator can support the negotiators in a brainstorming session about possible solutions. During a brainstorming session, every idea is a good idea. Ideas are never criticized during a brainstorming session. In addition, it should be clear that the negotiators are not bound to any idea generated during a brainstorming session nor are any deemed to have been put on the table (II-12 and I-8). Brainstorming must be separated from making decisions and committing to specific solutions. All options are taken into account and are often recorded on a flip-chart. The mediator stimulates brainstorming by asking questions (III-10) and by encouraging 'outside the box' thinking. Evaluation does not take place until all ideas have been explored (see hint under this section and III-15.2).

In addition to subjective criteria (interests), objective criteria can be formulated that a (theoretical) solution should meet (III-16.1). To facilitate negotiations about what solutions will be selected, the best options from the brainstorming session can be compared to these objective norms during the negotiation phase. Consider a second round of brainstorming sessions for the options that survived the tests of evaluation and comparison with the subjective and objective criteria. Perhaps these solutions can be further improved.

Hints to facilitate brainstorming sessions:

- Keep the focus on the problem to be solved; do not spend time on unproductive side-issues.
- Do not criticize each other or each other's ideas. Criticism inhibits creativity.
- Ensure all parties are able to contribute to the brainstorming.
- Create an enthusiastic, open atmosphere.
- Do not dwell on one theme or idea for too long.
- Encourage the parties to invent solutions for each other's issues or problems.
- Pick up ideas and try to improve upon them.

15.2 Other methods for generating options

In addition to brainstorming there are other methods by which the mediator can enable parties to discuss alternative solutions without holding them to any:

- **Expand the pie**
  Impasses can often be attributed to a 'fixed pie assumption' (IV-1.2). The negotiators assume that there is only a limited amount of resources to be divided between them; the more one party gets, the less there is left for the other party. You can break through this assumption by searching for interests and exploring matters that are not necessarily part of the conflict but can contribute to finding a solution. This expands the field of reciprocal interests and leaves more pie to be shared. The pie can also be expanded by redefining a problem and by asking questions which cause the parties look differently at the problem (III-6, III-11).
- **Prepare lists and discuss them**
  The negotiators and party advisors can each prepare a list with as many options as possible. Next, these possible solutions are discussed in a joint session. If there are many parties or representatives involved in the mediation, the ideas can first be discussed in sub-groups. Each group decides what ideas will be discussed in the subsequent plenary meeting.

The concept of 'Wish Lists' involves parties compiling a list of what they want from the other party, and another list of what they think the other party wants from them. These lists are initially disclosed in confidence to the mediator. The mediator can review them in private and decide whether to negotiate a release from confidentiality, leading to an exchange of wish lists. He can subsequently decide whether there is a sufficient basis for a joint session to discuss a reciprocal exchange of Wish List items.

- **Develop one mutual vision**
  A shared vision is developed based on a mutual objective. Next, as many completely compatible solutions as possible are thought up.
- **Seek advice from experts**
  An expert can be invited to take part in the discussions, brainstorming sesions or the preparation of the optional solutions lists.
- **Let the mediator develop options as well**
  The mediator can actively participate in the brainstorming or one of the other methods described above. In this case, the mediator would not just facilitate, but also offer suggestions.
- **Consult external sources**
- **Stimulate creativity and let go of narrow lines of thought, use different thinking frames**

It is wise always to bring up at least two solutions or options as a mediator. Offering only one suggestion carries the risk of being seen as 'mediator advice' (I-7).

16 Reaching agreement

Definition/description	Application	Example of application
	Objective criteria	
An objective standard, principle or benchmark can be used for those components of the dispute that lack sufficient subjective criteria (interests) to enable the parties to reach settlement. The mediator and the parties can look for objective criteria such as market value. The development and application of objective criteria also facilitates reaching agreement with the parties' constituencies.	If the parties fail to generate enough feasible solutions based on subjective criteria (interests), objective criteria can be applied as a second step. These facilitate reaching agreement by comparing a solution with an objective standard.	**Possible objective criteria**: - What output does the Board expect from the team? - How do other teams cooperate? - How were similar difficulties handled within the company or how would another company deal with them? - If the conflict escalated and was brought before a court, how would a judge rule? - What does the human resources department say? - What arrangements were made between the team members at the start?

16.1 Develop objective criteria and select options

In principled negotiations, as defined for example in the Harvard Project on Negotiation (II-4), the development of objective criteria is seen as an important tool. It can be used to neutralize bluffing and coercion. In addition, it helps to persuade the opposing party and is a guideline for fair and reasonable solutions.

In a mediation setting, objective criteria can help assess alternative solutions and the options that were developed during the brainstorming phase. This is especially important when the negotiators failed to develop sufficient subjective criteria (interests) (II-7) or where it is difficult to generate enough options that meet the interests. Moreover, objective criteria can facilitate acceptance by a party's own constituency (I-2.7.2 and IV-6.1).

The negotiation between the parties is facilitated when different options can be compared with the objective criteria that a theoretical solution should meet. Furthermore, neutral criteria simplify the negotiation about concessions and exchange, as well as the determination of the (comparative) value of an or interest.

In a mediation objective standards are sometimes unnecessary because the developed options meet all the subjective standards of the parties (interests). However, applying an objective criterion can greatly facilitate the negotiation about what options should be selected. Therefore, if decisionmaking based on subjective criteria fails, the mediator can draw upon the objective criterion as another important tool to reach agreement. A solution that is supported by an objective benchmark also increases the acceptance of the chosen solution by the parties and by their constituents.

An objective criterion should be clear and unambiguous. Additionally, it must be possible to determine an objective criterion apart from the (personal) intentions of the parties. Examples of objective criteria:

- market value;
- the customary method of appraising value in a market;.
- fairness and reasonableness;
- precedent;
- the state-of-the-art in science or an expert opinion;
- the initial value less depreciation;
- cost of replacement;
- code of conduct (written or unwritten);
- efficiency;
- effectiveness;
- ethics;
- principles and values;

- equal treatment;
- tradition;
- reciprocity;
- what has been agreed;
- reasonable impressiosn or expectations in the circumstances;
- what was/would be settled or agreed with a third party in the circumstances.

More on objective criteria in Fisher, Ury, Patton (1999) GETTING TO YES: NEGOTIATING AGREEMENT WITHOUT GIVING IN.

16.2 Other methods

Other methods of reaching agreement:

- **The one text procedure (III-12)**
- **Developing a mutual vision (III-15.2)**
  The mediator can formulate a higher objective or mutual objectives, based on which a joint vision can be developed. Next, the mediator and parties can decide which solutions best support this higher objective.
- **Structured process of 'give and take'**
  The mediator asks each party what interests or positions they may be willing to concede and what they would expect from the other party in return. This is the basis for a process of reciprocal exchange or 'give and take'.
- **Call in experts (III-15.2)**
  An expert can be involved to assess different initial steps towards solutions (I-7). This expert evaluates the solution based on his or her general knowledge and principles, or standards that have been agreed previously, for example objective criteria or the parties' interests (if these are identified clearly).
- **Mediator advice (III-15.2)**
  The mediator can also play the role of an external expert as described above, if the parties expressly ask him to do so. However, this is not without risks and consequences. Therefore, the mediator must make an informed choice before he takes on the role of expert. Moreover, conditions and safeguards are required (I-7).

16.3 Reactive devaluation

Reactive devaluation is the effect that a perfectly reasonable proposal can have on somebody who distrusts the source of the proposal: *'It is your proposal, so it must be unfavorable for me.'* The vicious circle in mediation is that reactive devaluation can also play a role in initiating a mediation procedure. The opposing party often thinks that the person proposing the mediation must have an ulterior motive or is in a weak position.

Consequently, it is often very difficult to get both parties to the mediation table. A similar effect can be observed if one party presses hard to appoint a specific mediator.
In the phase in which the negotiators need to reach agreement on the solution, it is also important to avoid the negative impact of reactive devaluation. A mediator can reduce this effect by not referring to certain issues, proposals, agenda items, or proposed solutions in terms of 'belonging to' or originating with one or the other party. It is far better to prepare a joint overview with ideas on agenda and other issues, and skate over the ownership of the idea. See the hint for making a negotiation agenda (I-6). Please note: the mediator can be the cause of reactive devaluation as well.

If you know how reactive devaluation works, you can also make use of its effect. By accepting a proposal from the opposing party, you can create an advantage for yourself, for example by accepting the mediator preferred by the opponent or by agreeing that a specific person takes part in the mediation on behalf of that party. You can also accept the location for the negotiation proposed by the other party. The advantage of doing so is that the opposing party will probably trust this mediator or representative, or feel comfortable at that specific venue. This ensures that reality testing or proposals are less vulnerable to reactive devaluation, for it is their mediator, their representative or their venue.

16.4 Loss minimizing

Social psychology has shown that people instinctively dislike losing something, so will try harder to avoid a loss than to secure a prospective gain. If a risky decision must be made, a party will more readily comply with a proposal if they think they can prevent a loss. However, an opportunity to gain something is a less powerful motivation for accepting an offer. Minimizing loss is therefore more important in decision making than maximizing gains is.

A mediator or negotiator can use the phenomenon of loss minimizing by reframing a proposal or an offer in terms of avoiding loss, instead of emphasizing its quality in terms of possible gain. This can even be done literally by putting something tangible on the table, for example, a bank draft or a draft settlement in a mediation. If the opponent does not accept the offer or draft, it can be helpful to physically remove this tangible representation of the offer from the table (i.e. returning the paper to your suitcase), thereby visualizing the 'loss'.

17 Use of voice and silence

Definition/description	Application	Example of application
Use of voice and silences		
Interventions are also possible through use of voice (or, conversely, silence) and the way the voice is used.	Manage communication and control the process by respecting silences and the use of the voice.	**Silences**: - Be comfortable with silences. - Bring prolonged and unhelpful silences to an appropriate end. - Make 'silent parties' participate in the mediation. **Using the voice (technique):** - Vary with the voice and intonation: volume, pitch, tone, speed. - The way of speaking: hesitant, timid, bold. - In the case of intense emotions or a great deal of noise, speaking slowly and in a clear and quiet tone can be helpful.

Making effective use of silence means:

- daring to observe silence;
- breaking through prolonged (unproductive) silence;
- getting 'silent parties' to participate more vocally in the process.

Whether and how you should intervene depends on the reason for the silence.

- If the silence can be attributed to insecurity or confusion or if a party does not know what else to say you can bring that up. You can reframe it into a feeling as well, to let the party involved know that such a feeling is acceptable.
  'Our discussion has progressively become more complex. Let's recap to see where we are.'
  'I can imagine that it is probably hard for you to make a decision like that.'I notice that it is tough for you to ....'
- If the reason for the silence is anger, you can ask questions or use an acknowledgement to encourage more expression:
  'Could you tell us more about this?'
  'I have the impression that this makes you angry. Is angry the correct word?'
- If the silence is caused by someone thinking or needing time for internal reflection after an emotional outburst, respect that silence.
- If the silence is caused by an impasse, it can be very wise *not* to intervene. The situation or the silence can become so uncomfortable that the parties will continue or even make a unilateral proposal (IV-1).
- The mediator can offer a (content) reflection (III-5.1) on the silence to avoid the impression that the mediator himself feels uncomfortable with it.
  'You have been silent for a long time. Can you tell me the reason?'
  'I can see we are all thinking hard to find the right way forward. (I might have an idea ...')
  Or give an acknowledgement:
  'Such a long silence can feel uncomfortable, can't it?'

Whether or not you want to intervene in a silence can also depend on the phase of the mediation, as well as your mediation strategy (I-2.1). At the outset of the mediation process, it is usually wise to be proactive to avoid losing control for the rest of the process. There is also a risk that one party will start dominating the entire session if the mediator is too reactive in the beginning. From the exploration phase onwards, it can be advisable to respect silence - depending on what caused it - and to watch what happens. To expedite this, the mediator can also use paradoxical intervention (III-19).

Paul Ekman, together with the Dalai Lama, has created a wonderful website called "The Atlas of Emotions". It is an interactive tool designed to help describe emotions and expand your vocabulary when discussing them. The goal is to gain a better understanding of what triggers emotions and how to respond to them, both individually and with others. The website features a beautiful layout and a clear, organized categorization of emotions, along with a timeline of how these emotions are triggered. It covers not only negative emotions such as anger, fear, disgust, and sadness, but also positive ones such as joy. You can explore this valuable resource at https://atlasofemotions.org/.

18 Non-verbal behavior

Definition/description	**Application**	**Example of application**
	Non-verbal interventions and non-verbal communication	
Clarify interactions or confront parties, for example, by pointing out any discrepancies between what the parties are saying and how they are behaving. Demonstrate the impartiality and the commitment of the mediator. Regulate communication between the parties, and between the parties and the mediator.	By bringing attention to the non-verbal communications of the parties, the mediator is able to clarify or magnify issues or to confront parties (III-10.4). Through body language, the mediator can emphasize his commitment to the mediation and his impartiality. In this way, a mediator can also manage the process.	**Pointing out body language of the parties** : - *'I notice that you are smiling.'* - *'While you are saying this you shrug your shoulders.'* **To show that you are listening (III-2)**: - Facial expression (smiling, looking interested, frowning). - Maintain eye contact without staring. - Gestures (nodding, jotting down key words, hand gestures). - Attitude (relaxed, facing the parties). **Non-verbal communication**: - Give a sign, for example hold the palm of the hand up to indicate 'stop.' (But beware - different gestures may have different meanings in different cultures). - Emphasize verbal communication. - Shrug shoulders. - Express emotions. Reflect feelings in facial expression or body language. - Control the communication. Supporting 'uh-huhs' and 'mmms', nodding, etc. Look somebody in the eye or look away. Stand up or walk around. - Subconscious actions. - Keeping a distance and touching.

The mediator intervenes with his eyes, hands, facial expression and by changing positions. By using non-verbal interventions, a mediator can correct the behavior of a negotiator who constantly interrupts the other party, for example by making eye contact. If the discussion seems to deteriorate or if the parties are not listening to the mediator, the mediator can stand up or look one of the parties squarely in the eye in order to command attention. In addition, intentionally and noticeably leaning back can be an adequate non-verbal intervention.
The use of non-verbal interventions expands the range of interventions and can demonstrate the mediator's commitment and neutrality.

Non-verbal communication
Mentioning non-verbal communication clarifies matters. There are several ways to communicate non-verbally:

- **Effective listening**
  The most important non-verbal intervention (III-2).
- **Giving signs**
  An unambiguous sign, which can be 'translated' immediately into a word or a sentence. Examples are: thumbs up (OK), waving an arm in the air (hello), holding the palm of the hand up (stop) or motioning (come here). Signs are often defined culturally and the same sign can have different meanings in different cultures.
- **Gestures to emphasize the verbal communication**
  Examples are: indicating proportions, banging one's fist on the table, shrugging.
- **Express emotions**
  Feelings reflected in the facial expression or body language, for example anger, rage, fear, aversion, joy, grief and happiness, appear to be universal. People from various cultures seem to be able to interpret these feelings correctly.
- **Control communication**
  Supportive 'uh-huhs' and nodding. Standing up or walking around. Frowning, turning towards somebody, or turning away. Looking somebody in the eye or looking away.
- **Subconscious actions**
  These are often recurring movements that are part of one's manner. Examples are: rocking, biting nails, scratching the nose, playing with a ring or pen, putting your glasses on and taking them off. These actions usually increase in intensity and frequency when a person is stressed or anxious.
- **Keeping distance – more or less**
  Touching another person can range from brute force on one end of the spectrum to a friendly pat on the shoulder, or a light touch on the hand on the other. The distance that somebody observes is also a form of non-verbal communication: In most western

countries[51] you only stand close (closer than 45 centimeters or approximately 19.5 inches) to a person with whom you have a close personal relationship. The distance between people who socially interact is between 45 cm and 1 meter (approx. 19.5 inches - 3.3 feet). The standard 'social distance' to strangers is approximately one to two meters or yards (approx. 3.3 - 6.6 feet). This distance is culturally defined. In Latin-American and Arab countries the distance is usually much less. Literally keeping one's distance also says something about the relationship.

- **Silence** (III-17).

Interpretation of a reaction on non-verbal communication

The mediator should react to non-verbal signals of the parties. This reaction can be verbal. A mediator can for example name his observation and check to see if it is correct. He can give brief affirmations like 'hmm', 'yes', or ask questions (III-10). The mediator can also give a non-verbal reaction; for example, through his attitude, his charisma, nodding or by the way he looks at someone. See also the chart listening in III-2.3.

More information about non-verbal communication can be found on f.e. www.vhml.org: there is a scholarly article on non-verbal communication with illustrations in the workshops section. www.kevinhogan.com describes decoding and interpreting body language, also with pictures, in the section body language reading. Other web references are included in the webography in Resource H.

19 Paradoxical interventions

Definition/description	Application	Example of application
Paradoxical intervention		
By applying a paradoxical intervention, a mediator can reflect on specific behavior in a contrary way (thus magnifying it in a sense) or break deadlocks. Superficially the goal of a paradoxical intervention appears be to achieve the exact opposite of what would be expected or appropriate.	A paradoxical intervention is used to break resistance. The parties are given the opportunity to correct inappropriate or unhelpful behavior and at the same time try to get the mediation moving again. A paradoxical intervention causes a shock effect that can break an impasse (IV-1.3.2). Moreover, a paradoxical intervention can make the parties want to prove that things can be done differently.	*'Fine, if she leaves the team the problem is solved. So the dispute is settled now.'* *'Would you like another cup of coffee?'*

At first sight a paradoxical intervention seems to aim at the exact opposite of the next advisable step. The parties, and sometimes also their advisors, often have the tendency to offer resistance to the mediator as well as the process of finding a solution. With

51 www.lichaamstaal.com.

the help of a paradoxical intervention, you utilize this mechanism. Instead of applying 'counterpressure' to try to break the resistance, you redirect the control of the process entirely to the parties. The surprise effect of not offering the expected resistance allows you to break through the mechanism of opposition of the parties involved.

Somebody who is constantly talking and keeps on interrupting the other parties, is told that the mediation is *'progressing extremely well'* due to their contribution or is encouraged to tell more. A mediator can, for example, observe that the clients are especially good at discussing unimportant matters and that *'It is fine that you do not want to touch on controversial issues. It is not necessary to discuss all issues, is it? That will only lead to lengthy discussions.'*

The observation by the mediator that there is no progress at all and that he is considering discontinuing the mediation is usually also a paradoxical intervention.

Another way to intervene paradoxically is taking a side-path that is unrelated to the issues of the mediation: *'What do you think? Is there enough snow in the Swiss mountains to go on a skiing holiday?'*

If there is no forward movement at all, an absurd solution can be proposed (paradoxically): *'You know what, why don't all of you just donate $30,000 to the works council. They can organize a huge salsa party for all your employees. That will settle the matter I should think.'*

Not every mediator will be able or willing to apply a paradoxical intervention. You must think about it before you use this intervention. You need to know how to do it and it must suit your own style as a mediator. In addition, a paradoxical intervention cannot be applied in every phase of the mediation without consequences.

As with confronting questions (III-10.4) and reality testing (III-11), the mediator must not use these interventions too early in the mediation. It takes a good working relationship based on trust to be able to perform this intervention effectively and without damaging the neutrality and position of the mediator. A paradoxical intervention is a kind of 'crowbar' that a mediator can use if the parties continue to resist each other, or you as a mediator, or the mediation process.

Many mediators become very authoritative in these circumstances or point out the ground rules once again: 'We said that we would let the other party finish and not interrupt one another' or 'We agreed that we would try our best to cooperate to find a solution.' Other mediators become more assertive and constantly emphasize the positive aspects or joint interests. Mediators also frequently start to push and pull parties in the 'right' direction, for example compelling a party to show understanding for the other party or demanding an apology, repeatedly asking circular questions (III-10.2.2), or using reality testing (III-11). If the parties resist, these techniques do not always have the desired effect. On the contrary, often they only evoke even more resistance. Consider the use of a paradoxical intervention in these circumstances.

However, take care not to use it as a trick. In order to apply a paradoxical intervention effectively, you must move along with the parties and put control in their hands instead of applying force. If you are not willing or ready to do that, it is better not to use a paradoxical intervention.

Ballou (1995), editor, PSYCHOLOGICAL INTERVENTIONS: A GUIDE TO STRATEGIES.[52]

52 For those in command of Dutch we recommend: Prein (2005) *De waarde van paradoxale Interventies* (The value of paradoxical interventions).

IV. Challenging situations & selected topics

1	Overcoming deadlocks effectively	211
2	Differing perceptions	217
3	Tricky tactics and difficult behavior	223
4	Dealing with emotions	228
5	Varying cultural backgrounds	235
6	Multi-party mediations or mediations with many individuals	237
7	Escalation phases of a conflict	239
8	Online mediation	249
9	Dealing with brains, tips for mediators from neuroscience	257

Part IV. Challenging situations & selected topics

The structure of part IV can be found in row IV of the checklist. This part, about methods for specific situations, can be consulted in case of special circumstances. Several methods and techniques for overcoming a deadlock are discussed. You can find answers to questions like: 'How do I handle parties or their advisors who use difficult tactics?'
In addition, attention is paid to methods for clarifying different perspectives. Several psychological processes which could lead to having different perceptions are addressed. In this part you can find checklists for mediations with several parties or parties with different cultural backgrounds. Additionally this part contains tools for dealing with emotions.

1 Overcoming deadlocks effectively

1.1 Characteristics of a deadlock

A deadlock in a negotiation or a mediation can manifest itself by:

- making no forward progress – moving around in circles;
- not reaching agreement;
- uncoordinated and difficult communication;
- emotions running high; these cannot be normalized and (no longer) contribute to a productive dialogue;
- recurring arguments or issues;
- persistent resistance to you or to the process.

1.2 Causes of deadlock

See also causes of the conflict (II-8.2).

Communication
A deadlock can be caused by parties communicating ineffectively. This is usually not caused only by an inability to express oneself or not being able to listen actively, but because there are other complicating factors. Examples of complicating factors: both parties have different information or they make different assumptions. See the ladder of inference (IV-2.2).
Poor communication can cause parties to get off the right track and become entangled without being able to recover the situation.

Relationship

Deadlocks caused by the relationship often originate in long-standing relationships. They may be caused by dysfunctional patterns of communication that have developed over time. Examples are recurring negative interactions like aggression, settling old scores, or severe incidents from the past (for example abuse or fraud). Personal differences of opinion or antipathy may also be the cause of a relational deadlock.

Financial

Being deadlocked on financial aspects is often connected with the so called 'fixed pie assumption' (III-15.2): Parties assume that the amount or quantity to be divided is limited, so the more one party gets, the less remains for the other party. Moreover, a deadlock can be caused by having different priorities regarding the allocation and utilization of financial resources.

Legal

A deadlock on technical-legal grounds can arise from different expectations regarding the answer to the question whether all parties complied with certain rules or procedures (law), or from different interpretations of the jurisprudence.

Emotions

Emotional deadlocks are generally caused by one party being overwhelmed by emotions and therefore being unable to look at (other) options, which makes effective communication impossible. Whether latent or expressed, emotions play a part in literally every conflict (IV-4).

Distrust

Parties in a conflict often assume 'the other' party does not act in good faith and therefore cannot be trusted. This often has to do with perspective and interpretation (IV-2). Reactive devaluation also plays a part (III-16.3). Furthermore, in many negotiations, a hidden agenda comes into play which only surfaces when trust is fully restored. If a hidden agenda or the underlying interest are not brought out into the open, this can result in a deadlock.

1.3 Techniques and methods

1.3.1 Interim evaluation of the mediation process[53]

In the initial contact phase (preparation) and the beginning of phase one of the mediation (opening statements).

- Is there balance and neutrality (II-2), also in the language (III-7), tone and non-verbal communication (III-18) of the mediator? The balance of power – has it been taken into consideration (II-3)?
- Did the mediator establish a psychological contract with the parties and did he inspire enough confidence in himself and the mediation process (II-1)?
- Have the parties or their advisors shown any resistance (III-19)?
- Have clear ground rules been agreed and are they being observed (I-5)?
- Are all relevant parties taking part in the mediation and are they being represented by the right delegates? Are any other parties involved in the conflict (I-2.6) who are not represented in the mediation?
- What about mandates? Who makes up the constituency and what role do they play (I-2.7)?
- Is it clear to the parties and their advisors what their role is during the mediation (I-2.8 and I-3)?
- Has there been a preliminary procedural consultation with the lawyers (I-2.8)?

At the beginning of phase two: first exchange between parties.

- Did all parties have enough time and opportunity to make their statement?
- Did the mediator properly summarize the parties' statements, and therefore is it clear to all what the dispute is about? The summary – was it complete (III-4)? Have all important issues been addressed (II-7 and II-8)? The negotiating agenda – has it been drawn up neutrally and does it pay equal attention to each of the parties (I-6 and III-7)? Common interests – have they been mentioned (III-13)?
- Is it clear what each party expects from the mediation? Do the parties know what the other one expects? What do they think they can achieve? Do they participate in the mediation voluntarily (I-1.1 and I-2.3)?

In phase 2, exploration.

- Has communication between parties been reestablished?
- Did the blocking issue become clear? Has this been discussed or is it still unresolved between the parties? What are the causes of the conflict (II-8)?

53 This model is based on information from NCRCs (at the time SDMC) training manual 1998/1999.

- Is there resistance from parties and are you as a mediator aggravating it by pulling or pushing too much or by over-emphasizing the common or positive aspects (III-19 and III-6.1)?
- Did the negotiators show an understanding of the perspectives and the intentions of the other party?
- The underlying interests - have they all been discussed? Is there recognition (III-2.1)? The important issues for one party - have they been acknowledged by the other party (II-7 and IV-4.5)?
- Did you adequately manage the emotions, which means normalizing them without trivializing, and making them functional as part of the mediation (IV-4)?

In phases 3 and 4: generating options and negotiation.

- Did you pay sufficient attention to the balance of power (I-3) and the empowerment of parties (I-6)?
- Are there any other options to explore? Did each party contribute to the search for possible solutions (III-15)?
- Do all options meet the subjective criteria (interests) (II-7) or were objective criteria established to support the decision of parties in favor or against a solution (III-16)?

In phases 5 and 6: reaching an agreement & closure, follow-up and implementation (finalizing and deliberating with the constituency).

- Did the mediator actually become a (non-)binding advisor trying to impose his own solution on the parties?
- Does either of the parties fear loss of face? Did you address how to minimize potential loss of face?
- Are there any problems with the constituency (I-2.7.2)? And did you support the party in their deliberations with their constituency? Are there enough objective criteria to make the outcome acceptable for the constituency (III-16.1)?

If your evaluation results in the conclusion that you have omitted certain issues, is it advisable to repeat the relevant phases?

1.3.2 Techniques

1.3.2.1 Deadlocks caused by persons

- ☐ **Re-contextualizing** (III-6)

  If the use of language hampers the continuation, you can reframe positively/neutrally or in an interest. The mediator can do this himself or he can try to empower the parties to adapt their use of language. Be careful though not to overdo it. There is a point where continuous positive or neutral re-contextualizing becomes detrimental (hint in III-6.1).

- ☐ **Reflecting on the proceedings** (III-5.3)

  You can mention the progress by asking the parties to make an inventory: 'Issues that have been discussed and agreed upon'. You can also do this yourself.

- ☐ **Changing the participants or the location**

  It is not always possible to switch the representatives, for example with a divorce, a labor dispute or an exit mediation (a mediation which is aimed at carefully ending an employment relationship). Especially in business mediations, it can be a good idea to change the composition of the negotiating team. For example, you can replace the immediately involved managers by more senior or lower-ranking colleagues. Proceeding with the mediation at another location, or just taking a walk or another kind of break, can also be helpful. This also applies to letting parties change places during a mediation session. The mediator can also be the cause of the conflict, for example when he has lost his (perceived) neutrality and has therefore, in a way, become a party himself. Or when parties and the mediator have conflicting styles or personalities. In these cases it is advisable to pull back and to bring in another mediator.

- ☐ **Change the game and its rules** (IV-3.3.2)

- ☐ **Keep the emotions manageable without trivializing them – normalizing** (IV-4.4)

  If the progress of the mediation is seriously hampered because parties cannot let go of their emotions, it can be advisable to adjourn the mediation and refer the parties to a therapist.

- ☐ **Let parties listen actively by paraphrasing (or having them paraphrase)** (III-3)

  Do not use this technique too often. It can become tedious.

- ☐ **Try to change communication patterns**

  To change dynamics, you could try to find out who communicates with whom and subsequently try to alter this, for instance by having the party advisors speak to each other or with their opponent. If the party advisors continuously have the floor, you could hand it to the party representatives. Having the communication go through the mediator for a while is another useful option.

- ☐ **Try to find out if there is a risk of loss of face**

  This is easiest to determine during a caucus (II-16). If a negotiator seems to risk loss of face, you should support both the parties as well as the constituency with face-saving techniques (I-2.7 and IV-6.1). The opposing party can also be involved here. Try to make this a subject for discussion or an issue for which a common solution must be found. Always, however, respect cultural considerations.

- ☐ **Do nothing, or intervene paradoxically** (III-19)
  Not intervening during a deadlock situation can be a good intervention. It also depends on which phase the mediation is in at the time. A silence or a very obvious deadlock situation can become so painful that the parties want to proceed themselves or make a proposal. To accelerate this effect, the mediator could intervene paradoxically (III-19). If there is stiff resistance from the parties, intervening paradoxically can be used as a means of reducing it.
- ☐ **A caucus** (II-16)
- ☐ **Stopping the mediation**
  If you notice that parties really do not want or are unable to move forward, you should terminate the mediation.

1.3.2.2 Deadlocks about content

- ☐ **Try to structure the mediation process** (II-15) **and fractionalize the points at issue** (II-15.4)
- ☐ **Draw up a negotiating agenda** (I-6)
  Working diligently to solve the dispute, mediators can sometimes provoke a deadlock themselves by starting with the most difficult issues. Do not go into too many details or move towards a solution too quickly. Make sure that all interests are on the table and that a sufficient number of options are generated. Are you enlarging the pie or are you merely dividing it ('fixed pie assumption')?
- ☐ **Try to put themes in a different or a broader perspective**
  For instance: *'We need to look for some kind of compensation for this'* instead of *'They have to pay for it'.* Try to enlarge the pie. Put things in a different perspective by asking different questions or looking at matters in dispute in a new way. See reframing (III-6) and generating options (III-15).
- ☐ **Try asking circular questions** (III-10.2.2) **or try mirroring** (III-10.2.4)
- ☐ **Reflect the deadlock situation or the progress** (III-5)
  'We are not moving one step forward. What could be the cause of that?'
  'Does it make sense to continue the mediation?'
  'We have come far. Issues a, b and c are already clear. We now only have to solve the following issues'.
- ☐ **Find out if sufficient objective criteria have been elaborated** (III-16)
  Try switching to another theme or reaching agreement about other issues first.
- ☐ **Find out if the parties need more information or more time to get comfortable with a proposal**

- ☐ **Give them 'homework' to do or bring in an expert, adjourn the mediation or plan a follow-up mediation session**
- ☐ **Reality testing** (III-11).
- ☐ **Use BATNA, RATNA, WATNA or ZOPA or analyze leverage** (III-14)
- ☐ **Let the negotiators decide about the conflict and the deadlock**:
  'How do you want to proceed?'
- ☐ **Do nothing or intervene paradoxically** (III-19).
- ☐ **Try to determine whether all parties are acting in good faith** (I-1.2)
  Is a party using the mediation as a delaying tactic or as a means to gather information? Is a party participating in the mediation only because of the pressure applied by a third party, like a referring court or the constituency? All this can be effectively explored and assessed in a caucus (I-1.2 and II-16).
- ☐ **A caucus** (II-16)
- ☐ **Stop the mediation**
  Do not endlessly continue the mediation in a deadlock situation. Accept that a deadlock sometimes cannot be resolved and that there are mediations which do not lead to an agreement.

2 Differing perceptions

Definition/description	Application	Example of application
Clarify assumptions and perspectives		
Clarify differing observations, lines of thought, points of view and perceptions. Clear up and evaluate bias and preconceived ideas.	Through the clarification of misunderstandings and inconsistent perspectives, mutual understanding of the positions of the other party is increased.	**Example of perspective**: **A:** B is a professional and valuable employee but she fails to stick to agreed actions and thus undermines my authority. **B:** A is a decisive manager. Unfortunately, her assignments are often unclear to me. Moreover, there are frequent last-minute changes. That is why I usually don't immediately carry out an assignment. These constant changes waste too much time, because I have to do the same work twice.

Everyone involved in a mediation or a negotiation has to contend with differing perspectives, including the mediator. Empowering parties to look in a more 'rational' or cooperative manner at the conflict and at the mutual relationship is not enough to solve the problems. Many conflicts evolve from differences in perspectives. Everybody perceives and interprets matters differently. After you analyze the various perceptions, you must consider to what extent they differ from one another or impede progress. If they do not, you could consider not exploring the issue any further. Otherwise you have to help the parties clarify the differences in their perceptions.

2.1 Reconciling differing perceptions

You can assist the parties to reconcile differing perceptions in many ways:

1. You could actively explore with the parties information which would prove the opposite of a certain outlook. This could be achieved by asking confronting questions (III-10.4.1) and reality testing (III-11).
2. You could ask the negotiators to imagine themselves in the perspective assumed by the other party. This can be done by asking relational questions (III-10.2), mirroring (III-10.2.4) or circular questions (III-10.2.2).

2.2 The 'ladder of inference'

2.2.1 The development of differing perceptions

A differing perspective can be explained with the 'ladder of inference' (Argyris, 1990). Everybody perceives a situation in his/her own unique way, and then draws certain conclusions which form the basis for proposals or action. Because all parties can draw their own conclusions, this can lead to all kinds of misunderstandings. According to Argyris this process can take place in milliseconds. Putting it simply, in three steps parties can adopt totally different perceptions of the same situation. Subsequently this can give rise to a conflict.

Step 1: Selection from the multitude of impressions

Everybody makes their own unique selections from the multitude of impressions. This may cause parties to start from different data or other information. The information you use depends, among other things, on what you actually have at your disposal, the selection you made based on your interests and the assumptions you make.

Step 2: Assumptions

Even if you begin with the same information, the image generated can be different. Based on their personal and cultural backgrounds, their habits and assumptions, parties assign their own meaning to the selected information. So this information can be interpreted in a different way.

Step 3: Conclusion

Even if you depart from the same data and you have comparable assumptions, this is not enough. You might still draw other conclusions. Both parties go through a process of drawing conclusions which could lead to misunderstandings and differences. Many blocking issues (II-8) originate in this process.

Example of the ladder of inference

A says to his colleague: *'You are hard to cooperate with'.* B interprets this as a criticism on his way of working and reacts with: *'How can you say that? I am definitely more experienced than you are.'* As a result A leaves the room angry and he concludes: *'Just what I thought.'* What happened? When A and B are visiting a customer, B monopolizes the conversation and he frequently interrupts A. The inference made by A: B is continuously interrupting me and it annoys me (fact for A). You constantly interrupt somebody if you think he is not able to do certain things (assumption by A). The inference made by B: When A and I are visiting a customer, we nearly always secure an order (fact for B). We form a good team and I am a successful salesman (assumption by B). I do not understand what is happening with A. It's a pity, he has great potential, but apparently there are some problems he needs to work on (conclusion from B). It would have been better if A had expressed the facts (*'You constantly interrupt me'*) and the conclusion he draws from them. The same applies to B.

2.2.2 Techniques

How can you make the negotiators, who are on different rungs of the ladder of inference, climb down the ladder together?

1. Recognize the process. During the mediation ask yourself frequently if parties are miscommunicating because they are on different rungs of the ladder of inference. Check the assumptions, including your own.
2. Support the negotiators, so that they can be clear and specific. Make sure you find out exactly which information parties are starting from, how this information is interpreted, and which conclusions are being reached. This can be achieved for example by summarizing (III-3), paraphrasing (III-4), asking questions (III-10) and re-contextualizing (III-6).
3. Ask questions about how parties draw their conclusions, what facts they are based on, and how they are being interpreted. Be careful not to let it turn into a cross-examination. Inform the parties what you are doing and make sure they understand you want to explain the perspective. Communicate to all parties that they have a valid reason for their perception and that you want to give both sides the opportunity to clarify their own perspective.

Another example of clarifying perceptions. The parties in a mediation are a manufacturer of bottles (A) and a manufacturer of cleaning products (B). They jointly developed a new bottle. A offered this bottle to another manufacturer of cleaning products who wants to sell it in a country where B is not represented. After both parties' statements, party B concludes with: *'The agreement clearly states that the bottle may not be sold to competitors. So this amounts to a breach of contract and you have to pay compensation.'* And A concludes their contribution with: *'We have complied with the contract. B's allegations are pure slander.'*

The mediator clarifies the assumptions, conclusions and perceptions.

> *'As I understand it, you both emphasized during the contract negotiations the fact that B is represented in nearly every country in the world, and is still expanding. (***Fact for B.***) I understand that based on that, B assumed that the agreement that the bottle would not be used by B's competitors, meant that A would not offer their bottle to any other manufacturer of cleaning products. (***Interpretation by B.***) If I understand correctly, that is the reason why B speaks of a breach of contract. (***Conclusion drawn by B.***) Am I right?'*

And subsequently:

> *'In all contracts A inserts the clause that a product should not be offered to a competitor. (***Fact for A.***) This clause was intended to mean that only a limited group of direct competitors is excluded. (***Interpretation by A.***) I observe that, based on this, A assumed that 'competitors' refers to only those immediate competitors who are active in a country where B is represented. (***Conclusion by A.***) Am I right?'*

2.3 Clarifying differing perceptions is difficult

There are several psychological processes that interfere with communication, observation of facts and people's perceptions. Some of them are described below.

2.3.1 Cognitive dissonance

If a discrepancy arises between one's own perception and facts or observations, people try to avoid it or rationalize it. This is called cognitive dissonance. People are inclined to look for arguments that support their own perception, because it is uncomfortable to observe an inconsistency between their own convictions and their actual observations or actions they took.

Cognitive dissonance can be corrected by:

- deciding that the inconsistent information is not relevant;
- looking for other opinions or convictions which could restore the balance;
- undertaking steps to resolve the discrepancy, for example by changing behavior or getting rid of the causes of the conflict;

The next example presents possible reactions to cognitive dissonance: You have bought a laptop for a special price. At home you notice it is very heavy and has less memory than you would like.

- You could say to yourself you rarely have to carry the laptop, because you always take your car to work. So the weight is not very relevant. Furthermore, you use the laptop only to work on short texts and emails so you don't need that much memory.
- You contemplate that the laptop has a beautiful design, an indestructible metallic cover, and all kinds of hardware has been installed: two DVD burners/players, a big touch screen, wifi, built-in projector, voice recognition, etc. This is why the laptop is heavy, but it's worth it.
- You come to the conclusion the laptop is not what you need and you return it to the shop. This last option requires a degree of self-reflection.

It is not pleasant to have to admit you are wrong. The consequence of cognitive dissonance in a conflict or a negotiating situation is that parties prefer to look for information that supports their opinion, and are usually less open to information that could prove the opposite.

2.3.2 Naïve realism

Parties assume the world is the way they perceive it. 'Reality' as it is observed is constructed by the way the brain functions and by the way it processes information combined with real or constructed input from the environment.

- Social psychologists speak of naïve realism (Naïve Realism, Ross, 1995 and Turchin, 2005): everybody thinks the world is how they perceive it. You believe your own convictions are based on a rational interpretation of this reality and that your actions are consistent with it.
- Everybody assumes others should have the same perceptions they have, simply because it is the right way to look at things.
- If others have a different way of looking at the world, this is because they are unable to observe certain events in the correct way. For example:
  - The other person has false or insufficient information, so if I provide the right information and explain how it should be interpreted, he will realize I am right.
  - The other person is stupid, stubborn or dominant, so he is not capable of logical interpretation. He reaches the wrong conclusion or he makes irrational decisions.
  - The other person is not able to see the world objectively. He has certain prejudices, fixed opinions, self-interests.

Parties in a mediation or during a negotiation often assume the opponent is prejudiced or has a false view of matters, which makes them look at the dispute from different perspectives. However, they often forget the same principle applies to themselves. The mediator can also be affected by naïve realism. So it is perfectly normal for parties who are involved in a mediation, a conflict or a negotiation to have a totally different perception of the dispute, the facts, the events and the possible solutions. Also, the other party's as well as one's own part in the origin and development of the conflict is valued differently. Negotiators often regard their own conduct more positively than the conduct of their opponent (IV-2.4). Also see reactive devaluation (III-16.3).

The Theory Into Practice Database (TIP) contains short summaries and examples of important theories about learning and transferring information (http:/tip.psychology.org).

2.4 Dysfunctional behavior

The following checklist contains an overview of general (psychological) processes and approaches which may explain what makes parties in a negotiation or mediation act irrationally – according to others. In this context irrational behavior refers to: the behavior that is experienced by the other party as dysfunctional, regarding effectiveness and efficiency of the negotiation. Finding a solution is hindered. In such a situation a mediator could try to show parties the dysfunctional character of their position in the context of the mediation. Intervention techniques which support efficient behavior (in the above described sense) during the negotiation or mediation are described in the checklist below.

Dysfunctional behavior

- ☐ **Fixed pie assumption** (III-15.2)
  Parties see that which is being negotiated as only a piece of the pie that has to be divided during the negotiation. As a result each negotiator is inclined to think: *'The more the other party gets, the less remains for me'.*
- ☐ **Irrational escalation of commitment**
  Having invested too much in a negotiation, a position or being right, as a result of which you continue to follow the same path, against your better judgment.
- ☐ **Anchoring** (III-10.7)
  As soon as a number, an offer or a proposal is on the table, this will be used as a frame of reference in the discussion.
- ☐ **Loss minimalization** (III-16.4)
  People tend to try harder to prevent a loss than to pursue a gain.
- ☐ **Reactive devaluation** (III-16.3)
  A proposal made by the other is by definition unfavorable for me, so I am against it.
- ☐ **Cognitive dissonance** (IV-2.3)
  People are inclined to look for arguments that support their own perception, because it feels uncomfortable if an inconsistency is observed between one's own conviction and the actions one has already taken.

- ☐ **Winner's curse**

  If you get something too easily, or if the other party agrees too quickly on a proposal, it makes you uncomfortable. If something is that easy to achieve, there must have been room to get an even better deal. For a mediator, securing a SMART and well-balanced settlement agreement (II-13) and working with package deals (II-12), is a good method to neutralize the effect of the winner's curse.
- ☐ Different perspective:
  - **Naïve realism** (IV-2.3)

    Everybody thinks the world is as he sees it. So if somebody has a different perception, he must be ignorant, stubborn or prejudiced, or he has too little or incorrect information.
  - **Overestimating yourself** (III-14)

    Many people experience their own alternatives as more beneficial than they really are, or they overestimate the value of their offers to the opponent.
  - **Ladder of inference** (IV-2.2)

    In several stages (rungs) misunderstandings can develop because parties reach different conclusions based on the same facts. In addition, they sometimes start from different facts, which are then interpreted differently, and other conclusions are drawn.
  - **Self-serving biases and rationalizations** (IV-4.5)

    Attaching more importance to information and arguments which support your own position. Your part in the origin and development of a dispute or deadlock is often valued in a more positive way than the conduct of the opponent. The same is true for your own proposals or offers. This, combined with naïve realism, often convinces a person his perspective is the right, and he is fulfilling a positive role in the process.
  - **Emotions** (IV-4)

    Emotions always play a part in a conflict, only the degree in which this happens varies. A party who is overpowered by his emotions often cannot continue to think clearly.

Ariely (2008), PREDICTABLY IRRATIONAL: THE HIDDEN FORCES THAT SHAPE OUR DECISIONS deals with unproductive rationalizations of own behavior and the own role in a conflict.

3 Tricky tactics and difficult behavior

3.1 Parties experienced as difficult

In a mediation or negotiation you can be confronted with parties who exhibit conduct you experience as difficult. Whether this really is the case is not a question for the mediator to answer. Because of the need for neutrality and preventing narrow-minded thinking (II-2), a mediator should take care not to label people as being difficult, awkward, etc. However, behavior and action that affects the efficiency and effectiveness of the mediation or negotiation are of major importance, and a mediator should deal with it in a functional way (IV-2.4).

Examples of parties with behavior that is experienced as difficult:

- **The victim**: the helpless, carrying no responsibility. The other party or the circumstances are solely to 'blame' for what has happened.
- **The bully**: the aggressive party who uses personal attacks or outbursts of anger.
- **The power-player or the macho exhibitionist**: the dominant party who completely outplays and overrules the opponent.
- **The Nirvana-party**: the quiet party who hardly participates in the mediation and is absent-minded.
- **The chameleon**: the party who is constantly changing her mind, adopts different positions and does not want to commit.
- **The poker face**: the sphinx who does not show emotions, who (unlike the Nirvana-party) does participate in the interaction of the mediation, but does not want to show his cards.
- **The scaredy-cat**: a party who surrenders too easily or gives in quickly to 'get off the hook'.
- **The paranoid**: the party fixated on the conviction that the opponent is acting in bad faith, has evil intent and is untrustworthy.
- **The emotional volcano**: the party having continuous emotional outbursts to the point that they are hampering the progress of the mediation or negotiation.

3.2 Tricky tactics

In addition to dealing with difficult parties, you can be confronted with parties or party advisors who use tricky tactics. For example:

- **Introducing phony deadlines**: *'This offer is valid for 24 hours. If there is no decision by then, it will expire'.* Due to the time pressure the other party will be inclined to give in faster to prevent losing the deal. It also makes it more difficult for that party to evaluate their options and think clearly.
- **Good guy/bad guy**: Nice and nasty representatives of a party taking turns. The theory is that the opponent is more inclined to agree with (far-reaching) proposals made by the 'nice' person. This mind game can also be played by a single person alternating between being nice and nasty.
- **A limited mandate**: the representative is willing to move, but only as far as ....but first she needs the approval of.... And in order to persuade the constituency, another concession is needed. An alternative could be: to return to the mediation or negotiation table with additional demands made by the constituency about the (final) deal. The negotiator is willing to agree, but unfortunately his constituency is adamant.

- **Walking out**: with the expectation of being called back to the mediation table with a certain concession as a bait. The other party concedes.
- **Making 'concessions'**: continuingly making small concessions with a great deal of noise, but expecting the opponent to offer something substantial in exchange.
- **Rethinking an (excessive) demand**: the initial demand is totally unrealistic and is rejected by the opponent. Subsequently the negotiator presents a toned-down demand, making it look like a concession, but in fact he is only aiming for a realistic opening bid. However, the opponent is inclined to respond to the 'concession' by making a real one.
- **The personal attack**: the negotiator starts playing the man not the ball. For instance, he tries to injure the integrity or professionalism of the mediator or the opponent. He is not taking the process or the negotiators seriously, and tries to make them look foolish.
- **Unseemly behavior**: not making eye contact, being indifferent regarding a possible resolution of the dispute, a total lack of interest, lying, grossly exaggerating or understating, or refusing to speak.
- **Salami tactics**: constantly making small (additional) demands, that together add up to a considerable concession to be made by the opponent.
- **Escalation of demands**: if the opponent does not give in, the negotiator immediately responds with higher demands or even threats. This is done with the expectation that the opponent will give in quickly to prevent additional demands.
- **Escalation of the value of 'giving in'**: the negotiator meets a request of the opponent. After an agreement has been reached, the negotiator then informs the other party that he wants more in exchange for his concession.
- **Last minute grabs**: the deal has been closed and one party states: *'Oh, I forgot to mention ... we just need ...'*
- **Stonewall**: not moving an inch.

Lax and Sebenius (2006) in 3-D NEGOTIATION illustrate three dimensions of negotiations. The first dimension is tactics. However, a tactical focus alone is not enough to reach a mutual gain deal, especially not when faced with difficult parties, multiple-parties and/or hard tactics. The second dimension is deal design, meant to uncover sources of value creation. The third dimension is the setup, i.e. things a negotiator can do to improve her situation while being 'away from the negotiation table', for example preparation, having the proper parties with the proper issues to negotiate about.

Tactics and strategies are often confused with one another:

- A tactic is a method, adapted to the circumstances, to help achieve a certain goal.
- A strategy is the route or plan for achieving the goal.[54]

Also see negotiating with difficult people (II-4.3).

3.3 Techniques

3.3.1 Do not react

Regaining balance and analyzing:

- A helicopter view: What is happening between you? Are they reacting to something I am doing?
- Their perspective: Why are they doing this?
- My perspective: What am I doing? Why?

3.3.2 An appropriate reaction

Definition/description	Application	Example of application
Play their game (tit-for-tat) or name the game		
Techniques to manage a complicated conversation or negotiation, to deal with people that act in a way you perceive as difficult, or who use tricky tactics. The objective in using these techniques is to try to change the negotiating style of the (other) party and/or the rules of the negotiation game towards a more effective way of dealing with each other, for example principled negotiation (II-4). Tit-for-tat means doing the same to the other party as they are doing to you. You play the same (negotiation) game they do in order to make them change the way they play it. Another approach to accomplish this is to name the game they are playing.	How to deal with difficult people or tricky tactics: - Analyze what is happening. - Play their game (tit for tat IV-3.3.2). - Give in or walk away. - Change the game and the rules of the game by listening (III-2), reframing (III-6), naming the game or changing the players (IV-3.3.2).	**Play their game (tit-for-tat)** *'Don't project your own frustration on her.'* *'You can't demand that everybody accommodates your style of working.'* **Name the game** *'Do you want to confront her with an accomplished fact?'* *'I'm under the impression that you're trying to power play here. Do you think that will solve the problem? Don't you think it is better to ...?'*

Play their game (tit-for-tat)

Tit-for-tat still is considered a very effective negotiating strategy. This technique can be used by the mediator or the parties in a mediation. Hard-core principled negotiators like Fischer (1989) advise using the tit-for-tat approach only with respect to content matters, not for relationship issues. According to Fischer you need to be 'unconditionally constructive' with respect to the relationship.

54 www.wikipedia.com.

Tit-for-tat works as follows:

- The line of approach is being cooperative, assuming '*integrative*' or '*principled*' negotiation (II-4), unless you are provoked.
- If you are provoked, you respond to the other party in the way they are behaving to you: you copy the behavior of the other party, so to speak.
- You forgive and forget quickly. This means you do not hit back harder than necessary, and you do not want to be seen as scoring points. As soon as you reach your goal, i.e. the other party adopts a more constructive attitude, you follow suit.
- To prevent escalation, it can be helpful to describe the interaction after you applied the tit-for-tat approach - including your own part in it - and propose to continue in a different way.

An example of the tit-for-tat approach in a mediation: A party continually interrupts the mediator and the other party. The mediator can point out the rules that everybody agreed to (I-5), he can intervene paradoxically (III-18) or opt for a tit-for-tat approach. When choosing the tit-for-tat approach, the mediator interrupts this party several times. However, this should not be exaggerated, so do not shout down the negotiator or raise your voice while interrupting. On the other hand, the other party needs to notice the tactic, and it should make them uncomfortable. You subsequently discuss the interaction: *'I do not think we will make any progress in this mediation if we keep interrupting one another'* (deliberate shared blame). If the party sticks to the new rule of not interrupting, you will do the same, with no hard feelings.
A tit-for-tat approach may affect the perceived neutrality of the mediator. See the hints under confronting questions (III-10.4).

Giving-in or walking out
You give in if an issue is more important to the other party than it is to you, or if the other party turns out to be right, or they have a better proposal. The walk-away alternative can be used when you think the issue underpinning the deal is not worth the trouble, if you do not succeed in reaching a negotiated solution and you need to resort to another method, or if there is an acute danger, or you 'agree to disagree' (II-11.3). Using the walk-away alternative, or indicating you might do so, is sometimes applied to increase pressure or as a paradoxical intervention (III-19). Both the mediator and the parties can announce they want to stop the mediation (III-14).

Changing the game and the rules of the game
If a game is being played, you could try to switch to another game in which parties treat each other more creatively, or positively, or you can try to change the rules of the game so it will be played more productively,

The following techniques may be helpful:

- **Listening**
  Look for the interest behind the 'attack' or other kind of undesirable behavior. Be curious, ask questions (III-10). Effective listening here means:
  - *Attitude*
    Stay focused, be curious, no personal offense taken.
  - *Action*
    Verify your assumptions and those of the other(s).
    Paraphrase (III-4): Repeat in your own words in order to clarify understanding, which is not the same as agreeing with the (other) party.
    Try acknowledgement, reflecting feelings (III-5.2).
  - *Active listening with paraphrasing and summarizing* (III-2.2)
    These methods can be applied in emotional circumstances, when communication is difficult, if you are not certain you understand the developments or what is being said, or when parties are not listening to you or each other.
- **Reframe**: neutrally or in an interest, a feeling, options or objective criteria (III-6).
- **'Name the game'** that is being played.
  Try to describe the interaction and its possible consequences. Propose to continue in another way.
- **Change the players**
  New participants on either side of the table or add a (new or additional) third party (IV-1.3.2.1).

Apply mediation tools

See part III, especially paraphrasing (III-3), acknowledgement (III-5.2), asking questions (III-10), reframing (III-6), summarizing (III-4) and verifying assumptions (IV-2.2).

4 Dealing with emotions

The extent to which emotions play a part in a conflict varies. During a business dispute or a conflict involving a government body, emotions are often less important or more controlled than during dismissal, neighborhood, or family disputes. However, in any dispute or conflict, including business conflicts, emotions form a part of the negotiations. Examples are: fear of loss of face, anger over not being taken seriously, being distressed because you have not been listened to, rage about impolite treatment, frustrations over tactics or other delays, or having had enough of something repeatedly going wrong. But also positive emotions: like anticipation about a good deal, happiness that things are finally out in the open, or a party feels heard, relief to have been able to have to tell some 'home truths'.

4.1 'Emotional pitfalls' for a mediator

In general, emotions are hard to deal with. There are a few tempting pitfalls for a mediator.

4.1.1 Exploring extensively

Dwelling on emotions, continually looking for the causes behind them and constantly focusing on emotions is in contradiction with the essence of mediation. A mediation is about looking for interests, generating options, smooth proceedings and looking ahead. A mediator is not a therapist and consequently he should handle emotions functionally. This implies allowing them to be discussed to the extent that this is necessary to find a solution of the conflict. The mediator has to try to separate the emotions from content issues (III-8). For example, he can discuss them because they constitute a blocking issue or one of the causes of the conflict (II-8), or because someone has to let off steam. But if parties are allowed to dwell on their emotions, they automatically focus on the past and on a possible fear of the future. Yet the resolution of a conflict is in the future. The past cannot be changed, but the future can. Both the mediator and the negotiators have to keep this in mind.

4.1.2 Pretending emotions do not play a role

Banning emotions from a mediation completely is also counterproductive. If the mediator continuously ignores emotions, while the parties need to recognize the emotional obstacles, the mediation could reach a deadlock. The mediator must make emotions a subject of discussion if it is necessary for the opponent to acknowledge some issues, or if the emotion is a blocking issue.

4.1.3 Adopting emotions or going along with them

A mediator is only human himself. During a mediation, heated emotions can be expressed. Moreover, themes can come under discussion which might be painful for the mediator himself. In this way, he could become emotionally involved. Heated emotions from others do not just evoke recognition in others. They can also be extremely annoying. If a party continues to react aggressively or if he is stuck in the role of victim, the mediator is often affected too. Feelings of irritation or frustration could arise. Self-reflection and self-knowledge are therefore very important for a mediator. You must decide to discontinue the mediation if you feel you are getting too caught up in the emotions of the negotiators, or if your own emotions start interfering with your ability to function as a mediator. The way to deal with emotions is referred to as 'normalizing emotions without trivializing them'.[55] This means:

- noticing emotions and naming them;
- if necessary reflecting on feelings (magnifying III-5.1, or reframing them (putting them in another framework III-6, or neutralizing them);
- respecting feelings and showing they are being understood (reflection on feelings III-5.2);
- checking if the emotions have been interpreted correctly;
- subsequently look to the future.

Books on dealing with emotions in a mediation (normalizing them):

- *Thompson, (6th edition 2014), THE MIND AND HEART OF THE NEGOTIATOR.*
- *Stone, Patton and Heen (2010), DIFFICULT CONVERSATIONS: HOW TO DISCUSS WHAT MATTERS MOST.*
- *Cloke (2010), THE CROSSROADS OF CONFLICT: A JOURNEY INTO THE HEART OF DISPUTE RESOLUTION.*
- *Fisher and Shapiro (2007), BEYOND REASON: USING EMOTIONS AS YOU NEGOTIATE.*
- *Fisher and Shapiro (2004), THE ART OF MANAGING EVERYDAY CONFLICT: UNDERSTANDING EMOTIONS AND POWER STRUGGLES. Praeger Publishers.*
- *Jones and Bodtker (2007), Mediating with heart in mind: addressing emotion in mediation practice, 17 Negotiation Journal.*
- *Ury (2007), THE POWER OF A POSITIVE NO: HOW TO SAY NO AND STILL GET TO YES.*
- *Ury (2000), THE THIRD SIDE: WHY WE FIGHT AND HOW WE CAN STOP.*

4.2 Positive emotions

Positive emotions like happiness, relief and gratitude also occur during a mediation. Mostly these emotions do not interfere. Conversely putting too much emphasis on positive emotions seldom leads to a solution. Positive emotions can be helpful during mutualizing (III-13). Also the progress of the mediation can be underlined by specifically naming the positive issues.

4.3 Negative emotions

Haynes (1994) distinguishes negative emotions by categorizing them as offensive and defensive.[56]

55 Bonenkamp (2003).

56 Haynes (1994), THE FUNDAMENTALS OF FAMILY MEDIATION. Pages. 60-64.

4.3.1 Offensive

Offensive emotions are directed outward. Examples of offensive emotions are: reproaching the opponent, anger and irritation. One party blames the other and holds them responsible instead of taking their own responsibility. The mediator needs to pay attention to these emotions. An effective intervention could be recontextualizing these emotions into the underlying interest (III-6.3): *'You feel...is important', You want... differently'.*

However, paying too much attention to offensive emotions could cause a downward spiral. Moreover, this way parties are not encouraged to take responsibility themselves or address their own part in the conflict. If offensive emotions keep blocking progress, reality testing (III-11) or asking confronting questions (III-10.4) could be used to normalize these emotions. If they tend to develop into personal attacks, or manifest themselves as aggression or potentially violence, the mediator can try to control the process by establishing clear ground rules (I-5).

4.3.2 Defensive

Defensive emotions are directed at oneself or at one's own conduct. Here the blaming and the reproaches are directed inward. Grief, shame or insecurity say something about an underlying interest. It is therefore sensible to pay attention to them. However, the pitfall of paying too much attention to these emotions is that you run the risk of stimulating victim behavior. Reality testing (in a face-to-face conversation) may discourage this kind of conduct.

The terms 'positive and negative emotions' are actually inappropriate. The emotion itself, the effect it has on all parties and its impact on the progress of the mediation can all differ. Positive emotions do not always help to solve a conflict and not all negative emotions have a negative effect on the parties. Provided that emotions are expressed functionally and are managed correctly, all emotions can actually be channeled to have a positive effect. Additionally, if they are bottled up and not expressed, it is often not possible to solve the conflict. It would therefore be better to speak of warm or manifest emotions and cold or hidden emotions. Warm emotions can be expressed so the mediator and the parties can use them to reach a solution. Cold or hidden emotions do play a part below the surface, but they are not expressed and accordingly their existence is often denied, or not recognized. They can severely obstruct the progress of the mediation.

4.4 Interventions for managing emotions

See part III Techniques and Interventions.

See IV-9.3 'Neuro'-Interventions, and IV-9.4.

Interventions for managing emotions

- ☐ **Active listening** (III-2.2)
  - Acknowledging that the speaker has been 'heard'.
  - Verifying that the intentions of the speaker have been fully understood.
  - Showing that it is acceptable to have feelings and to express them.
- ☐ **Asking questions** (III-10)
  - Clarify the relationship between emotions and interests or conflict issues. *'I see issue X stirs up emotions. Could you name one?'* Answer: *'Anger'. 'What does feeling this anger cost you?' 'And what does it bring you?' 'What can be done to change these emotions?' 'Why are you having these feelings of anger?' 'What other emotions do you experience?' 'What can the other party do to help you cope with your emotions?'*
- ☐ **Paraphrasing** (III-3)
  - Clarifying emotional issues.
  - Enabling 'hearing' what is being said, confirming someone is being listened to and checking it has been understood correctly.
- ☐ **Reality testing** (III-11), asking confronting questions (III-10.4) or, conversely, asking questions which put things in perspective.
  - Breaking through the role of victim.
  - Empowering parties to solve the matter and stimulating them to change the situation by themselves (IV-4.5 and IV-4.4.6).
- ☐ **Adjourning, time-out** (II-14).
  - Enabling parties to cool down or to consult an advisor, such as a lawyer or a therapist.
  - Caucus (II-16).
  - Letting off steam or trying to temper emotions without the other party being present.
  - Reality testing or asking confronting questions without running the risk of damaging the mediator's neutrality.
- ☐ **Reflecting** (III-5)
  - Reflecting on content (magnifying) by bringing up emotions or by reflecting on the content: *'Do you always communicate in this way?'*
  - Acknowledge and clarify that the emotion and its relevance are 'understood'.

- ☐ **Mutualizing** (III-13)
  - Emphasizing joint interests and positive or common issues to break through negative stereotyping and stimulate confidence in the progress.
- ☐ **Recontextualizing in an interest or in a feeling** (III-6.2)
  - Normalizing outbursts and transforming them into an interest, for example the desire for understanding.
  - Recontextualizing cold or hidden emotions in a feeling: *'It can be quite frustrating if certain events stir up (certain) feelings, while at the same time they can be difficult to express. Is that right?'*
- ☐ **Maintaining the ground rules** (I-3)
  - Treating the other party with respect and as an equal partner.
  - Stimulating the parties to make an effort to resolve the conflict.
  - Guaranteeing a smooth proceeding of the mediation.
- ☐ **Ignoring**
  - Not all emotions or outbursts need to be addressed. Not every cold emotion needs be explained explicitly.

4.5 Recognizing your own role in the conflict

Parties often find it difficult to recognize their part in the origin and continuation of the conflict. As a result, responsibility for one's conduct is often denied. One's own conduct during a conflict is often justified after the event with rational explanations (rationalization). For example – it was the situation, or the other party, or it is consistent with generally accepted standards. The real motives are often not faced and it can be difficult to find these genuine, underlying reasons. J.P. Morgan once observed – *'There are two reasons for everything: a good reason and the real reason'.*

As with meta-communication, it is more efficient to mention the (possible) rationalization in an indirect manner (III-9). Not: *'You rationalize your conduct afterwards, but in fact you yourself....'* This could lead to a *'Yes it is; No it isn't'* discussion and may damage the mediator's neutrality. Try to use the observations as an instrument for analysis. Only mention rationalization if it interferes with the progress of the mediation, and name it indirectly by pointing out the effect it could have.

> *'Sometimes it is difficult to look at your own role and determine the effect it could have on others. This is particularly true when issues have had a different impact than intended.'*
> *'When you hear the story from another perspective, things might look totally different. As a result you can start looking at the situation differently yourself'.*

Reality testing can also be a good approach:

'Do you think party A is willing to make concessions if you continue to blame her for the situation as it evolved? In retrospect, what could you have done to prevent this situation?'

In this respect Prein (2005) speaks of unproductive rationalizations of one's own conduct and one's own part in the conflict. He describes a procedure through which parties can feel more responsible for their conduct and the underlying motives. In short, this means you can make the parties use different language by reframing (III-6) and reflecting (III-5). The mediator can achieve this by setting an example.

- Changing *'it', 'you', 'them'* into *'I'*.
- *'Cannot'* becomes *'will not'*; *'is necessary'* becomes *'would like to'*
- *'I have to'* becomes *'I choose to'*
- Changing *'but'* to *'and'*
- 'Interrogative form' (a veiled proposition) becomes 'stating form' (beginning of III-10).
- No value judgments.
- Changing a *'why'* question into one beginning with *'how and what'* (III-10.4.2).

4.6 Change is difficult

For several reasons victims often get stuck in their role. Reality testing (III-11) could jog a party into wanting to change the situation. Background information which could help with asking relevant questions (III-10) and reality testing:

- **Change generates anxiety**
  The old situation, however undesirable, is familiar and that gives a certain sense of security. A new situation is by definition unknown and therefore produces anxiety.
- **The other party is wrong**
  Being recognized as a victim implies you can safely state that others are to blame for the situation and consequently they must change, not you. The responsibility can be passed onto others or to external circumstances.
- **An annoying situation can ultimately be profitable**
  - In a certain way, the conflict has become a life fulfillment, or a common stereotype of the enemy unites you with a third party. Besides, a lot of effort may already have been invested in proving you are in the right.
  - Changing requires effort. It seems easier to continue as before.
  - An undesirable situation can also have positive side effects and you don't want to lose them. For example, the attention you get as a victim, or not having to deal with yourself or other problems as a result of the conflict. In addition, an annoying situation can also yield tangible benefits.

5 Varying cultural backgrounds

A mediator should recognize intercultural influences and neutralize and if necessary clarify the effects they have on the mediation. In addition to recognizing and making the cultural influences a subject of discussion, it is also possible to introduce structures in the set-up of the mediation which can help to neutralize these effects. For example, by engaging an interpreter or by introducing co-mediation with complementary mediators who have the same or similar cultural backgrounds as the parties. Another possibility is introducing a mediator with a background which is totally different from all the parties. A mediator should be well aware of the possible intercultural effects during a mediation. On the other hand you should not ascribe all problems during an international mediation to intercultural influences. Techniques for dealing with intercultural influences:[57]

1. Constantly verify if everything that is said has been understood correctly, both by you and by the parties (III-10.5.2).
2. If possible, you should make all important written documents available to all parties in their national language.
3. If necessary use an interpreter.
4. Do not depart from your own cultural norms or values, or the values of one party.
5. If something is not clear to you, or if things are happening you are not used to, ask for an explanation (III-10.1.3).
6. Ensure parties have a mutual understanding for each other's cultural background and the perceptions and the conduct based on it (IV-2.1).
7. Be inquisitive, patient and flexible.
8. Use the intercultural components to stimulate creativity and 'outside the box' thinking.

Cross cultural references

- *ABORIGINAL CULTURAL GUIDE FOR MEDIATORS. ACT Network. Family Pathways Branch, Attorney General's Department. Canberra, Australia.*
- *Bauman (2006). Final Report of the Indigenous Faciliation and Mediation Project Report 2003/2004. – Findings, Recommendations and Implementation. INDIGENOUS FACILITATION AND MEDIATION PROJECT. Native Titles Unit, Australian Institute of Aboriginal and Torres Strait Islander Studies, Canberra.*
- *Brigg (2003). Mediation, Power, and Cultural Difference. CONFLICT RESOLUTION QUARTERLY 20 (3) 287-306.*
- *Kingham and Bauman,(2006). Native Title mediation: Issues identified, lessons learnt: proceedings of IFaMP workshops with Native Title Indigenous and Non-Indigenous Mediators, February & March 2005. No.5 INDIGINEOUS FACILITATION*

57 Delaney (2002).

AND MEDIATION PROJECT. Native Title Research Unit, Australian Institute of Aboriginal & Torres Strait Islander Studies, Canberra. Australia.

- *Lebaron, (2004). COMMUNICATION TOOLS FOR UNDERSTANDING CULTURAL DIFFERENCES. CULTURE BASED NEGOTIATION STYLES. CROSS-CULTURAL COMMUNICATION.*
- *Williams, (2005). Native Title Mediation Practice: The Commonalities, the Challenges, the Contradictions of Native Title Mediators, INIDIGENOUS FACILITATION AND MEDIATION PROJECT REPORT No. 3 Native Title research. Australian Institute of Aboriginal and Torres Strait Islander Studies, Canberra.*

A mediator or negotiator must be highly aware of the potential intercultural effects during mediation or negotiation. On the other hand, for example, in an international setting, they should not attribute all issues to intercultural influences. To recognize when intercultural influences are at play in a conflict, a mediator must possess well-developed intercultural competencies and skills.

INTERNATIONAL MEDIATION: THE ART OF BUSINESS DIPLOMACY by Carroll and Mackie (2nd edition 2006) deals with international mediation and covers case studies of international disputes that have been resolved by using mediation. It describes relevant models and techniques for applying mediation in an international setting.

Mental images of cultural clusters

Wursten[58] (2002, 2006) developed based on the Hofstede-model mental images of culture clusters to facilitate the comparison between cultures in practice.

MENTAL IMAGES OF CULTURAL CLUSTERS

AUL, GBR, IRE, NZL, USA	DEN, NET, NOR, SWE, FIN	CHI, HOK, IND, IDO, MAL, PHI, SIN	BRA, CHL, COL, ECA, SAL, GRE, GUA, ITA SOUTH, KOR, MEX, PER, POR, RUS, TAI, THA, TUR, URU, VEN	BEL, FRA, ITA NORTH, SPA, SWI (FRENCH)	AUT, CZE, HUN, GER, SWI (GERMAN)
Contest	**Network**	**Family**	**Pyramid**	**Solar system**	**Machine**
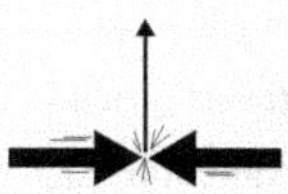				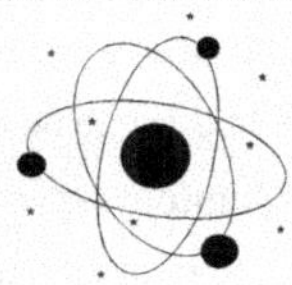	

CENTRAL CONCEPT

Competition	Consensus	Loyalty and hierarchy	Loyalty and hierarchy and implicit order	Hierarchy and impersonal bureaucracy	Order
PDI-	PDI-	PDI+	PDI+	PDI+	-PDI
IDV+	IDV+	IDV-	IDV-	IDV+	±IDV/+IDV
UAI-	UAI-/UAI+	UAI-	UAI+	UAI+	+UAI
MAS+	MAS-				

6 Multi-party mediations or mediations with many individuals

Multi-party mediations, or mediations with a large number of representatives, often are complicated. Instead of communication between two individuals and the mediator, you have to deal with interactions between many more individuals and also group dynamics. In addition to forging agreements between several external parties, you are also dealing with various mutual agreements between factions of the group. Moreover, you have to monitor many more communication flows and interactions. Multi-party mediations typically have a lower success rate of 38% against a general mediation success rate of 62% in court-connected mediations (WODC 2003). In multi-party mediations it is harder to identify all the relevant parties and all the relevant individuals.

58 With special thanks to Huib Wursten for making this model available for the Toolkit Mediation. More information: huib@itim.org.

6.1 Large groups

Tips for mediations with large groups

- ☐ Consider a **co-mediation** (I-2.5) if more than four people are taking part in the mediation.
- ☐ During the intake phase, help the parties **compose their team**: how many participants, which profile should they have?
- ☐ Try having a **delegation** with a restricted number of participants represent the other group members, or ask the group to appoint one spokesman or a limited number of participants to speak on their behalf. The other group members are then able to participate in the mediation, but the spokesman will be talking with the mediator and the other parties.
- ☐ If the groups are segmented and there are differing underlying interests, clustering the issues could prove to be difficult. You could consider asking the group to appoint an **internal group facilitator** who will act as their first spokesman and who will also arrange the contribution of the other team members in the mediation (an internal agreement about the positions in the group).
- ☐ Support the delegation or the negotiator with the **internal process of reaching agreement** with the constituency and the rest of the group (I-2.7.2), for example in a parallel sub-mediation or in a caucus (II-16).
- ☐ Try mapping the **interests** of the group as well as the subgroups and the individual group members.
- ☐ Try to discuss in advance, in a **procedural consultation** with the group (I-2.8), how reaching a mutual agreement will be managed.
- ☐ Ensure that an **implied division of roles** is **transformed** into a **formal division of roles**, for example with a chairman. Not everything has to be done by the whole group.
- ☐ Determine **how the decisions** within each group **are taking place**, and make an agreement about it:
  - discussion and consensus;
  - voting;
  - the 'boss or the opinion maker decides';
  - otherwise, that is.....
- ☐ Ensure that the **consultation with the constituency** is regarded as a **negotiating situation** and not as a routine conversation. This way there is a clear requirement for a decision structure within the group. Existing relationships, a common interest and the need to reach an agreement with other parties, can cause mutual differences of opinion to be ignored. As a result there is no clear consultation, which means a risk of future conflicts, for instance during the conclusion of the mediation. You must therefore allow different opinions to be expressed.

- ☐ Try determining the limits of the **mandate** of the party representative as well as the group (I-2.7.1):
  - complete mandate;
  - restricted mandate;
  - consulting about everything within the group;
  - further consultations of the group with the constituency;
  - reporting to the group;
  - otherwise, namely...
- ☐ Consider forming **subgroups**, consisting of participants from both parties, to tackle certain issues.

6.2 More than two parties

Tips for multi-party mediations

- ☐ Consider a **co-mediation** when more than two parties participate in the mediation.
- ☐ Mediations with more than two parties basically do not require different skills of the mediator. But he will have to be able to deal with more complexity. Because in addition to having more interactions between the parties, you also have to deal with **group dynamics** and possibly private discussions and the formation of coalitions and factions.
- ☐ You can use the fact that there are more parties, by working in **teams with a different composition**. For example when conducting a caucus with party A, you can let parties B and C develop certain issues jointly, or let them brainstorm together (III-15.1). Or you can facilitate a sub-mediation with parties B and C, and give party A the time to deliberate with their constituency or advisor, or some extra homework.
- ☐ Using a **caucus** (II-16) gives you the opportunity to discover hidden agendas or the interests behind them (II-7), which are not brought up in the presence of the other parties.
- ☐ Be **alert to the formation of an unwanted coalition**. Multi-party mediations require additional focus on the balance of power (II-3) and it is very important to agree in advance that they will be working with package deals (II-12).

7 Escalation phases of a conflict[59]

7.1 Glasl's stairway of conflict escalation

The diagnostic instrument developed by Glasl (2004, 1998, 1981) offers a good basis for analyzing conflict behavior. Almost every conflict develops in escalation phases according to an established pattern. The threshold to the next phase can be recognized by obvious behavior. Every barrier that is crossed implies a further escalation of the conflict. The stairs of conflict are a descending stairway. Deeper, more intuitive, layers are activated on every step. Falling further downward takes less effort than climbing up together. Gravity only operates in one direction. The further parties descend, the more skills, techniques and strength are needed to defy gravity and turn the escalation process upwards.

A mediator needs to be aware of the phases that a conflict passes through. It is a useful instrument to diagnose the scale of a conflict situation and to predict the reactions that can be expected. Moreover, it offers an aid to recommend appropriate interventions and to determine how the conflict can be resolved (II-8.2 and III-1).

This is the strength of the model: it demonstrates that one should not look for the guilty parties, but rather realize that parties in a conflict situation react to each other in a certain, predictable, way. It is the interaction which results from the pressure of the moment. One can observe a 'natural response' to conduct and reactions in a certain phase of the conflict. It is more difficult to turn the escalation in a more constructive direction than to 'slide down' in the escalation. The interrelated properties of the nine steps are an instrument for analyzing how far the conflict has progressed. A single property could be applicable in an earlier or a later phase. Glasl describes this as: *'As one little red spot is not enough to diagnose measles, a single property is not enough to determine the correct escalation phase'.*

In 1980 Glasl published a standard work about conflict management for people who deal with conflicts professionally: KONFLIKTMANAGEMENT. EIN HANDBUCH FÜR FÜHRUNGSKRAFTE, BERATERINNEN UND BERATER. In 1981 he published the model in a condensed form in the Dutch language (Glasl 1981). With CONFRONTING CONFLICT: A FIRST-AID KIT FOR HANDLING CONFLICT Glasl (1999) wrote a hands-on book which offers first aid to parties in a conflict situation. By asking questions like: 'How did each party contribute to the arising of the conflict?', 'How did I get involved?', 'What do I want to achieve?', 'What do I not want to happen?', 'To what extent is it my conflict?', a first step is taken towards de-escalation and resolution of the conflict.

59 I'm very grateful to Professor Glasl for his willingness to read the draft of this chapter and for his valuable additions.

7.2 The phases of conflict escalation

The stairs of conflict escalation by Glasl (1998)

In this model the dynamics of conflicts are described in nine degrees of escalation (steps), subdivided into three main phases. Parties in a conflict exhibit different behaviors, depending on the step they occupy. This behavior develops in nine steps, and every transition to the next step implies crossing a barrier and a further escalation of the conflict.

Glasl's stairway of conflict escalation

Main Phase I Conflict seen as win-win Cooperation, dialogue. Conflict is about the conflict			**Main Phase II** Conflict seen as win-loose No dialogue: distrust. Conflict about winning
◄—— Dialogue	◄————►	End of Dialogue ——►	◄—— Distrust/
1. Hardening	Own solution		
Interests translated into positions	2. Debate & polemic	Own solution with informal help 3rd	Trained 3rd
Only own point of view counts	*Tactical moves, manipulation instead of dialogue*	3. Action instead of words	
Interpretation, facts leading life of their own	Verbal abuse, confrontations	*No consultation, one-sided actions*	4. Image + coalitions
Hardening	Polarization	No more talking, fait accompli	*Personal attack*
Less dialogue	Conflict becomes personal, irritations	Misinterpretation	Black-white: positive self-image, negative image opponent (knows nothing)
Impasse	Move from rational arguments to emotions and power issues. Scoring in front of 'spectators'	Negative spiral: accelerated escalation	Forming coalitions
Less understanding		Empathy diminishes	Avoid loss of face
		Finding a solution not seen as mutual responsibility	
Cooperation > competition	*Transition from cooperation to competition*	*Competition > cooperation*	

and be put in the right		**Main Phase III** Conflict seen as lose-lose Animosity. Conflict is about causing damage		
animosity increases →		←	No more communication →	
Professional 3rd	Professional 3rd	Professional 3rd	Formal intervention of trained/professional 3rd	Formal intervention trained/professional 3rd
5. Loss of face				
Attack on moral integrity	6. Threat strategies			
Distrust, see the other negatively	*Demands and sanctions*	7. Cause damage		
Manipulation, sabotaging	*Loss of control and deadlocked in dynamic of (counter) threats*	*Execute threats*	8. Destruction of enemy	
Foul games	1. demands 2. announce sanction 3. show sanction-potential	No reaction expected	*Physical, economical or psychological destruction*	9. Into the abyss together
	Conflict + psychological processes more complex	No communication	Direct attacks	Destroy at the cost of self-destruction
	Difficult to control	Target is to cause damage	Self-preservation	No way back
		Loss for enemy = winning		

Recommended interventions according to the escalation stage of the conflict

Main Phase I Conflict seen as win-win
Cooperation, dialogue. Conflict is about the conflict

← Dialogue ↔

1. Hardening			
Interests translated into positions	Interventions	2. Debate & polemic	
Only own point of view counts	*Focus: prevent escalation. Utilize (positive) potential*	Tactical moves, manipulation instead of dialogue	Interventions
Interpretation, facts leading life of their own	Translate positions into interests (II-7 and II-10)	Verbal abuse, confrontations	*Focus: managing from debate to dialogue*
Hardening, less dialogue	Identify mutual interests (II-7.1) and blocking issues (II-8)	Polarization	Managing the communication (III-1)
Impasse	Separate the content/problem from the relationship issues/persons (II-8)	Conflict becomes personal, irritations	Ground rules (I-5)
Less understanding.	Restore trust, clarify perspectives (IV-2.2)	Move from rational arguments to emotions and power issues. Scoring in front of 'spectators'	Structuring and fractionalizing (II-15)
	Structure communication (II-15) and establish ground rules (I-5)		
	Trigger the parties' determination to settle the dispute themselves (reality testing future oriented III-11.1), overcome impasse (IV-1)		
Cooperation > competition		*Transition from cooperation to competition*	

		Main Phase II Conflict seen as win-loose No dialogue: distrust. Conflict about winning and be put in the right	
	End of dialogue ⟶	⟵ Distrust / animosity increases ⟶	
		Trained third Profes-sional 3rd	Professional 3rd
3. Action instead of words			
No consultation, one-sided actions	Interventions	4. Image + coalitions	Contemplate calling in a professional/trained third party
No more talking, fait accompli	*Focus: conflict control, back to dialogue*	Personal attack	Interventions
Misinterpretation	Break down role patterns	Black-white: positive self-image, negative image opponent (knows nothing)	*Focus: conflict resolution, de-escalating, clarify perspectives and build trust*
Negative spiral: accelerated escalation	Work on the relationship, 'we' instead of 'you'. For criticism: use 'I'	Forming coalitions	Focus on interests (II-7 and II-10), reality testing (III-11)
Empathy diminishes	Dispel distrust, try to see each other as human beings	Avoid loss of face	Ask confrontation questions (III-10.4.1), argument questions (III-10.4.2) or mirroring (III-10.2.4)
Finding a solution not seen as mutual responsibility	Clarify perspectives (IV-2), reframe (III-6), reflect (III-5)		Deal with emotions (IV-4), break deadlocks (IV-1). Paradoxical interventions (III-19)
	Reality testing risk analysis (III-11.2), use leverage, test BATNA/WATNA/RATNA (III-14)		Regulate the group processes, address constituency (IV-6.2)
	Establish communication (make parties listen to each other III-2)		Cut across coalition lines
	Break deadlocks (IV-1), paradoxical interventions (III-19)		Make all involved feel responsible for solving the conflict
			Support deliberations with the constituency (IV-6.2), introduce objective criteria (III-16.1), look for a solution that takes into account the interests of all involved (II-7 and III-15)
Competition > cooperation			

Main phase I: Conflict seen as win-win by the parties

Here, there is still dialogue. Initially parties try to deal with the differences in a rational way. Then in a few steps the conflict escalates from solving problems together to competing with one another. And still both parties assume they can win. On steps 1 and 2 of the main phase I, parties can often solve the conflict themselves. After that moment, they need support.

Step 1 Hardening

At the beginning of step 1 a conflict can still turn out positively. It is a constructive conflict whose potential can be utilized. In this phase, a conflict can clear the air and conflicting opinions can generate new ideas and growth. Here it is often sufficient to facilitate the communication and ensure the conflict does not escalate (maintain the dialogue). It is important to focus primarily on the problem (separate the content from the relationship III-8) and at the same time also on the underlying relational problems. Positions can be reduced to the underlying interests and needs (II-7). As a result of several (psychological) processes (IV-2.4) hardening could occur. In addition, there is also a selective perception. At this stage it is important to guard against one's own interpretations assuming a life of their own (ladder of inference IV-2.2). If discussions degenerate into tactical maneuvering the conflict moves to step 2.

Step 2 Debate and controversy

On step 2 a conflict has to be managed actively and the conflict management skills of the parties involved come into play. The conflict expands, it is not only about the original issue; all kinds of other issues are now being introduced. In addition to the business conflicts, the manner in which the parties handle it also tends to provoke irritation. Positions harden further and there is a progression from dialogue to debate and allegations back and forth. Effective interventions are: controlling communications (III-1), introduce ground rules (I-5), structure the conflict (II-15), manage emotions (IV-4) and maintain the balance of power (II-3).
If direct personal communication is cut off (communication through third parties or by email) and unilateral actions are taken, the conflict moves to the third step of the main phase I.

Step 3 Putting one's plans into action

Starting from step 3, third party support is recommended. This can be an informal intervention made by a colleague, the executive, human resources, legal affairs, or a more formal intervention by an external advisor, such as a (negotiating) lawyer, a coach or a mediator. This third party should be aware of the dynamics of conflicts and be equipped to address escalating behavior. Effective interventions in this stage of the conflict are clarifying the perspective (IV-2), reality testing (III-11), reframing (III-

6), reflecting (III-5) and breaking deadlocks, for example by exploring the underlying relational issues (IV-1.3.2.1). On step 3, an escalation accelerates. Parties perceive the other as opponents and distance themselves (by avoiding direct contact and assuming formal behavior). Examples of conduct on step 3 are: communicating only in writing (email or letter) or via third parties:
'Could you let John know that...', 'I will not speak to him directly...', 'It is impossible to communicate with her...'

The transition to main phase II step 4 is characterized by the relationship/attacks becoming personal and parties trying to discredit each other.

Main Phase II: Perceiving conflicts as win-loose

There is no more dialogue, and mutual distrust and open hostility increase. The conflict is about winning and having the last word. The content of conflict issues is no longer addressed and the conflict becomes personal. Support is sought from others who take the same position. Here support is needed from a third party who is thoroughly trained in mediating conflicts. From step 4, support by an (external) professional is necessary.

Step 4 Image and coalitions

As the conflict becomes personal, a party creates a false image of the knowledge and skills of the other party and attacks the 'incompetent opponent'. However, they do not yet attack the opponent's morality. Stereotypes are created and maintained. Coalitions of shared positions are sought as a means of support. In addition to discussing the conduct of the opponent with others, a party will often resort to spreading rumors, by email (cc or bcc), letters, etc. and both parties try to establish a power block. The moment the opponents engage openly in mud-slinging (attack on morality), the conflict moves to step 5.

Step 5 Open attack and causing loss of face

The opponent is only seen in a negative way. Distrust, open hostility and 'distracting actions' are increasing. Parties have moral judgments about each other, and the integrity of the opponent is questioned and destroyed by open, targeted attacks. Steps are taken to damage reputations (manipulating, sabotage) and to alienate the other party. From step 5 it is almost impossible to resolve the conflict without professional help. At that moment strong psychological pressure is exerted openly, and the conflict enters step 6.

Step 6 Strategies to threaten

Before there were already hidden threats and 'warnings'. Now challenging demands are being made, followed by measures and actions. One party flexes its muscles and tries to harm the other if he does not comply. The conflict and the psychological processes become more complex and difficult to control. The parties lose control and get locked in an escalating spiral of action and reaction. First there is a threat to put pressure on a party (showing muscles). Submitting to the desires of this other party or not following through on their own threats, is perceived as a loss of credibility. Finally an ultimatum is presented which is usually answered with a counter-ultimatum. Each party still expects the opponent to respond (preferably by capitulating to the ultimatum). So this is a time of minimal communication. Parties are threatening with sabotage, legal action or media involvement, etc.

If the threatened sanctions are implemented the conflict enters main phase III, step 7.

Main phase III: Parties in a conflict regard it as a lose-lose situation

Now the conflict is mainly about harming the opponent. The parties think nothing can be won, but it is important to limit their own damage and maximizing the damage to the other party. To the extent that there is communication, it only leads to more distrust, misunderstandings and insinuations. In this main phase a formal intervention by a professional third party is necessary. Because the conflict has escalated seriously, external intervention initially needs to be aimed at preventing greater damage and stopping mutual harm, even violence.

Step 7 Damaging

The threats are being carried out. The opponent is attacked openly, although on a limited scale. The aim is to prevent the opponent from using sanctions and attacking. For example, causing a (management) crisis, leaking information to the press, starting summary proceedings or calling in the chief executive. The goal is to damage the opponent. Also actions are being taken which do not benefit the 'perpetrator'. However, as long as it damages the opponent it is perceived as gain. The difference with step 6 is that the other party is no longer expected to examine positions and interests. Any communication contributes more to escalation than to clarification. The opponent is attacked and a response is not expected. Attacking is no longer a warning or a threat, but an aim in itself. The transition to step 8 takes place when the limits self-restraint shift increasingly in the direction of total annihilation.

Step 8 Destroying the enemy

The other party has to be destroyed – physically, psychologically, or economically. This is only tempered by the opponent's wish not to suffer any serious damage themselves. Self-preservation sets a limit to the means deployed and the actions undertaken. However, a party is prepared to tolerate a degree of self-harm in the interests of inflicting greater harm on the opponent. Bringing about the dismissal of a colleague in such a way that he has little prospect of finding another job, or accusing the ex-partner of severe sexual offences like incest, or organizing a strike, are all examples of actions being undertaken.

Step 9 Ruining both yourself and your opponent

Parties have maneuvered themselves into a dead end, so there is no way back. Self-preservation is no longer important, destroying the opponent is all that matters, even if at the expense of self-destruction.

7.3 Interventions per escalation phase of the conflict

During steps 1 through 3, and possibly step 4, informal interventions by parties themselves or a third party are possible. Interventions the negotiators or a third party can use on steps 1 through 4 are presented in a diagram.

From Step 5 (Main Phase II) it is almost impossible to solve the conflict without the help of a (trained/professional) third party. Starting from step 5 it is very important for parties to recognize the gravity of the situation they are in.

See further Glasl (2006).

8 Online mediation

Online Dispute Resolution (ODR) has become common practice in courts and in arbitration and mediation procedures. Technology is constantly advancing, and users and their attorneys are increasingly embracing ODR to reduce costs and improve efficiency. This trend aligns with growing environmental awareness and the desire to reduce the carbon footprint of dispute resolution processes. Users seem to appreciate e-discovery, automated negotiation tools, analytics for finding mediators, and tools for predicting claim outcomes, even though there is some skepticism. Developments in this field are rapid, and mediators should stay informed.

Online Dispute Resolution (ODR) refers to the attempt to resolve a conflict using web-based applications, such as the internet or email. The most common form of ODR in

ADR is a mediation meeting via video conferencing, such as Teams or Zoom. A mediation process can take place entirely online or involve online elements, such as the intake. The mediation may also alternate between in-person and online sessions. In addition to video conferencing where the parties and mediator can see each other, e-mediation (via email) or teleconferencing (via phone) also falls under ODR. Therefore, most mediators incorporate ODR into (parts of) their practice.
While there is ongoing debate about whether AI can replace judges and arbitrators, it seems that the 'soft' skills required for mediation, including active listening and interpersonal interaction, will still be performed by humans for the foreseeable future. Mediation cannot (yet) be entirely reduced to algorithms. It is a social, emotional, psychological, and legal process that requires knowledge of human behavior, psychology, social and brain sciences, emotions, group heuristics, and more. Therefore, mediation will likely remain a process involving human beings.

For more on ODR and the development of new technologies, you can read articles 5.1 'Take Advantage of ODR's Full Potential' by Jeremy Lack, Ana Gonçalves, and Daniel Rainey, and 5.2 'Embrace and integrate relevant new technologies' by Francois Bogacz and Jeremy Lack in Michael Leathes (ed.), SEVEN KEYS TO UNLOCK MEDIATION'S GOLDEN AGE, mediate.com 2020.

Learn more about competency criteria for online mediators and the possibility of international ODR certification on the website of the International Mediation Institute (IMI).[60]

Checklist for the Challenges and Opportunities in Online Mediation[61]

When to Use Online Mediation

Reasons not to Use It:

- ☐ Logistics, responsibility for, and dependence on technology.
- ☐ You need to familiarize yourself with the technology and other mediation methods.
- ☐ Some non-verbal communication and interaction are missing.
- ☐ It can feel less important or impersonal.
- ☐ Participants (and the mediator) can lose focus or lose attention more easily.
- ☐ Potential cconfidentiality issues (for highly sensitive cases).
- ☐ It requires some technical proficiency from parties, which can be a barrier.
- ☐ Parties or you as the mediator may not want to or may be able to use it.
- ☐ Requires extra preparation, mindset shift, and planning in the beginning.

60 https://imimediation.org/orgs/cag-odr/.

61 Checklist prepared by Manon Schonewille and Jeremy Lack.

Reasons to Use It:

- ☐ Flexibility.
- ☐ 'The show can go on' under almost any circumstances.
- ☐ Participants and the mediator do not need to travel, in line with the Mediators Green Pledge and sustainable practices.
- ☐ Quick initiation, immediate crisis intervention possible.
- ☐ You can easily view and edit digital documents together.
- ☐ Since there is less direct confrontation and everyone is in their own (safe) environment, people often feel more comfortable sharing feelings and information.
- ☐ You can easily involve the constituency or stakeholder.
- ☐ You have full control and can set rules, such as allowing only one person to speak at a time or muting participants.
- ☐ Some programs offer a digital waiting room and separate breakout rooms for private conversations with individual parties during a caucus.

Step-by-Step Tips, Tricks, and Best Practices for Online Mediation

1. General

a. Check which platforms are available and take them for a test drive. Some providers like Skype, Zoom, and Teams offer free options. You can also use FaceTime or WhatsApp video calls. Or (if you want to talk without video) use the conference call feature on your iPhone or other conference call programs. Which one is the best? It depends on your preferences and the situation. Assess the facilities you need. Sometimes, the simplest application is sufficient, while at other times, managing separate rooms or working with subtitles might be important. Besides feeling comfortable with the technology, consider joining the platform that parties are used to or their organization permits from their work laptops. For highly confidential cases, also pay extra attention to security options.

b. Before starting your mediation, have the intended program ready and perform a test. Also, consider a backup plan. For example, a Zoom meeting as the primary option and a conference call as a backup. Inform the parties about this and have all contact information at hand.

c. Co-mediation with a second 'host' brings significant advantages, particularly in dealing with technical issues. Both mediators work with different internet connections, so there is a good chance that at least one of them can stay online. Additionally, if necessary, the co-mediators can also go to different breakout rooms separately.

d. Consider investing in a few good headphones with a microphone function, or use a quality table microphone.

e. Mention on your website, LinkedIn account, etc., that you also offer online mediation Online Dispute Resolution. Your clients and their advisors may not think of it themselves, and this can give them ideas on how you can serve them.

2. Before the mediation session

a. Send all participants an invitation to log in, including login procedures, practical steps, and an invitation for a 'test run' if the parties have no experience with digital meetings. In most cases, you can work with a general login link (as long as you ensure that you have a waiting room function or that the host needs to admit participants). For more complex cases, see below.

b. Have the email addresses and mobile numbers of all participants ready and stored in your phone and/or laptop. Ensure everything is set up in advance, so that you are linked via Teams and have also sent a Zoom invitation as a fallback option, or created a WhatsApp group. This way, if the online platform malfunctions or participants cannot log in, you will not have to scramble all information and options at that moment. It is wise to discuss fallback options with the parties.

c. Set up the documents or email correspondence that you may need during the mediation on your desktop and close all other applications. This way, you can screen share at any time, avoid disruptive notifications, and keep your laptop running smoothly.

d. Think about which visual communication or document sharing options you want to use. Since the attention span for online meetings is generally shorter than in-person meetings, it is also useful to vary activities. For example, have a flip chart behind you on which you write something occasionally. On your laptop, use a blank document (e.g., Word or a whiteboard function) for taking notes, especially to capture as many ideas as possible during brainstorming sessions.

e. If you wish to use them, have a number of supporting presentation slides ready (e.g., an initial welcome screen with the word 'WELCOME' and also 'CONFIDENTIAL' on it) to set the tone. If you prefer working with slides, there are also advanced options (see below).

f. Mediation agreement: have this signed in advance and returned. Various programs allow you to sign digitally (e.g., Docusign, Adobe), and some even offer additional verification options for a legally binding signature.
What should you do with parties who find digital signing complicated (or in case of technical issues)? Email the mediation agreement signed by you as the mediator to both parties and ask them to sign and initial their own copies and return them (this can also be a scan of a printed copy). Additionally, it is wise to include a provision in the mediation agreement like this one:

"If multiple copies of this agreement are separately signed, each copy shall be considered an original, and together, these copies form the mediation agreement."
Then, send both signed copies to the parties together via email.

g. If parties or you feel the need, you can arrange to be online earlier to test sound and video. To avoid any confusion (as people may log in and out repeatedly if not admitted immediately), inform them if you have a waiting room function in your program and that you will admit both of them simultaneously. For Skype or conference calls, you can call both parties simultaneously.
h. During your test, take a moment to see what the parties see when you turn on your camera. A real background with books or plants seems to create an impression of competence and trustworthiness. A neutral background (a wall) is also acceptable. The use of a virtual background, especially when blurred, appears to be less advisable. Research indicates that it generates less trust and does not convey the impression of expertise. [62]

3. At the start of the mediation

a. Ensure that you have a platform with the waiting room feature enabled (e.g., Zoom or Teams), and that you are the one who can admit both parties simultaneously.

Avoid the temptation to admit someone to your digital mediation room before the other party arrives. This is true even if someone is taking a long time to join. Instead, you can send a text message or email to both or leave a message in the waiting room's chat.

b. At the beginning of the session, take some time to discuss how you will handle the online session and, where necessary, how the technology works, so that everyone knows how to use the basic functions. In addition to practical aspects, this creates a shared learning experience, puts everyone at ease, and enables the mediator to guide the process. Unless you are working without video and all microphones are continuously open, make sure that everyone knows how to:
   1. Turn their own sound on/off.
   2. Turn their own video on/off.
   3. If you mute the participants' audio, how to digitally raise their hand or request a break.
   For advanced users (and typically only for longer sessions using these features):

62 https://journals.plos.org/plosone/article?id=10.1371/journal.pone.0291444, And Dress for the (Remote) Job You Want, Noah Zandan, Hallie Lynch, June 18, 2020 Harvard Business Review. https://hbr.org/2020/06/dress-for-the-remote-job-you-want. Seeing the actual room that you are in gives - according to research - the impression of: authenticity 65%, expert 52%, trustworthy 73%, vs a virtual / blurred background authenticity 4%, expert 4%, trustworthy 5%. A neutral wall gives the impression of: authenticity 31%, expert 43%, trustworthy 22%.

4. Share their own screen.
5. Send a chat message (make it clear that they should select a specific person and not 'everyone' if they want the message to be private!). Whether you use this depends on your mediation approach.
6. How to return from a separate meeting room to the joint session room, etc.
7. How to change their name (it is more convenient for everyone if it says Peter Smith Company X' rather than something like 'IPad PS1969'...).

c. Check confidentiality and explicitly ask if there may be others in the room who are (able to) listen in. Request that everyone reports if others enter their physical space during the mediation meeting. Since it is easier to make videos, audio recordings, etc., online, make sure to mention this explicitly. Include this also in the mediation agreement, stating that this is not allowed.
d. I personally find it convenient to share the mediation agreement via my screen at the beginning and walk through the articles with the parties.

4. During the mediation session

a. The attention span tends to be less online, so propose that everyone can indicate when they need a break, and you can take (shorter) breaks more frequently. Keep the participants engaged by limiting speaking time and occasionally doing something different. For instance, use a flip chart behind you and alternate with a digital whiteboard if it is available in your program, show slides, etc.
b. Some platforms allow you to pre-set whether participants can speak one by one or simultaneously. You can also mute everyone or a specific person. In online mediation, you are literally in control of the communication, at least you can control who speaks.
c. It is in general preferable to schedule several short sessions rather than one long session (unless...). For most parties, 1,5 or 2 hours is a good length.
d. Online mediation lacks some non-verbal communication (body language), but in my experience you gain the advantage that people feel more comfortable and secure in their own space. This often helps in sharing information and feelings and addressing challenging issues. Also, participants are not sitting directly across from each other, but they still see each other and are looking at the same screen.
e. It can feel a bit awkward to shift from a formal business introduction to addressing underlying issues instead of diving into the content. We are often accustomed to a business approach from telephone meetings. What works well for me is to discuss this and, for example, start with a visual like an iceberg, explaining that during mediation, the Problem, Process, and People will be addressed; and that you would like to start with what is beneath the surface. Where the emotion/blocking issues/resistance/concerns, etc., lie.

f. Depending on the issues and the parties, I sometimes ask if they would like to exchange their perspectives in advance in writing (I send them a list of questions). This helps to start the conversation about underlying issues, even in a digital meeting. If they have already exchanged a significant portion of the content, this sometimes seems to provide peace and space to first discuss the relationship and communication issues.
g. Summarize or paraphrase more often than you are used to and ask if it is accurate, especially regarding the relationship and the emotional/underlying issues, not just the content.
h. Silence feels more natural online, perhaps because we are also accustomed to technology causing occasional poor reception and break-offs. Therefore, make use of silence frequently.
i. I have noticed that during online mediation, partly due to the pacing and the typically shorter and more frequent sessions, I can leave more to the parties and have them do more work. For example, following up with an offer made during mediation by recording it in an email, so the other party can then review it calmly before the next meeting. Summarizing where they stand, etc.
Be careful: email or text message communication is tricky and is often interpreted more negatively than other forms of communication. Also, the party concerned may keep re-reading it and may be annoyed every time. So, think carefully if such an intervention suits the parties (check: if they are ready to formulate fairly neutrally and from a 'we' perspective).
j. Collaborating on a settlement agreement online with a one text procedure (II-12), in my experience, often works even better than having everyone with their own paper copy at the table.
k. The same applies to a mediator proposal (II-7).

5. Advanced applications

Here are some ideas for those who want to go further and leverage even more possibilities, or for mediations with large groups, cases that are sensitive to publicity, cross-border mediations, full-day online mediations (e.g., international trade cases), multiple involved (legal) advisors, and potentially complicated mediations, etc.

Whether you want to use the following depends on the type of mediations you conduct, the parties involved, and your mediation style.

Below are a few options for deeper exploration, meant as inspiration.

a) If you expect security issues, you can set passwords to limit access in advance, encrypt the call, and send prior invitations only to approved participants, so others cannot join, even if they have the access URL and password.

b) Set up individual digital rooms (break-out rooms): each room can be named after the party or a team, and you can also pre-assign rooms to individual participants. Additionally, you can create a separate break-out room for the mediator(s) where a caucus conversation can take place. You can also have a separate meeting room for lawyers or involved experts, etc. Even if these spaces are not used, it is helpful to have them ready for large commercial cases or cases with many (international) advisors/participants who are accustomed to working in this manner. In principle, you can digitally replicate everything you can do with physical spaces.

c) Since everyone is already on a digital platform, you can easily use digital/visual aids like PowerPoint presentations you have prepared in advance. These can set the tone, display visuals, make people more open to discussing sensitive subjects, or normalize/neutralize issues (e.g., an image of an iceberg with positions as the tip and interests underwater, Hofstede's cultural dimensions (IV-5)). You can also prepare a few slides for standard topics (e.g., interests vs. positions, a SWOT analysis) or for specific components, such as your mediator's opening statement, ground rules, cooperation-promoting exercises, or models like a list of interests and agenda items, or BATNAs, WATNAs, and R/PATNA analysis (III-14).

d) You can seamlessly present your own or all opening statements using visual presentations online. This is not only useful for discussing the ground rules but also for having a more structured discussion about the type of process the parties have in mind and where they stand. Handy slides to discuss with parties in this context include the Glasl stairs (IV-7) or the adapted Riskin grid to discuss your style (I-2.1).

   This can optionally be extended with (anonymous) polls to determine everyone's starting position.

e) You can also use the poll function to do a "how do you feel on a scale of 1-10" check at regular intervals. Polls can be done anonymously, and you do not have to share the results.

9 Dealing with brains, tips for mediators from neuroscience[63]

9.1 Our brain in evolution

Neurosciences represent an intriguing field, highly relevant to mediation. In neuropsychology, fascinating insights have emerged regarding decision-making processes, the role of emotions, and the effects of our neurobiology on our behavior in conflict or negotiation situations.
Our brain has evolved on three levels, referred to as the 'triune brain' by MacLean,[64] or the three-part brain. These three brain parts are interconnected but also have distinct functions.

1. The Reptilian Brain
The oldest part of our brain is the reptilian brain, which includes the brainstem. This part houses our survival mechanisms and aggression. It is also responsible for autonomous functions like breathing and heartbeat.

2. The Limbic System
The second level is the limbic system, also known as the mammal brain. This section is involved in emotions, motivation, social behavior, and emotional memory. Pain and reward are two significant drivers of our behavior. Research has shown that social and physical stimuli are processed by the same neural networks. This means that experiences like social exclusion or feeling unfairly treated cause responses similar to physical pain. The same principle applies to social cues such as having a good reputation, being treated fairly, and collaborating with others.
In the emotional brain, there is the amygdala, also known as an almond shaped cluster of nuclei, which plays a significant role in regulating our emotions. The amygdala connects information from different senses to emotions and stores it in memory so that similar situations can be easily recognized in the future and responded to appropriately. Some responses to stimuli, such as stimuli causing fear, can be automatic.

Thinking about your emotions causes a greater decrease in amygdala activity compared to self-reflection or doing nothing. This is likely a reason why reflecting on feeling or emotions (III-5.2) work well during mediation. There are strong connections between the limbic system and the most recent part of our brain, the neocortex.

63 With many thanks to Huub Liefhebber for his invaluable contribution to this chapter.

64 The 'triune brain hypothesis' was developed in the 1960s by the American neuroscientist Paul MacLean and extensively described in his book: MacLean, P.D. (1990), The Triune Brain in Evolution: Role of Paleocerebral Functions. Munich: Springer.

3. The neocortex

The third and most recently developed part of our brain is the neocortex. This section is responsible for complex cognitive functions such as language, reasoning, planning, problem-solving, abstract thinking, and consciousness. It enables us to learn from experiences, anticipate the future, and comprehend intricate social relationships.
The neocortex or the cerebral cortex occupies the largest part of our brain in terms of size. It is involved in higher functions where cognition, interpreting feelings, and conscious thinking take place.

Higher mammals and humans have a well-developed neocortex. The size of our prefrontal cortex (PFC) and its relationship with underlying brain areas make humans, from a neurobiological standpoint, unique compared to animals.
Evolutionarily, these three parts of our brain are stacked on top of each other, with the newest part, the neocortex, overlaying the older parts, the limbic system and the reptilian brain. This stacking of brain regions allows for the gradual development of more sophisticated cognitive and social abilities.
In practice, the three parts of the brain communicate with each other with difficulty, and it is the older brain parts that tend to dominate the more recent ones. While this strategy proves highly effective for species survival, a dominant reptilian brain is in general not very helpful in conflict resolution.

A comprehensive article on insights from neuroscience and their lessons for mediators and negotiators is provided by Birke (2010), "Neuroscience and Settlement. An examination of scientific innovations and practical applications".[65]

9.2 Mirror neurons and body language

In his book 'Mirroring people, science of empathy and how we connect with others', Iacoboni[66] describes the discovery of mirror neurons in an Italian lab. Animal experiments revealed that a mirror neuron is a neuron that becomes active not only when an animal performs an action but also when it observes another animal performing the same action. Research using functional MRI and electroencephalography has shown that humans also possess mirror neurons. Mirror neuron systems play a role in understanding and interpreting others' actions and learning new skills through imitation. They are also believed to play a role in understanding others' thought patterns (theory of mind) and empathy (II-5). Iacoboni concludes in his book that people use mirror neurons

65 Birke, R., (2010), 'Neuroscience and Settlement. An examination of scientific innovations and practical applications', Ohio State Journal on Dispute Resolution 2010, vol. 25, no. 2, p. 477-527.

66 Iacoboni, M. (2009), Mirroring people, science of empathy and how we connect with others. Picador.

for empathy, language processing, and self-awareness. Does this imply that we can better understand others' intentions using these mirror neurons?
The existence of a universal language would be possible only if people shared a universal emotional language. In the 1950s, the American psychologist Paul Ekman traveled the world as a young scientist, photographing faces of people from different cultures and showing them to others. It was found that a resident of Papua New Guinea could effortlessly recognize facial expressions of fear or anger in a white woman from San Francisco. The ability to recognize even the smallest changes in expression surprisingly transcended cultural backgrounds, demonstrating that facial expressions form a universal language. Evidently, humans possess physical features where specific facial muscles and mirror neurons in the brain can combine to create a form of communication easily understood by others.
This idea that we can 'read' others might advocate for having more frequent and longer joint sessions during mediations, or at the very least, encouraging more direct personal contact between the negotiators. More direct contact during mediations gives parties and their lawyers the opportunity to convincingly demonstrate their sincerity emotionally. It also allows them to assess whether the information provided is trustworthy or not.

9.3 'Neuro'-interventions[67]

Reality Testing (III-11):
In successful mediations, there comes a point where parties need to formulate concrete offers and are willing to compromise or concede where necessary. Mediators often encourage parties to think about the future as a tool for making a good decision, e.g., in the form of reality testing. Recent research indicates that encouraging people to think (briefly) about the future promotes 'helpful behavior,' and when individuals can contemplate the past or the future in a somewhat more positive manner, it fosters prosocial behavior.[68]
The assumption that people can accurately predict what will make them happy in the future is often incorrect. When people are asked to predict their feelings in the future, they tend to underestimate their mental state at the time of the prediction. In essence, it is not wise to make predictions during a conflict about how one will feel after resolving the conflict. Therefore, reality testing is more effective when combined with framing.

67 Based on: Liefhebber, H.J. (2017), 'Dealing with your brain. Een neurokompas voor mediators', Tijdschrift conflicthantering 4, jrg 2017, p. 22-26 (Dutch).

68 Cernadas Curotto, P., Sander, D., d'Argembeau, A. and Klimecki, O. (2022), 'Back to the future: A way to increase prosocial behavior', PLoS ONE 17(8): e0272340. https://doi.org/10.1371/journal.pone.0272340.

Framing (III-16.4):
A powerful tool a mediator has is the ability to frame parties' decisions in a way that maximizes the likelihood of reaching a solution. A useful technique is to leverage parties' tendency to avoid risks. Generally, people are willing to accept significant risks to prevent potential losses and are risk-averse when there are gains to be made. Concerns about potential losses seem to undermine the ability to think of winning scenarios. In short, fear of loss negatively affects creativity. Although it may seem unwise to induce a risk-averse frame of mind during a brainstorming session, it can be a very useful tool in a later stage of the mediation. If parties seem to reach an impasse toward the end of a mediation and cannot decide whether to accept a compromise or proceed to a lawsuit, the mediator can induce a loss frame of mind to guide parties toward a solution (III-11 Decision error).

Handling Emotions Carefully (IV-4):
Mediators and negotiators know from experience that it is important to let both parties tell their story, and in many disputes, there are more than two stories. Attorneys often have different interests and viewpoints than their clients, who in turn often have mixed feelings about the events leading up to the conflict.
Recapping events that preceded a conflict can often evoke strong emotional reactions from the party telling their story or the other party. Yet, the general notion is that it is beneficial for parties to vent their feelings beforehand, allowing them to enter the negotiation process in a more rational manner. Mediators assume that telling one's story with all the accompanying emotions ultimately leads to relaxation afterward, increasing the willingness to negotiate again. Modern brain research, however, seems to challenge this conventional wisdom.
In our brains, among the billions of neurons, a single neuron can form a chemical connection with several nearby neurons. When such a chain reaction occurs, it constitutes a neural network. While our brains consist of a staggering hundred billion neurons, the potential number of neural networks is exponentially larger. As these temporary configurations of neurons occur more frequently, the corresponding networks become more durable, helping us develop specific skills such as playing the piano or typing.

See also IV-4.4 Interventions for managing emotions.

Neuroscientist LeDoux[69] discovered that neurological networks associated with feelings of fear are among the most enduring. Fear is one of the most successful evolutionary strategies as it can prevent significant problems and is deeply rooted in the brain. It

69 LeDoux, J. (2003), The emotional brain fear and the amygdala: cellular and molecular biology, October 2003. Springer.

turns out that when a person describes events in detail that were painful for them, they activate the same neural networks that were active at the time of the original experience, essentially reliving everything. However, avoiding emotions entirely leads to a missed opportunity to explore the underlying interests of the parties involved. Suppressing emotions repeatedly negatively affects activating empathy in the other party and the mediator. If emotions are not adequately addressed, it can lead to a decline in communication quality or merely negotiating financial compensation. Therefore, the best advice for the mediator seems to be to allow parties to tell their story, including all the emotions involved, and then take a short break before continuing with negotiations or activities that require the parties' cognitive abilities. Next, ensure focus on the future.

9.4 The SCARF model and beyond reason

9.4.1 The SCARF model

In 2008, David Rock of the Neuro Leadership Institute introduced the SCARF model.[70] This model aims to enhance understanding of both one's own behavior and that of others, ultimately enabling the ability to influence this behavior. In numerous situations that may arise during a mediation, this model can serve as a 'neurocompass' for the mediator to neuro-effectively lead the mediation process.

SCARF represents basic human needs:
Status,
Certainty,
Autonomy,
Relatedness, and
Fairness.

These five domains activate the primary threat or reward networks in the brain. It is crucial to address all SCARF elements during interactions with others. For instance, a threat to someone's status activates the same network in the brain as when someone's life is threatened. Similarly, an increase in 'Fairness' experienced by parties activates the same network associated with receiving a salary raise, for example.

How to deal with SCARF in a negotiation or a mediation setting:
1. **Dealing with Status**, as the relative social position parties hold in relation to each other.
We process the assessment of our position and status relative to others using the same brain area we use for ranking numbers: unconsciously, you assign others a higher or

70 Rock, D. (2008), 'SCARF: A Brain-Based Model for Collaborating with and Influencing Others', Neuroleadership Journal, no. 1, p. 1-9.

lower score than yourself. Comparing oneself with others requires cognitive effort. An increase in status is processed in the same way as a financial windfall. Giving positive feedback or a compliment, especially in the presence of others, can elevate the feeling of status. However, offering advice or well-intentioned critical feedback can be perceived as threatening to one's status. Therefore, as a mediator, be cautious when giving advice. Asking open-ended questions (III-10.1) and using neutral language (III-7) are more effective. Reflecting on progress (III-5.3) and complimenting parties on their effort and what has been achieved in mediation also positively impact the feeling of status. Status is related to the relative position taken in comparison to others. Perhaps this explains the power of reframing (III-6).

2. **Dealing with Certainty**, the need for certainty and predictability in a mediation process.
Meeting an unknown person, such as the mediator, or the legal advisor of the other party, can trigger an automatic flight response. Therefore, it is beneficial to have contact with the parties before the first meeting (pre-mediation session I-1.1 and process consultation meeting I-2.8). Provide parties with certainty by creating safety and clarity about the mediation (opening statement and ground rules I-3).
'Uncertain pain' is a stronger stimulus than a 'certain reward'. Manage expectations and ensure that as a mediator, you are present as the process manager. Stick to agreements and be predictable. Not meeting an expectation has a significant negative impact. Structuring (II-15) and bringing order and clarity to the chaos that conflict usually entails also positively influence certainty.

3. **Dealing with Autonomy**, the need for parties to make their own decisions during the mediation and about the chosen solutions.
Autonomy is a good remedy against stress, and (the idea of) more autonomy provides a sense of reward. Our brain likes to make predictions and be able to have a say about the future. Empowering (II-6) the parties, ensuring party autonomy and letting them decide on a solution, have a positive effect on the feeling of autonomy. It is essential to emphasize that mediation is voluntary, and parties cannot obligate each other to anything during the mediation unless they specifically choose to make an agreement.

4. **Dealing with Relatedness**, the degree to which parties feel connected despite differences in opinions and perspectives.
Relatedness involves belonging to a social group or being outside it. Relatedness is closely related to trust (II-1). Our brain quickly categorizes: 'friend or foe', through mirror neurons (IV-9.2) facilitating non-verbal communication. Therefore, it is good to also hold joint sessions. Parties can establish through direct non-verbal communication whether the other party is genuine or trustworthy, or if they meant certain things differently.

Exaggerated enemy images can thus be adjusted. Set ground rules and ensure that parties treat each other with respect (I-3). It becomes more challenging to empathize when someone is perceived as an enemy or competitor.
We perceive 'social comfort' as a reward and its absence as a threat. Mutual trust can be achieved through optimal use of breaks and joint sessions, as well as something as simple as having lunch together or interacting on a mutually neutral topic (e.g., favorite vacation destination, hobby's or even the weather).

5. **Dealing with Fairness**, the mediator's proportional attention to parties, the space each party gets during mediation, and the solutions that not only need to make sense rationally but also need to feel right.
Fairness has a profound impact on negotiation situations. Unfair behavior is interpreted in the same brain region responsible for registering pain. Studies have shown that people can make choices that go against their own interests or rationality if they feel something is unfair.[71] A sense of unfairness for any party involved can be detrimental in mediation, whereas the presence of a feeling of fairness promotes willingness to cooperate. The mediator can contribute to this by paying attention to the people the process and the problem (content).
Perceived fairness can be enhanced in mediation or negotiation through transparency, communication, personal engagement, the use of objective criteria (III-16), and ensuring that both parties have equal influence over the process.

9.4.2 'Beyond Reason: Using Emotions as you Negotiate' by Fisher and Shapiro[72]

The conclusions of the SCARF model (IV-9.4.1) seamlessly align with those presented in the earlier published book 'Beyond Reason' by Roger Fisher and Daniel Shapiro. Similar to David Rock in the SCARF model, these authors offer a systematic approach for handling emotions during negotiations. Both authors recognize that emotions play an essential role in such processes and can sometimes be obstacles. Therefore, they consider it crucial to uncover the concerns underlying these emotions. In 'Beyond Reason: Using Emotions as You Negotiate', a framework is introduced for effectively managing emotions in negotiation situations. The authors advise shifting attention from emotions to the underlying concerns (core concerns). This approach proves to be much more effective than other interventions, such as attempting to ignore, stop, or address emotions.

71 For example, the ultimatum game, developed in 1982 by Güth, Schmittberger, and Schwarze: A is given an amount, for instance, €100, and must share it with B. A can make one offer, and B can choose whether to accept or reject that offer. There is no possibility of negotiation regarding the distribution. If B rejects the offer, both receive nothing. Rationally, B should accept any offer from A that gives him something since it is more than he has at that moment. However, in practice, 'unfair' distributions are often refused. The average offer that results in an agreement typically falls between 40 and 60% of the total amount.

72 Fisher, R., & D. Shapiro (2006), Beyond Reason: Using Emotions as You Negotiate. New York: The Penguin Group.

The five 'core concerns' that motivate people are similar to the SCARF model:

- **A**ppreciation: acknowledgment of ideas and emotions, expressing gratitude.
- **A**ffiliation: in a business setting: whether/how you are treated equally, as a colleague, having a relationship/bond where you feel connected.
- **A**utonomy: respecting others' freedom to make independent decisions.
- **S**tatus: acknowledgment of the position you hold.
- **R**ole: acknowledgment of the role someone else plays during a negotiation.

Working with core concerns and translating emotions into underlying concerns serves two purposes: (1) it helps to understand someone's emotional experience and behavior, and (2) it is a means to stimulate positive emotions during a negotiation situation. These functions can be fulfilled through this approach.

A key takeaway from both SCARF and the approach in Beyond Reason is that the mediator's role is to help parties recognize the importance of these five categories and guide them in these aspects. What does not work, according to these models, is trying to stop, smother or ignore emotions. Directly addressing them often backfires. So the best strategy seems to be to shift the focus from emotions to the underlying concerns.

9.5 A neurocompass for mediators

9.5.1 Neuro tips

Below are some general insights from neuroscience that can support mediators when conducting the mediation process.

- ☐ **Reflecting on feelings** (III-5.2) and discussing the cause of emotions with a party, for example in a caucus (II-14), can decrease amygdala activity, thus reducing the fight or flight response and the perception of threat or danger. Give room for emotions to be expressed but take breaks occasionally (IV-4).
- ☐ **Social reward stimuli**, such as feeling fairly treated, collaborating with others, and having a good reputation, stimulate the reward center and an 'approach/towards' response. Danger is more dominant than reward. The challenge for a mediator is to reduce the perception of danger/threat/fear in parties. Develop an awareness to recognize feelings of fear and threat in parties. Be empathetic, but do not get carried away by the parties' emotions (IV-4).
- ☐ **Create an environment where people treat each other respectfully and provide positive feedback** (status!). Ensure safety by being clear about the process, be predictable (certainty). Provide self-determination to parties (autonomy). Allow parties to collaborate with each other. Therefore, also conduct joint sessions (relatedness). Ensure all parties have equal influence

on the mediation process (II-3) and the development of solutions; create a mediation process perceived as fair by all parties (fairness).

- ☐ **Enable parties and their attorneys to communicate directly during a joint session** so the 'universal language' can work. As a mediator, articulate the intention behind an action (which might differ from its impact on the other party). Demonstrate desired behavior to activate mirror neurons (IV-9.2): listen attentively, look friendly and neutral, collaborate effectively with a co-mediator. If parties struggle to make decisions or not showing willingness to compromise, concede or make steps towards resolution near the end of mediation, induce a risk-averse frame of mind (II-11.2 and III-16.4. Enhance parties' perception of reward.

9.5.2 Neuroscience tips for different phases of the mediation process

Tips from neuroscience for phases (II-16) of the mediation process:

- ☐ **Opening statement:**
  Conducting a comprehensive joint session is better than going directly or exclusively into caucus (II-9).
- ☐ **Exploration and information exchange:**
  Social reward stimuli, such as feeling fairly treated, collaborating with others, and having a good reputation, stimulate the reward center, promoting willingness to collaborate. Therefore, give both parties equal opportunities to influence the process and tell their story. Summarize (also) common interests and reflect on positive interactions between parties. Reflect on the progress and the effort both parties are making. Take a break after intense emotions and especially decouple decision-making from emotional moments.
- ☐ **Reaching agreement:**
  A little push here and there, (re)framing (III-6), and clear guidance can help (loss minimization III-16.4). The solution should not only sound good from a rational perspective, but also feel good (reactive devaluation III-16.3, winner's curse, and self-serving bias IV-2.4 and IV-4.5).

on the mediation process (II-3) and the development of solutions; create a mediation process perceived as fair by all parties (fairness).

- ☐ **Enable parties and their attorneys to communicate directly during a joint session** so the 'universal language' can work. As a mediator, articulate the intention behind an action (which might differ from its impact on the other party). Demonstrate desired behavior to activate mirror neurons (IV-9.2): listen attentively, look friendly and neutral, collaborate effectively with a co-mediator. If parties struggle to make decisions or not showing willingness to compromise, concede or make steps towards resolution near the end of mediation, induce a risk-averse frame of mind (II-11.2 and III-16.4. Enhance parties' perception of reward.

9.5.2 Neuroscience tips for different phases of the mediation process

Tips from neuroscience for phases (II-16) of the mediation process:

- ☐ **Opening statement:**
  Conducting a comprehensive joint session is better than going directly or exclusively into caucus (II-9).
- ☐ **Exploration and information exchange:**
  Social reward stimuli, such as feeling fairly treated, collaborating with others, and having a good reputation, stimulate the reward center, promoting willingness to collaborate. Therefore, give both parties equal opportunities to influence the process and tell their story. Summarize (also) common interests and reflect on positive interactions between parties. Reflect on the progress and the effort both parties are making. Take a break after intense emotions and especially decouple decision-making from emotional moments.
- ☐ **Reaching agreement:**
  A little push here and there, (re)framing (III-6), and clear guidance can help (loss minimization III-16.4). The solution should not only sound good from a rational perspective, but also feel good (reactive devaluation III-16.3, winner's curse, and self-serving bias IV-2.4 and IV-4.5).

Resources

Resource A	Glossary	269
Resource B	Key procedural drivers	277
Resource C	Indicators predicting likelihood of settlement by mediation	279
Resource D	Checklist Cost – Benefit Analysis mediation vs arbitration and litigation	281
Resource E	Sample mediation agreement	284
Resource F	Sample settlement agreement	291
Resource G	5 NEGOTIATION KEYS to claim & create value	294
Resource H	Consulted Literature and other sources	297

Resource A Glossary

Acknowledgement	Putting an end to recurring (emotional) topics by highlighting the importance of the issue or the feelings associated with it and thereby communicate that the message and the feelings behind a statement are being 'heard'.
Active listening	A technique to listen effectively by constantly giving feedback through paraphrasing and summarizing. Often used in emotional situations, when communication is strained or if conversation is circular.
Agree to disagree	Parties involved in a mediation agree that they have differing opinions on a certain issue.
Anchoring	A concept from social psychology. The process of thinking takes a lot of energy, so our brain tries to use a shortcut wherever possible. A familiar quantity is an easy anchor. So the moment a number or proposal is mentioned, this is very often used as a reference point. A proposal or a number influences our ability to judge and can therefore influence the course of a negotiation or mediation.
Asking questions	The mediator asks questions to obtain information and to get important topics out in the open. Moreover, asking questions is a vital tool to manage or control a mediation and make progress as a result. They can be: closed, linear, clarifying, open, relational, circular, reciprocal, mirroring, peel-off, confronting, strategic, hypothetical, argumentative, tactical, verification and summarizing.
BATNA	BATNA is the acronym for Best Alternative to Negotiated Agreement. This is the most positive scenario that can be envisaged if the negotiators fail to reach a settlement.
Benchmark	A standard by which something can be measured or judged.
Blocking issues	A blocking issue is the reason why parties did not manage to resolve a conflict themselves. Blocking issues often are of an emotional nature.
Bottom line	The limit of what one is prepared to accept or give during a negotiation.
Brainstorming	Coming to a possible solution by generating options and ideas without criticizing them.
Caucus	In a caucus the mediator consults the party individually and in confidence in order to move forward to the next phase of the mediation.

Caucus mediation style	In a caucus the mediator consults the party individually and in confidence. The mediator will proceed to a caucus if he notices the discussion is deadlocked, if there is no forward movement in the process, or when blocking issues prevent the real interests from being discussed.
Cognitive dissonance	If a discrepancy arises between one's own perception and facts or observations, people try to avoid it or they try to reason it away. This is called cognitive dissonance. People are inclined to look for arguments that support their own perception, because it is uncomfortable to observe an inconsistency between their own convictions and their actual observations or even the actions they took.
Co-mediation	A mediation with two mediators. It can be two equally competent mediators who complement each other and it is often a combination of a mediator with content expertise and a facilitative mediator.
Communication-focused mediator	See relationship-focused mediator.
Confidential listening	During a mediation that is based on the principle of confidential listening the parties agree on letting the mediator confidentially know in advance their conditions and options to come to an agreement. This way the mediator can evaluate possible overlap where common solutions can be found. The mediator informs the parties only about a potential ZOPA, Zone of Possible Agreement, but tells nothing about the content.
Defensive emotions	Defensive emotions are directed to oneself or one's own conduct.
Deadlock	Making no forward progress - moving in a circle. Not agreeing. Impasse.
Empathy	Understanding and entering into another one's feelings. (Without agreeing. Empathy doesn't mean sympathy.)
Empowerment	Empowerment means stimulating independency, autonomy and the ability to make decisions on your own.
Evaluating mediator	Approach of the mediator. Solution-focused, directive both in the process and in the content.
Evaluative mediation	See solution-focused mediation.
Expand the pie	Searching for interests and exploring matters that are not necessarily part of the conflict but can contribute to finding a solution. This expands the field of reciprocal interests and enables more pie to be shared. The pie can

	also be expanded by redefining a problem and by asking questions which propel the parties look differently at the problem.
Exploring	Researching a theme, often used to proceed from positions to the interests behind them.
Facilitating mediation	See problem-focused mediation.
Facilitative mediator	The problem-focused, or facilitative, mediator puts more emphasis on process, the underlying interests and on clarifying conflict issues, rather than on finding a specific solution. This style of mediator feels no sense of responsibility for the specific outcome.
Fixed pie assumption	Parties assume that only a certain amount or quantity can be divided, so the more one party gets, the less remains for the other party.
Inference	Conclusion.
Interests	Wishes, needs, the reason for desire. An interest is a subjective criterion and is often being expressed as a point of view (demanding, being entitled to). A point of view is often the legal or positional rendering of an underlying interest.
Intervention	Action undertaken by the mediator or negotiator to interfere in the process.
Ladder of inference	Everybody perceives a situation in his/her own unique way, and then draws certain conclusions which form the basis for proposals or action. Because all parties can draw their own conclusions, this can lead to all kinds of misunderstandings (Argyris, 1990).
Listening effectively	True listening, and demonstrating that you are doing so, emphasizes your commitment as a mediator, facilitates your ability to hear a message and helps collect information. How to listen effectively and what to listen for depends on what is necessary at this stage of the mediation and what you want to achieve as a mediator. Listening is more than letting someone finish and absorbing their meaning. You also need to demonstrate that you are listening.
Loss minimizing	People instinctively strongly dislike losing something and will potentially try harder to avoid a loss than to secure a prospective gain. If a risky decision must be made, a party will more readily comply with a proposal if she thinks she can prevent a loss. However, an opportunity to gain something is a less powerful motivation for accepting an offer. So, in making choices, minimizing loss plays a more important role than maximizing gains.

Mediation agreement	The document containing the agreements and obligations between the parties being made during the mediation procedure.
Mediation clause	The provision in an agreement that parties shall endeavor to resolve future disputes by mediation.
Mediator advice	A mediator's advice on content issues; depending on the agreements made they can be binding.
Meta-communication	Meta-communication is communication about communicating. The purpose is to point out why certain things are being said and what consequences these implicit messages can have. Explaining the intention behind the words can help anticipate and clarify misunderstandings or differing interpretations, especially on relationship topics.
Mutual gain negotiating	A negotiation without a loser or winner. All parties concerned benefit from the solution.
Mutualizing	Emphasize common facts and mutual interests. Mutualizing offers clients the opportunity to look differently at themselves, the other party and at the problems that have arisen. The opportunity is not only in terms of your/my point of view, but also from a joint perspective. Advancement of the mediation can be demonstrated by highlighting shared interests and common concerns. Moreover, the understanding of the other party's position will be increased.
Naïve realism	Parties assume the world is the way they perceive it. The 'reality' as being observed is constructed by the way the brain functions and by the way it processes information combined with real or constructed input from the environment. Everybody assumes others should have the same perceptions as they have themselves, simply because it is the right way to look at things.
Narrative mediation	Narrative mediation (Winslade and Monk 2000) is a relationship-focused mediation style. Narrative mediation develops a new context and description of the conflict in which all parties concerned recognize their own roles in the origin and escalation of a conflict. The dispute becomes a mutual problem, as a result of which all parties involved have an interest in resolving the conflict. Under the guidance of a mediator, the parties more or less create a (new) story by exploring time and place (the setting), the events (the plot) and the parties concerned (the players, roles).
Negotiation agenda	Determining the order of the themes which have to be discussed during the mediation or negotiation.

Non-verbal interventions	By using non-verbal interventions, a mediator can, for example, correct the behavior of a negotiator that is constantly interrupting the other party by making eye contact with the negotiator who is interrupting. If the discussion seems to have degenerated or if the parties are not listening to the mediator, the mediator can rise to his feet or clearly look one of the parties in the eye in order to command attention. In addition, intentionally and noticeably leaning back can be an adequate non-verbal intervention. The use of non-verbal interventions expands the range of interventions and can demonstrate the mediator's commitment and his neutrality.
Objective criteria	In a mediation setting, objective criteria can help assess alternative solutions and the options that were developed during the brainstorming phase. This is especially important when the negotiators failed in developing sufficient subjective criteria (interests) or where it is hard to generate satisfactory options that meet all interests. It can be used to neutralize bluffing and coercion. In addition, it helps to persuade the opposing party and is a guideline for fair and reasonable solutions.
Offensive emotions	Offensive emotions are directed outward, pointing to another person.
One-Minute-Rule	When emotions run high, one tool is to let each party talk for one minute at most (the One-Minute-Rule; Schreuder Tromp, 1997). This is considered to be the maximum time that people involved in a conflict situation can effectively listen to each other.
Options	Develop ideas or ways to arrive at potential solutions, to find solutions that take in account all identified interests. Stimulate creativity and inter-connected thinking; expand the pie and find optimal solutions.
Out of the box thinking	Stimulating to see things from a different perspective and looking for a non-standard solution.
Package deal	In mediation, parties only commit themselves to a proposal or to an agreement if all issues have been recorded and signed in a settlement agreement or have been specifically agreed upon in a package. Until that moment all consensus is conditional.
Paraphrasing	Repeat in your own words what has been said. Express the same statement in other words. The content of the repetition needs to be identical to the original message, with only the choice of words being different. A paraphrase should not include your own conclusions. It is important to check whether the paraphrased account is correct.

Parroting	See reflecting on content.
Positions	Positional or legal demands. A position is often the legal translation of an interest behind it.
Problem-focused mediation	The problem-focused, or facilitative, mediator puts more emphasis on process, the underlying interests and on clarifying conflict issues, rather than on finding a specific solution. This style of mediator feels no sense of responsibility for the specific outcome.
Psychological contract	The psychological contract consists of mutual expectations and responsibilities. A clear psychological contract: stimulates confidence in the process; motivates the parties; generates the mediator's credibility.
Rationalization	Parties often find it difficult to recognize accurately and dispassionately their part in the arising and the continuation of the conflict. As a result, the responsibility for one's conduct is often denied. One's own conduct during a conflict is often justified after the event with rational explanations.
Reactive devaluation	Reactive devaluation is the effect that a perfectly reasonable proposal can have on somebody who distrusts the source of the proposal: 'It is your proposal, so it must be bad for me.'
Reality testing	The mediator can test the degree of realism in the parties' positions by asking risk analysis questions. These questions can also help to compare perceptions and to explore expectations with reality and probabilities. Reality testing can encourage parties to make an effort to resolve the dispute themselves. Therefore, it can empower the parties. It helps them focus on what the consequences might be if the dispute is not resolved.
Recognition	The process when a party realizes that the other party understands what the issue is really about for him is often a confirmation that his feelings regarding the conflict are acceptable.
Reflecting	Also called parroting or enlarging. Reflecting is an intervention that a mediator can use to make things plain such as to clarify what a party has said or to highlight what intentions or feelings the mediator sees. Further, he can remark on the progress of the process. Reflecting can be on the level of: Content: what is said, enlarge key words/parts of a sentence. Emotion/intention: how things are expressed, to make the

	underlying feelings or the intention clear. Process: emphasize the progress or forward movement.
Reflecting on content	Also called enlarging or parroting. Enlarge positions or topics, to point out themes explicitly. This way, both parties obtain more insight into their counter-party's positions and get the opportunity either to further explain their point of view or to revise their opinion. Also see reflecting and acknowledgement.
Reframing	Also called re-contextualizing. Through reframing the mediator places what a party says in a different frame of mind or a new context. Neutral or positive reframing makes it easier to transform a difficult issue into a topic that both parties are willing to discuss. Reframing is more powerful if done in: • an option • an interest • an objective criterion • a feeling
Relation-focused mediation	Approach of the mediator. Also see communication-focused mediation, narrative mediation and transformative mediation. A relationship-focused mediator mainly concentrates on the communication between parties and on providing insight into the different perspectives and perceptions and thereby on the underlying emotions. The mediation is less focused on the content and the clarifying and resolving of the conflict matters.
Settlement agreement	The document containing the final result of the mediation.
Settlement range	Range for possible solutions.
SMART agreement	Acronym for a clear and sustainable agreement. Such an agreement is: Specific, Measurable, Achievable, Realistic and it has a clear Time limit.
Solution-focused mediation	The solution-focused mediator is especially focused on reaching an agreement and feels partly responsible for reaching a workable solution. Some of these mediators are prepared to suggest solutions themselves or to give an advice, which in some situations could be binding, on how to settle the case.
Structured process of 'give and take'	The mediator asks each party what interests or positions they may be willing to concede and what they would expect in return from the other party. This forms the base for a process of reciprocal exchange or 'give and take'.
Summarize	Summarizing conveys the essence of the statements of several parties or of a range of issues of one party. This

is done in order to retain what has been said, to clarify topics, to sum up and (re)structure important issues and themes. Combining a summary with other techniques like mutualizing or reflecting is also possible. It is an essential tool to structure and control the mediation process (II-15).

Task-focused mediation	A task-focused mediator generally applies pressure on the parties to resolve their dispute and as a result is inclined to structure the mediation process in such a way that several stages are completed. He can be a solution-focused, an evaluative, a problem-focused or a facilitative mediator.
Tit-for-tat	The line of approach is being cooperative, assuming integrative or principled negotiation, unless you are being provoked. If you are being provoked, you respond to the other party in the way they are behaving to you: you are, so to speak, copying the behavior of the other party. You forgive and forget quickly. This means you are not hitting back harder than necessary, and you do not want to be seen as scoring points. As soon as you reach your goal, i.e. the other party is adopting a more constructive attitude, you follow suit.
Trade-off	See structured process of 'give and take'.
Transformative mediation	Approach of the mediator. The most consistent and distinct form of communication/relationship-focused mediation is the transformative mediation (Bush and Folger 1994) which strives for total empowerment (II-6) and recognition (II-6) of the parties involved. Reaching an agreement is not the main goal of this form of mediation. The mediator has a non-directive style and even leaves the control over the process to the parties. This is done to exclude any influence on the content by the mediator. The mutual interaction and the development of that (transformation) are central. The parties can get a different perspective on the conflict as well as clarity on their own needs and possibilities. A better understanding arises for one's own position as well as the other party's and, therefore, parties are better capable of resolving the problem themselves.
WATNA	Acronym for Worst Alternative to Negotiated Agreement.
ZOPA	Acronym for Zone of Potential Agreement. The ZOPA indicates the limits to possible settlement.

Resource B Key procedural drivers

The 8 key drivers that are central to diagnose and design customized processes as identified by Mundi Mediatores (www.mundimediatores.com) are:[73]

1. costs;
2. time;
3. control of outcome;
4. control of process;
5. reputations;
6. relationships;
7. enforceability; and
8. confidentiality.

A proprietary MM-RapiDR™ scoring system helps to provide a consistent, structured, and flexible way of working with one or more disputants to help them.

Mundi Mediatores
PROACTIVE BUSINESS MEDIATION

I. The MM-RapiDR™ Scan

8 key drivers to determine what type of ADR-process might work best.

These 8 procedural drivers give an indication for the most suitable process or combined processes to resolve your case.

1. COST: How important to you are the costs you will need to pay for resolving this conflict (including legal fees, experts' fees, neutrals' fees, etc.)? (For example, are you operating on a limited budget?)

NOT at all important	1 2 3 4 5	Very important

2. TIME: How important to you is the time it will take to resolve this conflict? (For example, is resolving it as quickly as possible or as slowly as possible important to you?)

NOT at all important	1 2 3 4 5	Very important

3. CONTROL OF OUTCOME: How important to you is control over the OUTCOME of the dispute? (For example, ensuring the outcome is business-oriented you can agree to, or

73 They are built on the 8 key drivers identified by the IMI, International Mediation Institute, Mixed Mode Taskforce: https://imimediation.org/about/who-are-imi/mixed-mode-task-force/ and https://imimediation.org/2021/05/04/introduction-to-the-series-of-articles-on-the-mixed-mode-task-force/.

something a tribunal can decide based on legal principles that you cannot control, but provides certainty of an outcome?)

Guaranteed outcome most important	1 2 3 4 5	Control over | acceptable outcome most important

4. CONTROL OF PROCESS: How important to you is control over the PROCESS by which the dispute will be resolved? (For example, flexibility in deciding what documents or evidence needs to be provided, when and where to meet, etc. or having all these factors decided by a tribunal?)

Procedure decided by a tribunal is most important	1 2 3 4 5	Control over process and flexibility are most important

5. REPUTATION: How important to you is the possible impact on the disputants' reputations?

NOT at all important	1 2 3 4 5	Very important

6. RELATIONSHIPS: How important to you are relationships (with the other party or third-party stakeholders involved in the dispute)?

NOT at all important	1 2 3 4 5	Very important

7. ENFORCEABILITY: How important to you is enforceability of the outcome? (For example, do you need it to be enforceable in any particular countries?)

Very important	1 2 3 4 5	**NOT** at all important

8. CONFIDENTIALITY: How important to you is CONFIDENTIALITY of the existence of the dispute itself and any INFORMATION that may need to be exchanged to resolve this process?

Very important	1 2 3 4 5	**NOT** at all important

Assessment:

If most of your replies are in:

- 1, 2 or on the left side of the scale: likely best options: arbitration, litigation, mediation.
- 4, 5 or on the right side of the scale: likely best options; negotiation, or mediation.
- 3 (combined with 2 and 4): likely best options: mixed mode procedures.

Answers in the lower range of the scale (e.g., 1-2 points) can also be combined with answers on the higher end of the scale (4-5 points) to provide mixed mode processes.

Resource C Indicators predicting likelihood of settlement by mediation

The tables below are intended to help you if you are seeking a quick indication whether a settlement (through mediation or any other form of facilitated negotiation) is likely to be successful. Practice suggests that **all disputed issues can be suitable for mediation but not all parties/participants** who are involved in the process.
Please put a check in each column where this applies and count and insert the total number of checks in the spaces indicated at the bottom of the last two columns in each table below.

1. Suitability of PEOPLE	Characteristics of a participant/party:	My party/me	Other party/ies'
	1. Willing or seeing the need to solve the conflict and issue(s)		
	2. Willing and able to also look at own contribution to the arising and continuation of the conflict		
	3. Willing and able to also look at/discuss things from the others side perspective		
	4. A positive contribution and support of the lawyers is to be expected (or at least not to hinder the process)		
	5. Commitment to willing to try to solve the issues and not only 'feeling forced or obliged' to mediate		
	6. Willing and able to negotiate about the conflict or are at least willing to talk to each other about it		
	7. The conflict/relationship is not escalated beyond repair (Glasl 8-9)[74]		
	8. Parties trust the neutral (mediator | the person leading the negotiatons)		
	9. During the process trust between the parties is likely to / may probably be (re)established		
	Total number of checks in each column		

74 *See the Glasl escalation stairs (IV-7).*

	Characteristics of the case / conflict:	My party/me	Other party/ies'
2. Suitability of PROBLEM	1. A solution on the short term is needed/preferred		
	2. It is important to control cost		
	3. Need for risk control e.g., as to publicity and timing		
	4. Parties will need and/or encounter each other in the future or prefer to carefully end their relationship		
	5. Confidentiality/privacy are/is essential		
	6. Control/influence on the process and process steps is preferred		
	7. Control/influence on the outcome or finding a business solution is preferred		
	8. A decision on the legal issue(s) will not end the conflict		
	9. Multiple parties or several participants/representatives per party		
	10. Multiple conflicts (legally unrelated) between the parties		
	11. A cross border case, jurisdictional issues		
	12. Intercultural aspects		
	Total number of checks in each column		

Assessment:

The more questions that are answered in the affirmative for both parties, the greater the likelihood of a settlement being reached through mediation.

Resource D Checklist Cost – Benefit Analysis mediation vs arbitration and litigation

You can use this as a tool for reality testing (III-11) and alternatives analysis (III-14) in a caucus or to help parties to further commit to searching for a mediated outcome instead.

Mediation	Costs	Litigation/arbitration	Costs
Sunk Costs of the dispute to date	**€**	**Sunk Costs of the dispute to date**	**€**
Time		**Time**	
☐ Missing deadline(s)		☐ Missing deadline(s)	
€ ___________ (estimation) =	€ ____	€ ___________ (estimation) =	€ ____
☐ Lost office hours executives/managers involved:		☐ Lost office hours executives/managers involved:	
Person 1: hours spent on solving conflict		Person 1: hours spent on solving conflict	
______ x € ______ (hourly pay/fee) =	€ ____	______ x € ______ (hourly pay/fee) =	€ ____
Person 2: ____ hours x € ______ =	€ ____	Person 2: ____ hours x € ______ =	€ ____
Person 3: ____ hours x € ______ =	€ ____	Person 3: ____ hours x € ______ =	€ ____
Person 4: ____ hours x € ______ =	€ ____	Person 4: ____ hours x € ______ =	€ ____
☐ Office hours spent on dispute by other departments (E.g. Legal services, HR):		☐ Office hours spent on dispute by other departments (E.g. Legal services, HR):	
______ x € ________ (hourly pay/fee) =	€ ____	______ x € ________ (hourly pay/fee) =	€ ____
True (ie including hidden) costs caused by the dispute		**True (ie including hidden) costs caused by the dispute**	
Reputational damage, negative publicity (estimation)		**Reputational damage, negative publicity (estimation)**	
☐ Negative impact on company relationships (estimation)	€ ____	☐ Negative impact on company relationships (estimation)	€ ____
☐ Projects/work postponed/delayed/ cancelled (estimation)	€ ____	☐ Projects/work postponed/delayed/ cancelled (estimation)	€ ____
☐ Negative impact on personal life of parties concerned (estimation)	€ ____	☐ Negative impact on personal life of parties concerned (estimation)	€ ____
☐ Negative impact on quality output of parties concerned (estimation)	€ ____	☐ Negative impact on quality output of parties concerned (estimation)	€ ____
☐ Fees for advisors/lawyers		☐ Fees for advisors/lawyers	
____ hours x € _________	€ ____	____ hours x € _________	€ ____
other costs	€ ____	other costs	€ ____
☐ Extra costs spent due to the dispute (E.g. media-consultant, PR campaign, etc.) (estimation).	€ ____	☐ Extra costs spent due to the dispute (E.g. media-consultant, PR campaign, etc.) (estimation).	€ ____
☐ Other costs (E.g. personal turnover, adjustment within the organisation or method of working, procedures, sabotage, absence, etc.) (estimation).	€ ____	☐ Other costs (E.g. personal turnover, adjustment within the organisation or method of working, procedures, sabotage, absence, etc.) (estimation).	€ ____
Subtotal costs to date	**€**	**Subtotal costs to date**	**€**

Mediation	**Costs**
(Future) Costs for resolving the dispute	**€**
☐ Fees for mediator ____ hours x € ____	
other costs (e.g. venue, travel expenses)	€ ____
☐ Fees for lawyer(s) ____ hours x € ________	€ ____
other costs (e.g. .administration, travel expenses)	€ ____
☐ Fees for experts/ assistants ____ hours x € _________	€ ____
other costs	€ ____
☐ Damage to reputation, negative publicity (estimation)	€ ____
☐ Negative impact on company relationships (estimation)	€ ____
☐ Negative impact on personal life of parties concerned (estimation)	€ ____
☐ Negative impact on quality output of parties concerned (estimation)	€ ____
☐ Additional costs (estimation)	€ ____
☐ Other costs (estimation)	€ ____
Time	
☐ Time involvement for resolving dispute for executives/managers:	
Person 1: hours spent on solving conflict ______ x € ______ (hourly pay/fee) =	€ ____
Person 2: ____ hours x € ______ =	€ ____
Person 3: ____ hours x € ______ =	€ ____
Person 4: ____ hours x € ______ =	€ ____
☐ Time involvement for resolving dispute by other departments (E.g. Legal services, HRM): ______ x € ________ (hourly pay/fee).	€ ____
Other potential future costs	**€**
☐ Costs for reaching agreement	€ ____
☐ Costs involved in reaching a partial agreement	€ ____
☐ Costs if no (partial) agreement	€ ____
☐ Cancellation/loss of projects/jobs	€ ____
☐ Loss of/ damage on important relationships	€ ____
☐ Other	€ ____
Total costs	**€**

Litigation/arbitration	**Costs**
(Future) Costs for resolving the dispute	**€**
☐ Costs legal proceedings	€ ____
☐ Fees for lawyer(s) ____ hours x € ________	€ ____
other costs (e.g. .administration, travel expenses)	€ ____
☐ Fees for experts/ assistants ____ uren x € _________	€ ____
other costs	€ ____
☐ Damage to reputation, negative publicity (estimation)	€ ____
☐ Negative impact on company relationships (estimation)	€ ____
☐ Negative impact on personal life of parties concerned (estimation)	€ ____
☐ Negative impact on quality output of parties concerned (estimation)	€ ____
☐ Additional costs (estimation)	€ ____
☐ Other costs (estimation)	€ ____
Time	
☐ Time involvement for resolving dispute for executives/managers:	
Person 1: hours spent on solving conflict ______ x € ______ (hourly pay/fee) =	€ ____
Person 2: ____ hours x € ______ =	€ ____
Person 3: ____ hours x € ______ =	€ ____
Person 4: ____ hours x € ______ =	€ ____
☐ Time involvement for resolving dispute by other departments (E.g. Legal services, HRM ______ x € ________ (uurloon)	€ ____
Other potential future costs	**€**
☐ Costs involved in winning/loosing partially (E.g. damages, negative publicity, etc.).	€ ____
☐ Costs for losing the lawsuit (E.g. damages, negative publicity, etc.).	€ ____
☐ Cancellation/loss of projects/jobs	€ ____
☐ Loss of/ damage on important relationships	€ ____
☐ Other	€ ____
Total costs	**€**

Mediation	Benefits
Benefits of the dispute to date	**€**
☐ Extra revenue(s), projects, work (estimate)	€ ____
☐ Costs for the opposing party / competitors (E.g. legal aid, involving experts, media, management time, etc.) (estimate)	€ ____
☐ Reputation opposing party / competitors affected (estimate)	€ ____
☐ Time taken up from the opposing party / competitor (estimate).	€ ____
☐ Positive publicity, PR, create awareness (estimate).	€ ____
☐ Other beneficial effects for the own company (estimate)	€ ____
Benefits of resolving the dispute	**€**
☐ Speed	€ ____
☐ (Limited) costs that can be controlled by the parties.	€ ____
☐ Own (business) solution, not being bound by (limited) range of legal solutions.	€ ____
☐ High compliance rate.	€ ____
☐ Opportunity to settle things that are not legally enforceable (E.g. behaviour, emotions and communication problems).	€ ____
☐ The real (underlying) interests can surface (in a caucus) and options can be explored in confidence	€ ____
☐ Confidentiality and privacy.	€ ____
☐ Maintaining a (workable) business relationship or cautiously ending it.	€ ____
☐ Settlement agreement.	€ ____
☐ Settle several disputes at the same time.	€ ____
☐ Solve disputes with several parties in one procedure.	€ ____
☐ Other ____________________	€ ____
Potential future benefits	**€**
☐ Preservation or new start of business relationship.	€ ____ € ____
☐ New opportunities.	€ ____
☐ Potential revenues of business solution	€ ____
☐ Other ____________________	
Total costs	**€**

Litigation/arbitration	Benefits
Benefits of the dispute to date	**€**
☐ Extra revenue(s), projects, work (estimate)	€ ____
☐ Costs for the opposing party / competitors (E.g. legal aid, involving experts, media, management time, etc.) (estimate)	€ ____
☐ Reputation opposing party / competitors affected (estimate)	€ ____
☐ Time taken up from the opposing party / competitor (estimate).	€ ____
☐ Positive publicity, PR, create awareness (estimate).	€ ____
☐ Other beneficial effects for the own company (estimate)	€ ____
Benefits of resolving the dispute	**€**
☐ Public rehabilitation/publicly prove who is right.	€ ____
☐ Delay settlement/dealing with consequences (utilize all available procedures).	€ ____
☐ Costs incurred to and time taken up from the opposing party / competitor.	€ ____
☐ Clear legal solution (win a case, loose a case, damages or not, explanation of (new) legislation or rules).	€ ____
☐ Third party who takes a binding decision.	€ ____
☐ Possible damages.	€ ____
☐ Discharge the responsibility to a third party (internal accountability towards constituency).	€ ____
☐ Implementation of acts that need a judicial order to be executed.	€ ____
☐ Precedent, leading case.	€ ____
☐ Publicity.	€ ____
☐ Enforceable title.	€ ____
☐ Other ____________________	€ ____
Potential future benefits	**€**
☐ Beneficial effects of winning a law suit.	€ ____
☐ Awarded damages.	€ ____
☐ Precedent or leading case.	€ ____
☐ Other ____________________	
Total costs	**€**

Resource E Sample mediation agreement

(without referring to any specific mediation rules).
Please note that this is meant as an illustration and inspiration for preparing your own mediation agreements in line with your own jurisdiction and does not constitute (legal) advice.

MEDIATION AGREEMENT

The undersigned:

[NAME(S)] (hereafter: mediator), jointly appointed by the parties to act as [co-]mediator(s) in the dispute described hereafter in article 2

and the parties:

A: [COMPANY]

....

Represented by:

....

[REPRESENTATIVE]

....

(hereafter representative(s) A)
(hereafter jointly: party A)

And: Legal Advisor

....

and:
B: [COMPANY]

....

represented by:
[REPRESENTATIVE]

....

(hereafter representative(s) A)
(hereafter jointly: party B)
And: Legal Advisor

....

(hereafter: party A and party B jointly referred to as: parties)
(hereafter: representative A and representative B jointly referred to as: representatives)
(hereafter: legal advisor A and legal advisor B jointly referred to as: legal advisors)
The parties are responsible for ensuring that their representative(s) A and B are legally authorised to represent such party in the mediation and to perform all legal acts which are required in the context of the mediation, including the conclusion of a settlement agreement.
Upon the request of the mediator or one of the parties, the representative shall submit a written proxy that constitutes proof of the authority of the representative.

Agree as follows:

Article 1 | Mediation
The parties agree to try to resolve the dispute described hereinafter in article 2 by mediation, conducted by the mediator. They jointly instruct the mediator to conduct the mediation. The mediator accepts this instruction.
The mediator adopts a neutral position between the parties and is independent of all parties.
The parties and the mediator are bound towards each other by all obligations resulting from this agreement.

Article 2 | General description of the dispute
[DESCRIPTION]
(hereafter: the dispute)

Article 3 | General Procedure
3.1 The mediation commences upon the signing of the mediation agreement by the parties and the mediator.
3.2 The mediator determines in consultation with the parties how to conduct the mediation process.
3.3 Unless otherwise agreed in writing, the parties cannot be bound by positions they have adopted or proposals they have made during the mediation, nor by any statements they have made to the mediator or to the other party and/or to their legal advisors.
3.4 The activities of the mediator relate to the mediation sessions as well as to other activities such as reporting, any contact with the parties outside of the mediation sessions (e.g. in person, electronically, in writing, video-conferencing, text messaging or by telephone),

studying documents, contacts with third parties, and drawing up agreements or other documents.

3.5 The parties and the mediator shall see to it that the mediation progresses as expeditiously as possible.

3.6 The mediator can meet with the parties and/or their legal advisor(s) jointly as well as in separate meetings with each party and/or their legal advisor(s) (hereafter: caucus). The mediator as well as the parties and/or their legal advisor(s) can propose a caucus.

3.7 The mediator may seek secretarial and/or administrative assistance for the mediation from a person to be appointed by him.

3.8 With the permission of the parties, the mediator may allow or involve others in the mediation, including legal advisors or experts. When granting this permission, it will be decided how these persons need to oblige themselves to confidentiality and any other relevant obligations following this mediation agreement.

Article 4 | Voluntariness and conclusion of mediation

4.1 The mediation is conducted on a voluntary basis. Each of the parties and the mediator are free to conclude the mediation at any time in the way specified in this mediation agreement.

4.2 The mediation shall conclude:

(a) by the parties signing a settlement agreement pursuant Article 9 or the parties signing a list of arrangements;

(b) by a written notification of withdrawal by the mediator or by the mediator otherwise terminating the mediation without the appointment of another mediator pursuant article 4.3;

(c) by a written declaration by one party to the other party and to the mediator that it terminates the mediation;

(d) by a joint written notification to the mediator by all parties that they want to terminate the instruction of the mediator.

4.3 If the parties wish so the mediator should support the parties in identifying and appointing a different mediator.

4.4 After the conclusion of the mediation the mediator sends a neutrally formulated written notice of conclusion to the parties. This notice of conclusion states the date on which the mediation started as well as the date of conclusion of the mediation. Unless the parties and the mediator expressly differently agree in writing, this notice of conclusion is excluded from the non-disclosure and confidentially obligations pursuant article 5.

Article 5 | Non-disclosure, privacy and confidentiality

5.1. By entering into this mediation agreement, the parties waive the right to use as evidence against one another, in legal proceedings or otherwise, anything that was disclosed during the mediation in confidence. The confidentiality concerns information provided and/or recorded, or positions taken, or proposals made in any form during or in connection with the mediation, all the preceding to be taken in the broadest sense of the word. The parties agree not to take testimony from (or cause testimony to be taken from) as a witness or otherwise: the mediator, or any person or organisation involved in the mediation, including the individuals referred to in Articles 3.7, 3.8, and the Legal Representatives.

5.2 In respect of the confidentiality undertaking this agreement constitutes an agreement regarding evidence within the meaning of the law (Article 7: 900 paragraph 3 of the Netherlands Civil Code in conjunction with Article 153 Dutch Code of Civil Procedure).

5.3 The mediator shall treat any information provided to him by any of the parties and/or their legal advisors, in correspondence, discussions or otherwise, as confidential, unless agreed otherwise.

5.4 The mediator may communicate and obtain information separately and confidentially from any party and/or where applicable their legal advisor(s) through discussions, correspondence or otherwise. Information that the mediator receives from one party and/or where applicable their legal advisor(s) outside of mediation sessions - for example during phone calls, in text messages, email or any other written, oral or digital communication means - qualifies as a caucus as described in 3.6.

5.5 Information shared by a party and/or its legal advisor in a caucus is confidential and will not be shared by the mediator with the other party or parties unless agreed otherwise.

5.6 Anyone else besides the parties, including the individuals referred to in Articles 3.7, 3.8 as well as legal advisors, shall not be involved in the mediation without consent of the parties nor before and after they have signed a declaration of confidentiality or have co-signed the mediation agreement.

5.7 The obligation of confidentiality and the provisions of this Article 5 also apply to any discussions or correspondence preceding the mediation in which the parties and/or their legal advisors have provided information concerning the dispute to the mediator or any organisation or person involved in initiating the mediation.

5.8 The parties agree that they will not record, save, or otherwise capture any audio or video recordings.

5.9 The provisions of Articles 5.1 to 5.7 shall not apply in case of:

a) information concerning criminal acts in respect of which there exists a statutory obligation or right to report,

b) information concerning the threat of a crime,

c) complaints, disciplinary, liability or other proceedings against the mediator. In such event the mediator shall be released from the obligation to observe confidentiality insofar as may be necessary to defend against the claims and/or make a claim under professional liability insurance.

d) the notice of conclusion governed by Article 4.4.

Article 6 | Special obligations of the parties

6.1. The parties undertake to cooperate in the mediation in a constructive manner. They declare to be willing to listen to each other within the framework of the mediation and to cooperate to try to find a solution of the dispute that is mutually acceptable.

6.2. The parties agree to during the mediation refrain from actions or behavior that may seriously jeopardize or hamper the mediation.

6.3. The parties undertake within the framework of the mediation to provide only correct and complete information to each other and to the mediator.

6.4. If a party has instituted judicial or other proceedings in relation to the dispute, or parts thereof, or does so during mediation, that party shall be obliged to advise the mediator and the other party of this fact, either at the start of mediation or immediately after the initiation of any such proceedings.

6.5. In line with the mediator's code of conduct as referred to in Article 7, the mediator can on completion of the mediation invite all participants to provide feedback. The parties and, if applicable, their legal advisors agree to provide feedback on the performance of the mediator. This feedback can be provided anonymously if desired.

6.6. Each representative undertakes on his own behalf to comply with the non-disclosure confidentiality and privacy obligations provision specified in Article 5. Each Party shall ensure that all those present at the Mediation on its behalf or at its invitation and any person in receipt of any Confidential Information from that Party agrees to be bound by Article 5 of this agreement. This includes the legal advisors.

Article 7 | Code of Conduct mediator

The Mediator is bound by the IMI Code of Professional Conduct as well as the Dutch MfN Code of Conduct for Mediators (a copy of which shall be made available to the parties on request). If the parties or one of the parties believe that the standards established in the IMI Code for Professional Conduct have not been met, they may activate the IMI Professional Conduct Assessment Process. If the parties or one of the parties believe the standards established in the MfN Code of Conduct have not been met, the mediator is subject to disciplinary law according to the Rules and Regulations of the Foundation 'Tuchtrecht Mediators' (Disciplinary Law Mediators).

Article 8 | Costs of the mediation

8.1. The mediators fee is € [-, -] per hour excluding 21% VAT (btw) and shall be borne by the parties each 50% - 50%, i.e. for each party € [-, -] per hour.
In addition to the mediator's fee, if applicable, all other direct and indirect costs and expenses regarding the mediation, such as the renting of external meeting venue, travel expenses and hotel expense of the mediator, fees and costs as provided by Articles 3.8 and 9.1, costs of third parties involved in the mediation on request of the parties, as well as the applicable Dutch VAT, are to be paid by the parties and borne each 50%-50%. Further arrangements in this respect can only be agreed in writing.

8.2. The parties are held to pay the mediators fees and costs as well as the applicable VAT irrespective of the course and the outcome of the mediation.

8.3. Each party shall bear its own costs and expenses.

Article 9 | Settlement agreement, interim agreements

9.1. Any solution regarding the dispute between the parties that results from the mediation shall be laid down in writing in a list of arrangements or a written settlement agreement prepared by the mediator, an expert third party or the parties themselves (hereafter: SA).

9.2. The parties shall jointly decide and record in writing to what extent the contents of the SA shall remain confidential. The contents of the SA may in any case be submitted to a court if this is necessary to claim compliance with the agreement.

9.3 The parties themselves are responsible for the contents of the SA. The mediator is not liable for the contents of the SA concluded by the parties nor for any loss, claims, demands, costs or damages that may arise from the same.

9.4 Agreements made between the parties during the mediation (hereafter: interim agreements) shall be binding for them only insofar as interim agreements are made expressly as binding agreements and have been laid down in writing. The parties may stipulate in an interim agreement that the agreements concerned will not bind them if and as soon as the mediation is concluded without a SA.

Article 10 | Disputes and liability

10.1 In the event of disputes, resulting from any agreements as provided by Article 9 or agreements based thereon, the parties shall first try to solve these disputes by means of mediation.

10.2 If it is not possible to solve the dispute as provided by Article 10.1 by means of mediation, the dispute shall be decided upon by the competent court.

10.3 Any liability of the mediator in case of damage caused by any act or omission of the mediator in the mediation, shall be limited to the maximum amount payable under the mediator's professional liability insurance policy (a copy of which shall be made available to the parties on request). Except for intentional act on the part of the mediator *("Opzet door een verzekerde veroorzaakte schade voor zover deze schade het beoogde of zekere gevolg is van de door deze verzekerde gemaakte fout")*, the parties undertake to hold the mediator harmless and indemnify the mediator, including but not limited to legal expenses made in relation to this claim, in respect of all claims that a third party may institute against the mediator at any time related to acts or omissions of the mediator during the mediation or otherwise.

Article 11 | Governing law and competent courts

This agreement is governed exclusively by [Dutch] law and the [Dutch] courts in [Amsterdam] are exclusively competent to hear and determine any actions or proceedings that would be brought against the mediator.

Agreed and signed
On [DATE]

Mediator:

....

Party A:

....

Party B:

....

Legal advisor Party A:

....

Legal advisor Party B:

....

In case several copies of this agreement are signed seperately, every copy is valid as the original document and these copies together form the mediation agreement.

Resource F Sample settlement agreement

Please note that this is meant as an illustration and inspiration for preparing your own settlement agreements in line with your own jurisdiction and does not constitute (legal) advice.

SETTLEMENT AGREEMENT AS RESULT OF A MEDIATION

The undersigned:

Party A:

1.

....

....

If applicable: Party A is represented by:

1.

....

....

2.

....

....

and:

Party B:

1.

....

....

If applicable: Party B is represented by:

1.

....

....

2.

....

....

Jointly: the “Parties”

Considering that:

a. A dispute has occurred between the parties and the latter have decided together to solve this dispute by means of mediation.

For this purpose, the parties have concluded a mediation agreement on .... [Date] .... The mediation agreement [if applicable: as well as the [name] mediation rules, which were given to the parties in advance, are/] /forms an inseparably part of this agreement.

b. As part of the mediation agreement, meetings and negotiations were held on .... [Dates].. and presided over by mediator [NAME].

The parties wish to formalize the results of their negotiations in this settlement agreement.

c. Considerations underlying these agreements ....

d. [Add context and the objective of the mediation, e.g.:[75]

The mediation meetings were conducted to explore [fill in]. In these mediation sessions, their mutual communication was also analyzed, and ways to improve it were discussed. Additionally, during these discussions, the possibility of achieving [fill in] was addressed.

[And/or]

In both the individual conversations and joint sessions that took place, the parties shared information and expressed their feelings about the situation that had arisen, as well as their views on its causes. Various potential solutions were also explored during these conversations.

[And/or]

The parties have recognized that the crux of the existing conflict has been [fill in and optionally provide an example] / During the mediation, the parties noted that [fill in] / The parties have determined [fill in] / The parties have come to the conclusion [fill in] / The parties have expressed [fill in].

The above implies for the parties that it is important to arrive at a solution that is acceptable to each of them and that does justice to the common interests identified during the joint discussions, namely: •.......•.......• [etc. fill in the identified interests]

e. With the agreements made in this contract, the parties have in mind to [fill in].

75 Please keep in mind why you add this context and when this settlement agreement could potentially play a role:

a. When they review the agreements made at the end of the mediation (possibly together with their constituency who were not direct part of the mediation). Therefore, it is important to keep track of the interests and why parties made the agreements they did, recognition of joint contributions, etc.

b. When compliance or enforcement of the contract is initiated, for that it is better to use more general interests, needs, concerns, motivations here because a settlement agreement could be submitted to a court. Exactly for this reason (a judge or arbitrator will review the contract) it is important to give context in my opinion. In any case, mention that the agreement was made as a result of a mediation.

c. When something does not work out in the implementation or when future issues arise: for this reason it is important to keep track of the interests and why parties made the agreements they did, recognition of joint contributions, etc.

The parties agree as follows:

Article 1 The dispute

The parties' dispute is described in article 2 of the mediation agreement.[76]

Article 2 Negotiation result of the mediation

The Parties agreed the following:

....

....

....

....

Article 3 Modification of the agreement

1. This agreement can only be modified if the parties have reached an agreement about both the content of the modification and the consequences of this modification.
2. The modification only applies if it has been documented in writing and signed by all parties.

Article 4 Disputes

1. The parties agree that in the first instance they shall endeavour to resolve any disputes arising from this agreement or subsequent agreements concluded as a result of this agreement, with the help of mediation.
2. If it is not possible to solve the dispute as mentioned above with the help of mediation, the dispute shall be decided upon the request of the party taking the initiative: *[choose one]*
   - in accordance with the Arbitration regulations of .... ;
   - the competent judge.

Article 5 Applicable law

This agreement is governed by [Dutch] law.

Agreed and signed in [Place].................... copies, [Number].................... on [Date]....................

Party A: Party B:

....

Representative for Party A: Representative for Party B:

....

76 I prefer not to write a new dispute definition in the settlement agreement but refer to what is written in the mediation agreement to avoid any discrepancies.

Resource G 5 NEGOTIATION KEYS to claim & create value[77]

THE ACADEMY OF LEGAL MEDIATION

1: The Master Key to claim & create value: Create the process and prepare

- Planning and Preparation Toolkit:
  - Who: participants, constituency, external influencers?
  - What: objective & topics, information strategy (give, get, protect)
  - Why interests | concerns | needs, legitimacy | Reasonableness = subjective and objective criteria
  - What if: no deal alternatives
  - How: options

Other keys for effective negotiators

2: Create the playing field and players | Game rules

- Own mindset: joint problem, information sharing, high expectations
- Relationship and interaction, rules of thumb (e.g. Harvard):
  - Be 'unconditionally constructive' on the relationship
  - Separate the people from the problem
  - Don't try to fix the relationship by giving away substance
  - Establish trust early and build it throughout the process
- Negotiate the process first
  ⇨ Choose your approach and distinguish between 3 process levels

77 Negotiation Keys | 5 Negotiation Keys to claim and create value © Manon Schonewille | Toolkit Company 2020 - 2023

3: Create value and unlock creativity | Unfolding of the game

- Focus on interests (subjective criterions), needs & concerns to unlock new value | positions
- Unlock Skills Triangle: perspective taking (empathy, understanding) assertiveness (speaking, effective communication) creativity (inventing)
  - ⇨ Techniques Toolkit: Ensure 2-way communication:
    - Listen, be curious and show that you have heard
    (paraphrase: repeat in own words + control question and/or acknowledge)
    - Asking questions
    - Summarizing
    - Brainstorming separate from deciding
    - (Re)framing

4: Claim value | Winning moves

- Focus on legitimacy (objective criterions)
- Anchoring, opening offers
- Reaching & implementing agreement (Prioritizing, trade-offs, contingencies, (multiple) proposals | options, SMART commitments, decision making)

5: Have your safety Toolkit in place | Fall back tactics

- Leverage, focus on No-Deal alternatives
- Tit-for-tat
- Package deals and other game rules to set up a good process
- Dealing with sequential games, unexpected moves or circumstances, problem solving

Negotiation Preparation and Planning Toolkit:

The Master Negotiation Key[78]

<table>
<tr><td>Who:</td><td colspan="2">Participants | Relationship:

Expected approach | mindset:

Constituency:
External influencers?</td></tr>
<tr><td>What:</td><td colspan="2">Objective | Commitments:

Topics:
•
•
•
•

Information strategy
• Give:
• Get:
• Protect:</td></tr>
<tr><td>Why
Legitimacy

Subjective criteria</td><td>My interests | concerns | needs

Joint?</td><td>Their interests | concerns | needs

Joint?</td></tr>
<tr><td>Why
Legitimacy |
Reasonableness

Objective criteria</td><td>My preferred objective criteria</td><td>Their preferred objective criteria</td></tr>
<tr><td>What if:</td><td>My No-Deal alternatives

Best? | How to improve?</td><td>Their No-Deal alternatives

Best? | How to improve?</td></tr>
<tr><td>How</td><td colspan="2">Potential options
•
•
•
•</td></tr>
</table>

78 Negotiation Keys | 5 Negotiation Keys to claim and create value © Manon Schonewille | Toolkit Company 2020 - 2023.

Resource H Consulted Literature and other sources

Books

Abramson, H., Mediation representation: advocating in a problem-solving process. Boston: Aspen Publishing 2013.
Abramson, H.I. (2004), Mediation Representation: advocating in a problem-solving process, Louisville: NITA.
Alexander, N. (2006), Global trends in mediation. 2nd edition. Netherlands: Kluwer Law International.
Alexander N., J.R. Coben, S. Rudolph Cole, C.A. McEwen, N. Hardin Rogers and, P.N. Thompson (2022-2023), Mediation law, policy, and practice. Thomson Reuters.
Alfini, Press, Sternlight and Stulberg (2nd ed. 2006), Mediation theory and practice.
Argyris, C. (1990), Overcoming organizational defences, facilitating organizational change. Boston: Allyn & Bacon.
Ariely, D. (2008), Predictably irrational: the hidden forces that shape our decisions. HarperCollins Publishers.
Ballou, M (Editor, 1995), Psychological interventions: a guide to strategies. Praeger Publishers.
Barendrecht, J.M. & E.J.M. van Beukering-Rosmuller (2000), Recht rond onderhandeling. Den Haag: Boom Juridische Uitgevers.
Barendrecht, J.M. & P. Kamminga (red.) (2004), Effectief conflicten oplossen. Amsterdam/Antwerpen: Uitgeverij Business Contact.
Beer, J. and E. Stief (1997), The mediator's handbook. New Society Publishers.
Bennett, M.D. and S. Hughes, (2nd ed. 2005), The art of mediation. Louisville: NITA.
Bilikoff, G. (2004), 'Helping Others Resolve Conflicts: Empowering Stakeholders' 19-20. Regents of the University of California.
Bonenkamp, H.J. (2003), 'Het mediationproces'. In: A.F.M. Brenninkmeijer, H.J. Bonenkamp, J. van Bruggen & P. Walters (ed.), Handboek mediation, 2e herz. druk. Den Haag: Sdu Uitgevers, p.109–160.
Bonenkamp, H.J., K. van Oyen, H.C.M. Prein & P. Walters (ed.), Handboek mediation, 3e geheel herziene druk. Den Haag: Sdu Uitgevers.
Boulle, L. (2nd edition 2005), Mediation: principles, process, practice. Sydney: Lexis Nexis.
Boulle, L. and M. Nesic (2001), Mediation: principles, process, practice. London: Butterworths.
Boulle, L.J., M.T. Colatrella Jr., A. P. Picchioni (2008), Mediation: skills and techniques. Lexisnexis.
Bowling, D. and D. Hoffman Editors (2003), Bringing peace into the room: the personal qualities of the mediator and their impact on mediation. Jossey Bass.

Brandon, M. and L. Robertson (2007), Conflict and dispute resolution: a guide for practice. Melbourne: Oxford University Press.
Brenninkmeijer, A.F.M. (2005), 'Onderhandelen'. In: A.F.M. Brenninkmeijer, H.J. Bonenkamp,
Brenninkmeijer, A.F.M., I. Kabbes & K. van Oyen (2004), Mediation en verwijzen. Editie 2004/2005. Den Haag: Sdu Uitgevers.
Brunet, E., C, Craver, E. Deason (3rd ed. 2007), Alternative dispute resolution: the advocate's perspective.
Bush, R.A.B. and J.P. Folger (2005), The promise of mediation: the transformative approach to conflict. John Wiley & Sons Pub.
Bush, R.A.B. and J.P. Folger (2004), The promise of mediation: the transformative approach to conflict. San Francisco: Jossey Bass [e-book].
Bush, R.A.B. en J.P. Folger (1994) The promise of mediation; responding to conflict through empowerment and recognition. San Francisco: Jossey Bass.
Calkins, R.M. and F. Lane (2006), Mediation practice guide, Ch. 5 'The Attorney and Mediation'. Aspen.
Carroll, E. and Mackie, K., (2nd edition 2006), International mediation: the art of business diplomacy. Tottel Publishing and Kluwer Law International.
Cauffman, L. (2010), Simpel, oplossingsgerichte positieve psychologie in actie. Amsterdam: Boom Lemma. Dutch publication. English version: Solution focused coaching, simple works best, Brave New Books (2020).
Cloke, K. (2001), Mediating dangerously: the frontiers of conflict resolution. Jossey Bass.
Cloke, K. (2003), Mediating dangerously: the frontiers of conflict resolution. John Wiley & Sons.
Cloke, K. (2010), The crossroads of conflict: a journey into the heart of dispute resolution. Janis Publications.
Cloke, K. and J. Goldsmith (2011), Resolving conflicts at work: a complete guide for everyone on the job. 3rd edition. Jossey Bass.
Cole, S.R., C.A. McEwen & N. Rogers (2nd Ed. 2006), Mediation: law, policy, and practice.
Combrink-Kuiters, L., E. Niemeijer & M. ter Voert, m.m.v. N. Dijkhoff, M. van Gammeren-Zoeteweij & J. Kuppens (2003), 'Ruimte voor mediation. Evaluatie van projecten bij de rechterlijke macht en gefinancierde rechtsbijstand', WODC-reeks Onderzoek en beleid, nr. 210. Den Haag: Boom Juridische Uitgevers.
Cooley, J.W. (1996), Mediation advocacy. Louisville: NITA.
Crawley, J. and K. Graham (reprint 2005), Mediation for managers. Resolving conflict and rebuilding relationships at word. London, Boston: Nicholas Brealey Publishing.
Dana, D. (2001), Conflict resolution. New York: McGraw-Hill.
De Palo, G. and M.B. Trevor (2007), 'Arbitration and mediation in the Southern Mediterranean Countries'. In: Global trends in dispute resolution, series editor N. Alexander. Alphen aan den Rijn: Kluwer Law International.

Deutsch, M., P.T. Coleman and E.C. Marcus, (Editors 2006), The handbook of conflict resolution. 2nd edition, Jossey Bass.

Dreu, C.K.W. de (2005), Bang voor conflict? De psychologie van conflicten in organisaties. NSVP-reeks. Assen: Koninklijke Van Gorcum.

E. Schutte, E. & J. Spierdijk (2021), Juridische aspecten van mediation. 5e herziene druk. Den Haag: Sdu Uitgevers . [Dutch]

Eijsbouts, A.J.A.J. & M.A. Schonewille (2005), 'Zakelijke mediation'. In: A.F.M. Brenninkmeijer, H.J. Bonenkamp, K. van Oyen, H.C.M. Prein & P. Walters (red.), Handboek mediation, 3e geheel herziene druk. Den Haag: Sdu Uitgevers, p. 343–351.

Euwema, M. and E. Giebels (2017), Conflictmanagement en mediation. Groningen/ Houten: Noordhoff Uitgevers. [Dutch].

Falcone, P. (2019), 101 tough conversations to have with employees: a manager's guide to addressing performance, conduct, and discipline challenges. HarperCollins Leadership.

Fisher, E.A. and S. W. Sharp (2004), The art of managing everyday conflict: understanding emotions and power struggles. Praeger Publishers.

Fisher, L. and M. Brandon (2002), Mediating with families: making the difference. Malaysia: Prentice Hall.

Fisher, R. and D. Shapiro (2007), Beyond reason: using emotions as you negotiate. Penguin Group.

Fisher, R. and S. Brown (1988), Getting together: building relationships as we negotiate. Harvard Negotiation Project. New York: Penguin Books.

Fisher, R., & D. Shapiro (2006). Beyond Reason: Using Emotions as You Negotiate. New York: The Penguin Group.

Fisher, R., W. Ury and B. Patton (1999). Getting to yes: negotiating agreement without giving in. Harvard Negotiation Project, 2nd edition. New York: Penguin Books.

Folberg, J. (ed.), D. Golann, L.A. Kloppenberg and T. Stipanowich (2005), Resolving disputes: theory, practice and law. New York: Aspen Publishers Inc.

Folger J. and T.S. Jones (eds. 1994), New directions in mediation-communication research and perspectives. Thousand Oaks: Sage Publications.

Fowler. C.E. (2023), rising above office conflict: a light-hearted guide for the heavy-hearted employee (Volume 4), The ACR Practitioner's Guide Series. Rowman & Littlefield Publishers.

Frenkel, D.N. and J.H. Stark (2008), The practice of mediation. Aspen Publishers.

Furlong (2020), Conflict resolution toolbox: models and maps for analyzing, diagnosing, and resolving conflict. 2nd edition. Jossey Bass.

Gallo, A. (2017), HBR guide to dealing with conflict (HBR Guide Series). Harvard Business Review Press.

Galton E. (1994), Representing clients in mediation. Dallas: American Lawyer Media/ Texas Lawyer Press.

Galton, E.R. (2004), Ripples from peace lake: essays for mediators and peacemakers. Trafford.
Glasl, F. (1980), Konfliktmanagement. Ein Handbuch for Fuhrungskrafte, Betraterinnen und Berater. Bern/Stuttgart: Haupt.
Glasl, F. (1998), Help! Conflicten. Heb ik een conflict, of heeft het conflict mij. Zeist: Christofoor.
Glasl, F. (1999), Confronting conflict: a first-aid kit for handling conflict. Stroud, Gloucestershire, Hawthorn Press.
Glasl, F. (2006), In: Tj. Bercx, A. Kil, R. van der Laan & L. Marinusse, Handboek conflicthantering en mediation. Een leidraad voor de P&O'er. Deventer: Wolters Kluwer business.
Golann, D. (1996), Mediating legal disputes.
Golann, D. and J. Folberg (2021), Mediation: the roles of advocate and neutral (Aspen Casebook). Aspen Publishing 4th Edition.
Golann, D. and J.P. Folberg (2006), Mediation: the roles of advocate and neutral. Chapter 13. Aspen.
Goldberg, S.B. (ed.), F.E.A. Sander, N.H. Rogers and S.R. Cole (4th ed. 2003), Dispute resolution: negotiation, mediation and other processes. New York: Aspen Publishers Inc.
Goodman, A.H. (2nd ed. 2004), Basic skills for the new mediator.
Grenny, J., K. Patterson, R. McMillan, A. Switzler and E. Gregory (2021), Crucial Conversations: Tools for Talking When Stakes are High. McGraw Hill Third Edition.
Haynes, J.M. (1994), The fundamentals of family mediation.
Haynes, J.M., G.L. Haynes and L.S. Fong (2004), Mediation: positive conflict management. State University of New York Press.
Herrman, M.S. (ed.) (2006), Handbook of mediation: bridging theory, research, and practice. Blackwell Publishing.
Hofstede, G., G.-J. Hofstede and M. Minkov (2010), Cultures and organizations, software of the mind: intercultural cooperation and its importance for survivaL. McGraw Hill.
Houben, M.C.P.H. (2005), 'Hanteren van machtsverschillen'. In: A.F.M. Brenninkmeijer,
Iacoboni, M. (2009), Mirroring people, science of empathy and how we connect with others. Picador.
Iest, K. en J. Spierdijk (2004), Zakboek mediation. Den Haag: Sdu Uitgevers.
IJzermans, Th. & C. Dirx (1999). 'Beren op de weg, spinsels in je hoofd'. Omgaan met emoties op het werk: de rationele effectiviteits training. Zaltbommel: THEMA, bedrijfs-wetenschappelijke en educatieve uitgeverij van Schouten & Nelissen.
Jordaan, B. (2022), negotiation and dispute resolution for lawyers. Belgium: Elgar..
Kimsey and McKinney (2005), Mediator communication competencies: problem solving and transformative practices.
Kolb, D. (1983), The mediators. Cambridge: MIT Press.
Kolb, D. and Associates (1994), When talk works-profiles of mediators. Jossey -Bass.

Kovach, K.K. (2003), Mediation (Law in a nutshell). West.
Kovach, K.K. (3rd ed. 2004), Mediation principles and practice.
Kraybill, R. (2005) Style matters: the kraybill conflict style inventory. Riverhouse ePress Publication.
Kressel, Pruitt and Associates, Mediation research. In: William A. Donohue, Communicative Competence in Mediators, Ch. 15, 322 (Jossey Bass 1989).
Krivis, J. (2006), Impovisational negotiation: a mediator's stories of conflict about love, money, anger and the strategies that resolved them. E Book Jossey Bass.
Landau, S., B. Landau and D. Landau (2001), From conflict to creativity: how resolving workplace disagreements can inspire innovation and productivity. Jossey Bass.
Lang, M.D. and A. Taylor (2000), The making of a mediator: developing artistry in practice. Jossey-Bass.
Lax, D.A., and James K. Sebenius (2006), 3D Negotiation: powerful tools to change the game in your most important deals. Harvard Business School Press.
Lewis, R.D. (2006 and 3rd edition 2018), When Cultures Collide. Leading Across Cultures (3rd edition). London/ Boston: Nicholas Brealey Publishing.
Lipsky, D.B., R.L. Seeber and R.D. Fincher (2003), Emerging systems for managing workplace conflict: lesson's from American corporations for managers and dispute resolution professionals. Jossey Bass.
Macfarlane, J. (2008), The new lawyer: how settlement is transforming the practice of law. UBC Press.
Madonik, B.G. (2001), I hear what you say, but what are you telling me? The strategic use of nonverbal communication in mediation. Jossey Bass.
Mayer, B. (2000), The dynamics of conflict resolution: a practitioner's guide. Jossey Bass.
Mayer, B. (2004), Beyond neutrality: confronting the crisis in conflict resolution. Jossey Bass.
Menkel Meadow, C., L. Love and A. Schneider (2006), Mediation: practice, policy, and ethics (Chapters 7, 8, 9). Aspen.
Mieras, M. (2010), Ben ik dat? Wat hersenonderzoek vertelt over onszelf (editie 2.0). Amsterdam: Nieuw Amsterdam.
Mnookin, R.H., S.R. Peppet and A.S. Tulumello (2000), Beyond winning: negotiating to create value in deals and disputes. Cambridge: Harvard University Press.
Moffitt, M.L. and R.C. Bordone (Editors 2005), The handbook of dispute resolution, Jossey Bass.
Moore, C.W. (2014), The mediation process. 3rd edition. San Francisco: Jossey-Bass.
Mosten, F.S. (1997), The complete guide to mediation, American Bar Association.
Newmark, C. and A. Monaghan (2005), Mediators on mediation: leading mediator perspectives on the practice of commercial mediation. Butterworths.
Nichols, P. (2006), Mediation survivor's handbook: a practical guide to mediation for the parties, Olathe, Kansas: Weir Publications.

Nolan-Haley, J.M. (2008), Alternative Dispute Resolution, Chapter 3, Nutshell Series.
Pel, M. (2004-2005), Doorverwijzen naar mediation, onder redactie van A.F.M. Brenninkmeijer, H.C.M. Prein, mediationreeks deel 3, Den Haag: Sdu Uitgevers.
Pel, M. (2007), Referral to Mediation, The Hague: Sdu Uitgevers.
Pel, M. en M.A. Vogel (red.) (2003), Mediation en vertrouwelijkheid. Den Haag: Sdu Uitgevers.
Phillips, B.A. (2001), The mediation field guide: transcending litigation and resolving conflicts in your business or organization. Jossey Bass.
Poirier Elliott M. L. (1999) 'The role of facilitators, mediators, and other consensus building practitioners' , Chapter 5 in: Susskind, L., S. McKearnan and J. Thomas-Larmer, The consensus building handbook: a comprehensive guide to reaching agreement, Sage Publications.
Pollack, J. (2020), Conflict Resolution Playbook: Practical Communication Skills for Preventing, Managing, and Resolving Conflict. RockRidge Press.
Prein, H.C.M. (2002), Trainingsboek conflicthantering en mediation. Houten/Diegem: Bohn Stafleu Van Loghum.
Prein, H.C.M. (2004-2005), Beroepsvaardigheid en interventietechnieken van de mediator, onder redactie van A.F.M. Brenninkmeijer, M. Pel, mediationreeks deel 2, Den Haag: Sdu Uitgevers.
Raiffa (1982), The art and science of negotiation. Harvard Univ. Press.
Raiffa, H. (1996), Lectures on negotiation analysis, Program on Negotiation at Harvard Law School.
Ripley, A. (2021), High conflict: why we get trapped and how we get out. Simon and Schuster.
Roediger (2003), H.L., E. Deutsch Capaldi, S.G. Paris, J., C.P. Herman & M. Brysbaert, Psychologie, een inleiding, 3e druk 2003. Gent: Academia Press.
Scanlon, K.M. (1999), Mediator's deskbook, New York: CPR Publications.
Schön, D. (1983), The reflective practitioner: how professionals think in action. New York: Basic Books.
Schonewille, M. and J. Lack, Mediation in the European Union and abroad: 60 states divided by a common word? Chapter 2, p. 19-44 (can be downloaded in the resources section on www.manonschonewille.com): in: M. Schonewille & F. Schonewille (2104), The Variegated Landscape of Mediation: A Comparative Study of Mediation Regulation and Practices in Europe and the World. Eleven International Publishing.
Schonewille, M.A. (2004), Mediation toolkit voor managers, Den Haag: ACBMediation.
Schonewille, M.A. (2005), Mediation toolkit voor juristen, Den Haag: ACBMediation.
Schonewille, M.A. (2007a), Pocket toolkit mediation, pre-publication, www. toolkitmediation.com.
Schonewille, M.A. (2007b), Toolkit mediation advocacy. Den Haag: Boom Juridische uitgevers.

Schonewille, M.A. (december 2004), Winst maken bij het oplossen van internationale geschillen: de rol van mediation binnen conflictmanagement. In: Handboek internationaal inkopen, 27e aanvulling. Deventer: Kluwer.
Schonewille, M.A. (May 2004), Winst maken bij het oplossen van geschillen: conflictmanagement en mediation in Nederlandse ondernemingen, Den Haag: ACBMediation.
Schreuder-Tromp, M. (1997), Praktisch opgelost, mediation als methode voor conflicthantering, ed. J. van Bruggen. Den Haag: Sdu Uitgevers, p. 147-175.
Shailor, J.G. (1994), Empowerment in dispute mediation: a critical analysis of communication. Praeger Press.
Shell, G.R. (2nd edition 2007), Bargaining for advantage. Negotiation strategies for reasonable people. New York: Penguin books.
Silver, M.P. and P.G. Barton (2001), Mediation and negotiation: representing your clients. Butterworths.
Smith, E.R. and D.M. Mackie (2000), Social psychology, 2nd edition. Psychology press Taylor & Francis Group.
Sourdin, T. (2005), Alternative dispute resolution. 2nd edition. Sydney: Lawbook Co.
Spencer, D. and M. Brogan (Jan. 2007), Mediation law and practice. Cambridge University Press.
Spencer, D. and T. Altobelli (2005), Dispute resolution in Australia: cases, commentary and materials. Pyrmont: Lawbook Co.
Spiller, P. (2007), Dispute resolution in New Zealand. 2nd edition. Melbourne: Oxford University Press.
Stone, D., B. Patton and S. Heen (2010), Difficult conversations: how to discuss what matters most. Viking.
Stone, D., B. Patton and S. Heen, Difficult Conversations. How to Discuss What Matters Most. Penguin books (2010).
Stone, D., Patton, B, Heen, S. (2010), Difficult conversations: how to discuss what matters most. Harvard Negotiation Project, New York: Penguin Books.
Stone, M. (1998), Representing clients in mediation. Butterworths Tolley.
Stulberg, J.B. (1987), Taking charge/managing conflict, Lexington Books.
The Arbinger Institute (2022), The Anatomy of Peace, Resolving the Heart of Conflict. Berrett-Koehler Publishers, 4th edition.
Thompson, L. and J. Nadler, (2000), Judgement biases in conflict resolution and how to overcome them. In M. Deutsch and P.T. Coleman, eds. The handbook of conflict resolution: theory and practice. San Francisco: Jossey-Bass Publishers, (p. 213-235). Abstract in http://crinfo.beyondintractability.org/articlesummary/10574/?nid=5606.
Thompson, L.L. (6th edition 2014), The mind and heart of the negotiator. Pearson Prentice Hall.

Trompenaar, F. and C. Hampden-Turner (2020), Riding the Waves of Culture, Understanding Cultural Diversity in Business. Mc Graw Hill, 4th edition.
Umbreit, M. Ph.D. (1995), Mediating interpersonal conflicts: a pathway to peace, CPI Publishing.
Ury, W. (1993), Getting past no: negotiating your way from confrontation to cooperation, Program on Negotiation at Harvard Law School, New York: Bantam Books.
Ury, W.L. (2000), The third side: why we fight and how we can stop. Penguin Books.
Ury, W.L. (2007), The power of a positive no: how to say no and still get to yes. Random House.
Ury,W. (2016), Getting to yes with yourself. How to get what you truly want. New York: Harper Collins publishers.
Van Winkle, J.R. (2001), Mediation: a path back for the lost lawyer. American Bar Association.
Wade J.H. (2000), Representing clients at mediation and negotiation, Dispute Resolution Centre, Bond University, April 2000, Queensland: Australia.
Wade, J. (2013), Systematic risk analysis for negotiators and litigators: how to help clients make better decisions. Dispute Resolution Centre, Bond University.
Wade, J.H. (2004), 'Systematic risk analysis for negotiators and litigators: how to help clients make better decisions'. Dispute Resolution Centre, Bond University.
Wade, J.H., Dueling experts, Chapter 60, pp. 523-534 taken from: Schneider, Andrea Kupfer and Honeyman, Christopher, editors, The negotiator's fieldbook: the desk reference for the experienced negotiator; American Bar Association, Section of Dispute Resolution, Chicago, 2006.
Watkins, M. (2006), Shaping the game. The new leader's guide to effective negotiating. Boston: Harvard Business School Press.
Weinstein, R.J. (2000), Mediation in the workplace: a guide for training, practice, and administration. Quorum Books.
Wiggins, C. and L.R. Lowry (1997), Negotiation and settlement advocacy: a book of readings. West.
Winslade, J. and G. Monk (2000), Narrative mediation: a new approach to conflict resolution. San Francisco: Jossey-Bass.
Zutter, D.L. (2005), Preparing for mediation: a dispute resolution guide. BC Canada: Trafford.

Articles

Aboriginal Cultural Guide for Mediators. ACT Network. Family Pathways Branch, Attorney General's Department. Canberra, Australia.
Abramowitz, A.J. and K. Webb (2020), 'Bring Objective Science to Mediation, 2nd Key: Data', in: Michael Leathes (ed.), Seven Keys to Unlock Mediation's Golden Age, mediate.com.

Astor, H. (2000) 'Rethinking neutrality: a theory to inform practice – Parts 1 and 2'. Australasian Dispute Resolution Journal. 11: 73-83; 145-154.
Astor, H. (2007) 'Mediator neutrality: making sense of theory and practice'. Social & Legal Studies. 16: 221-239.
Bauman, T. (2006). Final report of the indigenous facilitation & mediation project report 2003/2004. – Findings, recommendations and implementation. Indigenous Facilitation & mediation project. Native Titles Unit, Australian Institute of Aboriginal and Torres Strait Islander Studies, Canberra.
Bodenhausen, Galen V., Gabriel Shira and Megan Linneberger (2000), 'Sadness and susceptibility to judgmental bias, the case of anchoring, northwestern university, psychological science', American Psychological Society, vol. 11, no. 4, July 2000.
Bogacz, F. and J. Lack (2020), 'Embrace and integrate relevant new technologies, article 5.2. 5th Key Technology', in: Michael Leathes (ed.), Seven Keys to Unlock Mediation's Golden Age, mediate.com..
Bosnak, J.M. (2005), Boekbespreking Juridische aspecten van mediation van Brenninkmeijer et al., Tijdschrift voor Mediation 2005, nummer 3 p. 66-69. Den Haag: Boom Juridische Uitgevers.
Brigg, M. (2003). 'Mediation, power, and cultural difference'. Conflict Resolution Quarterly 20 (3) 287-306.
Currie, Cris M. (2004), 'Mediating off the grid', Dispute Resolution Journal vol. 59, no. 2 (May-July 2004).
Deason, E.E. (2001), 'Enforcing mediated settlement agreements: contract law collides with confidentiality,' 35 U.C. Davis. L. Rev. 33.
Delaney, B. (2001), 'Techniques for resolving cross-cultural disputes', www.mediate.com, first published at HR.com.
Delaney, B. (2001), Techniques for Resolving Cross-Cultural Disputes, www.mediate. com, first published on www.hr.com.
Festinger, L. 'Cognitive dissonance' http://tip.psychology.org.
Galinsky, A.D., W.W. Maddux, D. Gilin and J.B. White (2008), 'Why It Pays to Get Inside the Head of Your Opponent. The Differential Effects of Perspective Taking and Empathy in Negotiations', Association for Psychological Science, vol. 19, no. 4, p. 378-384.
Gonçalves, A., F. Bogacz and D. Rainey (2020), 'Create a Universal Code of Disclosure, article 4.4, 4th Key Professionalism', in: Michael Leathes (ed.), Seven Keys to Unlock Mediation's Golden Age, mediate.com 2020.
Hanson, R.A. and R. Becker (2002), 'Appellate mediation in new mexico: an evaluation,' 4 J. App. Prac. & Process 167.
Henderson, D.A. (1996), 'Mediation success: an empirical analysis,' 11 Ohio St. J. on Disp. Resol. 105.
Hochman, S.A. (2012), 'A Mediator's Proposal – Whether, When and How It Should Be Used', www.mediate.com.

Howell, R. (2019), Mining Frank Sander's Legacy – Triage And More In A Bold Australian Experiment, Kluwer Blog, May 22, 2019, https://mediationblog.kluwerarbitration.com/2019/05/22/mining-frank-sanders-legacy-triage-and-more-in-a-bold-australian-experiment/.
Ingle, E., 'The power of suggestion', Lindsey Wilson College, http://class.lindsey.edu.
Jones, T.S. and A. Bodtker (2007), 'Mediating with heart in mind: addressing emotion in mediation practice', 17 Negotiation Journal, No. 3, July 2001 pages 217-244.
Kil, A. (1999), 'Mediation: leren in plaats van vechten', Tijdschrift voor de Sociaal Juridische Dienstverlening, september 1999, www.juriat.com.
Kil, A. (2005), 'Toolkit mediation: een mijlpaal in de ontwikkeling van mediation in Nederland!' Boekbespreking M.A. Schonewille (2005). 'Toolkit mediation voor de mediator en onderhandelaar'. ADR Actueel uitgave december 2005, Sdu Uitgevers.
Kingham, F. and Bauman, T. (2006). 'Native title mediation: issues identified, lessons learnt: proceedings of IFaMP workshops with native title indigenous and non-indigenous mediators', February & March 2005. No.5 Indigenous Facilitation and Mediation Project. Native Title Research Unit, Australian Institute of Aboriginal & Torres Strait Islander Studies, Canberra. Australia.
Lack, J., A. Gonçalves and D. Rainey (2020), 'Take Advantage of ODR's Full Potential, article 5.1. 5th Key Technology', in: Michael Leathes (ed.), Seven Keys to Unlock Mediation's Golden Age, mediate.com.
Leathes, M. (ed.) (2020), Seven Keys to Unlock Mediation's Golden Age, 1st edition, published as a series of articles in mediate.com.
Lebaron, M. (2004). 'Communication tools for understanding cultural differences'. Culture based Negotiation Styles. Cross-Cultural Communication.
LeDoux, J. (2003), The emotional brain fear and the amygdala; cellular and molecular biology, October 2003, Springer
Lieberman, M.D. and N.I. Eisenberger (2008), 'The Pains and Pleasures of Social Life',
Liefhebber, H.J. (2008), 'De vergissing van Descartes en 60 bits per seconde voor ons bewustzijn. Kan modern hersenonderzoek een praktische bijdrage leveren aan de kwaliteit van besluitvorming in conflictsituaties?', Tijdschrift voor Mediation en Conflictmanagement, jrg. 12, nr. 2, p. 44-48.
Liefhebber, H.J. (2017), Dealing with your brain. Een neurokompas voor mediators. Tijdschrift conflicthantering 4, jrg 2017, p. 22-26.
Linden, Jon (2004), 'The expert mediator versus the subject expert', november 2004: www.mediate.com.
MacLean, P.D. (1990), The Triune Brain in Evolution: Role of Paleocerebral Functions. Munich: Springer.
McEwen & Maiman (1981), 'Small claims mediation in Maine: an empirical assessment,' 33 Maine Law Rev. 237.

Moffitt, M. (2003), 'Ten ways to get sued: a guide for mediators,' 8 Harv. Negot. L. Rev. 81.

Neuroleadership Journal, vol. 1, p. 1-6.

Newmark, C. (2003), 'Agree to mediate.... or face the consequences – A review of the English courts' approach to mediation', SchiedsVZ, Heft 1.

Nijman, D. & M. Pel (2004), 'Team- of co-mediation: alleen leerzaam voor de mediator of ook effectief?'. Resultaten van een praktijkonderzoek. Tijdschrift voor Mediation, 2004 (8), p.2-8.

Nispen, P. van & A. van Stralen (2010), Culturele competentie. De verrijking door verschillen. Assen: Van Gorcum. (Dutch)

Nolan-Haley, J.M. (1999), 'informed consent in mediation: a guiding principle for truly educated decisionmaking,' 74 Notre Dame L. Rev. 775.

Nolan-Haley, J.M. (2002), 'Lawyers, non-lawyers, and mediation: rethinking the professional monopoly from a problem-solving perspective,' 7 Harv. Neg. L. Rev. 235.

Prein, H.C.M. (2005), 'De waarde van paradoxale interventies', ADR Actueel, nr. 4, juni 2005, jaargang 9.

Rackham, N. and J. Carlisle, (1978), 'The Effective Negotiator — Part I: The Behaviour of Successful Negotiators', Journal of European Industrial Training, Vol. 2 No. 6, pp. 6-11.

Riskin, L.L. (1991), 'Mediator orientations, strategies and techniques,' 12 Alternatives to High Cost Litig. 111.

Riskin, L.L. (2003), 'The new old grid and the new new grid system,' 79 Notre Dame L. Rev. 1.

Rock, D. (2008), 'SCARF: A Brain-Based Model for Collaborating with and Influencing Others', Neuroleadership Journal, no. 1, p. 1-9.

Ross, Jr., W.H., D.E. Conlon and E.A. Lind (1990), 'The mediator as leader: effects of behavioral style and deadline certainty on negotiator behavior', Group & Organization Management, Vol. 15, NO. 1, 105-124.

Ross, Lee, and Ward, Andrew, 'Naive realism in everyday life: implications for social conflict and misunderstanding', In: T. Brown, E. Reed, and E. Turiel (eds.), Values and Knowledge, in press. http://faculty.babson.edu.

Sander, F. and L. Rozdeiczer (2006), Matching Cases and Dispute Resolution Procedures.

Schutte. E. and J. Spierdijk (2002), 'Het mediatorsproposal, een nuttig laatste redmiddel?', Tijdschrift Conflicthantering nr. 2, Kluwer (in Dutch).

Shack, J., (2023), What Makes Parties Trust a Mediator? Mediate.com.

Silbey, S. and S. Merry (1986), 'Mediator settlement strategies,' 8 Law and Policy 7-32.

Starr, A. and N. Page (March 2005), 'Dealing with nonverbal cues: a key to mediator effectiveness' : www.mediate.com/articles/starrpage1.cfm

Torregrossa, J.A. (2002), 'Appellate mediation in the third circuit – program operations: nuts, bolts and practice tips,' 47 Vill. L. Rev. 1059.

Turchin, J. and J.E. McGuire (2005), 'Social psychology and mediation: theory to practice', NE-ACR Newsletter, vol. 11, no. 1, Winter 2005, http://www.neacr.org.
Wackie Eysten, P.A. (2005), 'Drie nieuwe uitspraken van de tuchtcommissie mediators', ADR Actueel, nr. 3, mei 2005, jaargang 9.
Wackie Eysten, P.A. (2005), 'Tuchtrechtspraak mediators', ADR Actueel, nr. 1, januari 2005, jaargang 9.
Wackie Eysten, P.A., (2004), 'De afstraffende kostenveroordeling', TvA, 2004, 63.
Wertheim, E. (2005), 'Bounded rationality in mediation: the impact of framing and anchoring', NE-ACR Newsletter, vol. 11, no. 1, Winter 2005, www.neacr.org.
Williams, R. (2005). 'Native title mediation practice: the commonalities, the challenges, the contradictions of native title mediators', Indigenous Facilitation and Mediation Project Report No. 3, Native Title research. Australian Institute of Aboriginal and Torres Strait Islander Studies, Canberra.
Wissler, R. (2005), 'Barriers to attorneys' discussion and use of ADR,' 19 Ohio St. J. on Disp. Resol. 459.
Wissler, R.L. & R.W. Rack, Jr. (2004), 'Assessing mediator performance: the usefulness of participant questionnaires,' J. Disp. Resol. 229.
Wissler, R.L. (2002), 'Court-connected mediation in general civil cases: what we know from empirical research,' 17 Ohio St. J. on Disp. Resol. 641 (2002).

Research / surveys

Cernadas Curotto, P., D. Sander, A. d'Argembeau and O. Klimecki (2022), Back to the future: A way to increase prosocial behavior, PLoS ONE 17(8): e0272340. https://doi.org/10.1371/journal.pone.0272340.
Kiser, R.L., M.A. Asher and B.B. McShane (2008), 'Let's Not Make a Deal: An Empirical Study of Decision Making in Unsuccessful Settlement Negotiations', Journal of Empirical Legal Studies, vol. 5, no. 3, p. 551-591.
Koch, K., J. McLean, R. Segev, M.A. Freed, M.J. Berry III, V. Balasubramanian and P. Sterling (2006), How Much the Eye Tells the Brain.
Shack, J. and A. Abramowitz What do Mediators Do That Creates Trust?
Simon Thomas, M., E. Schutte, M. Schonewille and O. Korneva (2023), UU-PBM Onderzoek naar kansen en belemmeringen voor zakelijke mediation onder advocaten en bedrijven in Nederland, PBM en Universiteit Utrecht [Dutch].
Simon Thomas, M., M. de Kort-de Wolde, E. Schutte and M. Schonewille (2018), ZAM/ACB [Dutch].
Swaab, R. and J. Brett (2007), 'Caucus with Care: The Impact of Pre-Mediation Caucuses on Conflict Resolution', IACM 2007 Meetings Paper.
The Singapore International Dispute Resolution Academy (SIDRA) at Singapore Management University, N. Alexander, A.R.T. Abala, S. Lim Hui Feng, S. Lopez, J. Phang

Shih Ern and R. Tan Xi En, International Dispute Resolution Survey: 2022 Final Report, 3rd edition 2022. (SIDRA 2022).
Thompson, L.L. (2008), The Mind and Heart of the Negotiator (4th edition). Upper Saddle River, NJ: Pearson Prentice Hall.
Wissler, R.L. and G. Weiner (2017), 'How Do Mediator Actions Affect Mediation Outcomes? The Report of the Section's Task Force on Research on Mediator Techniques Offers a Few Clues', 24 Dispute Resolution Magazine 26.
Wursten, H. (2002), 'Mental Images: The Influence of Culture on Economic Policy', in: Report of the International Colloquium on Regional Governance and Sustainable Development. United Nations Publication ST/ESA/PAD/SER..E46. Culture and Change Management: www.itim.org/articleonchangemanagement.pdf.
Wursten, H. (2006), 'Is McWorld in the Wings?', in: M. Minevich, F.-J. Richter and F. Hoque, Six Billion Minds: Managing Outsourcing in the Global Knowledge Economy. Boston: Aspatore Inc., part 4.1, p. 219-238.

Syllabi, training manuals and reports

ACB (april 2005), Kennisbank 1998-2004.
ACB: workshop De toolkit van de mediator.
CEDR Mediator Training Course Handbook, 1997.
CPR Fall 2004 European Business Mediation Conference te Den Haag.
CPR Fall 2004 European Business Mediation Training van Lewis/Singer te Den Haag.
Harvard Program of Instruction for lawyers: advanced negotiation, 2000.
Harvard Program of Instruction for lawyers: negotiation, 2000.
National Alternative Dispute Resolution Advisory Council, Commonwealth Attorney General, A Framework for ADR Standards, 2001.
NCRC (SDMC), training maual 1998/1999.
Pilot mediation scheme evaluation report of Central London County Court; data collected over the first two years of the projectpublished in 1998; study conducted by Professor Hazel Genn of University College London.
Project Mediation naast Rechtspraak: Co-mediation. Een onderzoek naar de verhouding tussen de effecten en kosten van co-mediation, H. Nijman, juni 2003.
The Academy of Legal Mediation: Mastering Mediation Course 2023
Toolkit Company: Mastering Mediation Course for International Commercial Mediators, 2021.

Webography alphabetical order

(Websites last consulted November 2023)

www.aboutrsi.org/library/aba-section-of-dispute-resolution-report-of-the-task-force-on-research-on-mediator-techniques.
www.aboutrsi.org/model-surveys.

www.academylegalmediation.com/.
www.academylegalmediation.nl/.
www.adr.org. The website of The American Arbitration Association (www.adr.org/si.asp?id=4125 brings you to a Practical Guide for Drafting Dispute Resolution clauses; Under Section III are AAA approved clauses for Mediation).
www.ADRcenter.com/international. The website of ADR Center international technical assistance, a division of ADR Center.
www.ADRcenter.it. The website of the Rome based ADR Center SpA.
www.ag.gov.bc.ca. The website of the British Columbia government in Canada (rules can be found on: www.ag.gov.bc.ca/dro/regulations-rules/clauses-rules/mediation-rules.pdf).
www.ama.asn.au. Website for the Australian Mediation Association.
www.aminz.org.nz. The Arbitrators and Mediators Institute of New Zealand in mediation practice.
www.bcicac.com. The website of the Canadian British Columbia International Commercial Arbitration Centre (clauses can be found on: www.bcicac.com/bcicac_adr_model_arbmed.php).
www.beyondintractability.org the online knowledge center about conflict management of the University of Colorado.
www.beyondintractability.org/essay/communication_tools.
www.beyondintractability.org/essay/zopa, Spangler, B. (2003), 'Zone of Possible Agreement (ZOPA).' Beyond Intractability. Eds. Guy Burgess and Heidi Burgess.
www.bond.edu.au/our-university/our-faculties-and-academic-units/faculty-of-law/centre-for-dis pute-resolution. Website for the Bond University Dispute Resolution Service.
www.bond.edu.au/study-areas/law/centres/drc/index_drc.html
www.ccma.org.za. The website of the South African Commission for conciliation, Mediation and Arbitration.
www.cedr.com. DisputeResolution in Londen (mediationclause: www.cedr.com/commercial/resources/).
www.cidra.org. The website of Chicago International Dispute Resolution Association ((www.cidra.org/cidra-info.html) brings you to a Sample Mediation clause for CIDRA).
www.civilmediation.org. Website with an overview of certified mediation providers in the UK and Scotland.
www.cmap.fr. The website of a French mediation provider.
www.core-solutions.com. The website of Core Solutions in Scotland (mediation clause: www.core-solutions.com/mediationclause.htm).
www.cpradr.org. The website of CPR, the Centre for Conflict Prevention and Resolution in New York.
www.crinfo.org contains on https://www.beyondintractability.org/library/coreknowledge-alpha an extensive mediation knowledge base.

www.crossculture.com/the-lewis-model-dimensions-of-behaviour/.
www.doi.org/10.1371/journal.pone.0272340.
www.eeoc.gov. The website of the European Commission, containing information including general information on ADR in the various EU countries (ec.europa.eu/civiljustice/adr/adr_gen_en.htm), the EC directive, European code of conduct for mediators, etc. (http://ec.europa.eu/civiljustice/adr/adr_ec_code_conduct_en.pdf).
www.eeoc.org the website of the US Equal Employment Opportunity Commission (EEOC), www.eeoc.gov/mediate/mediation_qa.html, brings you to a Questions and Answers page about mediation for the EEOC. Discusses the aspects of mediation in general and more specific results under the EEOC employed mediation.
www.en.wikipedia.org/wiki/Triune_brain.
www.hkiac.org. The website of the Hong Kong International Arbitration Center (www.hkiac.org/hkiac/pdf/Rules/en_mediation.pdf brings you to mediation clauses).
www.hofstede-insights.com/country-comparison-tool.
www.iccwbo.org. The website of the International Chamber of Commerce containing ADR clauses in many languages including Russian, German, Spanish and Portuguese.
www.IMImediation.org. The website of The International Mediation Institute (an extensive overview of rules can be found on imimediation.org/resources/rules-and-clauses/).
www.imimediation.org/2021/05/04/introduction-to-the-series-of-articles-on-the-mixed-mode-task-force/.
www.imimediation.org/about/who-are-imi/mixed-mode-task-force/.
www.inta.org. The website of the International Trademark Association (a mediation, negotiation and arbitration clause can be found on: www.inta.org/resources/practice-tools/).
www.interculturalreadiness.com/.
www.JAMSadr.com. The website of JAMS, a US based mediation provider. Includes the downloadable newsletter JAMS dispute alert. ((https://www.jamsadr.com/adr-rules-procedures/ brings you to JAMS guide for dispute resolution clauses for commercial contracts, which includes mediation clauses.)
www.law.fordham.edu/adr.htm. The Conflict Resolution & ADR Program of Fordham Law School.
www.lawtech.ch/.
www.lawtech.ch/. The website of Jeremy Lack where you can also consult an overview of arbitration cost calculators and other useful information on: http://lawtech.ch/useful-information/.
www.leadr.com.au. Resolution Institute (LEADR) is an association for dispute resolvers in Australia and New Zealand.
www.manonschonewille.com/.
www.manonschonewille.nl/.

www.mediate.com. The site of the Mediation Information and Resource Centre. Contains many articles.
www.mediate.com/2nd-key-data-bring-objective-science-to-mediation/#_ednref3.
www.mediate.com/a-mediators-proposal-whether-when-and-how-it-should-be-used/.
www.mediate.com/mediation-and-sitting-protocol/.
www.mediatenz.com. Website for conflict resolution in NZ.
www.mediation.com.sg. The website of the Singapore Mediation Centre (https://mediation.com.sg/forms-download/our-services/ brings you to mediation-clauses).
www.mediationcentre.com.hk. The website of the Hong Kong Mediation Centre.
www.mfnregister.nl/. The website of the Mediatorsfederatie Nederland, MfN in The Netherlands.
www.mfn-tuchtrechtupdates.nl/.
www.mundimediatores.com/. The website of the ADR broker who worldwide brings together users and mediators, by providing shortlists and process design in particularly for cross-border cases.
www.nzdrc.co.nz/. The website of the ADR broker who worldwide brings together users and mediators, by providing shortlists and process design in particularly for cross-border cases
www.papers.ssrn.com/sol3/papers.cfm?abstract_id=4061216.
SAAM: South African Association of Mediators: www.saam.org.za.
www.sagemediation.sg/. The website of Signapore based mediation provider Sage Mediation.
www.sccinstitute.com. The website of the Mediation Institute of the Stockholm Chamber of Commerce (https://sccarbitrationinstitute.se/en/model-clauses) brings you to mediation clauses).
www.tokisa.com. The website of South African Mediation Provider Tokisa Dispute Resolution.
www.Toolkitcompany.com. The website of Toolkit Company where information can be found regarding international toolkit trainings as well as a downloadable additional toolkit checklist.
www.universaldisclosureprotocolmediation.com/the-protocol/.
www.usam.com. The website of the USA&M (United States Arbitration & Mediation) (brings you to a sample mediation clause).
vaniac.org. The website of the Vancouver International Commercial Arbitration Centre, VANCIAC (clauses can be found on: https://vaniac.org/arbitration/model-clauses/).
www.wikipedia.com en http://nl.wikipedia.org. The web encyclopedia.
www.wipo.int. The website of the World Intellectual Property Organisation (www.wipo.int/amc/en/mediation/contract-clauses/) brings you to mediation clauses in several languages).

About the author

Manon Schonewille is an internationally recognized Business Mediator, who has been actively mediating since 1996 in a wide range of business and workplace-related conflicts, especially in international context and intercultural settings. Manon specializes in contract disputes, business matters, labor disputes, and collaboration issues.
She mediates in Dutch, English, and German.
Manon is a knowledgeable partner in implementing mediation services, developing mediation policies, or corporate ADR policies (Appropriate Dispute Resolution) for companies, government organizations, and law firms.
In the 'Who's Who Legal', Manon has been recommended since 2014 as "a serious name in the industry" and "a source of innovative thoughts, which she utilizes in commercial disputes".
She is a sought-after speaker and has authored several Dutch and international publications in professional journals and standard books in the field of mediation and negotiation. Toolkit Mediation is also available in Dutch.
Manon is a director of the International Mediation Institute (IMI) and chair of the Task Force Mediation Advocacy, and she is also a partner in the internationally recognized training institute 'The Academy of Legal Mediation' (part of Toolkit Company) and a co-founder of 'Mundi Mediatores', both based in The Netherlands.
Although companies express a preference for mediation in conflict resolution, in practice, litigation or arbitration is much more commonly used, despite increasing dissatisfaction. Mundi Mediatores (MM) is a catalyst that addresses this 'mediation paradox' by removing the hurdles for businesses to initiate mediation.
The organization acts as a 'broker' connecting demand and supply in ADR by putting the users' needs at the center. This mediator matching service for business users has been established with the mission to facilitate business mediation across borders.
MM builds upon the standards of excellence set by IMI, and recent contributions to the field like ESG considerations, the Mediators Green Pledge and the Universal Disclosure Protocol for Mediation (UDPM).

Contact: manon@toolkitcompany.com
www.academylegalmediation.nl
www.mundimediatores.com
www.manonschonewille.nl

Index

123

3-I model 111
7-I model 111
10-I model 111
80/20 rule 129

A

acknowledgement 163, 168
active listening 156, 158
advisor 56, 57
agreement 121, 127, 197
- methods of reaching 199
alternatives analysis 281
amygdala activity 257
anchoring 183
argumentative questions 180
assumptions 217
authority 54
autonomy 262

B

backgrounds 235
balance 54
balancing power 93, 94
BATNA 190, 191
behavior
- difficult 223
- dysfunctional 222
beyond reason 263
bias 92
blocking issue 106
body language 258
brain 257
brainstorming 195, 196
building trust 88

C

catalyst 313
caucus 32, 120, 132, 281
- approach and technique 135
- pre-mediation 32
- reasons for using 134
- structure and steps 135
caucus in co-mediation 137
causes of a conflict 106
certainty 262
change 234
circular questions 177

claim value	295
closed questions	174
Code of Disclosure	81
code of professional conduct	81
cognitive dissonance	220
co-mediation	63, 64
- advantages	64
- advisable	64
- cost-benefit ratio	68
- disadvantages	65
- guidelines	66
- models	63
- not advisable	64
commitment	57
communication	171
compromise	104
conceding	99
conclusion of a mediation	80, 124
confidentiality undertaking	57
confidential listening	42
conflict	
- causes and interventions	107
- recognizing own role in	233
conflict cause-analysis	109
conflict escalation	240
conflicting interests	29, 96
confronting questions	179
constituency	54, 55
- consultation process	55
content expertise	
- advantage	46
- disadvantage	46
contract clauses	75
control over the process	52
'core concerns' that motivate people	264
Cost - Benefit Analysis	281
countertransference	100
CPD	81
create value	295
cultural	235

D

deadlines	129
deadlock	215, 216
- causes	211
- overcoming	211
- techniques and methods	213
de-escalating the conflict	32
dialogue	246
differing perceptions	217
disclosure protocols	82

distributive or positional bargaining 95
drama triangle 113
dysfunctional behavior 222

E

effective behavior for negotiators 98
effective listening 155, 158
effective negotiators 294
emotions 202, 228, 257, 260, 264
- defensive 231
- interventions 232
- negative 230
- offensive 231
- positive 230
empathy 100, 259
empowerment 42, 101
end the mediation 95
enlarge the pie 104
escalation phases of the conflict 240
- interventions 249
escalation stage of the conflict
- recommended interventions 244
evaluative approach
- advantages 40
- disadvantages 40
evaluative mediation 40
exchange and exploration 118
expert in mediation 47
expertise on content 46
exploration phase
- sample question 119
external specialist 70

F

facilitating approach
- advantages 41
- disadvantages 41
fairness 263
fear 260
feelings reflection 168
fees 30
fixed pie assumption 222
formulating neutrally 183
framing 260

G

generating options 120, 195
- methods 196
Getting Past No 97
Getting to Yes 95
Getting to Yes with Yourself 51

Glasl 240
go to 'the balcony' 51
ground rules 57, 61

I
icons
- use and overview 23
imbalance 54
IMI certified mediator 81
IMI qualified mediator 81
impartiality 90
implementation 122
individual intake
- advantages 31
individual meetings 31
- before mediation sessions 31
individual meetings prior to mediation 32
inequality of power 93
information 48
- processing 154
informed choice 21
initial contact phase 29, 116
inner BATNA 52
InnovADR 78
intake phase 29, 33, 116
- questions 32
- sample questions 33
- topics 29
integrative negotiation 95
intercultural
- effects 236
- influences 235
- settings 43
interests 102, 105, 122
- classifications of 105
- classifying 102
- differing 103
- irreconcilable differing 103
- joint 103
- reconcilable differing 103
Interests, Concerns, Needs, and Motivations (ICNM's) 105
interim settlement 125
international disputes 44

J
jargon 153

K
key procedural drivers 277

L

ladder of inference 218
language 153
language of the mediator 168
language processing 259
large groups 238
lawyers 56
legal aspects of mediation 74
legal mediation 19
legal mediator 19
leverage 192
- techniques to increase 193
likelihood of settlement 279
limbic system 257
listening 153, 155
logistical arrangements 30

M

managing emotions 232
managing expectations 30
managing the process 131
mediation
- approach 48
- approach and style 44, 47
- definition 19, 20, 21
- suitability 34
- with the government 55
mediation agreement 57, 284
mediation approach
- guidelines 43
mediation clauses 75, 78
mediation expert 46
mediation organizations 77
mediation paradox 313
mediation process
- classification 44
- stages of 114
- styles and approaches 45
mediation strategy
- caucus 41
- recommendation 45
mediation styles 43
mediator
- communication-focused 42
- evaluative 39, 40
- facilitative 41
- problem-focused 41
- relationship-focused 42
- solution-focused 39
- task-focused 39

mediator proposal
- advantages 71
- alternatives to a 72
- definition 72
- disadvantages 71
- example 74
- How to 72
- steps and rules 73
- testing the waters 74
mediator role 49
mediator's approach 87
mental images of cultural clusters 237
meta-communication 170
- technique 172
mindfulness 49
- definition 50
mirroring 177
mirror neurons 258
multi-party mediations 237, 239
Mundi Mediatores 78
mutualizing 189

N
naïve realism 221
name the game 226
narrative mediation 42
- advantages 43
- disadvantages 43
Negotiated Agreement NOW (NAN) 187
negotiating techniques 95
negotiation agenda 68, 69
negotiation keys 294
negotiation phase 121
negotiation preparation 296
negotiators
- average 98
- skilled 98
neocortex 258
neuroscience 257
neuroscience tips 265
neutrality and impartiality
- demonstrating 92
- techniques 92
neutral language 168
non-verbal behavior 202
non-verbal communication 202
non-verbal interventions 202
notice of conclusion 79
- example 80

O
objective criteria 197
omni-partial mediator 21
one text procedure 187
Online Dispute Resolution (ODR) 249
online mediation 249, 250
- advanced applications 255
- best practices 251
- reasons not to use 250
- reasons to use 251
online sessions 250
opening statement 49, 58, 60, 117
open questions 175

P
package deals 127
paradoxical interventions 204
paraphrase 159
partial solutions 125
parties 54
party autonomy 82
'peel-off' questions 178
perspectives 217
perspective taking 100
phases of conflict escalation 241
phasing and structuring 114
positions 122
positions to interests 123
power imbalance 93
power of attorney 54
pre-mediation caucuses 100
pre-mediation phase 117
Pre-mediation sessions 31
preparation 116
principled negotiation 95
proactive mediation 19, 20, 60
proactive mediator 19, 20
procedural consultations 56
- issues to be discussed 57
process issues 44
psychological contract 87
public body 54, 55

Q
quantitative information 130
questions 176
- circular 177
- clarifying 175
- confronting 179
- dealing with risky 169
- peel-off 178

- straight 175
- strategic 181

R

rationalization 223, 233
RATNA 190, 191
reality testing 185, 259, 281
- hypothetical/future oriented 186
- risk analysis 186
reasoning shifts 43
recognition 42
recontextualizing 165
recording agreement & closure 121
reflecting 161
reflecting on feelings 163, 257
reflective practitioner 48
reflect on content 162
reflect progress 164
reframing 52, 165, 200
- examples 167
- in a feeling 168
relatedness 262
relationship questions 176
reporting 62
reports 62
reptilian brain 257
respect 52
result of a mediation 124
Riskin 43
Riskin Grid 43
rules and clauses 81

S

scaling questions 40
SCARF model 261
seating arrangements 67
select options 198
self-awareness 259
self-determination 82
self-reflection 45
self-serving biases 223
settlement 126
settlement agreement 291
shadow of the law 20, 21
short-term memory 157
silence 201
SMART agreement 127
solutions 125
- responsability of mediator 94
specialization 46
- advantages 46

stages of a mediation process 4
- quick reference guide 4
stairs of conflict escalation 241
statistical data on mediation 131
status 261
strategic questions 181
structuring 131
structuring thinking 131
structuring tools 52
styles and strategies 45
substantive issues 44
successful mediation 89
suitability of people 279
suitability of problem 280
summarize 160
sympathy 100

T
tactics 223
time 128
tit-for-tat 226
tools
- managing and structuring 52
transference 100
transformative approach
- advantages 42
- disadvantages 42
transformative mediation 42
tricky tactics 224
trust 32, 88, 89, 96
type of ADR-process 277

U
underlying concerns 264
Universal Disclosure Protocol Mediation (UDPM) 31

V
video conferencing 250
visual information 154
vocabulary 202
voice 201
voluntary 57

W
WATNA 190, 191
weaker party 94
winner's curse 223
winners triangle 113

Z
Zone of Possible Agreement (ZOPA) 42, 191, 194

www.ingramcontent.com/pod-product-compliance
Lightning Source LLC
Chambersburg PA
CBHW061353240926
51846CB00007B/1394
* 9 7 8 9 0 4 7 3 0 2 0 2 5 *